"Sydney diocese occupies a strategic position in the world Anglican communion, and Moore College a uniquely influential role in the diocese. Except for a brief period before 1897, the college was always Evangelical in teaching, but the nature of its Evangelicalism varied over time. By explaining the stance of its three principals during the first half of the twentieth century, John McIntosh illuminates the trajectory of Australian Evangelicalism and global Anglicanism alike."

—David Bebbington
Professor, University of Stirling

"John McIntosh sets the portraits of these three principals of Moore College, Sydney on a much larger canvas. One comes away not only with a clear understanding of the thought of each, but also with a nuanced account of how they fit into the larger picture of British thought and theology in the rich and pivotal era of the first half of the twentieth century."

—George Marsden
Professor, University of Notre Dame

"This is a valuable specimen, rare in Australia, of the genre of historical theology. It is the fruit of the careful research of a conscientious and proficient theologian. The views of three influential principals of Sydney's Anglican theological college are here inspected with 'a theological eye'. Since theology is Moore College's chief claim to fame, that is the best eye to view it. Yet John McIntosh is the first to make a comprehensive analysis of it or trace the influences on it or of it. He does not assume in advance that he knows what the views of his subjects must have been on the grounds that they were all committed Evangelicals. . . . In these days of the lazy tolerance of subjectivity, McIntosh's approach is as refreshing as it is rigorous."

—Stuart Piggin
Conjoint Associate Professor, Macquarie University

"Moore College in Sydney occupies a central place in the history of both Australian evangelicalism and global Anglican education. John McIntosh's study uncovers a fascinating and neglected part of the story, from the early twentieth-century, full of theological rivalries and intriguing personalities with competing visions for the Anglican evangelical future."

—ANDREW ATHERSTONE
Latimer Research Fellow, Wycliffe Hall, University of Oxford

It is an honor to write a pastor's appreciation for this feast of a book—meticulous and comprehensive. John McIntosh is a scholar-pastor-missionary who has traced the graph of theological leadership at Moore College in Sydney over a significant half century (1897–1953). If the theological college shapes the pastors who teach the churches which affect the nations this study of a 'rise-fall-rise' in our history has lessons for everyone interested in the vital truth of Jesus Christ and its progress. No-one who reads this can fail to be edified, informed and sharpened.

—SIMON MANCHESTER
Senior Minister, St Thomas' Anglican Church North Sydney

Anglican Evangelicalism in Sydney 1897 to 1953

Australian College of Theology Monograph Series

SERIES EDITOR GRAEME R. CHATFIELD

The ACT Monograph Series, generously supported by the Board of Directors of the Australian College of Theology, provides a forum for publishing quality research theses and studies by its graduates and affiliated college staff in the broad fields of Biblical Studies, Christian Thought and History, and Practical Theology with Wipf and Stock Publishers of Eugene, Oregon. The ACT selects the best of its doctoral and research masters theses as well as monographs that offer the academic community, scholars, church leaders and the wider community uniquely Australian and New Zealand perspectives on significant research topics and topics of current debate. The ACT also provides opportunity for contributors beyond its graduates and affiliated college staff to publish monographs which support the mission and values of the ACT.

Rev Dr Graeme Chatfield
Series Editor and Associate Dean

Anglican Evangelicalism in Sydney 1897 to 1953

Nathaniel Jones, D. J. Davies and T. C. Hammond

JOHN A. MCINTOSH

Foreword by
MARK D. THOMPSON

WIPF & STOCK · Eugene, Oregon

ANGLICAN EVANGELICALISM IN SYDNEY 1897 TO 1953
Nathaniel Jones, D. J. Davies and T. C. Hammond

Copyright © 2018 John A. McIntosh. All rights reserved. Except for brief quotations in critical publications or reviews, no part of this book may be reproduced in any manner without prior written permission from the publisher. Write: Permissions, Wipf and Stock Publishers, 199 W. 8th Ave., Suite 3, Eugene, OR 97401.

Wipf & Stock
An Imprint of Wipf and Stock Publishers
199 W. 8th Ave., Suite 3
Eugene, OR 97401

www.wipfandstock.com

PAPERBACK ISBN: 978-1-5326-4307-1
HARDCOVER ISBN: 978-1-5326-4308-8
EBOOK ISBN: 978-1-5326-4309-5

Manufactured in the U.S.A.

With gratitude for the love of my first wife, Barbara, and her parents, Jay and Alice Jeltema, and of our children, Jane, Alison, James, and Katherine, and for the wise advice and loving support of my late wife Diana, vital in bringing this study to fruition.

Contents

List of Illustrations | viii
Foreword—Mark D. Thompson | ix
Preface | xiii
Acknowledgements | xvii
List of Abbrevaiations | xx

Introduction | 1

1. Challenges Intellectual and Ecclesiastical | 11
2. Evangelical Responses to the Challenges | 26
3. Moore Theological College 1856–1953 | 53
4. Evangelicalism Embraced: Formation of a Scholar-Pastor | 67
5. Evangelical Doctrine Stated | 81
6. Evangelicalism Maintained | 101
7. Liberal Evangelicalism Embraced: Formation of a Historian | 123
8. Liberal Evangelicalism Stated and Applied | 141
9. Liberal Evangelicalism Maintained | 163
10. Reformation Evangelicalism Embraced: Formation of an Apologist-Pastor | 187
11. Reformation Evangelicalism Defended and Expounded | 206
12. Reformation Evangelicalism Maintained | 229
13. Conclusion | 261

Bibliography | 269

List of Illustrations

Figure 1: Moore Theological College | 52

Figure 2: Nathaniel Jones | 66

Figure 3: D. J. Davies | 122

Figure 4: T. C. Hammond | 186

Foreword

IN 1840 THE LAST will and testament of Thomas Moore of New South Wales, ship's carpenter, master boat-builder, pastoralist, and magistrate, came into effect. By that will a college was to be set up for the training of Protestant youth. It would be nearly sixteen years before that college took in its first students but since that date Moore Theological College has been a vital part of the Anglican Diocese of Sydney. The college in great measure sets the theological temperature of the diocese and has given it the robustness and resilience to retain its evangelical character almost undisturbed for all of its history. The principals of Moore College (thirteen to date) have been immensely influential through their appointments of the college faculty and their theological leadership of the college and, in concert with the archbishop, of the diocese. It is difficult to understand the Diocese of Sydney without serious attention to Moore College. It is difficult to understand Moore College without serious attention to the character and theology of its principals.

This important study of the theology of three of the Moore College principals, spanning between them more than half a century of the college's history, will enable a better understanding of the college and the diocese in those turbulent years. The sustained attention to original documents, manuscripts, and letters opens up new questions and helps to resolve old ones. It clarifies certain misconceptions about these three influential men, in terms of their background, their theology, and the impact of their tenure as principal of Australia's leading theological college. It uncovers their personalities as well as their ideas.

Dr. McIntosh's work securely locates each of its subjects in their personal, ecclesiastical, and theological contexts. Nathaniel Jones is characterized as a scholar-pastor, D. J. (Ben) Davies as an historian and social thinker, T. C. Hammond as an apologist, polemicist, and pastor. In none of these is the subject narrowly defined by these labels. The wider interests of each are touched upon and in some cases developed (e.g., Jones's interest in the novels of Charles Dickens and in the social concerns elaborated within them).

The significance of this study is indicated on three levels. In the first place, it gives careful attention to the shaping of each man by their education and experiences in ministry prior to taking up the post at Moore College. Oxford of the 1880s, despite the emerging presence of liberal and critical teachers in the university, nurtured Nathaniel Jones, especially through the vibrant ministry of Canon A. M. W. Christopher at St Aldate's Church and the resources available at Wycliffe Hall. Cambridge in the earliest years of the twentieth century, and even his ordination studies at Ridley Hall (where he came into contact with the Reverend H. L. C. V. de Candole, a foundation member of the Group Brotherhood and the man under whom he would serve as curate) shaped the more liberal evangelical mindset of Ben Davies. In those same years, the Irish Church Missions College in Dublin and then Trinity College Dublin itself shaped the philosophically astute yet deeply evangelical and biblical mind of T. C. Hammond. Very little work has been done in researching these influences prior to what Dr. McIntosh has done in this volume. At point after point this study breaks new ground in the understanding of the thought of its subjects by this painstaking attention to detail.

Secondly, careful detailed attention to the literary deposit of each of these men, their published and unpublished works of theology, their letters, and their sermons and addresses, allows them very much to speak for themselves rather than be simply subject to later analysis, some sympathetic and some much less so. Time and again it becomes clear that there is still much to learn from what these men have written. Dr. McIntosh deliberately avoids caricature, acknowledging that all three of them, not just the two with whom he is in substantial theological agreement, sought to be faithful to Christ and his gospel. Davies's departure from orthodox Reformation teaching on the authority of Scripture and the meaning of the atonement is carefully documented so as not to say more than he said or less. There may well be scope for looking more widely at the events in which each man was involved as well as what remains of what they wrote before and during their times as principal, yet this methodical approach keeps their voices from being stifled by our selective observations.

Thirdly, the significance of this study lies in the contemporary and ongoing influence of these men on the life and thought of the Anglican Diocese of Sydney. In the current upheaval within the Anglican Communion, the Diocese of Sydney has emerged as an encourager and supporter of all who wish to stand under the authority of Scripture, proclaiming the gospel of Christ crucified and risen to a needy world. It is not the only center of evangelical and Reformed life and thought in the Anglican Communion, yet it is a very significant and influential voice. What has kept the Diocese of Sydney committed to the biblical, evangelical heritage of the English Reformation when this has been dispensed with by so much of the Anglican (Episcopal) world? A very important part of the answer to that question lies in the theological college that has served the Diocese of Sydney since 1856 and so in the men who have led that college throughout its history. "As goes the seminary, so goes the church," is a slogan that has proven tragically true right around the world. It is heartening to hear how that slogan might have a positive value as well under God's good hand.

I take much delight in commending the pages that follow to you, the reader.

Mark D. Thompson
Principal, Moore Theological College, Sydney

Preface

MY INTEREST IN REFORMATION theology and modern liberal theology began in my undergraduate days at the University of Sydney in the 1950s. I was a member of the Evangelical Union and became acquainted with T. C. Hammond's handbook of doctrine as well as hearing him in person. Soon after finishing my degree (largely in history) I read Gabriel Hebert's *Fundamentalism and the Church of God,* then J. I. Packer's *"Fundamentalism" and the Word of God.* Together they piqued the interest. At some time I read Marcus L. Loane's *Masters of the English Reformation* and also his *Centenary History of Moore Theological College.* In this he described Moore College Principal Davies as "liberal in scholarship," Principal Jones as embodying "the true Keswick teaching," and Principal Hammond as "a man of massive intellect and noble capacity."

The difference in principle between "Christianity and Liberalism"[1] came up at Westminster Theological Seminary where I studied from 1959 to 1963 and some of my essays there focused on liberal works. Teaching theology in the 1970s at an Indonesian seminary (sent by CMSA, the Church Missionary Society in Australia) brought me face to face with colleagues having a liberal education. While at Trinity Evangelical Divinity School in 1986 and 1987 studying for the Doctor of Missiology degree, I attended sessions on modern theology offered by Kevin Vanhoozer and audited a course on the subject at the Lutheran School of Theology in Chicago. For my DMiss project I combined my interest in both Reformation theology and its liberal contrast, setting out how the theology of Luther and Calvin might be taught to Indonesian students who were under some impact

1. Machen, *Christianity and Liberalism.*

from liberal theology, who had a tribal cultural background, and who found themselves in a majority Muslim context.[2]

At Westminster I noticed Cornelius Van Til's criticism of Hammond for his "moderate Calvinism." This sparked in me the idea of doing my own estimate. Much later I read Warren Nelson's very reliable biography of Hammond, where the careful account of his books and theology invited even further analysis. In 1988 I heard Janet West's Moore College Library Lecture on Davies ("A Principal Embattled"), which mentioned briefly his liberalism but did not examine whether that may have lain at the basis of his being "embattled." I determined that someday I must examine the nature of his liberalism. When I read Lawton's *A Better Time to Be* I noted that he described Jones's teaching in striking contrast with what Loane had implied. This challenged me to find out what was actually the case.

Not long before I reached retirement, I told Peter Jensen, then principal of Moore College, of my idea of looking at the thought of certain of his predecessors. He appointed me a visiting fellow of the college and the college committee generously supported his encouragement, which enabled me to access fruitful library resources in England and Ireland.

I began my research with Davies expecting to be in least agreement with his liberal theology and wanting to understand and present it accurately and fairly. I focused, though not exclusively, on his notion of biblical authority and his understanding of the atonement. His place in a broadening of the Anglican Evangelical spectrum was clear. A more complete analysis of his thought might include several other matters: "the social problem," the 1920s debate on the Prayer Book, and the issue of a constitution for the national Australian Anglican Church. Davies's history lectures to the University of Sydney Extension Board, his papers given at the meetings of The Heretics (I have treated several), and many sermon notes would furnish further material for additional research.

Coming to Jones, I looked to evaluating the emphasis both of his doctrinal convictions and of his teaching on Christian holiness and piety. His earlier diaries (journals), his published teaching manual on the Thirty-nine Articles as well as his writings on the Prayer Book, showed clearly the true character of his faith and piety, while his Katoomba Convention addresses and certain other addresses exhibited his practical application of holiness. More work could be done on Jones by looking also at his last journal, of 1907, some lecture notes, and material written up by his wife, Grace Jones. There is some extra material in church newspapers as well.

---

2. "Reformation Theology for Batak Indonesian Students," 1993 (unpublished).

For Hammond, I used work not previously commented on, such as his critique of a modernist "New Theology," early journal articles on theology, his engagement with the encroachment of Anglo-Catholicism in the Church of Ireland, and several publications relating to Roman Catholic claims. I also examined his important essay explaining the "divine fiat" nature of biblical authority as well as his brief chapter on Christ's atoning death, that heralded his long-used handbook of Christian doctrine, which opened his Inter-Varsity Fellowship "trilogy." All the above, together with his final dogmatic opus, was sufficient to reveal the character of his thought and place him with Jones in the spectrum of Evangelical Anglicanism of the time.

A fuller study of Hammond would take advantage of a wide range (some of it only touched on in this work) of pamphlets, booklets, scholarly journal articles and contributions to the *Protestant Dictionary* of 1933, his apologetic lectures, lunchtime talks and radio broadcasts in Sydney, his Christian convention and other addresses in Australia, contributions to church newspapers on current topics, and two substantial unpublished manuscripts.

It became clear that to understand the development of what became a *spectrum* of Evangelical thought,[3] certain nineteenth-century challenges and the responses of Evangelicals also needed to be explained, as well as the extension of the doctrinal position of many who adopted a premillennial eschatology and the holiness movement. Important too, was the story of how Moore College came to be founded as an Evangelical institution and how its history connected with the bishops (later archbishops) of the Anglican Diocese of Sydney and their theological convictions. The three principals studied here, their thought and influence, could then find their context—the Evangelical succession, such as it was, in the history of the diocese with which the college was connected.

---

3. I owe to Dr. Geoffrey Treloar, co-supervisor of my thesis, the notion of an "Evangelical spectrum" and of the "IVF trilogy."

Acknowledgements

I AM GRATEFUL TO many people who have helped me along the way in writing this book.

Dr. Janet West's Moore College Library Lecture of 1988 on D. J. Davies provided information and initial stimulus for further exploration. The Reverend Doctor William (Bill) Lawton's published work on Nathaniel Jones likewise motivated me, and he personally informed me of the important Masonic Lodge source that preserves some of Davies's work.

The late Archbishop Marcus Loane and Bishop Donald Robinson were unstintingly generous in correspondence and interview time, as was the late Reverend Dr. Alan Cole. The late Professor Ken Cable provided information about Davies. Mrs. Carl Hammond, daughter-in-law of Hammond, and Mr. William (Bill) Andersen, active in the Sydney University Evangelical Union in the early 1940s, recalled their memories of Hammond for me. The late Dr. Stuart Barton Babbage, Dean of St Andrew's Cathedral (1947–1952) kindly supplied his personal memories of Hammond and of Archbishop Mowll. The late Reverend Noel Pollard of Cambridge located the service books of Holy Trinity Church and helped me record the entries for Davies. Mrs. Stephanie Bennett of Newtown, Victoria, daughter of Stephen Jones, kindly provided me with copies of published sermons and addresses by her grandfather, Nathaniel Jones. Also in Victoria, Dr. Darrell Paproth made available material he had written on evangelical movements in that state at the turn of the nineteenth century. My friend from undergraduate days, Dr. David Dockrill, formerly Senior Lecturer in Philosophy at Newcastle University, NSW, supplied me with published material on Professor John Anderson of Sydney University.

ACKNOWLEDGEMENTS

Emeritus Professor Brian Fletcher did me the favor of recommending the History Department at the University of New South Wales for my PhD. I am grateful to Associate Professor Stuart Piggin for inviting me to attend his postgraduate seminars at Macquarie University, thus providing academic fellowship and stimulus. My thesis supervisor, Professor John Gascoigne and co-supervisor Dr. Geoff Treloar were of unfailing help, encouragement, and guidance. Before I thought of enrolling for a PhD, Dr. Treloar lent me of his expertise for my visit to the libraries in England and Ireland. Dr. Bruce and Mrs. Lyn Winter and Dr. David and Mrs. Elizabeth Baker, both of Tyndale House, Cambridge, kindly allowed my wife, Diana, and me the use of their residences during research in Cambridge, and extended warm hospitality, as also did Dr. Stuart and Mrs. Mee Yan Cheung Judge in Oxford. At the Irish Church Missions office in Dublin, the Reverend Eddie Coulter, then superintendent, enabled access to source material on Hammond. Also in Ireland, the Reverend Warren Nelson, author of a carefully researched biography of Hammond, supplied me with unpublished material to do with the editing for publication of Hammond's first major book; he and his wife, Phyllis, were warmly hospitable to us.

Librarians have been unfailingly helpful. They include, in Australia, those of Moore Theological College Library (now the Donald Robinson Library), especially its former head, Kim Robinson, whose knowledge of the library's archival resources was essential; more lately Julie Olston, Library Manager, Annabel Bristow and Erin Mollenhauer, Special Collections Manager; also the librarians of the Leeper Library, of Trinity College in the University of Melbourne; and Hazel Snair, manager of the Archives of the Anglican Diocese of Melbourne. In England, I received help from the staffs of the University of Cambridge library and Mr. Jonathan Smith of the Wren Library of Trinity College, Cambridge; also from librarians of the Bodleian and Radford libraries of the University of Oxford; in Ireland, librarians of the Manuscript Department of the library of Trinity College, Dublin, of the Church Representative Body Library, and of the Catholic Library, Dublin.

The research could hardly have been done without the support of Dr. Peter Jensen, when still principal of Moore College. He made me a visiting fellow of the college, which entailed full faculty library privileges. Financial help funded my visit to libraries in England and Ireland.

Mr. Bill Breeze of Moore College's information technology department enabled the technological side of writing to go smoothly. Miss Heather McLeod kindly assembled and typed up the thesis bibliography.

To my editor for the book, the Reverend Doctor Chris Mulherin, I owe much for his advice and ensuring that the house rules of the publisher have been incorporated. And to Dr. Stuart Braga I am very grateful for his expert compilation of the index.

Especially, I must thank my wife, Diana, who so sadly passed on before this book could be published. She suggested that I submit the research I was undertaking to the PhD process. She diligently helped me in the search for material in the British and Irish libraries and in the Moore College Library microform material, and for proofreading the final drafts of the thesis. Her encouragement and patience were unfailing and ongoing in support for publishing the book.

I have also enjoyed encouragement and indications of interest from many others, both in the writing of the thesis and in its preparation for publication. To everyone I give my thanks.

List of Abbreviations

ACR	*The Australian Church Record.* Sydney, Australia: The Church Record, 1879–1987.
ACL	Anglican Church League.
ACQR	*The Australian Church Quarterly Review.* Sydney, Australia: D. S. Ford, 1910–1911. Continues as *The Australasian Church Quarterly Review.* Sydney, Australia: Church Book Store, 1911–1915.
ADB	*Australian Dictionary of Biography.* National Centre of Biography, Australian National University. http://adb.anu.edu.au.
ADEB	*Australian Dictionary of Evangelical Biography.* Edited by Brian Dickey. Sydney, Australia: Evangelical History Association, 1994.
AV	Authorized Version (King James) of the Bible. 1611.
BDE	*Biographical Dictionary of Evangelicals.* Edited by Timothy Larsen. Leicester, UK: Inter-Varsity, 2003.
DNB	*Dictionary of National Biography.* London: Smith, Elder, 1885–1899. *Dictionary of National Biography.* Supplement Vols. 1–3. London: Smith, Elder, 1912.

DSCHT	*Dictionary of Scottish Church History and Theology.* Edited by Nigel M. de S. Cameron. Edinburgh: T & T Clark, 1993.
ECEBC	Fausset, A. R. *The Englishman's Critical and Expositional Bible Cyclopaedia.* London: Hodder and Stoughton, 1878.
EQ	*The Evangelical Quarterly.* London: Paternoster, 1929–.
FEC	Fellowship of Evangelical Churchmen.
ICM	The Society for Irish Church Missions to the Roman Catholics.
ICQ	*The Irish Church Quarterly.* Dublin: Church of Ireland, 1909–1917.
ISBE	*The International Standard Bible Encyclopaedia.* London: Henry Camp, 1915.
IUBM	Hammond, T. C. *In Understanding Be Men: A Handbook on Christian Doctrine for Non-Theological Students.* 5th ed. London: Inter-Varsity, 1954.
IVF	Inter-Varsity Fellowship of Evangelical Unions
Lucas	*Lucas: An Evangelical History Review.* Sydney, Australia: Evangelical History Association, 1987–.
MitchLib	Mitchell Library, State Library of New South Wales.
NBD	*The New Bible Dictionary.* Edited by J. D. Douglas. London: Inter-Varsity Fellowship, 1962.
NIDCC	*The New International Dictionary of the Christian Church.* Edited by J. D. Douglas. Exeter, UK: Paternoster, 1974.
ODCC	*The Oxford Dictionary of the Christian Church.* 3rd rev. ed. Edited by F. L. Cross and E. A. Livingstone. Oxford: Oxford University Press, 2005.

PD	*The Protestant Dictionary: Containing Articles on the History, Doctrines, and Practices of the Christian Church.* New ed. Edited by Charles Sydney Carter and G. E. Alison Weeks. London: Harrison Trust, 1933.
PTR	*Princeton Theological Review.* Vols. 1–4. Philadelphia, PA: MacCalla, 1903–1906. Vols. 5–27. Philadelphia, PA: Princeton University, 1907–1929.
RV	Holy Bible: Revised Version. Oxford: Oxford University Press, 1885.
SCM	Student Christian Movement
SDM	*Sydney Diocesan Magazine: The Official Organ of the Lord Archbishop Month by Month.* Sydney, Australia: Church of England, 1910–1958.
SMAMoore	Samuel Marsden Archives, Moore Theological College Library (now Donald Robinson Library).
TCD	Trinity College, Dublin.
ThL	Licentiate of Theology
TSLR	*Transactions of the Sydney Lodge of Research, No. 290, U.G.L., NSW.* Sydney, Australia: The Lodge, 1914–1955.
USydArch	University Archives, University of Sydney Library.
WTJ	*Westminster Theological Journal.* Philadelphia, PA: Westminster Theological Seminary, 1938– .

Introduction

MOORE THEOLOGICAL COLLEGE IN Sydney, Australia, along with the Diocese of Sydney, is unique in the history of Anglican Evangelicalism,[1] at least in English-speaking countries. The diocese, although never in fact monochrome, is well known as Evangelical. If some view it as therefore less than Anglican, others contend that a sound evangelicalism is truest to the intent of the English Reformers.

There is no doubt the college has been Evangelical for most of its history, but there is no thorough analysis of the kind or kinds of evangelicalism taught in any period. Of the thought and influence of the principals of the college no *overall* analysis and assessment of any one principal has yet appeared.

Of the college's thirteen principals from 1856 to 2016, the three subjects of this study—Nathaniel Jones, David Davies, and T. C. Hammond—held office in succession from 1897 to 1953. This era was important because of a series of changes in the Evangelicalism taught in the college and at the same time represented by the archbishop of the diocese. Most problematic for conservative evangelicals was the theologically liberal movement among Evangelicals that organized itself in England early in the twentieth century. It became very influential at Ridley Hall, Cambridge and Wycliffe Hall, Oxford, in the Church Missionary Society, and on the Church of England's episcopal bench. This self-styled "Liberal Evangelicalism" impacted both the college and the diocese in the persons of the principals and the archbishops. Less of a problem was the rise in England of a premillennial expectation of Christ's return and of the holiness movement known as "Keswick."

From the time of its foundation the college became the single main theological institution where clergy of the Diocese of Sydney had their

---

1. *Evangelical* is spelled with both lower and upper case in this book. With upper case it refers to the Evangelical school of thought, or sometimes the Evangelical party, within Anglicanism. Lower case is used for a more generic sense of the term.

training. The diocese has always been the numerically largest in the country. In its first half-century the college also trained some clergy for other dioceses, especially Melbourne at first, as well as the dioceses of Bathurst and Goulburn, which were carved out of Sydney in the nineteenth century. It has also educated clergy who became missionaries, played a role in the training of deaconesses, and provided training to lay candidates for the Church Missionary Society of Australia. Less well known, perhaps, is that the college's graduates were never a majority of Sydney clergy until the last part of the era under study.

Bishop Barker, the second bishop of the diocese, founded the college in 1856 to be an Evangelical place of training of clergy. From the first, its principals were set against "rationalism and ritualism." But to explain how Moore College became the institution it was by the mid-twentieth century, the story needs to be told of what the three principals from 1897 to 1953 believed and taught. Each principal was the dominant figure in the college and important in the diocese. Each left his own living legacy—the men taught in the college (and women in the associated Deaconess House from 1891)—and his own literary remains. Perhaps the most important example of a living legacy was seen in the decisive action of a group of Nathaniel Jones's former students at the synod held in 1933 to elect a new archbishop. They succeeded in reestablishing in the diocese, and thereby in the college, the central features of the Evangelicalism their revered teacher had represented.

Just what were the ideas and convictions that motivated them? The history of Evangelicalism in Sydney has attracted scholarly historical interest and attention, most of which provides only an outline of what the several principals of the college believed. Some of the most critical writers appear to have the sketchiest knowledge and yet are the most confidently adverse in judgment.

Several writers focusing on the era following 1897–1953 attribute much to the influence of D. B. Knox, principal 1959–1985. Their verdicts reveal a long-standing antipathy on the part of some Anglicans to the Evangelical tradition of Moore College and the Sydney diocese. Criticism to do with issues such as Sydney's position on the ordination of women as presbyters (priests) and active homosexuality among ministers have been only a symptom. The historian David Hilliard is correct when he writes of "the new chasm" that has opened since the 1960s between "those who are labeled 'liberal'" and "those who see themselves as 'traditional' or 'orthodox.'" The chasm "slices across" the old divide between Evangelical and Anglo-Catholic.[2]

2. Hilliard, "Dioceses, Tribes and Factions," 65.

INTRODUCTION

Three works exemplifying the depth of the new chasm have claimed attention in recent years: those by Peter Carnley (2004),[3] Chris McGillion (2005),[4] and Muriel Porter (2006).[5] Tom Frame points out that they have "not always helped the cause of greater understanding or widened scope for empathy."[6] Archbishop Carnley of Perth, Primate of Australia 2000–2005, came to believe that Principal T. C. Hammond had taught a subordinationist view of Christ's position in the Godhead. Carnley at one time thought that this was what lay at the root of the Sydney Doctrine Commission's opposition to ordaining women as presbyters.[7]

Chris McGillion, a Roman Catholic and senior lecturer in print journalism at Charles Sturt University, tries to explain how it was that the Diocese of Sydney "took a sharp turn toward a more extreme and conservative form of Protestantism."[8] Muriel Porter is a member of General Synod and grew up in a Sydney parish, but now lives in Melbourne and is married to an Anglo-Catholic clergyman. She declares her hand: "My aim in this book is not to report on Sydney objectively and even-handedly." She, like McGillion, talks of Sydney's "extreme form of Evangelicalism."[9]

Frame faults all three writers: In sum, the books are distorted accounts of what the church does, because a prior commitment to social progressivism blurs each author's vision of the internal nuances of some Anglican belief.[10]

Frame has his own strictures on the current Evangelicalism in the diocese.[11] But his overall characterization of Sydney Evangelicalism is balanced by a positive assessment of principals T. C. Hammond and D. B. Knox and "the present teaching faculty at Moore College."[12] However, Frame also notes Stuart Piggin's point that "Australian Anglicans appear to [have] little memory and little sense of [their own] tradition."[13] This judgment is further

---

3. Carnley, *Reflections in Glass*.
4. McGillion, *Chosen Ones*.
5. Porter, *New Puritans*.
6. Frame, *Anglicans in Australia*, 1–2.
7. He later withdrew this accusation.
8. McGillion, *Chosen Ones*, xi.
9. Porter, *New Puritans*, 42.
10. Frame, *Anglicans in Australia*, 11.
11. Frame, "Tradition or Tribe?," 16–21.
12. Ibid., 29–30.
13. Frame, *Anglicans in Australia*, 13; cf. Stuart Piggin, "Towards the Renewal of the Anglican Church of Australia," 2.

justification for writing a close study of three Moore College principals of a key period.

Two recent histories of the Anglican Church in Australia and one of the Diocese of Sydney by Bruce Kaye contain little about Moore College and its principals in the period before D. B. Knox.[14] Kaye's earlier book, *A Church Without Walls*, faults the Moore College of Nathaniel Jones as "consolidating a very conservative kind of pietistic Evangelicalism."[15] He is probably dependent on William Lawton's pioneer reading of some of Jones's primary material. Lawton concluded that Jones was a source of "ardent millennialists," who neglected concern with society to focus their attention on the inner life of believers, the "Little Flock."[16] M. L. Loane, however, the only historian of the college,[17] knew the key Jones graduates personally. He severely questioned both elements of Lawton's conclusion.[18] Lawton also concluded that under Jones, Moore College "fashioned a clergy . . . who failed to interpret [God's mind] to a secularized society,"[19] whatever such an interpretation might have been. Lawton also faulted the Moore College under Jones for inculcating a Kantian intuitionist ethical theory.[20] If so, such instruction was probably from the vice-principal (from 1904 to 1911), G. A. Chambers, who had received his Master of Arts in philosophy from the University of Sydney under the idealist Professor Francis Anderson for a thesis entitled "The Idea of Development as Applied to Religion."[21] Probably unaware of Loane's comments, Lawton also subsequently reiterated his "Little Flock" theory. He is more likely correct, however, to speak of Archbishop Mowll's desire to prioritize preaching for evangelism by his clergy.[22]

Judd and Cable's history of the diocese mentions all three principals here studied, Judd being the author of the relevant chapters. His account of Jones and Moore College under him assumes Lawton's conclusions.[23] Judd refers to Principal Davies as a "Liberal Evangelical" but gives no account of his thought, recording only the "freedom of enquiry and study" that the

---

14. Kaye, *Anglicanism in Australia*.
15. Kaye, *Church Without Walls*, 32.
16. Lawton, *Better Time to Be*, 2, 210, 211.
17. Loane, *Centenary History*.
18. Loane, Review of *The Better Time to Be*, 42–43.
19. Lawton, "Nathaniel Jones," 374.
20. Lawton, *Better Time to Be*, 84–85.
21. Sibtain with Chambers, *Dare to Look Up*, 8–9.
22. Lawton, "Australian Anglican Theology," 183–85, 187–88, 190.
23. Judd and Cable, *Sydney Anglicans*, 155–56.

Anglican Fellowship formed after Mowll's election stood for.[24] Judd rightly draws attention to Hammond's emphasis on Scripture and the Reformation and to his outstanding intellect and scholarship. But his account of "The Memorial" episode (1938)[25] does not touch the root issue that Archbishop Mowll and Hammond perceived as implicit—the liberalism of the protesters. They sensed that they were being shut out from their previously significant roles made available to them under the comprehensive policy of Archbishop Wright (1909-1933). Judd overlooks Mowll's response to them,[26] crafted by Hammond, as well as his admiration for Bishop Barker's goal of an Evangelical diocese. Mowll's emphasis on evangelism accords well with Barker's aim, towards which he founded Moore College and chose its first three principals. Kaye's *A Church Without Walls*, following Judd and Cable, correctly implies that the Jonesian influence in the diocese brought to it both Howard Mowll and T. C. Hammond.[27]

From a non-Evangelical point of view, Brian Fletcher, the retired Foundation Bicentennial Professor of Australian History at Sydney University, has written a scholarly and succinct history of Anglicanism in Australia. He gives some account of "the difficult and complex problems arising from the diversity of belief that lies at the heart of Anglicanism."[28] He does not mention Jones, but acknowledges Davies as "the liberal-minded intellectual Principal of Moore College," who was concerned to present the relevance of the church's message to "the plain man."[29] On Hammond, he recognizes his "fine intellect and an unexcelled reputation as a debater," but sees him as "imprisoned within a narrow form of Puritanism that had been shaped by his experience in Ireland."[30] Fletcher seems unaware of the breadth and depth of Hammond's reading and writing, and of just where he stood and why. The latter questions (where and why?) also apply to Fletcher's remarks on Davies, which this book examines. Fletcher is rightly positive about Hammond's role in achieving an agreed constitution.[31]

Marcus Loane explicitly denied that he was himself a theologian,[32] and in his history of the college he gives only a few generalizations about the

---

24. Ibid., 227, 232-34.
25. Ibid., 238-40.
26. Loane, *Archbishop Mowll*, 147-48.
27. Kaye, *Church Without Walls*, 32.
28. Fletcher, *Place of Anglicanism*, iii.
29. Ibid., 82.
30. Ibid., 126.
31. Loane, *Centenary History*, 188.
32. Interview with Loane, June 5, 2001.

thought of the principals. Thus, Nathaniel Jones "turned the true Keswick teaching into daily life and habit," and Archbishop Wright praised "his sainted life and rich stores of theological knowledge."[33] Loane's later vignettes of Sydney clergy include seven who illustrate the long-lasting impact of Jones on the ministry within the diocese.[34] Of Davies's convictions (Loane was a student in the college under Davies) he says only that he was "a Protestant in churchmanship, a Liberal in scholarship," while also being "a man of fatherly interest and great kindness ... whose friendly counsel is still gratefully remembered."[35] Hammond's introductory lecture, as he remembered it (Loane was then a tutor in the college), was on "Transcendentalism."[36] Years later, perhaps questionably, he wrote that Hammond's "approach to Theology always emanated from the background of Philosophy" rather than being "rooted in sound exegesis" like the English writers.[37] That was certainly Loane's impression. He also records something of the positive effect of Hammond's intellectual stimulus on the students and his influence on committees and in synod. He notes too his generosity, wit, and love of humanity.[38]

Marcia Cameron's valuable doctoral study on the history of Anglican theological education in Australia[39] underlines the gap in our knowledge of Moore College's principals. She is strong on their influence but only touches on their thought. Her earlier study of Moore College under Jones gives informative details about the institution, but has only a little on Jones's doctrinal views and focuses more on his thinking about the spiritual development of students.[40]

Stuart Piggin is necessarily sketchy on both Davies and Hammond in his 1997 essay that traces the history of theological education in Australia, though he is trained in theology.[41] Later, in the revised edition of his history of evangelicalism in Australia, he repeats Lawton's stance on Jones's "futurism," and seems to assume the correctness of Lawton's view of the kingdom of God.[42] He mentions Davies (along with Dean A. E. Talbot)

---

33. Loane, *Centenary History*, 98–99, 112–13.
34. Loane, *Mark These Men*.
35. Loane, *Centenary History*, 137.
36. Ibid., 140.
37. Loane, *Mark These Men*, 71.
38. Loane, *Centenary History*, 152–53.
39. Cameron, "Aspects of Anglican Theological Education."
40. Cameron, "Moore College Under Nathaniel Jones," 96–123.
41. Piggin, "History of Theological Education," 31, 35.
42. Piggin, *Spirit of a Nation*, 76–77.

only for debating "the underlying causes of the economic malaise," making "pronouncements on social issues," and supporting "radical and political changes"[43]—the last being more applicable to Dean Talbot than to Davies. But he gives many details on Hammond, relating that he countered sinless perfectionism with "withering logic," along with the Evangelical C. H. Nash in Melbourne and G. H. Morling (Baptist) in Sydney,[44] and that "according to Geoffrey Bingham" he thought Walter Marshall's *The Gospel Mystery of Sanctification* (1692) was "spot on."[45] (Bingham was one of the abler students in Moore College in Hammond's last years.) Piggin calls Hammond "a genuinely Anglican theologian in the Evangelical tradition."[46] His essentially sound description of Hammond piques one's curiosity for a further and fuller analysis. Jones and Davies also warrant a much closer look into their own writing for an accurate understanding of what each believed and taught, *and* of the critical difference between Davies and the other two.

In a specialized study, Benjamin Edwards documents some of Hammond's public engagement with Roman Catholicism and gives useful quotations.[47] Treloar has added an article on Hammond as a controversialist, with regard not only to Roman Catholicism, but also to the "Memorialists" episode of 1938 and the "Red Book Case" of the 1940s.[48] He rightly emphasizes Hammond's Irish Protestant-Roman Catholic background in controversy. But he omits Hammond's firm engagement with liberal theology and with High Church and Anglo-Catholic notions of episcopal authority and ritualism before he came to Sydney.

The biographical studies also confirm the need for greater knowledge. Even Loane's biography of Archbishop Mowll, which narrates his leadership of the Cambridge Inter-Collegiate Christian Union in the matter of the authority of Scripture, gives only a sketch of the theological issues. On Mowll's convictions, Loane mentions his affirmation of "the doctrine of Justification by Faith only" at his public welcome to Sydney of March 13, 1934, and of the role of the Bible as "the principal means of grace in the hands of the Holy Spirit."[49] David Garnsey's biography of his father, Arthur Garnsey, Warden of St Paul's College (an Anglican college within the University of Sydney) 1916–1944, tells of the liberal theological views of this close friend of Prin-

---

43. Ibid., 88.
44. Ibid., 107, 115, 116, 120, 122.
45. Ibid., 150.
46. Ibid., 131.
47. Edwards, *WASPS, Tykes and Ecumaniacs*, 96–97, 127, 130–32, 133, 135, 157–58.
48. Treloar, "T. C. Hammond the Controversialist," 20–35.
49. Loane, *Archbishop Mowll*, 59–60, 133, 143.

cipal Davies but throws no light on the latter's beliefs except by implication. On Hammond, Arthur Garnsey seems to have lacked any knowledge or appreciation of the reasoning that underlay his thought.[50]

Warren Nelson's biography of Hammond is carefully researched and deserves a wide readership. His chapter on Hammond's most important books constitutes a valuable overview of the latter's theological convictions. As such, it invites a more comprehensive analysis of the Hammond *oeuvre*.[51]

Dictionary articles too confirm the need for further investigation. In *The Australian Dictionary of Evangelical Biography* (1994) Brian Dickey's entry on Nathaniel Jones depends only on Lawton's work. Stephen Judd on David Davies adds nothing to what he had written in *Sydney Anglicans*. Nelson summarizes his biography of Hammond just mentioned.[52] Kenneth Cable on Hammond (1996) in the *Australian Dictionary of Biography* thought that Hammond produced well-trained clergy, but essayed no account of his theology.[53] The best dictionary article on Hammond is by G. R. Treloar, in the *Biographical Dictionary of Evangelicals*. Like Piggin, he mentions Hammond's "moderate Calvinism," "strongly objective theology," and his handling of the Memorialists episode and the Red Book Case.[54]

Nothing written about the views of these three principals has been specifically related to the intellectual currents flowing in the British Isles in their student days. Apart from Nelson's writing on Hammond, no one has examined what confronted (or supported) each of them in their university education and ecclesiastical environment. Nor has any account thrown light on their thought with regard to the developments that these men addressed in their maturity.

The greatest lack in the literature is the examination with a *theological* eye of the writings of each of these Evangelical principals. No analysis has yet appeared of Davies's published works or of his unpublished papers, such as those he gave at meetings of The Heretics. Nothing seems to have been published on Hammond's view of the key Protestant issues with Roman Catholicism. In addition, a more complete account of his published work before coming to Moore College now seems fitting. The same applies to the substance of his major works from 1936 to 1953, the years of his principalship of the college.

50. Garnsey, *Arthur Garnsey*, 74, 145, 151, 157.

51. Nelson, *T. C. Hammond*, 131–44.

52. ADEB. See "Jones, Nathaniel," "Davies, David John," and "Hammond, Thomas Chatterton,"

53. Cable, "Hammond, Thomas Chatterton," 367–68.

54. Treloar, "Hammond, Thomas Chatterton," 586–87.

The English Baptist historian David Bebbington has usefully defined the nature of evangelicalism as common to Anglican, Nonconformist and Scottish Presbyterian (Church of Scotland and derived) churches—indeed across all the British churches from the 1730s to the 1980s. His necessarily broad-brush approach covers a variety of "evangelicalisms" from conservative to liberal. He calls his defining summation "a quadrilateral of priorities," "special marks of Evangelical religion."[55] Most recently he has stated them in the order: *biblicism*, "a particular regard for the Bible," *crucicentrism*, "a stress on the sacrifice of Christ on the cross," *conversionism*, "the belief that lives need to be changed," and *activism*, "the expression of the gospel in effort." He has explained them carefully as they apply to the second half of the nineteenth century.[56] Of course, the High Church school in Anglicanism also required conversion, and Anglo-Catholics might also be said to do so and be crucicentric and activist. Evangelicalism put biblicism at the foundation of all three. But did Evangelicalism's resistance within its Anglican context to the Anglo-Catholic school make some difference to itself? With that question in mind for the three principals, the historian may take these four qualities together as distinguishing the Evangelical from other Anglican schools.

The South African-born New Zealand Baptist, Brian Harris, who lives and works in Perth, Western Australia, has critiqued the most recent trends in Evangelicalism broadly.[57] But his view applies less aptly to Moore College from the late 1890s to the early 1950s, and hardly since.

This study will attempt to elucidate the Anglican Evangelicalism of Moore College's principals with the "Bebbington quadrilateral" in mind.[58] The questions are: What was each principal's understanding of Evangelicalism which he believed, taught to his students, and promulgated by his preaching and writing? What was the background—experiential and intellectual—that led each to his own set of convictions? What was the lasting influence of each man (as far as can be determined) on the clergy he taught, and the clergy and laity he preached to and wrote for? What were the historical consequences in Moore College and the Diocese of Sydney of the perceived incompatibility of the broadened, liberal portion of the Evangelical spectrum of the day with orthodox Evangelicalism?

This work, therefore, essays to fill a lacuna in the theological history of Moore College by focusing on the three successive Evangelical principals:

55. Bebbington, *Dominance of Evangelicalism*, 23–61.
56. Bebbington, *Evangelicalism in Modern Britain*, 2–3.
57. Harris, "Beyond Bebbington," 201–19.
58. Noll, *Rise of Evangelicalism*, 17–18; Bebbington, "About the Definition," 5.

Nathaniel Jones (1897–1911), David John Davies (1911–1935), and Thomas Chatterton Hammond (1936–1953). Their era largely and critically coincided with that of the three successive archbishops of Sydney who chose them: William Saumarez Smith (1890–1909), John Charles Wright (1909–1933), and Howard West Kilvinton Mowll (1933–1958). Jones, Davies, and Hammond each represented a variant of Evangelicalism, though that of Jones and Hammond will be found to be very similar in most respects, except for their beliefs concerning the millennium. Just what the variations were is the central question this work attempts to answer more fully and exactly.

I

Challenges Intellectual and Ecclesiastical

Introduction

BY THE MID-NINETEENTH CENTURY Evangelicals and others faced growing "rationalistic infidelity"[1] in society and ritualistic innovation in the Church of England. They set up Wycliffe Hall (1879) in Oxford and Ridley Hall (1881) in Cambridge to resist both challenges.

By the turn of the century there was still appreciable Christian religious life, even revival. But more and more, people had taken on the idea of human autonomy in the pursuit of truth: that the human mind could establish and understand truly scientific and historical fact as well as moral and religious truth independently of commitment to revealed, Christian ultimate beliefs and moral values.[2] Many of the more educated people in society were explicit agnostics, some even atheists. The response of some theologians was to adapt to this by adjusting aspects or even the whole of their faith to a non-Christian view of reality.[3]

Two Liberal Evangelical historians, both contemporary with our three Moore principals, recorded their view of the era. Vernon Storr (1869–1940) described English theological developments to 1860 in some depth.[4] Another, L. E. Elliott-Binns (1885–1963), an Emmanuel College student when Davies was teaching there, continued the story to 1900. He noted that by the

---

1. See Cooper, *Brief Defence*.
2. Hoffecker, *Understanding the Flow*, 227.
3. Lints, "The Age of Intellectual Iconoclasm," 281–317.
4. Storr, *Development of English Theology*.

end of the century the church's "point of view could no longer be taken for granted,"[5] at least for intellectuals.

On the other hand, at least one highly educated unbeliever, the English philosopher and statesman, A. J. Balfour (1848–1930), became an active defender of orthodox Christian thought; the eighth edition of his *Foundations of Belief* appeared in 1901.[6] There were also some from among the able self-educated promoters of anti-Christian secularism among the working classes who returned to active Christian faith.[7] Indeed, for the many more-than-nominal believers, the Christian message was still very much alive, if not always well. Movements promoted by Evangelicals, especially the Church Missionary Society, even expanded after 1860. In England, there were also great and successful evangelistic campaigns which benefited the church at home and abroad. Movements for the promotion of the personal Christian life such as Keswick flourished and spread to Australia.[8]

The Challenges

In the late-nineteenth and early-twentieth centuries five main challenges demanded a response, within Anglicanism, especially from the Evangelicals. First and most basic was the rise of a new, liberal concept of God and, related to that, of his revelation. The second was the question, therefore, of the nature and authority of the Bible and how it should be understood in the light of historical criticism and the natural sciences. A third challenge was posed by the rejection of the doctrine of the atonement. These first three were probably what Evangelicals meant by the term "rationalist infidelity." The Darwinian explanation for the origins of the human species posed a fourth challenge. A fifth was peculiar to the Church of England and the Church of Ireland (independent after 1869), namely the Tractarian or Anglo-Catholic movement (also known as the Oxford Movement) and its associated ritualism.

The first four developments affected all the churches in England, Scotland, and Ireland, as well as elsewhere in the English-speaking world (including Australia) and beyond. The Anglo-Catholic movement became pervasive within the Church of England at home and abroad, though much

---

5. Elliott-Binns, *Religion in the Victorian Era*, 495.
6. Balfour, *Foundations of Belief*.
7. Larsen, *Crisis of Doubt*, 1–17.
8. Pollock, *Keswick Story*; Braga, *Century of Preaching Christ*; Neill, *History of Christian Missions*; Bebbington, *Dominance of Evangelicalism*, 196–97.

less so in Ireland.⁹ Moore College principal T. C. Hammond was a son of the Church of Ireland.

Challenge 1: The Concept of God and Revelation— Philosophy and Doctrine

The most basic challenge to Evangelicals was to the concept of God as the self-existent and distinct creator of the universe, and, with that, Holy Scripture as his special revelation. The Evangelicals held a wholly orthodox doctrine of God the Holy Trinity. Perhaps most of them were "moderate" Calvinists like J. C. Ryle, E. A. Litton, and Handley C. G. Moule. But, like others, they had to rely for the defense of Christian theism on the classic works of non-Evangelicals. Required reading at Cambridge and Oxford and Trinity College, Dublin in the nineteenth century and into the twentieth were the High Church Bishop Joseph Butler's *Analogy of Religion* (1736) and William Paley's *Evidences of Christianity* (1795), including his famous "watchmaker" argument for the existence of God. These works assumed an element of human autonomy with regard to knowledge of God. As the century wore on many Evangelicals adopted a greater or lesser Semi-Pelagian or Arminian tendency, thus allowing some autonomy or "free will" with regard to God's sovereignty in salvation. This tendency compromised their notion of God's saving power.¹⁰

Butler and Paley's works were persuasive for the converted believer. But even by the time Frederic Barker was consecrated Bishop of Sydney (1855) and before either Darwin's *Origin of Species* appeared in 1859 or *Essays and Reviews* by seven Oxford academics in 1860, Matthew Arnold was saying that the age was already one of doubt.¹¹ "All intellectual theories, including those of morality, were insecure."¹² Common questions included: "Does God exist, and if he does is he personal or not?" "Is there a heaven or a hell?" "Is Christianity the true religion, and if so, which kind of Christianity?" Such concerns also "invaded ethical theory and the conception of man,"¹³ raising the question of the freedom of the will and of whether conscience was the source and authority of moral right and wrong. T. H. Huxley (1825–1895), famous in his day as the promoter of Darwinism, coined the

---

9. Acheson, *History of the Church of Ireland*, 180–82.
10. Van Til, *Christian Theory of Knowledge*, 12.
11. Houghton, *Victorian Frame of Mind*, 10–11.
12. Ibid.
13. Arnold, "Stanzas," in Houghton, ibid., 11–12.

term "agnostic" to describe his own position of doubt—that it was impossible to know whether God existed or not.

Both the future Archbishop of Sydney, John Charles Wright, and the future principal of Moore College, Nathaniel Jones, were Oxford students in the first half of the 1880s. E. A. Knox, an Evangelical fellow and tutor at Oxford, listed what he felt to be amongst the leading challenges to Christian faith. For Knox, they were both *philosophical* (especially J. S. Mill's *Utilitarianism*, which denied any orthodox idea of God) and *theological* (for example, the denial of the Christ of the Bible by D. F. Strauss and Ernest Renan, Bishop Colenso's "attack on the Pentateuch, and . . . the conclusions drawn from Darwinism").[14] J. S. Mill, for example, was committed to seeking truth by means of reason alone, rejecting the need of the divine perspective of special revelation in Scripture.[15] Mill did allow that religion provided the motivation to overcome human selfishness,[16] an important theme in D. J. Davies's thought. Thomas Rawson Birks (1810–1883), an Evangelical and Knightbridge Professor of Moral Philosophy in Cambridge (1872–1878) was a prominent critic of Mill.[17]

By the end of the century Ernst Haeckel's *Riddle of the Universe*, the "text-book of post-Darwinianism," which kept materialism very much alive, was being very widely read.[18] Materialism is the view that all life, even human consciousness itself, finds its origin purely in the *matter* which the universe consists of. Both Davies and Hammond were concerned with this challenge to the orthodox Christian view of the world.

For Davies and Hammond the most important current in philosophy was idealism, stemming from Immanuel Kant and still alive in the 1940s. The Romantic poet S. T. Coleridge (1772–1834) was also a philosopher-theologian and used idealism as a means of reconciling himself (and others) to an apparently orthodox Christian faith. Coleridge's doctrine that God is immanent (indwelling) in humans did not intend to deny that the self-existent Creator is distinct from his dependent creation. But did he make clear that God remains distinct from and transcendent over his creation even while present within humanity?[19] Coleridge profoundly influenced F.

---

14. Knox, *Reminiscences*, 112.

15. Storr, *Development of English Theology*, 392; Passmore, *Hundred Years of Philosophy*, 33, referencing Mill, *Three Essays on Religion*.

16. Mill, *Utility of Religion*, 109, cited in Storr, *Development of English Theology*, 391.

17. Birks, *Modern Utilitarianism*.

18. Passmore, *Hundred Years of Philosophy*, 42.

19. Pym, *Religious Thought*, 15–19, does not seem to clarify this point.

D. Maurice's thought,[20] and Maurice in turn influenced many other theologians. Archdeacon William Cunningham, for example, an important teacher of D. J. Davies at Trinity College, Cambridge, was a lifelong follower of Maurice's theology and social ideas.[21]

The widespread adoption of idealism can in part be attributed to the standard reading of Plato in the university Classical education of the time.[22] Idealism became the dominant philosophical school until the early twentieth century and even later. Many saw it as a means of restoring Christian faith in the face of J. S. Mill's views. But rather than restoring Christian orthodoxy, it had "an important influence on the development of our liberal form of Christianity."[23] The idealist, Thomas Hill Green (1836–1882), fellow at Balliol College, Oxford from 1860 and tutor from 1866, became Whyte's Professor of Moral Philosophy in 1878. Green readily accepted what he took to be Hegel's "main conclusion" concerning "the one spiritual self-conscious being" expressed in the world, and human beings as "partakers in some inchoate measure of [that] self-consciousness."[24] This immanentism threatened to deny that God was distinct from his creation.

Green "embodied and shaped late-Victorian Oxford"[25] and although he died in early 1882, his "powerful intellectual and moral force . . . would be found, from about 1880 to about 1910, penetrating and fertilizing every part of the national life."[26] Although not to be exaggerated, he had a significant influence on the *Lux Mundi* (1889) school of Oxford Tractarians. They developed a liberal Anglo-Catholicism, [27] though conservatively, outstandingly in the person of Henry Scott Holland,[28] as well as in Charles Gore.[29] Gore would be an important later influence on the Liberal Evangelical D. J. Davies. At Cambridge, William Cunningham, a mentor of Davies, acknowledged Green as "the man whom I looked on as my master in all that I care about in philosophy."[30]

20. Christensen, *Divine Order*, 295.
21. Cunningham, *William Cunningham*, 22.
22. Brown, *Philosophy and the Christian Faith*, 123.
23. Stirling, *Secret of Hegel*, quoted in Passmore, *Hundred Years of Philosophy*, 51.
24. Passmore, ibid., 57.
25. Goldman, *Dons and Workers*, 50.
26. Passmore, *Hundred Years of Philosophy*, 56, quoting Collingwood, *Autobiography*.
27. See Ovey, "Is Christ's Incarnation the Culmination?"
28. See Paget, *Henry Scott Holland*.
29. Ramsey, *From Gore to Temple*, 6–7, 12–15.
30. Cunningham, *William Cunningham*, 50 (from a letter written soon after Green's death).

Challenge 2: The New Concept of the Bible and "Critical-Historical Method(s)" Applied to its Literature and Religious Teaching

The authority of the Bible was of major concern for all three of the Moore College principals in this study. Coleridge's idealist notion of the inspiration of Scripture (as coming from the divine within man) had opened the way for a new critical approach. This had an impact on Matthew Arnold, on F. D. Maurice (especially), on F. J. A. Hort, and (perhaps indirectly) on B. F. Westcott.[31] It was after *Essays and Reviews* (1860) that matters such as the authority of Holy Scripture moved more to the public center of debate. Much of the scholarly work assumed that the human mind is autonomous, can reason independently of God, and that the research task can aspire to be religiously neutral.[32]

In fact the criticism of the Bible in *Essays and Reviews* was premised on the several essayists' view of reality. The Tractarian, E. B. Pusey (1800–1882), Regius Professor of Hebrew at Oxford, had for a time embraced the negative-critical approach. Later he noted the rationalistic spring from which the negative conclusions of the German biblical critics flowed.[33] With regard to the contributors to *Essays and Reviews* (1860), he made the insightful claim that "disbelief had been the parent, not the offspring of their criticism."[34]

John William Colenso (1814–1883), founding Anglican missionary Bishop of Natal (1853) and critic of the Pentateuch, was a man of theologically liberal presuppositions and on that basis attempted to apply his mathematics (his "major" at Cambridge) to the numerical data in the Pentateuch. In 1862 he publicly questioned both the historicity and the Mosaic authorship of the first five books of the Bible.[35]

Similarly inspired criticism of the New Testament gospels had appeared in Germany in the late eighteenth century.[36] Its roots went back to the English deists and their assumptions, which bore fruit in radical negative German criticism of the New Testament gospels, notoriously that of D. F. Strauss in *The Life of Jesus Critically Examined* (1846), and the work of F. C. Baur's "Tübingen School."

---

31. Ramsey, *Maurice and the Conflicts*, 13–20, 102–5. Ramsey cites Hort, in *Cambridge Essays,* on Coleridge.

32. See Packer, *"Fundamentalism" and the Word of God* for a full statement of the issues.

33. Pusey, *Historical Enquiry.*

34. Pusey, *Daniel the Prophet*, v.

35. Colenso, *Pentateuch and the Book of Joshua*, 3–37.

36. Reimarus, *Fragments.*

Thus all three of the future principals of Moore College of the period 1897 to 1953 grew to adulthood in an environment where the educated, at least, were aware that the new historical approach could and did induce skepticism with regard to the Christian message. Christian theism as the necessary presupposition of thought was either *a priori* ruled out, or at best reinterpreted along the immanentist lines of philosophical idealism. While the scholar quite properly examined the past in the light of its time and culture, and with strict attention to documentary evidence, this was only as *perceived within a rationalist framework* with its underlying assumptions that included ongoing autonomous human moral and intellectual progress, and the methodological need to exclude the supernatural. These writers all presupposed that human reason must be self-legislating: it must not depend on any external authority (such as the text of the Bible). It must come from within, following Immanuel Kant's maxim "*sapere aude*," "dare to be wise!"[37] There could be no infallible revelation of God's mind in Scripture as such.

The fundamental issue for Old Testament theology was whether the religion required of Israel was a *natural* historical development, following Hegel,[38] like that of the other Near-Eastern religions, or whether it was God's special revelation to them. The negative critics interconnected two fundamental approaches: first they presupposed a natural historical development in Israel along with attendant moral development, and, secondly, they developed a particular methodology for ascertaining the sources of the first five books of the Bible. Putting the two approaches together they estimated the relative dating of the sources. A further challenge was the question of the historicity or historical truth of the Old Testament narratives, and the truth of prophecy—as both "forthtelling" and "foretelling."

The trend of the shift in worldview of the time gave increasing weight to the findings of negative criticism, which were moderately stated by S. R. Driver (1846–1914).[39] Driver succeeded E. B. Pusey as Regius Professor of Hebrew and Canon at Oxford in 1883, even as Nathaniel Jones began his second year as a student.

At least until Albert Schweitzer's *The Quest of the Historical Jesus* (1906 German; 1910 English), the rigorous scholarship of the "Cambridge Triumvirate" of Lightfoot, Westcott, and Hort had made the reliability of the New Testament gospels' witness to Christ seem secure. What remained at issue was how to interpret them. In 1882, the year Jones went up to Oxford,

---

37. Horace, *Odes* 1.2.40, quoted in Kant, *What Is Enlightenment?* See Onora O'Neill, "Vindicating reason," 299; Schniewind, "Autonomy, Obligation, and Virtue," 309, 310.

38. See Welch, *Protestant Thought*, 96, 97, 99.

39. Driver, *Introduction to the Literature of the Old Testament*.

the conservative Anglo-Catholic, John Wordsworth (1843–1911) became the first Oriel Professor of the Interpretation of Scripture. In the same year, William Sanday was made the Dean Ireland's Professor of Exegesis. Later, while Davies and Hammond were students, Trinity College, Cambridge fellow V. H. Stanton published the first volume of his careful study of the New Testament gospels.[40] And in Dublin, the redoubtable George Salmon, known as the "hammer of the Germans" for his attacks on the Hegelian inspired Tübingen criticism of the New Testament, was still an authority in the divinity school. Shortly before his death he supplemented his standard New Testament introduction by a substantial work on the gospels.[41]

Challenge 3: The Nature of the Atonement

F. W. Macran, the Donnellan Lecturer of 1903 to 1904, pointed out the thoroughly anti-Reformation character of Coleridgean thought with regard to original sin and the atonement.[42] Coleridge regarded the historic doctrine as a "counterfeit" of its spiritual truth.[43] Following him, F. D. Maurice "claimed that a traditional understanding of the atonement 'outrages the conscience.'"[44] In his essay "The Doctrine of the Atonement," Benjamin Jowett of Balliol College, Oxford likewise accused the traditional doctrine of being "horrible and revolting" and "inconsistent with truth and morality";[45] and "God, if he transcend our ideas of morality, can yet never be in any degree contrary to them."[46] In 1889 the liberal Anglo-Catholic essay on the atonement in *Lux Mundi* also rejected the penal substitutionary view of Christ's death because "the punishment of the innocent instead of the guilty is unjust."[47] The underlying assumption was the supposedly growing autonomous human moral consciousness.

At the opening of the twentieth century R. C. Moberly utilized the idealist emphasis on personality in *Atonement and Personality* to put forward a

---

40. Stanton, *Gospels as Historical Documents*.

41. Salmon, *Historical Introduction to the Books of the New Testament*.

42. Macran, *English Apologetic Theology*, 103–4.

43. Pym, *Religious Thought of Samuel Taylor Coleridge*.

44. Maurice, *Theological Essays*, 138, cited by Atherstone, "Benjamin Jowett's Pauline Commentary," 139.

45. Jowett, *Epistles of St.Paul*, 2:474, quoted by Atherstone, "Benjamin Jowett's Pauline Commentary," 141.

46. Jowett, ibid., 472, quoted by Atherstone, "Benjamin Jowett's Pauline Commentary," 141.

47. Lyttleton, "Atonement," in Gore, *Lux Mundi*, 309.

theory of Christ's vicarious repentance. This work of wide influence argued for more than a merely moral-influence atonement, which was what the previous writers could accept.[48] The meaning of Christ's atoning death remained one of the major challenges around the turn of the century to some Evangelicals.

Challenge 4: Darwin's Theory of Evolution

Darwin's *On the Origin of Species by Means of Natural Selection, or the Preservation of Favoured Races in the Struggle for Life* appeared in November 1859. *Essays and Reviews* came out (see Challenge 2 above) the following February.

The idea of evolution was nothing new: at least all Classics students of Darwin's day knew of the great Latin poem *De Rerum Natura* by Lucretius (lived probably 94–54 BCE), which was based on the philosophy of Epicurus (341–271 BCE). The poem narrated the natural development of living species in a random universe through the survival of the fittest.[49] Before Darwin was born, anti-religious working-class radicals noted earlier pressed this very notion in their propaganda. The work of the deist skeptic, Thomas Paine (1737–1809) in *The Age of Reason* (1794) and that of Baron d'Holbach in his *System of Nature* (1797) strongly advocated a naturalistic evolution.

Darwin's explanation confirmed for the majority of the radicals their thoroughgoing materialism.[50] On the other hand, Darwin's grandfather, Erasmus Darwin, believed in a purposive evolution. The younger Darwin himself had read the idea of a struggle for life in the book by Thomas Malthus (1766–1834) published over sixty years before his *Essay on the Principle of Population*.

As well as biology, geological discovery also caused some rethinking of traditional views. At the time Darwin was finishing his studies at Cambridge, Charles Lyell's *Principles of Geology* (1830–1833) was proposing a uniformitarian theory of the earth as sufficient explanation of geological history. Leading scientists opposed this, but according to Owen Chadwick, by the 1840s even a child in an educated church-going family "learn[ed]

---

48. Moberly, *Atonement and Personality*; Mozley, *Doctrine of the Atonement*, 193–95. See also Mozley, "Reformation and Post-Reformation Concepts," in *Doctrine of the Atonement*, 141–201.

49. Lucretius, *De Rerum Natura*, 5. See "Lucretius" and "Epicurus," in *Oxford Classical Dictionary*, 622–24 and 390–92.

50. Cf. Larsen, *Crisis of Doubt*, 247.

at mother's knee that the seven days of Genesis Chapter 1 are not to be taken literally, and Noah's flood too for it would not have covered the whole earth." Chadwick writes: "We [the child] should think of the earth as very old ... for already we should have children's picture-books about dinosaurs and pterodactyls. ... We should feel no tug between school-learning and religious practice."[51] This knowledge made Darwin's new theory of 1859 more believable. His hypothesis was that new species of life had arisen by the *natural* selection of incremental *chance* variations through the mechanism of the survival of the fittest. Exactly how this *natural selection* might achieve *new* species as distinct from the variety *within* species achieved by the animal-breeder's *deliberate selection* Darwin did not explain. His *Origin of Species*, however, followed in 1871 by *The Descent of Man*, put a large question mark against William Paley's argument for God from the evidence of *design* in the world.[52] Darwin's proposal of a "purely mechanistic operation,"[53] a *materialistic* concept, was a view which, for most, made the notion of purpose in the creation and in human life a question,[54] not an assumption.

Many scientists had doubts and Darwin was aware of the problems, but T. H. Huxley, Professor of Natural History at the Royal School of Mines, embraced and promoted *Origin of Species* widely, as did many others. The views of Huxley, along with those of the philosopher Herbert Spencer, were commonly canvassed and well known. McCabe's translation from German of Haeckel's *The Riddle of the Universe*, became the "text-book of post-Darwinian naturalism," selling 100,000 copies by 1900.[55] A new edition of Darwin's *Descent of Man* had come out in 1901,[56] the year Davies went up to Cambridge University and when Hammond was well into his studies at Trinity College, Dublin; neither could afford to ignore the naturalistic challenges to orthodox faith.

In England the liberal biblical scholars did not ease this challenge for Evangelicals. Liberal Anglo-Catholics thought that the "facts of sin and the disorder of the world" could be accounted for without the fall of Genesis 3, as did the liberal Old Testament scholar S. R. Driver. G. Henslow,

---

51. Chadwick, *Secularization of the European Mind*, 182.

52. Paley, *Evidences*.

53. Barzun, *From Dawn to Decadence*, 570. See also Barzun, *Marx, Darwin, Wagner*, 10–11, 25–126.

54. Barzun, *Marx, Darwin, Wagner*, 28.

55. Chadwick, *Secularisation of the European Mind*, 177, with reference to Haeckel, *Riddle of the Universe*.

56. Darwin, *Descent of Man*.

a Cambridge botanist, wrote of humans having been "on a uniformly low level of barbarism for an incalculable length of time."[57]

The interested Australian public was well-versed in such matters, reading in both the local secular press and the church magazines about almost everything talked about in "the home country." Many read the books published in England and Scotland, and no lack of thought and discussion arose from Darwin's theory of natural selection.[58] Both church leaders and scholarly clergy addressed the matter.[59] The attitudes of leading clergy were important in the culture, and a few had even been educated in the sciences, among them the Reverend William Branwhite Clarke, the "father of Australian geology."[60] Clearly the sheer materialism of conclusions drawn from Darwin's theory not only challenged the notion of creation's design but was also inconsistent with God's changeless holiness in his relations with humanity, with the possibility of obedience to his moral law, and with sin as *voluntary* departure from rectitude.

Challenge 5: The Rise of the Tractarian or Oxford Movement[61]

Anglican Evangelicalism came to New South Wales with the chaplain of the First Fleet in 1788, the Reverend Richard Johnson (1755–1827), followed in 1793 by the assistant chaplain, Samuel Marsden (1765–1838). The Crown appointed William Grant Broughton (1788–1853) in 1829 as the second archdeacon of Australia, then appointed him as Bishop of Australia in 1836. One of those High Churchmen who would lean to the new Anglo-Catholic movement, Broughton brought in clergy of the same mind, thus posing a challenge to the next bishop, Frederic Barker, himself an Evangelical.

The immediate occasion for the rise of Tractarianism was the Reverend John Keble's Oxford Assize sermon of July 1833. The 1832 Reform Bill of the Whig government had just lowered the number of Church of Ireland bishoprics, and Keble, fearing an Erastianism that might also see the government abolish bishops from the Church of England, viewed this legislation as, in principle, an act of "National Apostasy."[62]

---

57. Henslow, in *Liberal Churchman*, 222–23, as cited in Orr, *Sin as a Problem Today*, 188n2; title of article not cited by Orr.
58. See Frame, *Anglicans in Australia*..
59. Robin, *Charles Perry*, 131; Judd and Cable, *Sydney Anglicans*, 118–19, 126–27.
60. See Young, *This Wonderfully*, 133–49.
61. Cf. Chadwick, *Victorian Church: Part II*.
62. Keble, "National Apostasy."

The long-term product of the movement was twofold: doctrinal and liturgical. Its followers thought the English church before the Reformation represented the authentic Christianity of the earliest centuries: the Reformation understanding of the sinner's justification was wrong; a "real presence" of Christ in the consecrated elements of the Lord's Supper must be affirmed (and the Holy Table called "the Altar"); and a tactual succession of bishops from Christ's apostles must be insisted on. This latter idea denied the validity of the ministry of the other Protestant churches, as had the old school High Churchmen. The series of tracts the movement published resulted in the epithet "Tractarian" for its followers. From 1838 the name "Anglo-Catholic" was used of them and later still, "Ritualists"; most adopted rituals in public worship that had been removed from the Church of England before the reign of Elizabeth I.

The new movement appealed to many of the older "historic High Churchmen," who were in fact, at least originally, "Protestant" in doctrine.[63] As the Evangelical Handley Moule put it, the teaching of the Anglo-Catholics on the vital necessity of episcopacy, on justification, on regeneration, and on the nature of the eucharistic presence was not that of the historic High Churchmen.[64]

Historians do not always note, however, that the High Churchmen had, in principle, turned back a little Romeward; among other things, they were confused about justification by faith. The exposition by the old High Churchman Bishop Bull (1634–1710)[65] appealed to some Anglo-Catholic writers. It was also hard-line episcopalian High Churchmen who in 1661 removed from the Ordination of Priests in the Prayer Book the New Testament passages that equated "elders" with "bishops" (Acts 20:17–35 and I Tim 3:1–16).

When Bishop Barker arrived in Sydney all the city clergy except Archdeacon William Cowper were High Churchmen and "unsympathetic to Barker's Evangelicalism."[66] Nathaniel Jones, later principal of Barker's Moore College, had gone up to Oxford in good time for the semi-centenary of Keble's sermon of July 1833. John Henry Newman was a fellow Tractarian leader with Keble until 1845 when he seceded to Rome, and his work reinterpreting justification was republished while Jones was a student.[67]

---

63. Upton, *Churchman's History*, 17.
64. Moule, *Evangelical School*, 29.
65. Bull, *Harmonia Apostolica*.
66. Maple, "Barker," 23.
67. Newman, *Lectures on Justification*.

CHALLENGES INTELLECTUAL AND ECCLESIASTICAL

Ritualism was the second and related part of the challenge of the Oxford Movement: actions being so obvious they could have more impact than words. The early Tractarians themselves reintroduced no new liturgical practices, and some never adopted any. But ritualism fitted their notions of the sacraments. Warre-Cornish pointed out that until the nineteenth century "the practice [in the Church of England] was the leanest ritual,"[68] and observed tellingly that

> ritual is the expression of doctrine.... When the growth of the High Church school of thought ... had brought high eucharistic and sacramental doctrine forward, and when the mediaeval [English] church became an object of veneration, it was to be expected that a revival of ritual should take place; the more so because symbolism of all kinds was attracting more and more attention.[69]

In England and in Ireland there had long been a few (exceptional) precedents[70] believed by the ritualists to be actually required by the Prayer Book rubrics. Newman adopted some ritualist practices in 1837 to 1839, while the future Bishop Frederic Barker was still a parish minister. John Mason Neale and others founded the Cambridge Camden Society "ostensibly 'to promote the study of Ecclesiastical Architecture and Antiquities,'" then "reorganized and renamed [it] 'The Ecclesiological Society'" in 1845.[71] In practice the society promoted the restoration of the Gothic church architecture of 1260 to 1360. By 1842 the Society's journal, *The Ecclesiologist*, was mandating "the building of chancel" (for an east-end communion table and a choir) "and the substitution of [stone] ALTARS for TABLES."[72] The churches built by the first chaplains in Sydney as well as some later ones had no chancels. The great architect A. W. N. Pugin (1812–1852), designer of the present English Houses of Parliament, was "the inspirer and initiator of the "Gothic Revival" in England and was a convert to Roman Catholicism.[73] St Andrew's Cathedral, Sydney, was modelled after Gothic examples.[74] By the first decade of the twentieth century "ritualism had had an impact on

---

68. Warre-Cornish, *History of the English Church*, 1:64.
69. Ibid., 2:1.
70. Yates, *Anglican Ritualism*, 10–39.
71. Toon, *Evangelical Theology*, 47.
72. Ibid., 66–69.
73. See "Pugin," in *ODCC*, 1356.
74. Johnstone, *St Andrew's Cathedral Sydney*, 21.

virtually every diocese in England and Wales, [but] its manifestations were patchy. . . . [But it] . . . was clearly beyond [being] successfully controlled."[75]

Some of the extremes reached by the turn of the century in England included "sacrifice of the Mass, elevation and reservation of the sacrament, extreme unction, the doctrine of purgatory, prayers for the dead, invocation of saints, and 'the whole body of Tridentine doctrine.'"[76] This "body of doctrine" was the Roman Catholic response to Reformation teaching formulated at the Council of Trent (1545–1571). Some ritualists encouraged fasting before Communion and even auricular confession beforehand. Perhaps it was Cranmer's retention in the Prayer Book of the word "priest," actually rooted in the New Testament word for "elder" (Gk. *presbyteros*), that made things easier for Anglo-Catholics to associate a real sacrifice of Christ's body and blood with the Holy Communion.

Two city parish churches in Sydney became flag-bearers of ritualism— St James' Church, King Street and, in 1885, Christ Church Saint Laurence, near Central railway station.[77] Ritualism remained a live issue in the diocese and hence for all three Moore College principals of this study. It spread to the other dioceses in New South Wales, where lay people who moved to the country from Sydney often found a local Baptist church more theologically and liturgically comfortable.

The ritualists themselves were the first to organize and to resort to the courts against Evangelicals. They established the English Church Union in 1860, in order to "defend and maintain unimpaired the doctrine, discipline and ritual of the Church of England . . . and to combat Erastianism, Rationalism and Puritanism."[78]

While one might sympathize with the High Churchmen's opposition to Erastianism and rationalism, it is more difficult to condone their attempted prosecution of the Evangelical Bishop Samuel Waldegrave for heresy (his "outspoken defence" of the Evangelical stance on the Reformation), as well as their attacks on the Evangelical clergy who held popular services in theatres to attract non-churchgoers.[79]

Since the Church of England was established by law, only Parliament could legislate for changes in its form of worship, Parliament being virtually the synod of the national church. The diocesan bishops were members of the House of Lords, so the civil courts could enforce church law. Questions of

---

75. Yates, *Anglican Ritualism*, 292.
76. Warre-Cornish, *History of the English Church*, 2:1.
77. Judd and Cable, *Sydney Anglicans*, 161–65.
78. Warre-Cornish, *History of the English Church*, 2:108–9.
79. Balleine, *History of the Evangelical Party*, 181.

its interpretation could go as high as the Privy Council and some ritualists went to prison rather than obey these "Erastian" courts; their "martyrdom" only aroused popular sympathy.

The matter was taken up in a Royal Commission of 1904–1906, which recommended that in non-doctrinal matters the Prayer Book might well be adjusted to modern needs, but for various reasons the Evangelicals did not take advantage of this opportunity.[80] In 1919 Parliament created the National Assembly of the Church of England, which proposed a revised Prayer Book containing concessions to Anglo-Catholic doctrine and ritualism. After "a stormy time in Convocation and Church Assembly" and having "already aroused considerable controversy in the country at large" this so-called "Deposited Book" was twice defeated in Parliament—in 1927 and 1928—to Bishop E. A. Knox's great surprise and relief.[81]

The Irish Book of Common Prayer of 1878 was important background of the Irish clergy who came to Sydney in the nineteenth century and for T. C. Hammond in the twentieth. This prayer book was a slightly modified version of the Book of Common Prayer (hereafter also called the Prayer Book) of 1662, intended to prevent the very liturgical chaos of ritual innovation that was threatening the English church. It added wording from the twenty-eighth of the Thirty-nine Articles to the Catechism, to clarify the manner in which the body and blood of Christ are received in the Lord's Supper. It accommodated, however, the old-school High Church tradition within the Irish church on the meaning of regeneration in baptism.[82]

Conclusion

As we have seen, nineteenth-century Evangelicals experienced a series of challenges—philosophical, theological, historical, scientific, and doctrinal-liturgical—to various core theological convictions: their understanding of the nature of God and what he did in Christ; the interpretation and authority of the Bible; their understanding of the English Reformation and the Prayer Book, and of Prayer Book liturgical practice. How Evangelicals responded to the above movements of thought and practice will be described in the following chapter.

---

80. Bromiley, "Appendix I," 254.
81. Knox, *Reminiscences*, 311–12.
82. Acheson, *Church of Ireland 1691–2001*, 207–10.

2

Evangelical Responses to the Challenges

Introduction

THE COURSE OF EVANGELICALISM in Sydney in general and at Moore College in particular from the 1890s to the 1950s reflected the responses of Evangelicals in England, and also in Ireland, to the challenges of liberalism and ritualism described above. As the thought of Christian thinkers, like that of philosophers,[1] bore the stamp of the intellectual trends of their times, so did that of the Evangelicals, including the principals of Moore College in the period from 1897 to 1953. This led to some weaknesses as well as strengths.

Two new doctrinal factors in the "home country" were to extend the character of conservative Evangelicalism. By the mid-nineteenth century, postmillennialism (the expectation of Christ's reign on earth as the climax of the conversion of the world through the preaching of the gospel) was being replaced. Now the personal advent of Christ and the resurrection of the saints was expected to precede the millennium (hence the term *premillennial*), a hope which a widespread pessimism made popular. The second half of the century also saw the rise of a desire for greater Christian holiness, which resulted most notably in the Keswick form. Both of these additions to the Thirty-nine Articles *cum* Prayer Book extended the spectrum of doctrinal thought for many Evangelicals, but caused little disturbance in their ethos and unity of mind. A liberal trend concerning biblical authority, however, stretched or broadened, not just extended the spectrum for some: it

---

1. Acton, "Inaugural Lecture," in Acton, *Lectures*, 35.

introduced a difference in principle, which had implications for other questions of doctrine, especially the authority of Scripture and the atonement.[2]

While Nathaniel Jones included both a premillennial expectation and Keswick holiness doctrine in his conservative Evangelical convictions, Hammond accepted only the latter. D. J. Davies, for his part, soon made his liberal outlook that of the teaching at Moore College. The Evangelical spectrum of the college would return from this shift to the left only when Archbishop Mowll appointed Principal Hammond to succeed him.

God and Revelation

The Christian doctrine of God entails the concept of God's revelation, both in creation and in Scripture, with the latter being necessary for the proper understanding of the former. However, by the nineteenth century the thoughtful in all the church denominations of Britain continued to rely on the High Churchman (and so theologically Arminian) Bishop Joseph Butler's *Analogy of Religion* (1736) to defend the Christian faith, and upon the Broad Church William Paley's *Evidences of Christianity* (1795).

As the nineteenth century wore on some Evangelical churchmen, though more naturally Calvinists, inclined to a Semi-Pelagian or Arminian shift with regard to "free will."[3] This was partly in reaction to T. H. Huxley's mechanistic notion of the human person, which seemed to do away with personal freedom. But their move implicitly compromised the notion of God as sovereign over all things including the human will.[4]

The Evangelical thinker, Thomas Rawson Birks avoided this mistake. From 1866 Birks was vicar of Holy Trinity Church, Cambridge, and also Knightbridge Professor of Moral Philosophy, Casuistry and Moral Theology from 1872 to 1878. His *Modern Utilitarianism*, a copy of which Nathaniel Jones purchased in Sydney in 1906,[5] penetratingly exposed J. S. Mill's implicit rejection of the need for a theistic perspective, namely presupposing God as revealed in Scripture:[6] "Utilitarianism, whenever it is advanced as a complete theory . . . must involve a negative Theology . . . the worship

---

2. Bromiley, "Appendix I," 262.
3. Bebbington, *Age of Spurgeon and Moody*, 130.
4. Van Til, *Christian Theory of Knowledge*, 12.
5. Jones's personal copy held in Moore College Library.
6. See Storr, *Development of English Theology*, 392; Passmore, *Hundred Years of Philosophy*, 33.

of blind Chance, of blind Fate, or of a personal Divinity, omnipotent and supreme, but lawless and arbitrary, and devoid of all moral perfections."[7]

Birks then laid down the doctrine of God necessary for an intelligible ethics: "But when once we acknowledge a true and living God, the Holy Governor of a moral universe, the true limits of the doctrine are restored."[8]

Birks was similarly consistent with a theistic, at least less neutral apologetic in his "Introduction" to Paley's *Evidences*[9] and, *pace* Bebbington, in his last major work, on ethics.[10] It is not clear that Jones, or even Hammond, clearly grasped this transcendental critique of non-Christian systems of thought.

E. A. Litton, the Oxford Evangelical theologian and near contemporary of Birks, was also more theologically consistent in his editing of Paley.[11] In his *magnum opus, Introduction to Dogmatic Theology: On the Basis of the XXXIX Articles*[12] he too addressed both Mill's logic and, especially, his theism,[13] as well as the thought of other figures intellectually important for his day—David Hume,[14] Immanuel Kant, and Henry Mansel of Oxford[15] among them. Nor did Litton overlook Baden Powell's contribution, "Evidences," in *Essays and Reviews*[16] or Benjamin Jowett's earlier "Essay on Natural Religion." [17]

Other Evangelicals, too, noticed the thinkers and issues of their day. T. P. Boultbee's work on the Thirty-nine Articles (1871) quoted a perceptive critique of contemporary thought by Francis Jeune, Bishop of Peterborough (1864–1868), whose "opinions were of the evangelical order,"[18] though "probably not a definite evangelical."[19] He ranged over *Material Atheism, Pantheism* (from Hegel), *Positivism, Suicide of Philosophy*, and *Destruction*

---

7. Birks, *Modern Utilitarianism*, 240.

8. Ibid.

9. Birks, "Introduction", 7–12.

10. Birks, *Supernatural Revelation*, 35; cf. Bebbington, *Age of Spurgeon and Moody*, 110–11.

11. Litton, "Notes."

12. Litton, *Introduction to Dogmatic Theology*, 52–66.

13. Mill, *Essay on Theism*, and *System of Logic*.

14. Hume, *Treatise of Human Nature*.

15. Mansel, *Limits of Religious Thought*.

16. Powell, "Study of the Evidences," 94–144.

17. Jowett, *Epistles of St Paul*, 2:480–94.

18. Boase, "Jeune, Francis," 373.

19. Reynolds, *Evangelicals*, 173.

of Morality (Spinoza),[20] perceptively tracing these to human reason's "successful revolt against all authority."[21] Handley C. G. Moule's *Outlines of Christian Doctrine* (1889) also drew attention both to the problem raised by philosophical idealism,[22] namely "Pantheism," and to agnosticism.[23]

The Scottish Presbyterian, James Orr, whom Hammond had met, "stressed to advantage the importance of presuppositions and of one's starting point," even if he also allowed some intrusion of idealistic and rationalistic elements into his thought.[24] *The Anglican Church Handbooks* series edited by W. H. Griffith Thomas published the Irish philosopher-theologian C. F. d'Arcy's *Christianity and the Supernatural*.[25] This explicitly treated the transcendence and immanence of God. Nathaniel Jones appears to have escaped the issues of philosophy in his student years at Oxford, while Davies accepted idealism as the true philosophy and Hammond would often quote pertinent *individual insights* of Green when teaching at Moore College.

Criticism of Scripture

The place and nature of the Bible became, perhaps, the key presenting issue in this period. Evangelicals responded to the negative biblical criticism that was brought to notorious prominence by *Essays and Reviews* in 1860 and by Colenso's *The Pentateuch and Book of Joshua Critically Examined* of 1862. Much of it presupposed, as J. I. Packer has succinctly put it, "that the Bible may contain falsehoods purporting to be truths."[26] In the early 1870s the American Presbyterian, Charles Hodge (1797–1878) had trenchantly noted (Anglicans were not so trenchant) that "most of the objections . . . are founded on unscriptural views of the relation of God to the world, or on the peculiar philosophical views of the objectors as to the nature of man or of his free agency."[27]

Soon after *Essays and Reviews*, the Evangelical dogmatics writer E. A. Litton examined "whether it can be satisfactorily made out that the Bible is

---

20. Boultbee, *Commentary on the Thirty-nine Articles*, 5–6, quoting Bishop Francis Jeune.
21. Jeune, "Primary Charge," 20.
22. Green, *Prolegomena to Ethics*; Bosanquet, *Knowledge and Reality*.
23. Moule, *Outlines of Christian Doctrine*, 14–16.
24. Knudsen, "Progressive and Regressive Tendencies," 281–82.
25. D'Arcy, *Christianity and the Supernatural*.
26. Packer, *"Fundamentalism,"* 140–41.
27. Hodge, *Systematic Theology*, 1:168.

from God, and is sufficient to instruct us in the way of life."[28] He rejected what he understood to be "the older theory [of inspiration] . . . which regards the sacred writers as merely amanuenses . . . of the Spirit"[29] (perhaps what Coleridge meant by "mechanical dictation"—a phrase much used by Principal Davies). Litton distinguished between the revelation received by prophets, for example, and the Holy Spirit's special inspiration that "supernaturally preserved [the writers] from error, and enabled [them] to transmit . . . the original revelation *as they received it*."[30] He could retain the notion of "plenary inspiration" of the author of Acts by allowing that he had truly reported Stephen's speech along with its alleged errors.[31]

In 1882, the year Nathaniel Jones enrolled at Oxford, Litton had argued somewhat differently—that the statements in the Psalms that "seem to jar our feelings as Christians," are not to be attributed to their inspired collector but taken as "a warning that even the most exalted rapture of devotion" does not exclude some human failing.[32] Not all Evangelicals adopted an acquiescent approach to those Psalms that call down judgment on the wicked.[33]

Evangelicals by no means neglected what remained the chief critical problem until the early twentieth century—that of the Old Testament. T. P. Boultbee addressed the moral problems in a relatively early lecture,[34] and Litton had touched on one mentioned above. But by 1900 Charles Henry Hamilton Wright (1836–1909), a Church of Ireland Evangelical and a learned Old Testament theologian, pointed to a need of more "scholars properly trained in Biblical science and able to uphold the truth as taught by Christ and His Apostles."[35] This must have "rung a bell" in T. C. Hammond's acute mind as he studied for his Divinitatis Testimonium examinations. Yet Wright, though widely read in the literature, made no mention of the Hegelian philosophy underlying the Graf-Kuenen-Wellhausen development hypothesis concerning the redaction of the Old Testament.[36]

A number of works by Evangelicals attempted to respond to the negative critical Old Testament scholarship. In 1894 Robert Sinker (1838–1913),

---

28. Litton, *Guide to the Study of Holy Scripture*, iv.
29. Ibid., 119.
30. Ibid., 110. Emphasis added.
31. Ibid., 124.
32. Litton, *Introduction to Dogmatic Theology*, 25.
33. E.g., Manley, *Gospel in the Psalms*, 124–25.
34. Boultbee, *Alleged Moral Difficulties*.
35. Wright, *Introduction*, vii.
36. Ibid., xxi.

librarian of Trinity College, tutor in Old Testament at Ridley Hall and friend of its principal, Handley Moule, wrote on the contested date of Deuteronomy in his contribution to *Lex Mosaica*.[37] Other contributors to that volume were the professor of Assyriology at Oxford, A. H. Sayce, and George Rawlinson, former Camden Professor of Ancient History at Oxford, both Presbyterians, as well as Henry Wace (1836–1924). The late Evangelical Bishop of Bath and Wells, Lord Arthur Hervey (1808–1894), concluded from his own analysis of the Pentateuch "that in the Pentateuch we have either true history, or a most ingenious, skilful, and unique fiction."[38] Wace's overall "Summary" of *Lex Mosaica* argued that the evidence showed that theories denying the traditional belief concerning the Law (ceremonial) and the subsequent history of Israel were "extremely precarious."[39]

Robert Sinker's own book a few years later, *"Higher Criticism,"*[40] may well have provided one basis to Howard Mowll and other students in the CICCU (Cambridge Inter-Collegiate Christian Union) in 1910–1911 for their stance on the inspiration and authority of Scripture. Sinker had read *The Higher Criticism of the Pentateuch*[41] by William Henry Green (1825–1900) of Princeton, and was well-read in German as well as English on both sides of the controversy. On Wellhausen's and others' development hypothesis of Israel's religion, Sinker cited the Scot, James Robertson's "masterly book,"[42] *The Early Religion of Israel*,[43] which Henry Wace also admired.

Early in 1902, the Bible League, instituted some ten years earlier, whose vice-presidents included Handley Moule (Norrisian Professor of Divinity, 1899, Bishop of Durham 1901), and Principal W. H. Griffith Thomas of Wycliffe Hall, organized a conference at Oxford chaired by Wace.[44] The speakers, Wace explained, were "cordially welcoming [of] critical and archeological investigations," and not motivated "by the least hostility to criticism" (that is, as such). The real question was "whether, in the main, the story of the course of Divine revelation from Abraham onwards is trustworthily narrated in the course of the Old Testament."[45] Wace hoped for better criticism as seen in the case of New Testament studies, notably the work

---

37. Sinker, "The Seventh Century," 449–90.
38. Hervey, "Introduction," xxxiv–xxxv.
39. Wace, "Summary," 610, 617.
40. Sinker, *"Higher Criticism."* Published previously as articles in *The Record*.
41. Green, *Higher Criticism*, cited in Sinker, *"Higher Criticism,"* 39, 48, 100.
42. Sinker, *"Higher Criticism,"* 70.
43. Robertson, *Early Religion of Israel*.
44. Wace, *Criticism Criticized*.
45. Ibid., 12.

of the "Cambridge Triumvirate." The Old Testament critic, August Dillman (1823–1894), he noted, had maintained that "the main course of the Old Testament narratives is substantially true."[46] But did not Wace then walk his reader along the edge of an apologetic precipice? He cited (as he had in his "Summary" of *Lex Mosaica*)[47] the rationalist dictum of Joseph Butler's *Analogy of Religion* for the reading of the Bible: "Let reason be kept to, and if any part of the scripture account of the redemption of the world by Christ can be shown to be really contrary to it, let the scripture, in the name of God, be given up."[48]

Wace's reading of works in German since 1894 appears to have overlooked Ernst Troeltsch, who in 1898 had set forth another principle of analogy—that history is a sequence of analogously *natural* events.[49] This was the ground of Adolph Harnack's rejection of New Testament miracles.[50]

Strong contributors to *Criticism Criticized* included D. S. Margoliouth (1858–1940), Laudian Professor of Arabic at Oxford from 1889 (he resigned his chair in 1937), J. J. Lias and R. B. Girdlestone, and also C. H. H. Wright on "The Book of Daniel and Modern Criticism," a point of contention later in the Diocese of Sydney and at Moore College under Hammond. One may assume that the student Hammond noticed *Criticism Criticized* in 1902, and James Orr's *The Problem of the Old Testament* and *The Bible Under Trial* in the early years of his ordained ministry. Each of these works touches on the worldview assumptions that constrained the methodology of the negative critic.[51]

But it was a son of the well-known Evangelical Bishop J. C. Ryle, namely Herbert Ryle, Hulsean Professor of Divinity at Cambridge from 1888 to 1901, who represented the new liberal broadening of the Evangelical spectrum of theological conviction. Though "welcomed by the CICCU, for he preached a clear evangelistic message,"[52] his "Preface" to *The Canon of the Old Testament* states that those who charge all biblical critics with "repudiating Revelation and denying the Inspiration of Scripture" show "either . . . want of acquaintance with the literature . . . or their disinclination to distinguish between the work of Christian scholars and that of avowed

---

46. Ibid., 10, citing Dillman, *Alttestamentliche Theologie*.
47. Wace, "Summary," 611.
48. Butler, *Analogy*, 2:275.
49. Troeltsch, "Historical and Dogmatic Method in Theology."
50. Harnack, *Dogmengeschichte*, 1:50n4, as cited in Denney, *Studies in Theology*, 259, note D; for English see Harnack, *History of Dogma*, 1:65n3.
51. Orr, *Problem*, 1–24; Orr, *Bible Under Trial*, 56–60.
52. Pollock, *Cambridge Movement*, 146.

antagonists to religion." His view was that mistakes due to "rashness, love of change, or inaccuracy of observation" will be corrected by "the Christian scholarship of another generation."[53] Herbert Ryle did not broach the prior issue of worldview. One is tempted to think that Robert Sinker included this Cambridge contemporary of his among "those 'Higher Critics' . . . who make desperate efforts to blend their neo-critical conclusions with their old beliefs . . . to the amazement or amusement, one would judge, of some of their Continental allies."[54]

Concerning the authority of Scripture, Ryle is an example of those Evangelicals who were beginning to move towards "a newer type of Evangelicalism which should be positive, and active, and liberal in outlook."[55] It was Evangelicals of this kind who formally inaugurated the private "Group Brotherhood" in 1907, with Archdeacon John Charles Wright of Manchester as chairman, which later renamed itself the "Anglican Evangelical Group Movement." Members included H. L. C. V. de Candole, the vicar of Holy Trinity Church, Cambridge, and A. J. Tait, who was about to become principal of Ridley Hall, Cambridge. De Candole's curate D. J. Davies also joined the Brotherhood.[56]

In the first decade of the twentieth century the New Testament became more overtly subjected to a negative higher criticism. James Orr could write in 1907, following upon the 1906 German original of Albert Schweitzer's *Quest of the Historical Jesus*: "Only folly could imagine that it was possible to stand permanently with an advanced liberal leg in the Old Testament and a conservative leg in the New."[57] Many in the Group Brotherhood, however, believed that they could so stand. They found supportive scholarship for the reliability of the gospels in Professor V. H. Stanton.[58]

With regard to Scripture, none of the Evangelicals, liberal or not, seems to have taken note of the recently published translation of Abraham Kuyper's seminal work on the principles of theology.[59] He laid out, what had been foreshadowed by Birks and others noted above, the antithesis between the thinking that characterizes the regenerate Christian mind and human autonomy. Hammond may have noticed Kuyper's book, and probably the strictures of Geerhardus Vos of Princeton on the current danger-

---

53. Ryle, *Canon of the Old Testament*, viii–ix.
54. Sinker, "Higher Criticism," 4–5.
55. Binns, *Evangelical Movement*, 70.
56. Davies, "Our Late Archbishop," 10.
57. Orr, *Bible Under Trial*, 150.
58. Stanton, *Gospels as Historical Documents*.
59. Kuyper, *Encyclopedia of Sacred Theology*.

ous tendency to relegate the saving works of God to the background by focusing on the human experience recorded in the Bible "hand in hand" with naturalism.[60]

Nathaniel Jones, newly installed at Moore College, was a member of the Sydney Anglican synod of 1897 when the topic of biblical criticism was addressed. The report of the 1897 Lambeth decennial conference of bishops on "The Critical Study of Holy Scripture" had arrived and had been prepared by bishops Saumarez Smith, Alfred Barry (the previous Bishop of Sydney), B. F. Westcott, and E. A. Knox. It appeared to have no appreciation of worldview assumptions that might determine the slant of critical study, and stated: "The Bible in historic, moral, and spiritual coherence, presents the Revelation of God, progressively given." (The term "progressively" was undefined.) Despite Orr's recent work, *The Christian View of God and the World*, they were confident that the critical study of the Bible would produce gains for the New Testament comparable with those already achieved for the Old, and would prove "the handmaid of faith" and not "the parent of doubt."[61]

Archdeacon Günther (presiding) summed up to Synod even more optimistically: "The results of . . . what is known as higher criticism, need cause no alarm. . . . The Holy Scriptures, as inspired and authoritative declarations, are admitted by all who have carefully studied these subjects."[62] One can only wonder what Nathaniel Jones and his friend Mervyn Archdall thought. Archdall read theology in several European languages. He was one of the last clergy Barker recruited on a visit back to England in 1882, a firm anti-ritualist and scholarly Evangelical theologian. He had graduated from Cambridge (BA 1870) when Lightfoot and Westcott were already prominent and T. R. Birks had become vicar of Holy Trinity Church. He brought with him to Sydney his new bride, Martha, daughter of a German Lutheran pastor in the Pietist tradition.[63] They would complement the ministry of Nathaniel and Grace Jones in Sydney.

The Atonement

Objections to a substitutionary atonement were another factor that led to the liberal broadening of the theological spectrum among Evangelicals and

---

60. Vos, "Christian Faith," 289–305.
61. Davidson, "Report of the Committee."
62. Günther, "Presidential Address," 31–32.
63. Andrews, "Archdall, Martha," 8–9, and Baker, "Archdall, Mervyn," 85–86.

to the formation of the Group Brotherhood. D. J. Davies was one of those who rejected the historic church doctrine.

The essentially Anselmic view of Christ's death found in *Cur Deus Homo*, "of course as corrected,"[64] was common to both the Roman Catholic Church and the churches of the Reformation.[65] It underlay the Book of Common Prayer service of the Lord's Supper as well as the Articles of Religion on the subject. It was tied to accepting "from the threshold . . . the inspiration and consequent authority of Scripture."[66] In the nineteenth century, the Congregationalist R. W. Dale's famous work on the atonement, addressed the rise of the liberal views and saw new editions in the student years of Jones, Davies (almost), and Hammond.[67] T. R. Birks had written briefly on the doctrine, and Handley C. G. Moule and E. A. Litton had given extensive space to the Anselmic view.[68]

In 1892 James Orr had also critically examined, albeit appreciatively, the views of the main figures challenging the long received doctrine—including F. D. E. Schleiermacher,[69] Horace Bushnell,[70] and Albrecht Ritschl,[71] all of whom recognized only a moral influence, not a saving historical accomplishment in the death of Christ. F. D. Maurice[72] acknowledged *some* objective ground for God's forgiveness in Christ's work.[73] Orr's summary statement of these and others' views rightly attempted to include the "elements of truth" in every one.[74] T. C. Hammond's Scottish Presbyterian connections through his wife may have enhanced his awareness of the work on the atonement of the Scots, Orr—whom he met in person—and James Denney, and of the American, B. B. Warfield. Warfield's overview appeared in the year Hammond graduated.[75]

Denney, a colleague of Orr, undertook in his famous *The Death of Christ* (1902) simply to lay out the actual New Testament teaching, without

---

64. Warfield, "Modern Theories of the Atonement," 375.
65. Litton, *Introduction to Dogmatic Theology*, 229–33.
66. Denney, *Atonement and Modern Mind*, 6.
67. Dale, *Atonement*.
68. Birks, *Difficulties*; Moule, *Outlines of Christian Doctrine*, 75–92; Litton, *Introduction to Dogmatic Theology*, 225–39.
69. Schleiermacher, *Christian Faith* 425–63.
70. Bushnell, *Vicarious Sacrifice*.
71. Ritschl, *Justification and Reconciliation*.
72. Maurice, *Theological Essays*, 127–51.
73. Orr, *Christian View*, 299–314.
74. Ibid., 316–18.
75. Warfield, "Modern Theories."

assuming Scripture's inspired authority. Denney's wife had drawn his attention to C. H. Spurgeon's writings, where Christ's atoning death was the "absorbing theme."[76] But Denney defined his own "simplest possible expression" of the atonement—simply, "Christ died for our sins."[77]

Liberal Evangelicals rejected the Anselmic for an Abelardian or moral influence theory of the atonement on the earlier grounds that assumed human autonomous moral development. Thus J. K. Mozley, who appears in the photograph of an early Group Brotherhood conference, found the views of those such as E. A. Litton and Charles Hodge "morally disquieting."[78] But those holding the satisfactionist view perceived this judgment as "an arraignment of the moral character of the Scriptures," the source.[79]

In 1898 the American Baptist William Newton Clarke (1841–1912), an evangelical liberal (in the American sense),[80] published an attractive-sounding statement of the moral influence theory in his long-used textbook for theological students.[81] It may well have been D. J. Davies who prescribed this work for the education of prospective Anglican clergy in Australia from 1913.[82] When the Group Brotherhood became the Anglican Evangelical Group Movement in 1923, the moral influence theory was the public position of the Liberal Evangelicals.[83]

Evangelicals and Science

Peter Toon noted that "the Evangelical response to the new ideas on Scripture and science from 1855 onwards has yet to be written."[84] More recently, Nicolaas Rupke has surveyed the response of some Christian thinkers to the "cognitive dissonance" about cosmogony seen in "the disappearance of the language of design from scientific discourse,"[85] and the monism promoted by E. H. Haeckel (see chapter 1 above). However, Rupke does not detail the important responses of the ablest evangelicals who, from the

---

76. Ross, "Denney, James," 239–40.
77. Denney, *Atonement*, 10–11.
78. Mozley, *Doctrine of the Atonement*, 177.
79. Warfield, Review of *Doctrine of the Atonement*, 474.
80. Toulouse, "Evangelical Liberalism," 411.
81. Clarke, *Outline*, 340–68.
82. "List of Suggested Books," 42.
83. Howard, "Work of Christ," 121–46.
84. Toon, *Evangelical Theology*, 207.
85. Rupke, "Christianity and the Sciences," 164–80.

mid-nineteenth century, said significant things with regard to the new ideas on Scripture and science. By and large, they experienced no great crisis of faith.

Thus, in the field of geology, Hugh Miller, a devout evangelical of the Free Church of Scotland, upheld the idea of God as Creator in his *Footprints of the Creator* (1849) and *The Testimony of the Rocks* (1857).[86] E. A. Litton had already dismissed the notion that Scripture might be intended "to convey accurate knowledge" on matters of natural science, pointing out that it was nonsensical to criticize Scripture for its phenomenal language that spoke of the earth as stationary.[87] The amazingly learned premillennial Evangelical, A. R. Fausset, held that the language of Genesis was not scientific description. For him, the real discoveries of science could not be opposed to revelation, but would resolve in time with a better understanding of Scripture. His single-handed *Critical and Expository Bible Cyclopaedia* took the discoveries of geology into account; the biblical Flood, for example, had to be a local if vast event, not universal.[88]

In Sydney, the Reverend William Branwhite Clarke (1798–1878) had been a student at Cambridge (BA 1821) in the days of Charles Simeon and had attended the lectures of Adam Sedgwick, the Woodwardian Professor of Geology. An Evangelical (perhaps like Professor Heurtley at Oxford noted above) and the rector of North Sydney (1844–1871), Clarke became the "father of Australian geology." He was offered but did not accept a professorship in geology and mineralogy in 1856 at the fledgling University of Sydney five years earlier.[89] He too was careful to distinguish the claims of Scripture from those of science.

In biology, the response of theologians to Darwin's *Origin of Species* was cautious. In 1870 the conservative Tractarian H. P. Liddon, and in 1871, the old-school High Churchman, Bishop E. Harold Browne, both cautiously withheld judgment. A. R. Fausset, on the other hand, adopted a modified uniformitarian view concluding, from a theistic point of view, that the plan of creation is progressive development modified by continual superintendence and occasional interpositions of the Creator just at the points where required to make the theory of Darwin possible.[90]

E. A. Litton, on the other hand, argued that theories of evolution impugned God's miraculous agency but were as yet "only theories, which do

---

86. Demster, "Miller, Hugh," 564.
87. Litton, *Study of Holy Scripture*, 124.
88. Fausset, "Noah," 516.
89. Mozley, "Clarke," 420–22.
90. Fausset, "Creation," 140–44.

not explain all the facts." An antiquity of humanity stretching back 20,000 years was not a problem for him. But he made an important point: the difference of the human from an ancestor must be a religious difference, and that not an accident.[91] Litton was writing scarcely more than a decade after Darwin had published *The Descent of Man* in 1871.

By 1889 Handley C. G. Moule could allow that Genesis chapter 1 was written in the form of *symbolic* representations, not of a "mechanical operation." The *observed phenomena* cannot exclude "a properly 'new departure'" for humanity as "at once spiritual and material, who should resemble, know and love the Creator." At the same time, "not one word" of Scripture rules out the human being as "moulded of the same matter . . . and on the same plan" as its "predecessors and coevals."[92] Herbert Spencer's agnostic-evolutionary philosophy "swept the world."[93] Moule noted its "general prevalence" among so many people of science, and insisted that observers of "verifiable phenomena" passed beyond their competence as observers "to say that the beast can be true ancestor of the man."[94]

On Darwin's theory of natural selection church leaders and scholarly clergy in Australia who addressed the public thought that a *naturalistic* theory of evolution presented a problem.[95] Bishop Charles Perry of Melbourne, senior wrangler (i.e., first in mathematics) in his Cambridge BA (1828) as well as highly placed in classics, was cautious. In his final lecture on evolution (1869) he found unanswerable objections to the idea of natural selection, but noting that the hypotheses were "fluid" he suspended judgment.[96] While "clergy typically adopted a wait and see attitude,"[97] at this time, there was a general public acceptance of Darwin's theories by the 1880s,[98] and "Evangelicals in general had come to accept" that they "could be interpreted within a Christian framework."[99]

---

91. Litton, *Introduction*, 81, 115–17.
92. Moule, *Outlines of Christian Doctrine*, 153–54.
93. Passmore, *Hundred Years*, 40.
94. Moule, *Outlines of Christian Doctrine*, 155.
95. Robin, *Charles Perry*, 131; Judd and Cable, *Sydney Anglicans*, 118–19, 126–27; Frame, *Anglicans in Australia*, 91–108, 109–24.
96. Frame, *Anglicans in Australia*, 112–14, quoting Bishop Perry's lectures published in the *Church of England Record*, IV (1860) 140, Charles Perry, *Science and the Bible*, the *Church of England Newspaper*, 8 September, 1870, and Robin, *Charles Perry*, 140–46.
97. Frame, *Anglicans in Australia*, 109–14.
98. Finney, *Paradise Revealed*, 97–112; cf. Moyal, *Bright and Savage Land*, 144–47.
99. Bebbington, *Dominance of Evangelicalism*, 168.

Back in England the Christian Association of University Colleges in London organized a broad-ranging series of addresses, *Christian Apologetics* in 1903. They focused on the rationalism and materialism of the day that was associated with Darwin's theories and touched on the key issue of the presupposed worldview. Lord William Thomson Kelvin (1824–1907), a devout Scottish Presbyterian, stated in a vote of thanks that Cicero's "fortuitous concourse of atoms" was utterly absurd in respect to the coming into existence, or the growth, or the continuation of molecular combinations presented in the bodies of living things. And, he concluded, "if you think strongly enough you will be forced by science to belief in God."[100] Unsurprisingly, Kelvin's remarks generated considerable correspondence in *The Times* of London.[101]

G. T. Manley, a Cambridge senior wrangler and later influential in the Inter-Varsity Fellowship of Evangelical Unions, addressed T. H. Huxley's term "agnosticism,"[102] along with a quotation from Herbert Spencer's *First Principles* that began, "Evolution is an integration of matter and concomitant dissipation of motion." For Manley, this was "enough to prove abundantly . . . that Agnosticism . . . is . . . a purely materialistic presentation of human knowledge."[103]

The following year, W. H. Griffith Thomas, close friend of Nathaniel Jones, summarized part of the common stock of Christian thought about science. He concluded that "evolution at the very most only indicates a precise *method* of origination." It was "a magnificent conception" but did not set aside the need for a Creator, and even if this working hypothesis "should prove the *one and only* method . . . 'In the beginning God'" would still stand as needed.[104] George Salmon, the distinguished provost of Trinity College, Dublin, also struck a theistic note: "No presumption *against* God's working is caused by our being able to trace the prevalence of a law which universally dominates in God's natural world."[105]

While a student at Trinity College, Dublin from 1901 to 1904, Everard Digges La Touche had been converted from acute doubt through T. C. Hammond. In 1910 he published *Christian Certitude* and Trinity College awarded him the LittD for a learned Butlerian probability treatment

---

100. Seton, *Christian Apologetics*, xi, 24–26.

101. Orr, *Bible Under Trial*, 205.

102. Manley, "Materialism or Christianity," 106–7, citing Huxley, *Science and Christian Tradition*, 33.

103. Manley, "Materialism or Christianity," 107–8, citing Spencer, *First Principles*, 44–54.

104. Thomas, *Catholic Faith*, 65–66.

105. Salmon, *Evolution*, 7.

of Christian evidences which argued that both history and scientific theory had given "immense antiquity" to humanity. Yet (here making the same point as Griffith Thomas), "the unfortunate confusion of the *fact* that God made man with the *methods* which He employed . . . did much to give the newer learning a hostile bias towards Christianity."[106] Against this confusion Digges La Touche made the point that "the theory of evolution reveals an order" which has revealed "the unutterable rationality of the universe."[107]

In 1913 Digges La Touche was Diocesan Missioner and Lecturer in the Diocese of Sydney and a lecturer at Moore College under Principal David Davies. His succinct manual *Is Christianity Scientific?*[108] now explained not the *probability* but the *necessity* of the Christian faith for modern science: perfect knowledge would require omniscience, which only God has; the very possibility of scientific enquiry necessarily presupposed the omnipotent and omniscient creator of an orderly universe, and human capacity for knowledge.[109]

Tractarianism, and Ritualism or Anglo-Catholicism

Before *Lux Mundi* (1889) there were great areas of agreement between Tractarians and Anglican Evangelicals, as well as those in other British churches. These included such matters as "the divine inspiration of Holy Scripture, the catholic doctrines of the Holy Trinity and the Person of Christ, the need to pursue holiness both in the visible Church and in the individual life, the blessed hope of the Second Coming of Christ, the resurrection of the dead, and the life everlasting."[110]

Indeed, it was the Anglo-Catholic writer, Charlotte Yonge's 1853 novel, *The Heir of Redclyffe* that led a liberal minister of the Dutch national Reformed Church, Abraham Kuyper, to regain a living Calvinist faith.[111] Later, the Evangelical successor of Hammond at Moore College, Marcus Loane, would find fellowship with the conservative Anglo-Catholic Bishop Philip Strong in New Guinea during World War II; and today Evangelicals still use hymns written by Tractarians.[112] Kuyper became a powerful defender of

---

106. Digges La Touche, *Christian Certitude*, 20.
107. Ibid., 30.
108. Digges La Touche, *Is Christianity Scientific?*
109. Ibid., 5–7.
110. Toon, *Evangelical Theology*, 203.
111. Bratt, "Kuyper," 351.
112. Blanch, *From Strength to Strength*, 83; such hymns as Keble, "Blest are the pure in heart," Faber, "My God, how wonderful Thou art," and Neale, "A great and mighty

Reformation theology, whose works would be effectively used by evangelical and Reformed theologians.[113]

Nevertheless, by 1840 most Evangelicals were definitely opposed to the Tractarians for their use of "Tradition" with Scripture, and their doctrines of the church and the sacraments.[114] Supported by old school High Churchmen, Evangelicals founded the Parker Society in 1840 and republished fifty-four works of the English Reformers in the period from 1841 to 1855. The Evangelical organs, *Christian Observer* (founded in 1802 and replaced by *The Churchman* in 1879) and the more distinctly Calvinistic *The Record* (founded in 1828) addressed the issues that Tractarian teaching raised. John Henry Newman's *Lectures on Justification* of 1838 had provoked no little reaction, as did his *Tract XC* of three years later, which advocated an interpretation of the Thirty-nine Articles generally in accord with the decrees of the Council of Trent. In the year that Newman was received into the Church of Rome, Charles Abel Heurtley (1813–1897), not "a party-man" but effectively an Evangelical, delivered the Bampton Lectures at Oxford— on justification in reply to Newman.[115] Later he was one of Jones's professors of Divinity.

Evangelicals could find plenty to confirm the authentic Anglican-ness of their convictions. The leading theological writers, E. A. Litton (1813–1897)[116] and H. C. G. Moule (1841–1920) admired the learning of William Goode (1801–1868),[117] a Calvinist, and perhaps the ablest English anti-Tractarian writer of his period. As a new student at Oxford in 1882, Jones can hardly have missed John Charles Ryle's books,[118] and by 1897, when Jones came to Moore College, Moule's textbook, *Outlines of Christian Doctrine* of 1889, a work written for both nonconformists and Anglicans, had already sold many thousands of copies.[119] Litton completed his outstanding *Introduction to Theology* in 1892 and by 1897 T. P. Boultbee's textbook on the Thirty-nine Articles was also still in print.[120]

---

wonder."

113. E.g., Packer, *"Fundamentalism"*, and Van Til, *Defense of the Faith*.

114. Fry, *Listener in Oxford*, 173, cited in Toon, *Evangelical Theology*, 45.

115. Heurtley, *Justification*.

116. Litton, *Sermon on John iii*, 5. Litton, *Church of Christ*.

117. Goode, *Doctrine of the Church of England as to . . . Baptism*; *Doctrine of the Church of England . . . on the Orders*.

118. E.g., *Knots Untied* and *Light from Old Times*.

119. Moule, *Outlines of Christian Doctrine*; Litton, *Introduction to Dogmatic Theology*.

120. Boultbee, *Theology of the Church of England*; new title from 1884: *Commentary on the Thirty-nine Articles*.

These works argued for the Reformation understanding of the sacraments. Handley Moule emphasized that Tractarian or Anglo-Catholic teaching "on the nature of the Eucharistic Presence" was not that of the early High Churchmen.[121] Just as Hammond completed his own formal theological education, W. H. Griffith Thomas published his Oxford DD thesis, *A Sacrament of Our Redemption,* which was a positive exposition written in part to counter the Anglo-Catholic contention that the Lord's Supper itself was a sacrifice.

Anti-Roman Catholic feeling surfaced again in 1850 with the restoration in England and Wales of the Roman Catholic hierarchy. This was the background to public concern occasioned by Anglo-Catholics pressing "Romanising" ritual on the Church of England. It was rather concern for purity of worship, implicitly doctrinal, that motivated those like E. A. Litton to respond verbally to the challenge in 1854.[122] But the Tractarian and ritualist English Church Union, founded in 1859, tried to prosecute Evangelicals for holding mission services in theatres, and in 1862, even to prosecute the Bishop of Carlisle for heresy.[123] It was then that Evangelicals responded in kind—by establishing the Church Association in 1865. With the intention of resisting both rationalism and ritualism they founded Wycliffe Hall, Oxford in 1877, and Ridley Hall, Cambridge in 1879.[124]

The most learned Evangelical to defend the 1662 Book of Common Prayer as the liturgical expression of Reformation doctrine was Nathaniel Dimock (1825–1909), an Oxford man. Before Jones went up, Dimock had already published two anti-ritualist works.[125] Dimock's further labors against Anglo-Catholic innovations were readily available when Davies and Hammond were students.[126] T. W. Drury, principal of Ridley Hall from 1899 to 1907, was the significant Evangelical scholar on the Prayer Book in Hammond and Davies's early years.[127]

In Sydney, Mervyn Archdall (1846–1917), one of Barker's last hand-picked men from England (1882), had become a close associate of Nathaniel Jones. He founded the Protestant Church of England Union in 1898 in Sydney to preserve the historic Reformed character of the doctrine and liturgy

---

121. Moule, *Evangelical School,* 29.

122. Litton, *Gospel Not a Ceremonial Law.* See Reynolds, *Evangelicals,* 127.

123. See previous chapter. The Tractarians, not the Evangelicals, were the first to resort to the secular courts on such matters.

124. Bullock, *History of Ridley Hall,* 1:120–21.

125. Dimock, *Eucharistic Worship,* and *Confession and Absolution.*

126. Dimock, *Vox Liturgiae Anglicanae; Light from History,* and *Some Notes . . . Doctrine of the Holy Communion.*

127. Drury, *How We Got Our Prayer Book,* and *Two Studies,* and *Principles.*

of the Church of England in Australia. He also published his passionate *Liturgical Right and National Wrong* in 1901. One issue he treated that would arise for Archbishop Mowll and hence for Hammond was the "recognition" at Lambeth in 1897 of the bishop's so-called *jus* [*ius*] *liturgicum* ("liturgical right")—the claim that a bishop might alter or modify services beyond what the Uniformity Amendment Act of 1872 allowed.[128]

Nathaniel Jones had been principal of Moore College for nearly a decade and D. J. Davies and T. C. Hammond only recently ordained when the Royal Commission on Ecclesiastical Discipline of 1904–1906 produced its report.[129] This "justified the complaints of the Evangelicals (against ritualism) and vindicated their position,"[130] but it "left action largely in the hands of the bishops."[131] In the Diocese of Manchester Bishop E. A. Knox acted—using his licensing authority to exclude any clergy who insisted on the Eucharistic vestments and associated practices that the Ritualists contended for.[132]

Two successive archbishops of Sydney were admirers of Knox. John Charles Wright had been one of his students at Oxford and his archdeacon in Manchester. Howard W. K. Mowll had been ordained by Knox in 1913 and corresponded with him for advice from that time.[133] Wright implemented Knox's Manchester policy on arriving in Sydney, satisfying the rigorous Archdall with his strictly constitutional approach.[134] Jones, Davies, and Hammond were all in agreement with Wright's policy on ritual, which Mowll continued. The liturgical standpoint of these two archbishops and the three principals, Jones, Davies, and Hammond had the support of substantial Evangelical thought and learning, both in England and in Sydney.

Premillennialism and Holiness

Both premillennialism and holiness were two widely adopted extensions to nineteenth-century evangelicalism, but not direct and specific responses to the five challenges described in the previous chapter. For those convinced of the former there would have been some apologetic value to be drawn from

---

128. Ibid., 19–22, 60–63, 72–74. See Wright, "Rites and Ceremonies," 609.
129. *Report of the Royal Commission.*
130. Bromiley, "Appendix I '1900–1950,'" 253.
131. Wellings, *Evangelicals Embattled*, 120.
132. Knox, *Reminiscences*, 253–54, 304, 307.
133. Loane, *Archbishop Mowll*, 63, 125, 127. Knox died in January 1937.
134. Robinson, "Origins," 156–57, citing "the PCEU Handbook published 1910."

the view. It is surprising that those who preached the latter made little or no application of sanctification to scholarship.

A study by two recent historians has commented: "Outside medieval studies, the significance of millennialism has been consistently underestimated in the scholarly analysis of human thought and society."[135] Bebbington has encapsulated recent research across evangelicalism in general.[136] The following discussion views the Anglican side in general while the chapters on Nathaniel Jones will estimate its significance for him.

The English Book of Common Prayer and the Thirty-nine Articles of Religion quietly assumed the view of Augustine of Hippo that the "thousand years" of Revelation 20:1–6 stood for the interval between Christ's resurrection and his advent in glory. This non-literal interpretation of the 1,000 years was later called the "amillennial" view.

But during the Thirty Years War on the Continent of 1618–1648, and when Archbishop William Laud in tandem with Charles I was resisting the Puritans, the Cambridge biblical scholar Joseph Mede (1586–1638) expounded a premillennial view: Christ would first return to establish his reign of 1,000 years on earth before the Last Judgment.[137] This view was also to be found among some Church Fathers of the second and third centuries. In the eighteenth century, John and Charles Wesley adopted it, following the German Pietist New Testament commentator, Albrecht Bengel (1687–1752).[138]

The upheavals of the French Revolutionary and Napoleonic wars made the view more attractive and by 1815 it began to be adopted by more evangelicals, including Anglicans. As well, the originally High-Church-ordained Anglican in the Church of Ireland, J. N. Darby (1800–1882), developed the version of premillennialism later known as *dispensationalism*. The *Scofield Reference Bible* (1909), consisting of the Authorised Version [139] with references and notes added, popularized the view widely.

Writing in 1907–1908, G.R. Balleine, the historian of the Evangelical school in the Church of England stated that most Evangelicals did not adopt a premillennial interpretation.[140] But well before the 1880s, when Jones was at Oxford, some of the leading Evangelical churchmen, both clerical and lay,

---

135. Gribben and Stunt, *Prisoners of Hope?*, 1.
136. Bebbington, *Dominance of Evangelicalism*, 179–88.
137. Mede, *Clavis Apocalyptica*.
138. Gribben and Stunt, *Prisoners of Hope?*, 8.
139. *Pace* Bebbington, *Dominance of Evangelicalism*, 187.
140. Balleine, *History of the Evangelical Party*, 164–65.

had arrived at a premillennial view.[141] Elliott's *Horae Apocalypticae* (1842), a "high-water mark of historicism," which promoted one premillennial view, went through five editions.[142] Fausset's *Biblical Cyclopaedia* of 1878, noted above, confidently set forth a premillennial scheme.[143] And in London, William Pennefather (1816-1873), the vicar of Mildmay, brought it into his annual parish prophetical conferences. Mildmay's speakers included distinguished evangelicals, including (in 1878 for example) Fausset, W. R. Fremantle, at that time Dean of Ripon, the Earl of Shaftesbury and Hudson Taylor.[144]

At least two influential Evangelical bishops were of premillennial conviction: John Charles Ryle (1816-1900) and Edward Henry Bickersteth (1825-1906). Ryle, who was Bishop of Liverpool from 1880 to 1900, had taught and preached against a postmillennial expectation of Christ's return at least as early as 1856 in his *Expository Thoughts*,[145] and also in his collected sermons *Coming Events and Present Duties* of 1867. Events of his day supporting pessimistic this-world expectations included the 1848 Continental revolutions, the Crimean War and the Indian Mutiny in the 1850s, and in the 1860s, the American Civil War. In the sphere of religion and the church, Ryle had seen not only the rise of "Romanising" doctrine and ritualism, but also the skepticism so prominent in *Essays and Reviews* (1860) with its negative criticism of Scripture. Nevertheless, Ryle urged, as would Nathaniel Jones, that no one should "neglect present duties" even while saying confidently but pessimistically in 1867: "I doubt much whether there ever was a time in the history of our country, when the horizon on all sides, both political and ecclesiastical, was so thoroughly black and lowering.... Happy is he who has learned... to look steadily for Christ's appearing!"[146]

Ryle's *Coming Events and Present Duties* saw four editions in fourteen years. By the third edition of his *Expository Thoughts on the Gospels* (1879) there had occurred the forced unification of Germany under Prussia, the Franco-Prussian War (1870) and much domestic disturbance in England—the latter despite the premillennial Evangelical activist Shaftesbury's social reforms.

---

141. E.g., Bishop Bickersteth and the Seventh Earl of Shaftesbury.

142. Elliott, *Horae Apocalypticae*, noted by Bebbington, *Evangelicalism in Modern Britain*, 85-86.

143. Fausset, "Dispensations," 173-74, and "Thousand Years," 685-86.

144. Mildmay Conference, *"Our God Shall Come"*, iii-iv.

145. Ryle, *Expository Thoughts on St Matthew*, 313-16, 318, 321, 323, 327.

146. Ryle, *Coming Events*, xiii-xiv.

Edward Henry Bickersteth, the Bishop of Exeter from 1885 to 1901, was a poet and accomplished hymn writer.[147] His premillennial epic poem, *Yesterday, To-day and Forever*, covers the history and future of redemption in the customary twelve books of blank verse. It too was written against the background of "the solemn events" of his time. It saw twenty-three editions in twenty-seven years after its first publication (1866), thus demonstrating the attractiveness of this perspective to many in the Victorian Christian public.[148] Bickersteth's brother-in-law, T. R. Birks, was a popular writer as well as being an academic theologian; he published fifteen premillennial works on prophecy.[149]

The Christian hope had become a live public issue. From June to August 1887 the new "Advanced Liberal" religious newspaper, *The British Weekly*, published a "discussion," (that weekly's term), on the different eschatological expectations: between a postmillennialist—David Brown (1803–1897), three premillennialists—Fausset and the husband and wife team Henry and Mrs. Grattan Guinness—and two other protagonists. This attracted so much attention and correspondence that the paper published the debate in book form.[150]

Henry Grattan Guinness (1835–1910), an international lay evangelist, saw evidential value for the truth of the Bible in fulfilled prophecy: "Providence, by many, is denied. History we are boldly taught, is but a blind evolution. The ages drift without aim. . . . Prophecy [however] is none other than history written in advance."[151] Guinness's astronomical studies (inspired by biblical prophecy) led to his being made a fellow of the Royal Astronomical Society. While his world-historicist view set no date for Christ's return, he did predict that 1917 (and 1948!) would be years of special significance for the Jews.[152] It was a factor behind the so-called "Balfour Declaration" of 2 November 1917. General Allenby took Jerusalem a little more than five weeks later, which inspired the immediate formation of "The Advent Testimony and Preparation Movement."[153]

---

147. Julian, *Dictionary of Hymnology*, 141, 142.

148. Bickersteth, *Yesterday, To-day and Forever*, v.

149. Munden, "Birks," 54–55.

150. Fausset, et al., *Second Advent*.

151. Guinness, *Divine Programme*, iii.

152. Dowling, "Guinness," 272–74. The Guinnesses' works included *Approaching End of the Age*, *Light for the Last Days*, and *Divine Programme*.

153. Randall, *Spirituality and Social Change*, 141; also www.pwmi.org, website of Prophetic Witness Movement International (PWMI), initially "The Advent Testimony and Preparation Movement."

In 1889 Handley Moule had, without preference, carefully stated the various positions on the millennium in his *Outlines of Christian Doctrine*. He underlined the profound agreement of all parties on the central truths concerning the person of Christ, and counseled students against "unloving mutual criticisms."[154] After the Great War, however, Moule openly professed the premillennial view.[155] So although a minority, premillennial Evangelicals were not an insignificant one. The theologian E. A. Litton was an amillennialist, but omitted his critique of premillennialism in his 1902 edition of *Introduction to Theology* originally published ten years earlier.[156] In the early twentieth century, Henry Wace published his book on prophecy without so much as a footnote acknowledging the premillennial position.[157] At some stage Hammond purchased a copy of Wace's work in Sydney.[158]

While Evangelicals disagreed, no liberal could be a premillennialist. J. W. Hunkin's essay in the Group Brotherhood's *Liberal Evangelicalism* (1923) critiqued a "small book of this [premillennial] type."[159] In the ears of premillennial Sydney synodsmen in the debate on Hunkin's nomination for archbishop in 1933 his essay would have had a "modernist" ring to it. Leading graduates of Moore College under Jones were premillennial in outlook, but did not make it a cause of division among fellow Evangelicals, as Moule had counselled. "They didn't bang the drum."[160]

A response to another challenge was seen in "the Victorian frame of mind," which included a surge of moral earnestness in society[161] and manifested itself within the Church of England. "Holiness was intimately bound up with the spirit of the age" and the new teaching found fertile soil in Romanticism and was in turn influenced by it.[162] Within the Church of England, instructed Evangelical believers knew well that the Thirty-nine Articles spoke of an abiding inborn inclination to evil in the believer, and condemned any claim to a sinless life. The Articles also stated that justification by faith alone was not by a faith that was alone.[163] In church, people

---

154. Moule, *Outlines of Christian Doctrine*, 114.
155. Randall, *Spirituality and Social Change*, 136.
156. Wace, "Introductory Remarks," xv.
157. Wace, *Prophecy*.
158. In Moore Theological College library.
159. Hunkin, "The Kingdom of God," 174–93.
160. Robinson, interview.
161. Houghton, *Victorian Frame of Mind*, 218–62.
162. Bebbington, *Holiness*, 5, 78–86.
163. Articles 9 "Of Original or Birth-sin," 11 "Of the Justification of Man," 12 "Of Good Works," 15 "Of Christ alone without Sin," and 16 "Of Sin after Baptism."

prayed from the Prayer Book each Sunday both for God's forgiveness and his enablement to "live a godly, righteous and sober life"; they were exhorted to beseech God for "true repentance, and his Holy Spirit" to enable a "pure, and holy" life pleasing to God.

G. R. Balleine, the best church historian of Evangelicalism according to D. J. Davies, thought that the need for teaching on holiness arose in response to dissatisfaction felt at the quality of Christian life evident in many of the new converts of the Moody-Sankey campaign of the mid-1870s.[164] But earlier, and possibly as important for Nathaniel Jones as Keswick might have been, was the work of William Pennefather mentioned above. Educated at Trinity College, Dublin, Pennefather was of premillennial conviction and was concerned for the poor. Already in 1856 in his earlier parish of Barnet, near London, he had instituted his non-denominational parish conference for the purpose of also promoting "personal holiness, brotherly love, and increased interest in the work of the Lord." The conference moved with him in 1863 to Mildmay, also near London, and continued into the twentieth century.[165] Nathaniel Jones's wife was a Mildmay-trained deaconess-nurse.

Between 1859 and 1874, *The Higher Christian Life*, by the American New School Presbyterian, W. E. Boardman, sold 60,000 copies in England. It had several publishers. According to B. B. Warfield it contended that "full salvation" was received by "full trust" in Jesus our "full Saviour" by "two distinct acts of faith."[166] Two other Americans, Mr. and Mrs. Robert Pearsall Smith, were in England preaching a similar formula for moral victory in 1874–1875.[167] A convention in September 1874 in Oxford was attended by about 1,000 people, including "a large number of the Evangelical clergy" among whom was a former Tractarian, Canon Harford-Battersby, Rector of Keswick. For him the address by the Evangelical, Evan Henry Hopkins (1837–1919), proved decisive for the future of Evangelical Anglicanism. In 1875 he returned to his parish in the Lake District to begin what would become a significant global evangelical tradition—the Keswick Convention.[168]

The new "holiness by faith" of Keswick was definitively expounded by Hopkins in *The Law of Liberty in the Spiritual Life*.[169] He emphasized a "crisis"—a step of faith in Christ for the power of his imparted life to en-

164. Balleine, *History of the Evangelical Party*, 237.

165. Smith, "Pennefather," 514–16.

166. Warfield, *Perfectionism*, 227.

167. Balleine, *History of the Evangelical Party*, 238; Bebbington, *Dominance of Evangelicalism*, 194–95.

168. Smellie, *Evan Henry Hopkins*, 71–72, 76–78; Balleine, *History of the Evangelical Party*, 238.

169. Hopkins, *Law of Liberty*.

able the believer to refrain from sin. It was a permanent enhancement of Christian life, needing to be maintained, however, by a process of moment-by-moment trust in Christ. It was a second, distinct step additional to one's initial turning to Christ for forgiveness.[170] By the early years of the twentieth century the Keswick Convention was annually drawing 6,000 persons. J. C. Ryle, however, thought that the particular emphases of the Keswick movement were (in J. I. Packer's words) "unbalanced, shallow, unrealistic and dangerous to spiritual well-being."[171] Notwithstanding this criticism, Ryle had long been deeply convinced "that practical holiness and entire self-consecration to God are not sufficiently attended to by modern Christians in this country."[172]

At first most of the Evangelical leaders also regarded such teaching with suspicion, for perfectionism was "a real danger at the time."[173] In July and August of 1884 Handley C. G. Moule reviewed Hopkins's book negatively for the *Record* (an Evangelical Church of England newspaper). But after meeting and hearing him, Moule expressed his deep satisfaction. Hopkins's convincing disavowal of perfectionism, his challenge of self-surrender to Christ, his elevation of the divine promises, and his balanced doctrine of the union of the believer with Christ persuaded Moule: he told a friend that "he had learned to trust God in prayer," including the prayer to "keep us this day without sin."[174] Moule incorporated his new understanding into both his *Outlines of Christian Doctrine* and in his second and expository commentary on Romans at chapter 7.[175] Modern evangelical commentators have remained critical of that period of Keswick, even while appreciating its merits.[176] Many at the time incorporated Keswick holiness, like the premillennial hope, into their spectrum of thought. The young T. C. Hammond, however, appears to have successfully combined it with his amillennial outlook.

The effect of Keswick on Sydney Anglican Evangelicalism preceded but was firmly set by the mission of 1891–1892. This was led by the Church of Ireland evangelist, the Reverend George C. Grubb, who was sent to Australia by Keswick. In Melbourne, Hussey Burgh Macartney Jr., vicar

---

170. Smellie, *Evan Henry Hopkins*, 103-20.

171. Packer, "Preface," xi.

172. Ryle, *Holiness*, xvii.

173. Balleine, *History of the Evangelical Party*, 239.

174. Moule, "Introduction," 9-15; Smellie, *Evan Henry Hopkins*, 122-23.

175. Moule, *Epistle of St.Paul to the Romans* (1894); cf. Moule, *Epistle of Paul to the Romans* (1879).

176. Murray, review of Barabas, *So Great Salvation*, 281-85; Packer, "Preface," xii; Packer, *Keep in Step*, 148-63.

of St Mary's Caulfield from 1868 to 1898, had earlier started similar convention movements in Victoria, beginning in January 1873 before reading of the Oxford and Brighton events.[177] An interdenominational group of Melbourne ministers including Macartney brought about a convention at which Grubb[178] preached evangelistically in the Melbourne area, followed by Sydney, in the summer of 1891–1892. Grubb's preaching emphasized the possibility of personal holiness. Long-term results included the formation of a Church Missionary Association in both states, Victoria and New South Wales. Those affected included men who would one day be influential clergy in Sydney. One such was Robert Brodribb Hammond, who had a remarkable ministry in the city parish of St Barnabas, Broadway from 1918 to 1943.[179]

The Katoomba Christian Convention in the Blue Mountains near Sydney owes its beginnings to both Christian Brethren and Anglicans, including Principal Nathaniel Jones. A later principal, T. C. Hammond would one day be a valued speaker at Katoomba and similar conventions around the country and help set the doctrinal criteria.[180]

Conclusion

The varying response of Evangelicals to the challenges of the century resulted in changes to the general Evangelical spectrum of thought. These consisted in conservative extensions for some, while for others it meant a liberal broadening of their thinking. Such changes would directly impact Moore Theological College and the Diocese of Sydney.

Among the conservative Evangelicals who embraced a world-historicist premillennial eschatology, many added a Keswick piety. Although this was a movement seeking a more complete holiness, no Evangelicals within it (or beforehand except for Birks and possibly Litton) applied the effects of sin on knowledge, the "noetic" effects, to the workings of the mind in scholarship.[181] Most assumed that they could understand facts of this world for what they truly are apart from consciously seeing them in the light of the special revelation of Scripture—they seem to have assumed it was possible for scholarship to be religiously neutral. Conservative Evangelicals worked

---

177. Paproth, "Hussey Burgh Macartney, 8".
178. Paproth, "Deeper Life Movement in Victoria."
179. Loane, *Mark These Men*, 33–38.
180. Braga, *Century of Preaching Christ*, 39–44, 105.
181. See also Klapwijk, "John Calvin," 123–42, and Clouser, *Myth of Religious Neutrality*, 94–107.

to refine their statements on both the atonement and Scripture, but apparently without understanding this clearly. Hence the new historical criticism more easily affected liberal-minded Evangelicals as to their doctrine of the authority of Scripture: and their conscience, being autonomous, as they assumed it must be, also turned them away from the church doctrine of an objective atonement.

If geology and Darwinian evolution occasioned much discussion and debate, there was no movement resembling the "Young Earth Creationism" of recent decades; leading evangelical writers cautiously accepted thoughtful literary readings of the first chapters of Genesis that did not involve a commitment to twenty-four-hour "days" or an earth of only 6,000 or so years old. Although affected by philosophical idealism, the Liberal Evangelical group did not all compromise the doctrine of God's transcendence. While some Liberal Evangelicals accepted a measure of ritualism, Davies of Moore College firmly resisted it.

The next chapter will trace the history of teaching at Moore College from its beginnings to 1897, the year Jones was appointed, then outline the changes in step with successive archbishops—conservative, liberal, and conservative again.

Figure 1: Moore Theological College

3

Moore Theological College 1856–1953

FREDERIC BARKER (1808–1882), THE second Bishop of Sydney (1855–1882), founded Moore College in 1856 to be an institution of the Evangelical school of thought and churchmanship to supply clergy for his diocese.[1] From the beginning the bishop had the controlling say in the selection of the principal, for he must license him. Each new principal therefore would reflect the particular bishop's theological preference (or intention!).

A First Evangelical Bishop

When Barker arrived in Sydney in 1855 he had come to a diocese by now of mixed tradition. The first chaplains to the penal colony of New South Wales—to its garrison, convicts, and free settlers—had been Yorkshire Evangelicals. They were appointed through the influence of William Wilberforce. The first chaplain, the Reverend Richard Johnson (1755–1827) was an Evangelical graduate of Cambridge (BA 1784) who had possibly come under the influence of the mild Calvinism of Charles Simeon, Fellow of King's College and Vicar of Holy Trinity Church, Cambridge (1782–1836). Johnson came to Sydney with the First Fleet in 1788. The second chaplain, Samuel Marsden (1765–1838), had studied at Cambridge but left before graduating in order to join Johnson in 1793. He made use of Simeon's sermon outlines in his long ministry.[2]

A third chaplain, William Cowper, another Evangelical from the north of England, responded to Marsden's appeal (when on leave in England

1. Loane, *Centenary History*, 16–33; Maple, "Barker," 21–26, 30–32.
2. Simeon, *Horae Homileticae*. See Pettet, *Samuel Marsden*.

1806–1809) and came to Sydney in 1809 as a chaplain and the incumbent of St Philip's Church, Sydney.[3] His son, William Macquarie Cowper (1810–1902), was born in Sydney and studied at Oxford (BA 1835). He became a significant and long-serving Evangelical figure in the diocese.

In 1825, by crown appointment, episcopal supervision of the whole of Australia came under the Bishop of Calcutta, Reginald Heber, who died in 1826 and was followed by Daniel Wilson; it ended with Wilson's death. Both were Evangelicals. But clergy of other traditions came meanwhile and a High Churchman, William Grant Broughton, was appointed archdeacon in 1829. In 1836 the crown appointed him Bishop of Australia. The initial Church of England impulse in Sydney had been Evangelical,[4] but things could change with imperial whim. Broughton, an Oxford man, added to Sydney the High Church tradition, especially in the city parishes. He was also sympathetic with the new Tractarian movement. He established the first Anglican theological institution in Australia, St James' College, Sydney. It opened in 1845, and reflected the bishop's High Church convictions and Tractarian leaning. After 1848 it fades from the records.[5]

The Second Bishop, Frederic Barker and Moore College 1856–1884

The appointment of Frederic Barker would prove decisive for the future of the Evangelical character of the diocese and of Moore College. Barker had graduated from Jesus College, Cambridge, in 1831. He came under the influence of the Evangelicals associated with Charles Simeon in the latter's last years. Barker needed to supplement the clergy he could recruit from England and Ireland. The University of Sydney (established 1850, inaugurated 1852) permitted no education in theological subjects. There was some justice in the university founders' fear of sectarianism, for there was such feeling in the Colony of New South Wales. [6] The Roman Catholic Church, no small minority and mostly Irish, was well established and had its own parish schools. Barker would have understood. While he himself "made no secret of his opposition to the Roman Catholic Church,"[7] there seems to

---

3. Bolt, *William Cowper*.
4. Piggin, *Spirit of a Nation*, 1–23.
5. Loane, *Centenary History*, 13.
6. Johnson, "The Shaping of Colonial Liberalism," 90–122.
7. Judd and Cable, *Sydney Anglicans*, 319.

be no evidence of a special anti-Roman emphasis at Moore College then or later, not even under the Irish principal, T. C. Hammond (1936–1953).[8]

Following recently established English precedent Barker quickly established Moore College for training non-university graduates. He used the generous property bequest left by Thomas Moore (1762–1840).[9] The location was the township of Liverpool, some twenty-five miles or forty kilometres south-west of Sydney. A contemporary model was ready to hand— St Aidan's College, Birkenhead (across the Mersey River from Liverpool), founded in 1847,[10] of which Barker had been a visitor. The three trustees of the Thomas Moore Estate (who might and usually did include the diocesan bishop) formed the "governing board" of the college, to whom the principal was responsible.

Barker invited his friend in England, the Reverend William Hodgson (1809–1869), to be founding principal. Hodgson had graduated from Cambridge in 1832. Academically very able, he was bracketed at graduation with the later distinguished E. Harold Browne (divinity professor at Cambridge 1854, Bishop of Ely 1864, then of Winchester 1873).[11] Hodgson was an experienced parish man and teacher of new clergy under him, and shared Barker's Evangelical convictions.[12] Principal *pro tem* until Hodgson arrived was William Macquarie Cowper, who later became a trustee of the Thomas Moore Estate (1877–1902). He was archdeacon of Sydney, and dean of the new St Andrew's Cathedral from 1858 until his death.[13]

Assisted in the teaching by other diocesan clergy, Hodgson served Moore College for eleven years (1856–1867). At his farewell he affirmed, "I have endeavoured to guard those within the sphere of my influence alike from ritualistic innovations and from the old and oft-refuted objections of rationalistic infidelity."[14] Ritualism and rationalism were the same two concerns in the founding of the Evangelical institutions, Wycliffe Hall, Oxford and Ridley Hall, Cambridge in the late 1870s.[15]

Both of the following principals that Barker appointed were also Cambridge-educated Evangelicals. Robert Lethbridge King (1823–1897), born at sea on his Australian family's voyage to visit England, graduated from

---

8. Pace Edwards, *Wasps, Tykes and Ecumaniacs*; and see chapters 10–12 below.
9. Loane, *Centenary History*, 7–10, 16–19; Bolt, *Thomas Moore*, 1–6, 105–14.
10. Dowland, *Nineteenth-century Anglican Theological Training*, 64–79.
11. See "Browne" in *ODCC*, 201.
12. Loane, *Centenary History*, 16–33.
13. Braga, "Cowper," 80–81
14. Loane, *Centenary History*, 32.
15. Robin, *Charles Perry*, 83–84; Bullock, *History of Ridley Hall*, 1:80–87.

Cambridge in mathematics (BA 1846), but had also a "critical knowledge of the Greek Testament, and scientific tastes."[16] A convinced Evangelical with twenty years of parish experience, he was principal of the college from 1868 to 1878.[17] His successor was Arthur Lukyn Williams (1853–1943), a Hebrew scholar, budding authority on Judaism, and New Testament commentator, who had taken his degree in the newly instituted Cambridge Theology Tripos (BA 1875, first-class honors). He identified as an Evangelical, then and in his later years.[18] As principal, Lukyn Williams established higher scholarly standards with the students. But, after Bishop Perry of Melbourne, an Evangelical, returned to England in 1874, the stream of students from Victoria dried up, and the pool of suitably educated young men from New South Wales was too small to make the college financially viable.

Nevertheless, by 1884 Moore had trained fifty ordinands for Sydney, fifty-seven for Melbourne (i.e., until 1879), eight for Goulburn (separated from Sydney in 1866), nineteen for Bathurst (separated in 1872), ten for Ballarat (separated from Melbourne in 1875), seven for work in the Diocese of North Queensland (inaugurated in 1870), plus a few others—upwards of 160 in all.[19] Fully one-third of the Sydney clergy listed in the *Diocesan Directory* of 1886 had been trained at Moore College.[20] Not all, of course, were Evangelicals, but some of the ablest were.

A Broad Church Bishop and a Crypto-Tractarian Principal

With the death of Barker the Crown appointed Alfred Barry (1882–1889), "a Low Churchman of liberal opinions, speculative but orthodox,"[21] however that term be understood. The close connection between the character of the college's instruction and the theological and liturgical intentions of the diocesan bishop continued when Lukyn Williams returned to England in 1885. When Williams resigned, Barry sought, through his commissary in England, someone "of the school of Lightfoot or Westcott, who would refuse to identify himself with either [High or Low Church] party."[22] But Thomas Ernest Hill (1853–1923) was discovered to be a secret ritualist, and having

16. Loane, *Centenary History*, 35.
17. Cable, "King, Robert Lethbridge," 201.
18. Bullock, *History of Ridley Hall*, 1:293.
19. Ibid., 180–84.
20. See *Sydney Diocesan Directory 1886*.
21. Cable, "Barry," 90–94.
22. Loane, *Centenary History*, 68, citing "Trustees Minute Book No. 2," 256.

begun as principal in September 1885 he was on his way home by mid-1888.²³ Only four of his students became clergy in the diocese.²⁴ Barry's lasting contribution to the college was to move it from Liverpool to a position adjacent to St Paul's College, a college within the University of Sydney.

A Second Evangelical Bishop and a High Church Principal

Barry resigned in 1889, and, by then, the synod of the diocese could elect its own bishop, choosing a centrist Evangelical.²⁵ Bishop (Archbishop from 1897–1909) William Saumarez Smith arrived in Sydney in September 1890.

He was a cultured Evangelical with a distinguished academic record at Cambridge (BA 1858, first class in the Classical Tripos, also in the theological examination 1859, BD 1872, and DD 1889). He had just completed some twenty years as the successful second principal (1869–1889) of St Aidan's College, Birkenhead, earlier so well known to Barker. He was "clearly Evangelical,"²⁶ but showed signs of adjustment to the new Cambridge theology of Lightfoot and Westcott," (meaning that he accepted in principle a *degree*, so the present writer would qualify) of "reverent higher criticism."²⁷ Moreover, unlike Bishop J. C. Ryle of Liverpool or even Charles Simeon of Cambridge earlier, Saumarez Smith seems to have embodied an attenuation among Evangelicals of Reformation emphases sometimes characterized as "Calvinism." His place in the spectrum of evangelicalism was a kind of "mere Christianity"; conservative but perhaps more open to the Arminianizing trend (on free will) evident at the time in the English Evangelical paper, *The Record*.²⁸ Not that Saumarez Smith was any the less opposed to Roman Catholicism; it was as Primate of the Church of England in Australia that he insisted on precedence over the Roman Catholic archbishop of Sydney at the Federation of Australia Celebrations in 1901.²⁹

But why did Saumarez Smith choose to invite, in 1891, the young (b. 1859) Bernard Schleicher, a High Churchman, to be principal of Moore College? Was it because he held a comprehensive view of the Church of

---

23. Ibid., 132–33.
24. Ibid., 70–71.
25. *Pace* Ballantine-Jones (*Inside Sydney*, 6), who brackets him with Archbishop Wright.
26. See Smith, *Blood of the New Covenant*.
27. Treloar, "Smith," 345–47.
28. Cf. Lewis, *Mere Christianity*.
29. Bale, "Commonwealth Celebrations of 1901," 90–107.

England? Was it dismay over "disunity in his Church,"[30] indeed in his diocese? It may have been to do with Schleicher's elderly father, John Theophilus Schleicher (1819–1892), educated in Berlin, a former SPG missionary in India (where Saumarez Smith had served in the 1860s), who had become an incumbent in Sydney.[31] Was it therefore so that the younger Schleicher could thus be reunited with his elderly parents and join his sister—a deaconess in the diocese? Perhaps so, together with knowledge of the younger Schleicher's tuberculosis and short life-expectancy.

Bernard Schleicher was distinguished academically—in Hebrew and Aramaic—and learnedly opposed, like E. B. Pusey, to negative Old Testament criticism[32] but he was "a High Churchman of the old school . . . [who] held and taught the doctrine of baptismal regeneration."[33] He was also "a man of great charm and gentleness . . . [whose] personal character could not fail to endear him to all his students."[34] Bishop Saumarez Smith imposed the educational requirement that students of Moore College should have attained university matriculation. Schleicher permitted them to enter as probationers until they achieved that standard.

His illness grew worse, and he could not teach at all in the first term of the academic year 1896–1897. He resumed only for the Michaelmas term, and died in February 1897. Several Sydney clergy, none of them graduates of Moore, helped with lectures to finish the Lent term.[35] The college had collapsed again. Of the students of 1891–1897, twelve were ordained for Sydney, three for Bathurst, and one each for Goulburn and Grafton-and-Armidale.

Conclusion on the College to 1897

Under Bishop Barry the college had digressed from its Evangelical tradition established by William Hodgson, Robert Lethbridge King, and Lukyn Williams. Under the godly and endearing person of Bernard Schleicher (1891–1897) it remained biblically conservative.

A majority of Sydney clergy had trained elsewhere than at Moore College, which had, however, contributed widely—to Sydney, Melbourne, Ballarat, Bathurst, and Goulburn dioceses—and others.[36] Though most of

30. Cable, "Smith, William Saumarez," 675–77.
31. "Schleicher, John Theophilus," in *Crockford's*, 1048.
32. Schleicher, "Results," 18–19.
33. Loane, *Centenary History*, 92.
34. Ibid., 92.
35. Ibid., 96–7.
36. Ibid., 180–84.

the college's graduates would have been Evangelicals, we may be certain that "old school High Church" students also were trained at the college during both Alfred Barry and William Saumarez Smith's episcopates: Jones explicitly affirmed that students of "various schools of thought . . . but true to the principles of the Reformation" were wanted at the college.[37] We do not know of Barker's policy in this matter.

With regard to the clergy in Sydney, we must assume that under Barry and Smith both the High Church and the Tractarian elements in the diocese as well as Broad Church were now strengthened as the end of the century drew near. The historian can be less confident concerning the lay members of Sydney's synod. Some at least, like the majority of the clergy, would have come from England and Ireland, and a few from Wales, bringing their various convictions and churchmanship preferences with them.

The Diocese and Moore College 1897–1953

Moore College would continue to go through theological changes in principals, from now on Evangelical changes, *pari passu* with the particular outlook of each archbishop. Saumarez Smith would next choose an Evangelical, one of those in the later nineteenth-century extended spectrum. He would be a premillennialist (like the Earl of Shaftesbury and Bishop J. C. Ryle, and Handley C. G. Moule in his later years) and an advocate of Keswick holiness teaching—moreover one "who had turned [it] into daily life and habit."[38]

Saumarez Smith's Second Appointee: An Evangelical Principal

The college having virtually collapsed with Schleicher's death, Archbishop (title granted from Lambeth in 1897) Saumarez Smith needed again to revive the college. He appointed a principal much more in sympathy with Bishop Barker's intention, namely, Nathaniel Jones, though a man in whom the spectrum of Evangelicalism was extended by both a premillennial hope and a Keswick holiness emphasis. Clearly the large Evangelical body of both laity and clergy in his flock would not have been wholly pleased with another High Churchman; the stalwart Evangelical, William Macquarie Cowper, was not only Saumarez Smith's archdeacon of Sydney and dean of the cathedral but also a long-serving trustee of the Thomas Moore Estate,

---

37. Jones, "Moore College," 10.
38. Loane, *Centenary History*, 99.

hence a governor of the college. The Keswick-inspired George Grubb mission of 1891–1892, which had a particularly great impact in Melbourne,[39] in Sydney had touched the archbishop himself. So Saumarez Smith was now an Evangelical "recently imbued with a deep sense of interior piety and spiritual perfectionism of the 'Keswick' movement,"[40] (though "perfectionism" here should not be read as "sinless perfectionism").

Jones had graduated from Oxford (BA Theology, first-class honors) in 1886, a time of theological transition at the university—from *The Origin of Species* (1859) and *Essays and Reviews* (1860) to *Lux Mundi* (1889). The negative criticism of the Old Testament was being felt. Jones was the second principal of Moore College with an Oxford degree and the second (after Lukyn Williams) with his degree in theology as such. By 1897 he had behind him some eleven years' parish experience in Victoria. He had combined that with teaching stipendiary lay readers to prepare them for ordination. He was a regular contributor to *The Victorian Churchman* and had supported the George Grubb mission. Bishop Goe of Melbourne (1887–1902) must have at least mentioned a clergyman of Jones's qualities to his fellow Evangelical bishop Saumarez Smith at annual episcopal meetings. Jones had become well known in Evangelical circles of both Sydney and Melbourne as a shining Christian personality with outstanding gifts.

Jones began a new era in the influence of Moore College principals on Sydney and beyond by restoring Barker's vision. Firm doctrinal faithfulness to the Articles and strictly lawful liturgical practice were important for him. He worked well with the archbishop, and always found the former principal of St Aidan's, Birkenhead a source of valuable advice.[41] After twelve years under Jones the college had been rejuvenated by the time Saumarez Smith died (1909). Some of those trained under him were to play leading roles in the diocese, for example, Sydney James Kirkby, Sydney Edgar Langford Smith, Herbert Smirnoff Begbie, David James Knox, Richard Bradley Robinson, Arthur Leslie Wade, and Stephen Henry Denman[42]—especially in the election of Howard Mowll as Archbishop of Sydney in 1933.

A Liberal Evangelical Bishop and His Appointee

A change in the diocese occurred when the astute campaigning of Canon Francis Bertie Boyce, a Moore College graduate from the last year of

39. Judd and Cable, *Sydney Anglicans*, 150–52; Piggin, *Spirit of a Nation*, 57–58.
40. Cable, "Smith," 675–77.
41. Loane, *Centenary History*, 111.
42. See Loane, *Mark These Men*, 11–16, 23–27, 38–42, 45–53, 59–67.

Hodgson and the first of King, secured the election of John Charles Wright. The synod rejected Nathaniel Jones's nominee, his friend W. H. Griffith Thomas, principal of Wycliffe Hall, one also whose theologically-minded Evangelicalism embraced the Keswick and premillennial extensions. Synod opted for someone with a reputation for concern for society's condition, probably unaware of the theologically liberalizing, now broadened spectrum of Evangelicalism. Bishops and clergy of Sydney before had expressed themselves on socio-political issues, notably Bishop Barry and Archbishop Saumarez Smith. Boyce wanted a man who would also uphold the constitutional liturgical position of the Church of England.[43]

John Charles Wright (BA Oxford, 1884, second-class honors in history), had been tutored by E. A. Knox at Merton College. Since ordination he had served under Knox, now Bishop of Manchester, and had become his archdeacon. Although like Knox he was a strict constitutionalist, firmly opposed to illegal ritual practices, in doctrine he was comprehensive in what he would allow. Archdeacon Wright had been elected the first chairman (1907) of the newly organized Group Brotherhood, who were clergy of the new liberal broadening of the Evangelical spectrum. They were looking for a fresh, as yet undefined, approach to the issues of the day.[44] Wright determined to bring to Sydney men of theologically liberal perspectives to assist in addressing "the social problem," namely, material poverty.

The new archbishop's first presidential address to synod (December 1909) was his position statement. He was explicitly inclusivist of all major schools—High (not excluding Tractarian), Broad, and of course, Evangelical. He encouraged synodsmen to look for "the possibility of deep spiritual unity beneath the diversity of theological standpoint," and declared it "a sin . . . for any man to utter or even think suspicion of those who differ from himself."[45] Was he alluding to Jones's friend Mervyn Archdall, rector of St Mary's, Balmain, who had stringently critiqued the bishops controlling the Australian College of Theology?[46] He and Jones, together with other likeminded Evangelical members of synod, must have perceived a mere rump of the gospel they cherished as Wright went on: "The great principles of the [Evangelical] school [are]: the direct right of approach to God possessed by the individual soul, the supremacy of Holy Scripture, and the right of

---

43. See Robinson, "Origins," 159–60, citing Boyce, *Fourscore Years and Seven*, 146.
44. Elliott-Binns, *Evangelical Movement*, 69.
45. Wright, "President's Address," 36.
46. Archdall, *Liturgical Right*, 288–91.

private judgement."[47] This was a bare and minimalist statement, without doubt deliberately so framed.[48]

Wright admired Jones, but on his death (June 1911) set about bringing two young Liberal Evangelicals (as the Group Brotherhood later designated themselves), both graduates of Cambridge, to key positions in the diocese. David John Davies (BA 1904, History Tripos) began as principal of Moore College in November 1911. Albert Edward Talbot (BA 1904, Theology Tripos) came to St Andrew's Cathedral as dean in the middle of 1912, only the second dean in its history. Both Davies and Talbot were members of the Group Brotherhood.[49] Both, like the new archbishop, had a concern for "the social issue." The new principal had accepted the modern approach to the authority of Scripture and the meaning of the atonement. Under him the teaching in the college would shift to the new theologically liberal part of the Evangelical spectrum, but remain uncompromising, like Wright, in its stance toward Anglo-Catholic ritual.

Wright had unwittingly set Davies a hard task. Part of his difficulty would be the rising influence in the diocese of some of Jones's abler former students. Three of the five clergy that the standing committee of synod would elect to the Moore College Committee (formed by synod in 1919) [50] were graduates of the college under Jones, and at least two of the lay members were similarly disposed. By that time there had been two other Evangelicals present in Sydney to consolidate and inform their conservative stance. Both of them were both learned and conservative: the Irish theologian, Dr. Everard Digges La Touche (in Sydney from 1912 to 1915) and Mervyn Archdall (retired to suburban Sydney, 1913 to 1917). By 1933 the Jones graduates and like-minded Evangelical laymen represented an even stronger element on the college committee.[51] A separate part of Davies's difficulties as principal would be the chronic financial straits of the college.

The theological tension between the majority of the college committee and Davies did not prevent them granting him leave of absence in 1920–1921. He had just been awarded the coveted Cambridge BD for his book,[52] but there was already some concern for his health. Again in February 1934 they granted him leave to visit England for two terms. His health was now in serious decline. Their other decision at that same meeting is

47. Wright, "President's Address," 37.
48. See Jay, *Faith and Doubt*, 13–15, quoting Ryle, *Evangelical Religion*, 10–13.
49. Judd, "Talbot," 363.
50. *Sydney Diocesan Directory for 1920*, 447.
51. *Sydney Diocesan Directory for 1934*, 276.
52. Davies, *Church and the Plain Man*.

puzzling and seems a great pity. In 1927 they had consented to Mrs. Davies being employed to tutor first-year students in English and history, and in addition she had lectured *gratis* in church history for some years. Now in February 1934 they thought it "not in the best interest of the college that any Lady should conduct lectures or teaching in connection with Moore College."[53] The reason is not known. What is known is that at this time "the Diocese was split from top to bottom over questions of Modernism. All this lay behind the attitude of the college committee."[54] It was nearly twelve months since Mowll had been elected (April 1933) and he was about to arrive in Sydney.

In the twenty-four years of Davies's tenure (1911-1935) some 160 students of the college were ordained in Sydney. They included a number of traditional Evangelicals, some of whom continued to hold Jones's premillennial hope and his holiness teaching.

Howard West Kilvinton Mowll: A Bishop Barker Redivivus?

With the election of a new archbishop in April 1933, following Wright's death in the February, another new era in the Evangelical tradition in the history of the Diocese of Sydney and of its theological college was about to open. Howard West Kilvinton Mowll (1890-1958) was a characteristic conservative Evangelical of his day.[55] He resembled Frederic Barker both in tallness of body and conviction of mind; only his Evangelicalism was firmly touched, like that of Jones, by Keswick holiness teaching. It was also honed by his experience of liberalism from his student days. Coincidentally, also like Barker, he would preside over the appointment of three principals of Moore Theological College.

Mowll was also like John Charles Wright in two respects: his degree was in history (BA 1912), but from Cambridge, and he had a close association with Bishop E. A. Knox, who had suggested his name (along with two others) for Sydney in 1933. Mowll remained in correspondence with Knox until the latter's death in 1937.[56] At Cambridge Mowll had heard the lectures of some of the same divinity professors as Davies (Swete and

---

53. Loane, *Centenary History*, 133.
54. Loane, Letter.
55. Bebbington, *Evangelicalism in Modern Britain*, 2-4.
56. Loane, *Archbishop Mowll*, 140; Loane, *Makers of Our Heritage*, 140.

Gwatkin), and like him had spent a year at Ridley Hall, but under Arthur J. Tait,[57] one of the new Group Brotherhood of Liberal Evangelicals.

But Mowll was unlike both Wright and Davies in one critical respect—his place in the spectrum of Evangelicalism. "It was in the CICCU that his theology took shape."[58] Most important was his experience of the CICCU's disaffiliation in 1910 from the Student Christian Movement, which had moved in principle onto a theologically liberal footing. The CICCU's decision had hinged on the doctrine of the inspiration and authority of Scripture.[59]

In marked contrast with Wright's statement to synod in 1909 was Mowll's public announcement of his Evangelical stance in 1934. An observer of the occasion records that when he stood up to speak at the welcome following his induction: "he drew his New Testament from his pocket. He then affirmed with great simplicity his desire to uphold the doctrine of Justification by Faith only. It was as if Sydney Churchmen might know that here was a Bishop who would take up his stand on the divine authority of the Scriptures alone."[60] His biographer also records: "[Mowll's] declared aim was to leave the diocese more Evangelical than he found it." He had Barker's main achievements as his own goal.[61] We know that Mowll read Dean Cowper's history of Barker's episcopate.[62] Stuart Babbage (1914–2012), the dean of St Andrew's Cathedral from 1947 to 1952, remembered that Mowll personally stressed to him (Babbage) that he was "a *conservative Evangelical*."[63]

On Principal Davies's death in June 1935, Archbishop Mowll (being one of the Thomas Moore Estate's three trustees, with Bishop Kirkby and Mr. H. L. Tress) was persuaded to invite Thomas Chatterton Hammond to be the next principal. In Davies's last months, Mowll had made Marcus Loane resident tutor and chaplain in the college. Loane had close ties to D. J. Knox, who had trained under Nathaniel Jones and admired him. Loane

---

57. Loane, *Archbishop Mowll*, 41–42.

58. Ibid., 60.

59. Ibid., 44–45, 47; and see Pollock, *Cambridge Movement*, 171–74.

60. Loane, *Archbishop Mowll*, 133. One assumes that Loane would hardly have missed the occasion.

61. Ibid.

62. Cowper, *Episcopate*. Mowll's copy had been in the library of Archbishop Wright, inscribed by W. M. Cowper to Dr. Eugene Stock, the renowned editorial secretary of the CMS, who gave it to Wright, his son-in-law, probably on his election to Sydney. Loosely inserted inside the back cover is a list of churches built in Barker's time. Mowll ticked them off as he visited them. (Information kindly supplied by Dr. Stuart Braga.)

63. Babbage, "Archbishop Mowll."

continued on under Hammond until 1938, when he married Patricia, a daughter of Knox. He was appointed the college's vice-principal from 1939 until Hammond's retirement, then principal from 1953 to 1958.

Hammond took up the reins of his appointment in April 1936, and with the strong support of the archbishop Moore College began to flourish again. The men of the Jones tradition found themselves quite comfortable with Hammond's Evangelicalism with its Reformation emphasis—as they had on his visit in 1926.[64] They admired his great learning and valued both his defense of the more central doctrines that they held dear and his reasoned opposition to both liberal and Anglo-Catholic teaching and ritualism. When Hammond retired in 1953 after seventeen years as principal, the great majority of the clergy in the Diocese of Sydney, some 200 had been trained at Moore.[65] Fifty, even sixty years later, there were clergy still living who remembered and cherished his teaching.

---

64. See chapter 11 below.
65. Loane, *Centenary History*, 152.

Figure 2: Nathaniel Jones

4

Evangelicalism Embraced
Formation of a Scholar-Pastor

Introduction

WILLIAM SAUMAREZ SMITH'S APPOINTMENT of Nathaniel Jones to Moore Theological College in 1897 would lead to the restoration and long-term preservation of Sydney's Evangelical tradition. Jones's Evangelicalism was one extended by a premillennial expectation of Christ's return, plus "the true Keswick teaching"[1] as clarified by H. C. G. Moule[2] and widely accepted by evangelicals at that time. It fitted well in a Sydney impacted by the George Grubb mission of 1891–1892. But no evidence appears in Jones's diaries of his parish ministry or in his published sermons and articles that his premillennial hope of Christ's advent in glory was a preoccupation, such as to exclude concern with this world outside the life of the "little flock" of believers.[3] Jones's outlook was representative of many in the Evangelical school at that time, and even Moule later embraced the premillennial hope.[4] Like Moule, too, Jones adhered to the theology of the Thirty-nine Articles of Religion and to the 1662 Prayer Book—both understood in close accord with their framers in sixteenth-century Reformation England. At the same time he warmly embraced non-Anglican evangelicals. A fresh

---

1. Loane, *Centenary History*, 98.
2. Moule, "Introduction," 9–15 and Moule, *Outlines of Christian Doctrine*, 190–201.
3. Pace Lawton, *Better Time to Be*, 86–89.
4. Gribben and Stunt, *Prisoners of Hope?*, 91.

examination of his published and unpublished written work will spell all this out.[5]

Embracing Theology and Piety

Nathaniel Jones, born June 1, 1861, was the eldest son of John Jones,[6] a farmer whose land was a few miles north of Oswestry, Shropshire, and thus not far east of the mountains of north Wales. Jones grew up on the farm. He came to a clear faith in Christ, possibly following D. L. Moody's evangelistic campaign of 1873–1874. The Reverend Frederick Cashel, an Evangelical educated at Trinity College, Dublin, was the incumbent of Holy Trinity Church, the second of the two Anglican churches in the town. Jones's exact contemporary and later close friend, W. H. Griffith Thomas who lived in the town, had experienced a definitive conversion in 1878 and was active in the parish.[7] But it seems that they did not yet know each other.[8]

Was it Cashel's suggestion that Jones read *The Christian System*, a work by Thomas Robinson (1749–1813), which Jones outlined in detail? It was a clear, moderate Calvinist statement of basic Christian doctrine.[9] At some time Jones also made careful notes from *"Our God Shall Come," Addresses on the Second Coming of the Lord*, a collection of the Mildmay Park[10] conference addresses of 1878.[11] Sponsors and speakers in that year featured notable premillennialist evangelicals, most of them Anglicans, including the social reforming Earl of Shaftesbury. Chapter 2 above noted that William Pennefather, the vicar of Mildmay, had also promoted a doctrine of release by faith from the reigning power of sin at his earlier parish of Barnet, from 1852 to 1864, then at Mildmay Park. Perhaps it was Cashel who pointed Jones in both the holiness and premillennial directions; it is probable that Jones was a premillennial and pietist Evangelical before he pursued study for ordination.

---

5. See also Cameron, "Moore College," 96–123.

6. *The Argus*, Family Notices: Marriages, February 15, 1888.

7. Lawton, *Better Time to Be*, 70, citing Thomas, *William*, 16.

8. Jones, "Notes," *pace* Lawton, *Better Time to Be*, 70–71. (Jones, aged 47, wrote, supporting his nomination of Thomas, "I have known him for 24 years," that is, since 1885.)

9. Robinson, *Christian System*.

10. See chapter 2 above, "Evangelical Responses."

11. Jones, Oxford Student Notebook, 27–36.

To Oxford to Prepare for the Ministry

In October 1882 Jones enrolled in Oxford's relatively new Honour School of Theology. He was just in time to be present for D. L. Moody's brief mission to the university. Like other sons of families of modest means, Jones enrolled as a non-collegiate student.[12]

Jones must have found much at Oxford to support him in his tradition as well as much that was challenging. Jones nowhere mentions the skeptical intellectual life of the time, though it was then a place of doubt and loss of faith for many.[13] The challenges included those explained in chapter 1 above. Utilitarian philosophy of J. S. Mill was one strong cause.[14] Benjamin Jowett, of *Essays and Reviews* (1860) notoriety, was Regius Professor of Greek and vice-chancellor of the university. His influential rationalist-idealist colleague at Balliol from 1860, the moral philosopher Thomas Hill Green, had only just died.[15]

More directly challenging a student for the ministry was the growing influence of the Tractarian or Anglo-Catholic movement, in 1883 just fifty years old. T. H. Green's impact on it now contributed to forming a new *liberal* Tractarian or Liberal Anglo-Catholic standpoint, as set out and defended in *Lux Mundi*,[16] published two years after Jones arrived in Melbourne. Its essayists were all teaching at Oxford colleges when Jones enrolled. Francis Paget (1851–1911), author of Essay X, "Sacraments" in *Lux Mundi*, became Regius Professor of Pastoral Theology in 1885 and could be sympathetic to Evangelicals. The stalwart Tractarian, E. B. Pusey, Regius Professor of Hebrew, had recently died, but he was a strong defender of the Old Testament and an anti-rationalist.

Pusey's successor (1883) was the liberal S. R. Driver, a fellow of Trinity College from 1870.[17] Although Driver was only moderately critical, a contemporary could write of him: "Nothing can exceed his scorn for those who betray any lack of acquaintance with the utterances of German critics, [he] who never has condescended . . . to state what, in his opinion, are to be considered sound and safe principles of investigation."[18] In the year Jones went up to Oxford, the then also moderately critical William Sanday

---

12. *Oxford University Calendar* (1883), 246–47.

13. See Ward, *Robert Elsmere*.

14. Knox, *Reminiscences*, 112; Brock and Curthois, *Nineteenth-Century Oxford*, 95 and notes 140, 141.

15. "Mr. Grey" in Ward, *Robert Elsemere*.

16. Gore, "Preface," vii–xi.

17. See "Driver, Samuel Rolles," *ODCC*, 512.

18. Lias, "Witness of the Historical Books," 284.

became Dean Ireland's Professor of the Exegesis of Holy Scripture. At times sympathetic to Evangelicals,[19] he lectured on the Epistle to the Romans and with A. C. Headlam later produced a classic commentary on that letter.[20]

There were also those clearly opposed to key elements of Evangelicalism: the art critic, John Ruskin, reinstated in 1883–1884 as Slade Professor of Fine Arts after an interval of mental illness, "hat[ed] the doctrine of justification by faith alone" and explicitly disavowed belief in a substitutionary atonement.[21] So had F. D. Maurice and B. F. Westcott at Cambridge.[22] The Oxford of the mid-1880s, as foreshadowed by *Essays and Reviews* (1860), was thus on the cusp of moving generally to the assumptions of the liberal negative criticism of Scripture described in chapter 2 above. In 1885 Frederic Farrar, already famous for his best-selling *Life of Christ*, delivered his Bampton lectures, *History of Interpretation*. These embodied the liberal critical approach, which was intended to be an apologetic for the abiding message of the Bible by making negative assessments of disposable historical and doctrinal statements in it.[23] Farrar warmly dedicated his lectures to Benjamin Jowett.[24] In this intellectual environment it seems hard to imagine that a student of Jones's caliber could have naively ignored views threatening his own.

Encouraging for Jones, one presumes, were those both within the theology school and outside whose presence was supportive for orthodox students, whether Evangelical like Jones, old-school High Church, such as Bernard Schleicher (see chapter 3) or Anglo-Catholic. Pusey's anti-rationalist apologetic for the authority of the Old Testament must have helped, and the listed teacher for Prophecy was Alfred Edersheim,[25] who provided helpful historical background for retaining confidence in the Bible. George Rawlinson, professor of ancient history, was a defender both of the Bible and of the historic Christian positions;[26] the Assyriologist A. H. Sayce had just published (1883) the first of his several books on the Bible;[27] and Monier Monier-Williams, expert in Sanskrit, Hinduism, and Buddhism,

---

19. See "Sanday, William," *ODCC*, 1463; Reynolds, *Evangelicals*, 67–68.
20. Sanday and Headlam, *Critical and Exegetical Commentary*.
21. Larsen, *Creative Company*, 536.
22. Maurice, "On Justification by Faith," 189–213; Westcott, *Victory of the Cross*, 78–89.
23. Farrar, *History of Interpretation*, ix–xi.
24. Ibid., v.
25. Edersheim, *Life and Times of Jesus*. See *Oxford University Gazette 1882–1883*, 13.
26. Rawlinson, *Alleged Historical Difficulties*; Rawlinson, *Antiquity of Man*.
27. Sayce, *Fresh Light*.

was also supportive of biblical reliability.[28] The High Churchman, John Wordsworth, nephew of the Romantic poet, was the first Oriel Professor of New Testament Interpretation (1883–1885) and was "very conservative in his approach to higher criticism."[29] The scholarship of Westcott and Lightfoot (the latter described as a liberal Anglican on the right wing in the tradition of Coleridge)[30] was also reassuring to those seeking a *positive critical*[31] approach to the New Testament. In addition, Westcott and Hort's great work establishing the best Greek text of the New Testament had just been published.[32]

Another supporter of orthodoxy was Dr. William Ince, Regius Professor of Divinity from 1878. An old-school High Churchman, he was favorably impressed by the Moody mission to the university in Jones's first term, Michaelmas 1882.[33] "Especially in his latter days" he inclined "to Evangelical interpretations, and rejecting ritualism alike in form and doctrine."[34] His older colleague and friend was Charles Abel Heurtley, Lady Margaret Professor of Divinity since 1853, and an authority on the early creeds. His 1845 Bampton lectures, *Justification*, have been noted in chapter 2. Reynolds sees him as among the "undoubted champions of the Evangelical cause."[35] If he "deplor[ed] hasty and unmeasured condemnation of the 'higher criticism,'"[36] he finally cautioned against the excesses of that criticism. Jones's notes show that he attended Wycliffe Hall for tutorials on Christian evidences that he took down from Principal Girdlestone.[37] It is worthy of note that both Girdlestone's father and an uncle were Evangelical clergy active in the interests respectively of industrial and rural social reform[38] Jones, as the son of a small farmer, is likely to have appreciated this evangelical social concern.

28. Monier-Williams, *Bible and the Sacred Books*.
29. Hinchcliff, "Religious Issues," 100.
30. Treloar, *Lightfoot the Historian*.
31. Cf. Pusey, "Preface."
32. *New Testament in the Original Greek*.
33. Reynolds, *Evangelicals*, 36.
34. Clark, "Ince, William," 337–38.
35. Reynolds, *Evangelicals*, 92, 92n10.
36. Strong, "Heurtley, Charles Abel," 416–17.
37. Jones, "Notes from Canon Girdlestone," in Jones, Oxford Student Notebook.
38. His father was the Reverend Charles Girdlestone; his uncle, the Reverend Edward Girdlestone.

The Course of Study

The course for the "honour school of theology" was accepted by bishops as a qualification for ordination. To some extent it addressed the current challenges to Christian faith. But no more than the Ordinal in the Prayer Book did it presuppose that a clergyman was obliged to study socio-political theory to understand the society's contemporary needs. Rather, the rigorously academic course assumed that the pastor should be an informed and skilled expositor of Scripture grounded in a knowledge of Greek and, for a first-class degree, Hebrew as well. He should know key parts of the Bible thoroughly, understand the great dogmatic issues of the ancient past and of the Reformation—as resolved in the historic creeds (Apostles', Nicene, and Athanasian) and the Thirty-nine Articles of Religion. He must also be adequately grounded in the worship of the Church of England as laid down in the 1662 Book of Common Prayer. He was to know the traditional rational grounds for the Christian faith and have some understanding of church history. The syllabus for the examinations that Jones sat in 1886 listed the substantial works required to be read.[39]

Thus the theology honors school demanded not a general liberal education but a rigorous introduction to the study of Holy Scripture and theology. Part of the context was Tractarianism and the stream of rationalism continuous with *Essays and Reviews*. The apologetics part of the course did not explicitly come to grips with how J. S. Mill's or T. H. Green's philosophy might be critiqued. Green's view of Christianity as set out in his "Essay on Christian Dogma" foreshadowed modern radical "demythologisation."[40] The study of personal piety and devotion was no part of the course, although students were required to attend daily chapel services and Sunday worship. In fact the degree was designed "to squeeze the last drop of religion out of [theology]" and "make it historical."[41] Jones completed it in the four academic years from October 1882 to June 1886 and the final examination papers he sat reveal a high intellectual demand.[42] He graduated fifth in the list of the eleven who gained the BA in theology with first-class honors.[43]

The Evangelical churches in Oxford could supplement study with Christian nurture.[44] Notable Oxford rectors included Alfred Millard Wil-

---

39. Honour School of Theology, in *Examination Statutes*, 110–17.
40. Green, "Essay on Christian Dogma," 161–85.
41. Chadwick, *Victorian Church*, 451.
42. School of Theology, 1886, in *Oxford University Examination Papers*.
43. *Oxford University Calendar* (1887), 316.
44. St Aldate's, St Clement's, St Ebbe's, St Peter-le-Bailey, and St Thomas's.

liam Christopher at St Aldate's from 1859 to 1905, honorary Canon of Christ Church from 1886. Like Jones at Moore College later, Christopher was remembered for his radiant Christian personality.[45] It seems certain that St Aldate's was Jones's spiritual home. Christopher was a personal friend of J. C. Ryle, then Bishop of Liverpool, and disseminated Ryle's many tracts and other writings among the students. Saturday evening meetings in Christopher's rectory enabled men to hear Evangelical clergy such as William Haslam—converted by his own sermon on repentance—and these guests would preach the next day at St Aldate's.[46] Canon Christopher was also convinced of the Keswick message, strongly affirmed by Handley Moule in 1884 when Jones was midway through his studies.

In 1884 or 1885 Jones began a close friendship with W. H. Griffith Thomas,[47] then a student at King's College, London. There Thomas sat at the feet of Henry Wace, later Dean of Canterbury,[48] of Principal Alfred Barry (consecrated Bishop of Sydney in that year), and possibly of A. W. Momerie, a pioneer of the radical "New Theology,"[49] which T. C. Hammond would critique early in his ministry (see chapter 10 below). Encouraged by Griffith Thomas, Jones would later write an excellent small commentary on the Thirty-nine Articles (chapter 6 below) and plan a work on the Prayer Book. Only his early death prevented him from writing it.

We must conclude that Jones left Oxford in June 1886 retaining both the theological convictions and the piety characteristic of many in the spectrum of Evangelicalism at that time. However, his intellectual grasp of the Christian gospel and the authority of Holy Scripture, both as recovered by the Reformation, was to be tried and deepened. Through St Aldate's he was confirmed in the necessity of conversion and of the active expression of faith. He remained a convinced premillennialist, and a firm adherent of the authentic Keswick doctrine of sanctification, without a lessened adherence to the three ancient creeds, the Thirty-nine Articles and the Book of Common Prayer. Such was his Anglican Evangelicalism.

---

45. Anonymous, "Appreciation," 16–17.

46. Reynolds, *Evangelicals at Oxford*, 136–37.

47. Jones, "Notes," *pace* Lawton, *Better Time to Be*, 70–71.

48. Wace was Professor of Ecclesiastical History and became principal from 1884 (Atherstone, "Wace," 688–89).

49. Carlyle, "Momerie," in *DNB*, 1901 Supplement, 183.

The Forming of an Evangelical Principal

Ordained deacon in 1886 Jones began to serve under an Evangelical, the Reverend Doctor Mitchell, previously a physician, in the parish of New Wortley, a suburb of Leeds.[50] Jones soon experienced serious voice trouble and a lung problem was also detected, which led him early in 1887 to board ship for the more favorable climate of Victoria, Australia. Later he would play a decisive role in the history of Evangelicalism in Sydney. On the voyage Jones became acquainted with Grace Henderson, a deaconess-nurse trained at Mildmay Park; they would marry on January 13, 1888, in Melbourne.[51]

In Melbourne the newly consecrated Evangelical, Field Flowers Goe (1832–1910), had just been installed on April 14, 1887 as the third bishop of the diocese, which he would serve until 1902. At first Jones was assistant to the vicar in the parish of Portarlington, southwest of the city across Port Phillip, on the Bellarine Peninsula. In May 1888, now ordained presbyter, having accepted Bishop Goe's offer, he moved to the parish of Tarnagulla (with Newbridge). Tarnagulla was about forty-five kilometers (thirty miles) west of the large town of Bendigo, itself some distance north of Melbourne. He combined rural parish duties with teaching stipendiary lay readers with a view to their ordination, an initiative of Charles Perry, the first bishop of Melbourne. Jones moved in late July 1893 to the parish of St Luke's, White Hills (on the north side of Bendigo), where Perry Divinity Hall—named after the bishop—was now opened to continue teaching lay readers, now in residence.[52] Perry Hall moved into Bendigo itself in 1894. These years turned out to be further preparation to be principal of Moore College, to which the call came in 1897. The syllabus at Perry Hall, which Jones had used for teaching his stipendiary lay readers while at Tarnagulla, was that required by the Universities Preliminary Theological Examination.[53] B. F. Westcott (chiefly) had drawn it up in 1874.[54] Anglican bishops accepted it as an ordination requirement and Jones would use it at Moore College.

---

50. "Joseph Mitchell," in *Crockford's*, 821.
51. *The Argus*, Family Notices: Marriages, January 15, 1888, 1.
52. *Victorian Churchman*, August 18, 1893, 508; ibid., September 28, 1894, 234.
53. Goe, "President's Annual Address," 6.
54. Bullock, *History of Training*, 123–25.

Parish Experience 1886–1897

Jones's Reading

The Jones diaries record his fellowship on the voyage out with the Plymouth Brethren captain who conducted shipboard services.[55] It must have been he who loaned Jones some of J. N. Darby's works to read. Gracie lent him Charles Dickens's *Dombey and Son*, which contains a moving account of Dombey's repentance. Dickens remained an interest all Jones's life.[56] The novelist's deliberate aim, stated in his prefaces, to motivate change in Victorian institutions,[57] meshed with Jones's awareness of Shaftesbury's role in parliamentary reform legislation. Later Jones read Dickens's *Great Expectations* and Charles Kingsley's social-conscience-arousing novels—*Two Years Ago*,[58] and *Hypatia*.[59] Jones's Evangelical theology and piety did not isolate him from the literature depicting social distress. And he read works of fiction that had an edifying moral or pious aim, by authors hardly known today—A. L. O. E.,[60] A. K. Dunning,[61] Pansy,[62] and Sir Walter Besant, *All Sorts and Conditions of Men* on which last, "trashy" was Jones's emphatic comment.[63] He also read J. R. Green's classic history of England, most likely the *Short History*. All the above is hardly the reading of one preoccupied with Christ's advent in glory to the exclusion of interest in this world's social issues.[64]

Theological works that Jones read reflect in part his sermon preparation, in part the issues of his day, *and* those for teaching his stipendiary lay readers preparing for ordination. Jones read (again?) the standard works on miracles (both set reading at Oxford) of R. C. Trench and J. B. Mozley,[65] the latter, like Pusey on Daniel, seeing the essential issue as a matter of one's pre-

---

55. Jones, "Diaries," June 2, 1887.

56. Anonymous, "Rev. Canon Jones."

57. Swifte, "Charles Dickens."

58. Jones, "Diaries," February 21, 1893.

59. Jones, "Diaries," January 1, 1890.

60. A. L. O. E., *Prisoners of Pride* (sic Jones), correctly, *Pride and His Prisoners*. ALOE (A Lady of England) was the pseudonym of Charlotte Maria Tucker (1821–1893). See Jones, "Diaries," June 20, 1888.

61. Dunning, *Hampered*. See Jones, "Diaries," June 20, 1888.

62. Pansy, *King's Daughter*. See Jones, "Diaries," June 20, 1888.

63. Jones, "Diaries," August 28, 1890.

64. *Pace* Lawton, *Better Time to Be*, 67–74.

65. Trench, *Notes on the Miracles*; Mozley, *Lectures on Miracles*. See Jones "Diaries," January 8–15, 1890.

suppositions.⁶⁶ He records reading C. A. Row's Bampton Lectures of 1877 on Christian evidences, ⁶⁷ not just his recent apologetics *Manual* of 1886.

For use in his own sermons, no doubt, Jones at least dipped into F. B. Proctor, *Classified Gems of Thought*.⁶⁸ He must also have used J. C. Ryle's *Expository Thoughts* on Luke and John's gospels, for he assigned them to be read for sermons in a period when his voice was nearly or completely unusable for a long period.⁶⁹ He also assigned readings from D. L. Moody's *Bible Characters* and at least one chapter, "Abide—by faith," from Andrew Murray, the Scottish Presbyterian-Dutch Reformed holiness writer in the Keswick tradition.⁷⁰ Earlier, while on the Bellarine Peninsula, he had read Evan Henry Hopkins's new book, *The Walk That Pleases God*.⁷¹ He also read a well-known work, *Pastoral Office*, on the pastoral ministry.⁷² Jones also used and loaned to his parishioners biographies illustrating Christian conversion and life. One was the well-known William Haslam's autobiography, which recounted his conversion from a merely formal Tractarian commitment to a living faith that was Evangelical in conviction and message. This had huge sales with 125,000 copies printed in 1887.⁷³ Another was the biography of the Church of Ireland Archdeacon of Waterford, John Alcock.⁷⁴ Not only is Jones's evangelical conversionism and holiness commitment evident in his reading, but so also is his Anglican Reformation heritage as an Evangelical.

Jones's diary for 1893 (there being none for 1891–1892) records his preparation for teaching the Prayer Book and early church history to his stipendiary lay reader students in Perry Hall. On church history he read that by the "Broad Church Evangelical,"⁷⁵ F. W. Farrar,⁷⁶ who in this same year became Dean of Canterbury until 1903; on the Prayer Book he read Daniel Evans, a moderate High Churchman.⁷⁷ In 1893, too, he records that *The Victorian Churchman* has asked him to review a "pamphlet on The Church

66. Brown, *Miracles*, 160.
67. Row, *Christian Evidences*. See Jones, "Diaries," February 12, 1890.
68. See Jones, "Diaries," January 10, 1890.
69. Jones, "Diaries," June 8, August 4, 1890.
70. Probably *Abide In Christ* (1882). See Jones, "Diaries," July 17, 1890.
71. Jones, "Diaries," April 16, April 18, 1888.
72. Ibid., April 17, 1888.
73. Haslam, *From Death Into Life*. See Jones, "Diaries," September 20, 1888.
74. Alcock, *Walking with God*. See Jones, "Diaries," August 26, 1889.
75. ODCC, "Farrar," 602.
76. Probably Farrer, *Darkness and Dawn*. See Jones, "Diaries," January 23, 1893.
77. Daniel, *Prayer-book*. See Jones, "Diaries," February 7, 1893.

of God as Bride, Body and Building," the last chapter having "caused some to leave the church and shaken others."[78] Neither the review nor the pamphlet could be traced.

Preaching in the Parish

Jones's sermons and weekday Bible studies in parish ministry perhaps show the influence of Canon Christopher of St Aldate's, Oxford. They are almost wholly on two broad themes: the gospel demand of repentance, faith, and conversion, and holy living in the life of faith.[79] There is an occasional reference to Anglo-Catholic ritualism, as its doctrine touched the true nature of saving faith. His topic for Palm Sunday, 1888, for example, was "Religious Sentimentalism," and his address to the choir, perhaps, at St John's, Newbridge, recounted the conversion of William Haslam noted above. Only a little more frequent than references to ritualism were sermons on eschatological topics: one such, which he preached on August 12, 1888, was "The Great Multitude" of the redeemed in heaven (Rev 7:9; 19:1–8).

From his early Tarnagulla days Jones preserved one sermon outline, a funeral sermon—on John 3:18–36, entitled "Saved and Condemned, Already." It was a challenge to his hearers to ensure that they turned and "received the kingdom of God as a little child."[80] The extant diary records only a very few sermons devoted to Christ's atoning death. In his confirmation classes of 1890, his topics "The Virgin Mary" and "The Confessional" suggest a cautioning needed in that parish against Anglo-Catholic teaching.

Beginning in June 1890, Jones began a series of Bible studies for *The Victorian Churchman* on Christian holiness, a fitting preparation of readers for the coming George Grubb mission of 1891 in Victoria.[81] The first explained the typical Keswick contrast of "the rest of forgiveness" with "the rest of deliverance from sin's dominion" and the need of "entire self-surrender."[82] Following the Grubb mission he contributed a sermon, "Practical Religion," in which he expounded the epistle readings of the Epiphany season[83] as they applied to the transformation of the Christian's life in church, home,

---

78. Jones, "Diaries," January 28, 1893.

79. Jones, "Diaries," September 20, 1888; Reynolds, *Evangelicals at Oxford*, 136–67; Downer, *Century of Evangelical Religion*, 31.

80. Jones, "Diaries," August 19, 1888.

81. *Victorian Churchman*, June 6, 1890, 138; July 18, 1890, 178; September 12, 1890, 226–27; and November 7, 1890, 269–70.

82. Jones, "Old Yoke and the New," 138.

83. Celebrates the manifestation of Christ to the Gentiles (the "Wise Men"), Matt 2.

society, business, and religion.[84] A series, "Texts Often Misunderstood"[85] followed, and at the ensuing Melbourne convention of 1895 he preached on the power of the Holy Spirit.[86]

The years at Tarnagulla included tragedy and his own health difficulties; four of Nathaniel and Grace's children died in infancy.[87] When they moved to Moore College, Sydney, in May 1897, they had with them only their second-born, Maisie, and their last, Stephen. Jones himself experienced hoarseness early on at Tarnagulla, perhaps a return of the earlier throat trouble, and by November 1889 it began seriously to impede his sermon delivery. It became mostly impossible for him to preach from January 1891 to March 1893 but finally a doctor in Melbourne was able to remove a growth on one of his vocal chords.[88] In this interval he composed sermons for his stipendiary lay readers to read at the services, or assigned them to read the plain speaking J. C. Ryle's *Expository Thoughts on the Gospels*[89] for the Prayer Book gospel readings from Luke and John. The *Expository Thoughts* on these two gospels were especially rich in the commentaries Ryle consulted. Jones also selected chapters from D. L. Moody's printed sermons.

The General Evangelical Concept of "Worldliness"

Moody's sketches of Bible characters at that time tell us what "worldliness" consisted of for an Evangelical like Jones.[90] Moody held up the young Daniel as the model for young Christians for resisting temptation and to encourage them to avoid moral and spiritual compromise: by his character and trust in God Daniel was a shining light.[91] Typical of the exemplarist, moralistic expositors of that time, Moody spoke much to the point, but he failed to ground his application in direct thankfulness to Christ for salvation, though he did emphasize Daniel's heartfelt love of God.[92] He was quite concrete as

---

84. Jones, "Practical Religion," 42.

85. *Victorian Churchman;* only May 20, 1892, and October 14, 1892 traced.

86. Jones, "Fulfilment of Promise," 162–63.

87. Printed card commemorating the four deceased infants (shown to author by Mrs. Stephanie Bennett, daughter of Stephen Jones, granddaughter of Nathaniel and Grace Jones).

88. Jones, "Diary for 1887," "Diary for 1888–1890," and "Diary for the Year of Grace 1893."

89. Jones, "Diary for 1888–1890."

90. Moody, *Bible Characters.*

91. Ibid., 7.

92. Ibid., 7, 8.

he illustrated "separation from the world." He first warned against the danger of the wrong start: "the first game of chance; ... the first night spent in evil company." As things to renounce he listed making "gods" out of money and position in society, religious compromise, fraud in business, falsehood, dishonest gain, blasphemy, talking as if you did everything in your own power, and setting one's heart and affections on a place in society, even at the cost of moral principle. As things to embrace, he instanced willingness to be unpopular, daring to be honest come what may, showing mercy to the poor, personal love and personal praise within the church, being blameless in life, having moral courage, standing firm under persecution, being willing to be thought eccentric (for example, by being a teetotaler), but pleasing God.[93] One should note that many liberal clergy too, urged "temperance" (actually total abstinence) to counter the evils of alcohol abuse, and some Roman Catholic priests also did so.

Moody urged a relatively new idea, that every Christian ought to be a verbal evangelist,[94] a notion heard at Keswick though apparently never taught either by H. C. G. Moule or Evan Henry Hopkins.[95] In 1996 it seemed almost canonical for many Moore College graduates in Sydney,[96] although this may have changed since then.[97]

Jones would have been quite in tune with Handley Moule as he read his careful recent address where Moule defined "the World, as the Scripture unfolds it" as "in its idea and essence, the antithesis" to all that "the Christian and his life purpose" is. Concretely, "it is men, who do not believe in and receive Jesus Christ with the heart as Saviour, and do not yield themselves to him, their King, as His possession."[98] This is, course, biblical, indeed Johannine.[99] Moule acknowledged difficulties of application in detail according to circumstance. In essence, he went on, the Christian must become "more and more sensitive to the pain and loss of whatever breaks communion with Christ, whatever impedes the longed-for growth of conformity to Him."[100]

---

93. Ibid., 10.

94. Ibid., 60. Bebbington quotes from the chief American Baptist newspaper, *Examiner and Chronicle* of January 2, 1868, in *Dominance of Evangelicalism*, 33.

95. Neither in Moule, *Outlines of Christian Doctrine*, nor Smellie, *Hopkins*.

96. Bates, "Email to Marcia Cameron." A meticulously executed survey (as described to the writer by Bates at the time) of seventy-one sermons preached in early 1996 by clergy in the Sydney diocese.

97. Jensen, "Good News about Preaching," 24–25.

98. Moule, "Christian's Relationship," 70.

99. See Gospel according to John, and the Johannine epistles.

100. Moule, "Christian's Relationship," 71.

The basic idea was virtually the biblical requirement that God's people be spiritually and morally distinct.

In these years, then, Jones was being well prepared to become principal of a theological college. He was filling out his Oxford degree in theology by subsequent reading, diligent pastoral work and preaching, and tutoring stipendiary lay readers. Not mentioned above is the fact that he was also maintaining his personal piety, recording and evaluating many of his daily early morning times of prayer.[101]

Conclusion

An attentive reading of his diaries reveals that by the end of nearly ten years of conscientious pastoral *cum* teaching experience, Nathaniel Jones, with Gracie, had experienced moving country, marriage, the trials and tragedies of their parishioners, as well as those of their own young family. He had applied his Evangelical convictions both in parish preaching and in teaching candidates for the ministry in rural Victoria. On coming to Sydney he would reinstate at Moore College the scholarly Evangelicalism of its first three principals. It was an Evangelicalism likewise rooted in the English Reformation but now extended since their day by a premillennial hope and Keswick holiness teaching. By the late nineteenth century these were accepted views in the doctrinal spectrum of many Anglicans in the Evangelical school.

---

101. Jones, "Diary for 1888–1890."

5

Evangelical Doctrine Stated

Introduction

When Dean William Macquarie Cowper, one of the trustees of the Thomas Moore Estate, wrote his note inviting Jones to head Moore College, he wrote to one already a tried and proven man. He was also well known to prominent Evangelical clergy in both Melbourne and Sydney. These included Henry Archdall Langley, working in the Melbourne diocese, and his older brother, John Douse Langley, now rector of St Philip's, Sydney and Archdeacon of Cumberland. Both had been trained at Moore College. Bishop Saumarez Smith, then absent at the Lambeth Conference of 1897 (which approved for him the title of Archbishop), had been present at the church congress held in Hobart in January 1894, where Jones spoke on the Prayer Book. He would likely also have heard Bishop Goe speak of his outstanding minister and must surely have consulted his fellow Evangelical diocesan before inviting Jones (through Cowper) to move to Sydney and Moore College.

What sort of Evangelical would a cultured, Cambridge-educated and theologically well-informed centrist Evangelical like Bishop William Saumarez Smith appoint to train his clergy? Would it be one who would focus on the "little flock" of the converted as in a putative Brethren assembly, merely cultivating personal holiness in expectation of the premillennial near return of the Lord?[1] The evidence from Jones's own hand confirms

---

1. Lawton, *Better Time to Be*, 67–75; Lawton, "Nathaniel Jones," 361–75; Dickey, "Jones, Nathaniel," 191–92 (dependent on Lawton); Bebbington, *Dominance of Evangelicalism*, 181–82 (also dependent on Lawton, but confined to premillennialism).

Marcus Loane's memory of prominent clergy trained by Jones, men whom he knew personally—that he had observed in them no such influence.[2] To embrace a premillennial hope and Keswick holiness doctrine did not require anyone to step away from the Reformation doctrines of the Thirty-nine Articles—most certainly not Jones. The fourteen years of Jones at Moore College would in fact restore the Evangelical tradition in the college, which had been interrupted by the hiatus of 1884 to 1897. Jones arrived in May 1897 and immediately put in place the requirements of the Universities Preliminary Theological Examination, which demanded, *inter alia*, knowledge of the Thirty-nine Articles.

The main period of Jones's literary work in Sydney was from 1900 to 1908, the heart of his fourteen years as principal. His publications fall into two main groups—small hardcover books, and pocket-sized booklets of a few thousand words each or less, reprints of articles or published addresses which had first appeared in church newspapers.[3] At all times Jones intelligently expounds and defends the conservative Evangelical spectrum of his day. In view of the suggestion of "Brethren" influence on him, the reality of the recent Anglo-Catholic thrust in England, the large Roman Catholic presence in Sydney, and the challenge of liberal thought, especially among the Presbyterians, Jones's slim manual on the Articles is worth close examination. Was Nathaniel Jones "faithful to the doctrine of our church"?[4]

Nathaniel Jones's Exposition of the Thirty-nine Articles of Religion[5]

Jones's aim was merely a "short and simple exposition of the doctrines of the Church of England" for "Lay Readers, Bible Class Teachers, and Churchmen generally," as well as to prepare lay reader and deaconess candidates for their examinations.[6] So he confined himself to "a plain exposition of the doctrines of the Articles with their Scripture proofs." He acknowledged his indebtedness[7] to the still standard commentary on the Articles by Bishop

---

2. Loane, Review, 41–42.

3. Scattered between Moore College Library, the Mitchell Library (State Library of NSW), and Jones's two surviving grandchildren, who kindly made them available for copying.

4. Anonymous, "Rev. Canon Jones," 17.

5. Jones, *Teaching of the Thirty-nine Articles*.

6. Ibid., 6.

7. Ibid.

Harold Browne (a required text in theology at Oxford),[8] to the pioneering Evangelical work of T. P. Boultbee,[9] who became a Prebendary of St Paul's Cathedral, London, as well as to the new Liberal Anglo-Catholic exposition of Edgar C. S. Gibson.[10] He did not use the extreme Anglo-Catholic "party" presentation of G. F. Maclear.[11] He also used H. C. G. Moule's textbook on Christian doctrine[12] and Charles Hardwick's classic historical answer to Newman's *Tract XC*.[13]

Following his student notes from Oxford,[14] where Professor Heurtley gave the lectures on the Articles, Jones set them out so as to show their "scientific order" (their systematic relationship with one another) under five groups: 1. "Fundamental Religion"; 2. "The Rule of Faith"; 3. "The Salvation of the Individual"; 4. "The Church: Its Ministers and Sacraments"; and 5. "National Religion."[15] His tone is moderate and measured.

Jones's exposition kept close to the Augustinian intention of the English reformers.[16] He neither glossed lightly over, nor especially highlighted, the articles that reject Roman Catholic teaching, even though at the time of his writing some Anglo-Catholics in England had become more stridently positive towards Rome. This was also at a time when liberal theology was making itself felt in Sydney, especially in St Andrew's College within the University of Sydney, where men studying to be ministers in the Presbyterian Church of New South Wales received their theological education.[17]

Group 1. "Fundamental Religion"

This group (Articles 1–5) "deals with the fundamental catholic doctrines laid down in the Creeds," namely the Doctrine of God, of the Son, and of the Holy Ghost, which all the Reformation churches accepted. Jones's Oxford professor, C. A. Heurtley, was the acknowledged expert on the early

---

8. Browne, *Exposition of the Thirty-nine Articles*.
9. Boultbee, *Commentary on the Thirty-nine Articles*.
10. Gibson, *Thirty-nine Articles of the Church of England*.
11. Maclear, *Introduction to the Thirty-nine Articles*. See Australian College of Theology, *Manual for the Year 1899*, 13, and Jones, "Australian College of Theology."
12. Moule, *Outlines of Christian Doctrine*.
13. Hardwick, *History of the Articles*.
14. Jones, Oxford Student Notebook; Jones, *Teaching*, 6.
15. See Jones, *Teaching*, 9, 37, 45, 79, 117.
16. See Thomas, *Principles of Theology*.
17. Those studying for the Methodist and Congregational churches in New South Wales also received part of their education with the Presbyterians in Sydney.

creeds. Jones explains the necessary limitation of man's creaturely, finite understanding of God. He accepts the natural theology universal in his day, that "the unity of God may be argued from human reason" and he does not touch on the challenge from philosophical idealism.

On the "The Doctrine of the Son" (Articles 2–4) he warned first against the "prevailing tendency of thought" in liberal theology. Losing sight of the divine in the earthly Christ, this found motivation for social reform grounded in the new *liberal* view of the human Christ—"man's leader in social reform." Nor did he accept a limitation of Christ's knowledge, such as found in Charles Gore's *kenosis* Christology, for that disqualified "his testimony to the authenticity and authority of the Old Testament writings."[18] Jones warned, secondly, against the Roman Catholic "tendency to lose sight of the human in the glorified Christ," and hence "the desire of some mediator" such as the Virgin or the saints "to come between man and Him."[19]

Still on Article 2, concerning the meaning of Christ's death, then a matter of intense debate, Jones grounded his students in a biblical crucicentrism: "This is the great central doctrine of the Christian faith. Everything in Scripture converges on it.... The Old Testament read apart from the death of Christ becomes 'a porch without an edifice, a cypher without a solution.'"[20] He quoted the Presbyterian, James Denney's *The Death of Christ* (a work respected by the Anglican theologian J. K. Mozley):[21] "The doctrine of the death of Christ and its significance was not St Paul's [speculative] theology, it was his Gospel. It was all he had to preach."[22]

Article 2 states that Christ died "to reconcile His Father to us." Jones corrected in some detail the error still propagated liturgically today,[23] that "reconciliation" in the Bible speaks of a change in *humankind's* attitude to God, not *God's* to humans.[24] Rather, "Scripture unmistakably represents sin as an obstacle that must be dealt with before God can act in grace toward the sinner"[25]—something Jones's archbishop had also emphasized.[26] Rebutting the notion that this represented God as "less ready to forgive than an earthly father," Jones argued the seriousness of the moral issue of sin for

---

18. Jones, *Teaching*, 18; Gore, "Holy Spirit and Inspiration," 358–61.
19. Jones, ibid., 19.
20. Ibid.
21. Mozley, *Doctrine of the Atonement*, 47, 52, etc.
22. Denney, *Death of Christ*, 109; Denney, *Death of Christ*, edited by Tasker, 66.
23. Anglican Church, *Prayer Book for Australia*, 133, 136.
24. Jones, *Teaching*, 21–24.
25. Ibid., 22.
26. Smith, *Blood of the New Covenant*, 15–16, 39–40.

God. He quoted a contemporary Australian-born Presbyterian: "[The problem] is to be eternally just, and also the eternal justifier of the unjust. . . . It is a problem for God, and a problem fit for a God."[27]

Jones was well aware, too, of the prevailing liberal denial of the "substitutionary character" of Christ's death, denied on the grounds of autonomous human ethical standards. It redefined Jesus's mission—making him a martyr to human hostility as he proclaimed "a great appeal of Divine love."[28] Jones did not, however, trace the liberal notion of the atonement to its root—the elevation of the liberal's human moral consciousness above scriptural divine authority. Even so, Jones's readers doubtless later found good reason here to resist Davies's liberal teaching and preaching on the subject.

Christ's resurrection (Article 4) enjoyed the status of "no better attested fact in history"; Jones listed the testimony of Mary Magdalene and "the other pious women" in the gospels, cited the "many infallible proofs" of Jesus's appearances to the apostles, and recounted the witness of the apostle Paul. The college used a standard apologetic text[29] and approach of the day—using good evidences without first engaging with the unbeliever's presupposed anti-supernaturalism. Jones applied the same method to rebut the old allegation of fraud and the hypothesis of hallucination.[30] Likewise, he argued, without the resurrection the rapid growth of the Christian church was "absolutely unaccountable."[31] This approach was doubtless convincing to those already presupposing the creator-sustainer and savior God of the Bible and the creeds, namely the Holy Trinity.

On the last sentence of Article 4 "Until He return to judge all men at the last day," Jones stated his premillennial extension to the spectrum of Evangelicalism. [32] It was the standard premillennialism of his day, and looked to the "thousand years" (for some read literally) "of Christ's reign over the earth."[33] Many well-read nineteenth-century evangelicals of all Protestant churches had made the "paradigm shift"[34] to this interpretation of Revelation 20:1–6. The great social reformer, the Earl of Shaftesbury, held the view, nor did it turn Jones against one's social responsibility, as the next chapter will show, but it did *focus* Evangelical activism on evangelism

27. Jones, *Teaching*, 23, quoting Simpson, *Fact of Christ*, 161–63.
28. Jones, ibid., 24.
29. Row, *Manual*.
30. Ibid., 171–87.
31. Jones, *Teaching*, 28.
32. Ibid., 32–33.
33. Fausset, "Thousand Years," 685–86.
34. Kuhn, *Structure of Scientific Revolutions*, viii.

at home and abroad.³⁵ Jones made no mention here of other theories of Christ's coming again, or of the liberal social gospel.

What of the historical ascension of Christ? Jones felt no need to say how the physical ascension of the resurrected Christ might be understood in a Copernican-Newtonian universe, although Westcott had done so.³⁶ Jones did, however, emphasize its doctrinal importance.³⁷

The third division under Group 1 "Fundamental Religion," is Article 5 "The Doctrine of the Holy Ghost."³⁸ Jones explains clearly the principle of subordination between the persons of the Trinity, as maintaining their co-eternity and co-equality of nature.³⁹ It was no new doctrine and he firmly resists any Sabellian or modern liberal misapprehension that the Holy Spirit is but an "influence."⁴⁰

Group 2. "The Rule of Faith"

Jones's second group covered Articles 6–8. They deal with the authority and canon of Holy Scripture (the Reformation's *sola scriptura*, "Scripture alone"), the Old Testament in relation to the New, and the authority of the three ecumenical creeds, the Apostles' Creed, the Nicene Creed, and the "Creed of Saint Athanasius."

Jones and his friend Mervyn Archdall had recently and publicly addressed negative higher criticism of the Scriptures.⁴¹ Here he expounded the Reformation watchword, *sola scriptura*, insisting that Scripture was "the primary and absolute norm" for what needed to be believed as an article of faith. Not only Roman Catholic but also Anglo-Catholic teaching thought that "unwritten traditions" had come down from Christ and his apostles.⁴² This article by itself was "sufficient to constitute the Church of England a

---

35. Robert, "Premillennialism," 783–84.
36. Westcott, *Historic Faith*, 71–99.
37. Jones, *Teaching*, 31–32.
38. Ibid., 34–36.
39. Ibid., 35, quoting Hooker, *Laws of Ecclesiastical Polity*, 5.51.1.
40. Ibid., 36. See Moule, *Outlines of Christian Doctrine*, 27, 150.
41. Jones, "The Manifestation of God." Jones cites the denial of the authority of the New Testament epistles and of the historical claims of the Old Testament. See also Archdall, *Analytical Higher Criticism*.
42. "Decree Concerning the Canonical Scriptures," in Schaff, *Creeds*, 80.

Protestant Church," and formed "its most distinguishing doctrine against Rome."[43] As usual, Jones follows with giving the New Testament support.[44]

On Article 7, the relation of the two testaments and of the authority of the Mosaic law for the Christian, he states briefly that the New Testament shows salvation by Christ alone to be the theme of the Old, which itself makes more than earthly promises. His view of the Christian's relation to the Mosaic Law was standard: the moral law, which Christ came "not to destroy but to fulfil (Matt v. 17)," remained binding on the Christian.[45] On Article 8, concerning the three ecumenical creeds above, he needed only to note that their authority was subordinate to and dependent on their agreement with Holy Scripture.

On these three articles Jones has upheld two of the four rallying cries common to Lutheran and Reformed branches of the Reformation:[46] Scripture alone (*sola scriptura*), and Christ alone (*solus Christus*). His exposition has illustrated already the Reformation roots behind the eighteenth-century revival in England and Wales. The challenge of Anglo-Catholicism in England and of Roman Catholicism, especially in Ireland, sufficiently accounts for the continuing Evangelical emphasis on the Reformation stance of the Church of England.

Group 3. "The Salvation of the Individual"

Jones's exposition of Articles 9–18 is important for three reasons. First, for how he understood the restoration and clarification of the gospel gained by the Reformation. Also, it shows the background to his teaching on holiness, and with that his perhaps unclear view of the freedom of the will. Finally, it demonstrates why, in his view, he believed that the articles on justification (11) and predestination (17), together with that on the sacrifice of the mass (31, in Group 4) were critical; for if "burned into the soul" they would remove a cause of basic conflict (with Anglo-Catholicism) from the Church of England.[47] The four heads—human sin, justification and works, holiness and indwelling sin, and the predestining love of God, plus the anathema against any who would deny the *solus Christus*—are all Reformation teachings that characterize centrist Evangelicals.

---

43. Jones, *Teaching*, 38.
44. Ibid.
45. Ibid., 42–3.
46. George, *Theology of the Reformers*, 120.
47. Jones, "Address," 5.

The articles on human sin (9 and 10) pronounced respectively on "man's lost condition by nature" and "his helplessness apart from Divine grace." Noting that Article 9's phrase "original sin" came from "the time of Augustine,"[48] Jones accordingly defined it as inherited from Adam, not acquired "by imitation" of him (the Pelagian view). In tune with Jones's holiness emphasis was his comment on the article's words "the flesh lusteth always contrary to the spirit": "man's sinful nature is in antagonism to . . . the new and Divine nature, and to the Holy Ghost, its author; they stand eternally opposed to one another."[49] The personal experience of believers and the exhortations of Scripture to them bore out that the "infection" of original sin always remained in the regenerate believer. Sinless perfection was not a realizable goal of Christian holiness.[50]

Article 10 prepared for Article 11: "The whole of Scripture shows the helplessness of man's natural state."[51] Against Roman Catholic and Anglo-Catholic understandings, Jones was careful to clarify the New Testament use of "grace" as "*God's unmerited favour towards sinners in saving them*" and "*the effect of this same favour within.*"[52] This article taught that "the first impulse towards a Christian life must proceed from God."[53] God's grace is his favor to sinners. God's prior, enabling grace must first incline the will of the unbeliever to turn to him in faith, and hence to act out of love for him. It then empowered the believer, who now has this renewed will, in all actual obedience.[54] Hence the believer's need of "constant dependence upon God in every step of the Christian life."[55] In the Book of Common Prayer "the Collects are full of the confession of man's weakness and helplessness"—a "protest against the Pelagianism of the human heart."[56] Jones was a 1662 Prayer Book Anglican.

Jones moved straight to application: his (mostly young) readers would be thankful for the relevance of Articles 9 and 10 against an evolutionary worldview, probably that of T. H. Huxley, with its assumption that humanity is "gradually rising . . . towards perfection," and the pure Pelagianism of "many novelists" seeking "to idealize human nature, and show that man

---

48. Jones, *Teaching*, 46.
49. Ibid., 48.
50. Ibid., 49–50.
51. Ibid., 51.
52. Ibid., 52.
53. Ibid.
54. Ibid., 51–52.
55. Ibid., 53.
56. Ibid.

is, after all, at the bottom, good."[57] He fully acknowledged something not always done among Sydney Evangelicals, what Calvin called God's "common grace": "The flesh may be cultivated and educated; it may be amiable flesh, benevolent flesh, aesthetic flesh." But it was "always contrary to the Spirit of God."[58]

The second head under Group 3 "The Salvation of the Individual" was Article 11 "The Justification of Man." This doctrine links Evangelicals unbreakably to the Reformation *sola fide*, *sola scriptura*, and *sola gratia*. Liberal Anglo-Catholics and Liberal Evangelicals, however, including D. J. Davies, would struggle with such a teaching.[59] Jones explained that in Scripture "justification" meant being "accounted righteous before God," and "to justify" meant "to acquit," "to pronounce a person not guilty," the opposite of "to condemn" or pronounce guilty. This excluded the Roman Catholic understanding—being "made righteous." Roman theology confused justification with sanctification, "a progressive work."[60]

Jones's analysis of Rome on justification was not quite precise, for under "justification" the Canons and Dogmatic Decrees of the Council of Trent included *both* remission (forgiveness) of sins *and* inward renewal.[61] So did Luther, but while the reformer highlighted forgiveness, Rome virtually obscured it; Hammond would be exact on this point.

The *ground* of justification, explained Jones correctly, is the merit of Christ alone, in total exclusion of our own merit.[62] Faith is the *means*, "the empty hand of the heart which receives God's free gift." He quoted what the article cites as "the Homily of Justification,"[63] which added that from sure trust in God's promises "doth follow a loving heart to obey His commandments."[64]

On the "salutary" (Article 11, "wholesome") nature of the doctrine, Jones added a touch from his experience of "the carnal mind" in evangelism and preaching for holiness: "It is no easy thing to break down man's pride and self-will and to get him to admit the helplessness and hopelessness of his

---

57. Jones supplies no references.
58. Jones, *Teaching*, 53.
59. See in chapter 7 below.
60. Jones, *Teaching*, 54–56, 58.
61. "Decree on Justification," in Schaff, 94–97.
62. Jones, *Teaching*, 56.
63. Titled "Homily of the Salvation of Mankind," in Griffiths, *Two Books of Homilies*, 24–35 (the edition which Jones would have used); Cranmer, "Homily of the Salvation of Mankind," 262–71.
64. Jones, *Teaching*, 57, quoting Cranmer, "Homily of the Salvation of Mankind," 270.

natural condition."[65] Does this imply that Jones used emotionally coercive methods at Moore College, as his letter to W. H. Griffith Thomas describing one occasion has been understood?[66] Vice-principal George Chambers, who had proposed the special meeting for prayer, spoke of a quite spontaneous response in the students praying.[67] On the doctrine's "consoling" efficacy (Article 11 has "very full of comfort"), Jones noted that it gives assurance of salvation to those who are "conscious how imperfect their best efforts are."[68] Jones had no tendency to sinless perfectionism.

Articles 12 and 13 explained the true relation of "good works" to justification. In contrast with Rome's "practically justification by works," Jones quoted the homily, which was Cranmer's and which excluded works from playing any part at all in God's forgiveness. But it joined them to the faith that justifies, faith which is not "a mere intellectual assent to the Gospel."[69] So also had Calvin taught ("it is faith alone that justifies, and yet the faith which justifies is not alone"), and so also Luther ("This faith will produce charity [love] and so good works").[70] Such works are "(a.) . . . *pleasing to God*," and although they "can never be our title to heaven they will win for us a reward at the judgment seat of Christ (see 2 Cor v. 10)." They are "(b.) . . . *the necessary proof of* [saving] *faith*," wrote Jones, following Article 12.[71] But before justification, *contra* Rome, works neither made one fit to receive nor fit to deserve God's saving grace (Article 13), for they are as "dead before God."[72] The reason? "Apart from Christ our righteousness, the taint of sin is in all our actions."[73]

But this was not to say that the actions of the justified had no such taint. "The Christian's Relation to Holiness and to Sin" (Articles 14–16) was a major emphasis in Jones's ministry. He sums up the thrust of these articles:[74]

(a.) No Christian can exceed God's standard of holiness [Article 14 "Of Works of Supererogation"].

---

65. Jones, *Teaching*, 58.

66. Lawton, "Better Time to Be," 81 (thus interpreting a letter of Jones to Griffith Thomas, July 16, 1905).

67. Sibtain with Chambers, *Dare to Look Up*, 7–8.

68. Jones, *Teaching*, 58.

69. Ibid., 59, quoting Cranmer, "Homily of the Salvation of Mankind," 264.

70. Ibid. (no references provided by Jones).

71. Ibid., 60.

72. Cranmer, "Homily or Sermon on Good Works," 283, 284 and n91.

73. Jones, *Teaching*, 61.

74. Not included by Jones, the specific articles are added in square brackets.

(b.) No one can even reach it, for no one in this life can attain to absolute sinlessness [Article 15 "Of Christ alone without Sin"].

(c.) A Christian may sin grievously and yet be restored [Article 16 "Of Sin after Baptism"].[75]

Jones explained that Article 14 denies the Roman Catholic "counsels of perfection," the doctrine that there were things (such as the vows of poverty and celibacy) over and above what God minimally asks for and that these "secure an excess of merit."[76] Rather, the commandment to love God with all one's heart, soul, mind and strength (Mark 12:30) showed that "God's standard of holiness is so high that none can attain it, much less go beyond it";[77] indwelling sin remained lifelong.[78]

Under Article 16 (that sin committed after baptism is not unpardonable) Jones examined various scriptural passages, using the recent Revised Version (NT, 1881) and a standard commentary for certain texts (Heb 6:4–6; 10:26–29).[79] A pastoral note concluded his commentary on "the unpardonable sin": the "very anxiety" of the troubled person "is an evidence that God's Holy Spirit is still dealing with him . . . therefore he is not beyond the reach of forgiveness."[80] The final sentence of Article 16 affirmed that by God's grace the true believer "may arise again and amend his life."[81]

Jones has seen in the articles two doctrines that the old school High Churchmen (such as John and Charles Wesley) did not fully grasp: man's total moral inability to please God apart from his grace in Christ, and (implicitly) the final perseverance of the true Christian. These two doctrines were also correctly taught in Robinson's *Christian System*, as well as in the standard Evangelical works that he consulted.[82]

Jones's exposition of Article 17 "Of Predestination and Election," however, begins by just leaning toward the Wesleyan Evangelical Arminian view.[83] Writing in the late nineteenth century Handley Moule noted: "a strong drift of modern thought" (probably including that of T. H. Huxley and J. S. Mill) "favours 'necessitarianism,' under which, in effect, man's

---

75. Jones, *Teaching*, 62.
76. Ibid., 63.
77. Ibid., 62–63.
78. Ibid., 64.
79. Conybeare and Howson, *Life and Epistles of St. Paul*, 798n7.
80. Jones, *Teaching*, 68–69.
81. Ibid., 69.
82. Moule, *Outlines of Christian Doctrine*, 46–47.
83. Elliott-Binns, *Religion in the Victorian Era*, 55. The work by Jones's friend Griffith Thomas, *Principles of Theology* has this same weakness.

will is but a phantom."⁸⁴ Against this, Moule affirmed "the harmony of the absolute sovereignty of the will of the Holy Creator, and the true freedom, and so true responsibility, of the will of the personal creature."⁸⁵

Though elsewhere he spoke of humanity's "guilty impotence" Moule failed to mention here the effect of sin upon the self and its choice to turn to Christ or not.⁸⁶ Jones's student notes record an unnamed lecturer's strong antipathy to Calvin,⁸⁷ and Jones regarded the Reformer's doctrine of election (as he had so received it) as falling short of the full scriptural view. Nevertheless he summed up the latter correctly: "The Bible teaches . . . on the one hand God's sovereignty, and on the other hand man's responsibility."⁸⁸ Oddly enough, in explanation he quoted the fine and orthodox theologian, H. P. Liddon, but a Tractarian and hence semi-Pelagian, who had retired as Dean Ireland's Professor of Exegesis just before Jones went up: "the Divine sovereignty must not merely be compatible with, but must even imply the perfect [sic!] freedom of created wills."⁸⁹

Had Jones read the very best nineteenth-century Evangelical dogmatics,⁹⁰ he might have distinguished (a) the will's power to make alternate choices (between actions not touching one's fundamental moral-spiritual disposition), from (b) the will's inability to choose to act contrary to that disposition—which was consistent with Article 10. But the trend was against this. In a fairly recent issue of *The Churchman* the editor was advocating a notion of free-will ⁹¹ that resembled what the Liberal Anglo-Catholics had adopted and future Liberal Evangelicals would follow—the philosophical-idealist emphasis on free personality⁹² and its notion of free-will.

On the other hand, Jones began well on "Predestination": "In Article XVII we stand at the top of the ladder which reaches from earth to heaven, just as in Articles X and XI we stand at the bottom."⁹³ He quoted a help-

---

84. Moule, *Outlines of Christian Doctrine*, 43. See Huxley, "Science and Morals," cited in Passmore, *Hundred Years of Philosophy*, 39.

85. Moule, *Outlines of Christian Doctrine*, 164–65.

86. Ibid., 50.

87. Jones, "Oxford Student Notebook," on predestination and free will, under the heading "Doctrines of the Churches" (pages not numbered).

88. Jones, *Teaching*, 72–73.

89. Ibid., 73, quoting Liddon, *Some Elements of Religion*, 191. Liddon is still respected for his defense of the deity of Christ.

90. Litton, *Introduction to Dogmatic Theology*, 180–82.

91. Sinclair, "St Augustine of Hippo," 374–87.

92. Illingworth, *Personality*, 227.

93. Jones, *Teaching*, 70.

ful analogy—that we are like "insects creeping across some vast cathedral floor" suspecting the building's unity but seeing only "unconnected pillars"; one day we will see "the great roof that connects them all."[94] He correctly pointed out that the article insists that predestination excluded neither the need to offer salvation to all[95] nor yet the obligation of all believers to obey God. Only by obedience, the evidence of the fruit of the Spirit in the self, could one's election to life be known.[96] Of course, this assurance did not apply to the person who "lives in sin."[97] But the "final perseverance" of believers he found clearly taught in Scripture (referencing John 10:27, 28; Rom 8:28–30). Hence Article 17 spoke of the "comfort" to believers to be found in predestination because of the assurance of faith it brought and the fervent love for God it enkindled. Jones aptly quoted the scriptural sources.[98]

On Article 18 "Salvation only by the Name of Christ" Jones applied the Reformation watch cry, *solus Christus*. It condemns, he observed, the Latitudinarian (he might have said "Broad Church") spirit, which maintained that sincerity and general moral uprightness were sufficient for salvation. The article insisted that Christ was the uniquely required object of faith that saves. Jones did not here connect this insistence with a home or foreign missionary obligation to preach the gospel.

Group 4. *"The Church: Its Ministers and Sacraments"*

Jones's exposition of this group, Articles 19–34, is important for two reasons. First, it shows how an Evangelical of the time needed to and might indeed rebut Anglo-Catholic claims about "church." In 1883 at Oxford the fiftieth anniversary of John Keble's sermon *National Apostasy* was celebrated. Anglo-Catholic views were on the increase and their liberalized form was soon to be expressed in *Lux Mundi* (1889). When Jones arrived in Sydney, two city churches—St James's Church, King Street, and Christ Church, St Laurence (George Street, Sydney, near Railway Square)—were already places of Anglo-Catholic doctrine, ritual, and associated vestments.[99]

Jones's exposition is important, secondly, because it demonstrates how far he was from being influenced by some putative "Brethren" doctrine of

---

94. Ibid., 73. Jones gave no reference.
95. Ibid., 72.
96. Ibid., 78.
97. Ibid., 75.
98. Ibid., citing 2 Tim 1:12; Rev 7:10; Ps 115:1.
99. Garnsey, *Arthur Garnsey*, 8; Judd and Cable, *Sydney Anglicans*, 161–62.

the church.[100] New Testament scholars knew perfectly well that the Greek word *ekklesia* meant "assembly," though usually translated "church" in the New Testament, and Jones knew that "assembly" was not always the precise meaning in New Testament usage. Jones's Brethren friends used the term for their local congregations, basically in fidelity to the Greek term. But they made no claim that their assembly comprised the whole of the "church" in any particular locality.[101] Here at last we find Jones's answer to the troubling pamphlet by a Brethren public evangelist.[102] The term "ecclesia" had different senses as it is used in the New Testament.[103]

Sometimes, he writes, the term is applied to the universal aspect of the church,[104] to "the whole company of believers in all times and places." And this is "sometimes called the invisible Church," of which a part is already in heaven. On earth its membership is known only to God, "who alone can read the heart."[105]

Jones thought that "ideal" was a better term than "invisible" to describe the church "as it now exists in the mind and purpose of God."[106] Did this express philosophical idealism, taken from C. A. Auberlen's presumed Kantian idealist thought?[107] Probably not, because Jones took the term that Moule used in exactly the same way, namely "as fully known only to God": "in Ephesians . . . that *ideal* which is also in this matter the ultimate *real*," the church, consists of those persons joined to Christ "in the supreme sense." Moule was expressing Hooker's notion mentioned above, of the distinction within this article.[108] Jones's friend Mervyn Archdall, a promoter of C. A. Auberlen, was explicitly not a philosophical idealist.[109]

---

100. Pace Lawton, *Better Time to Be*, 72–73.

101. Coad, *History of the Brethren*, 126n.

102. The pamphlet was "The Church of God as Bride, Body and Building" in Jones, "Diaries," January 28, 1893.

103. Jones, *Teaching*, 80.

104. Litton, *Introduction to Dogmatic Theology*, 364.

105. Citing Moule, *Outlines of Christian Doctrine*, 202–04, who quotes *in extenso* Hooker, *Laws of Ecclesiastical Polity*, Book 3.50.

106. Jones, *Teaching*, 80–81; Litton, *Introduction to Dogmatic Theology*, 365; Litton, *Church of Christ*, 70–71, 74, 152.

107. Lawton, *Better Time to Be*, 72–73, but compare Auberlen, *Divine Revelation*, 25, 200–201, 278.

108. Moule, *Outlines of Christian Doctrine*, 202–6, quoting Hooker, *Ecclesiastical Polity* 3.50.2–3, 6, 7, 8, 9; so also Litton, *Church of Christ in its Idea*, 77n, 158–59, 164). These theologians seem to have adopted philosophical vocabulary without entailing, or presupposing, an idealist worldview.

109. Archdall, *Mervyn Archdall*, 23, 43–46.

Jones also writes that the visible counterpart of those persons joined to Christ, "the definitely ordered society" (he did not say "meeting"!), which can ensure its own dissemination (A. R. Fausset)[110] is "very frequently" designated church (*ekklesia*) in the New Testament. It is applied both to "a particular body of Christians" either in a city or in a house, and sometimes it "embrac[es] all living Christians in one great society."[111] Thus "it is clear that the Church, taken as the aggregate of all living professing Christians, is regarded in the New Testament as one."[112] Similarly when defining "faithful" in this article Jones indicated that even in New Testament times the churches were a mixture, as Article 26 stated.[113] He illustrated this mixed and universal character from the Book of Common Prayer and the Canons of the Church of England.[114] Jones's doctrine of the church was mainstream biblicist and Reformation Evangelical, in the common tradition of the Reformation churches and common to Evangelicals in Sydney until the dynamic "church-exists-in-meeting" concept was taught at Moore College after the time of T. C. Hammond.[115]

As against both High Church and Tractarian or Anglo-Catholic views on the marks or notes[116] of a true church, Jones proved conclusively that the Church of England never intended "to refuse to non-episcopal organisations any place . . . in the visible Church." This was evidenced in the fact that the article did not make church *order* (its form of government) a mark of the church. The "Prayer for all Conditions of Men" and the "Bidding Prayer" (of the Canons of 1604) for use before sermons were prayers for the church universal, and the latter explicitly included the Church of Scotland, which was Presbyterian.[117] Jones did not mention William Goode.[118] Did he have the separatist and exclusivist *Plymouth* Brethren in mind[119] when he

---

110. Fausset, "Church," 130–31.

111. Jones, *Teaching*, 81, quoting Gal 1:13 and 1 Cor 12:28.

112. Jones, *Teaching*, 81. See Hort, *Christian Ecclesia*, 118–22 ("The many Ecclesiae and the one") and Archdall, "Doctrine of the Church," reprinted in Archdall, *Mervyn Archdall*, 46–47.

113. Jones, *Teaching*, 82.

114. Ibid., citing *Prayer for all Conditions of Men* (in "Prayers and Thanksgivings, upon several occasions"), *Prayer for the Church Militant* (in "The Order for the Administration of the Lord's Supper," in the Book of Common Prayer), and the *Bidding Prayer* before a sermon (from the Canons of 1604 [Canon 55]).

115. Robinson, "Church," 228–31; Robinson, "'Church' Revisited," 4–14.

116. Jones, *Teaching*, 82–84.

117. Ibid., 82–83.

118. Goode, *Vindication of the Doctrine of the Church of England*.

119. Thus *pace* Lawton, *Better Time to Be*, 73. See Coad, *History of the Brethren*,

insisted that in *no* church could the word of God be preached without "some admixture of error"? "Of necessity" it would often be done "in an imperfect way,"[120] answers the question.

No one in Sydney could be unmindful of the Church of Rome when this article stated that it had "erred not only in their living and manner of ceremonies, but also in matters of faith." The Homily for Whitsunday"[121] (Pentecost) reiterated this finding by the test of the three notes of the church—doctrine, sacraments, and ecclesiastical discipline. "On the other hand," Jones pointed out, "many of the Reformers recognised Rome as part of the Church."[122] Hooker, for example, wrote: "touching those main parts of Christian truth wherein they constantly still persist, we gladly acknowledge them to be of the family of Jesus Christ."[123] And T. C. Hammond, for his part, would be careful to acknowledge the extent of biblical truth embodied in decrees of the Council of Trent.[124]

Jones established that, as laid down in Articles 20–22, the authority spoken of was that of the particular or national church, as Article 24 established.[125] On "rites or ceremonies," Jones chose not to touch directly on the ritualism of Anglo-Catholics. He was content to point out that the New Testament principle was the edification of the believer and God's glory; only occasionally did it lay down a rule (1 Cor 10:14–16, 34). As "witness and keeper of Holy Writ" the church might not, negatively, decree rites or ceremonies contrary to Scripture.[126]

Likewise, teaching about what a person must believe for salvation must "directly rest on the authority of Scripture."[127] Jones was as biblicist as Article 21 "Of the Authority of General Councils," and Article 22 "Of Purgatory," and the other errors mentioned in this article. Both articles appealed to the biblical criterion, against the specifically Romish doctrines condemned in Article 22. Jones cited the specific witness of Scripture.[128]

116–19.

120. Jones, *Teaching*, 84.

121. "Homily concerning the Coming Down of the Holy Ghost," in Griffiths, *Two Books of Homilies*, 461–64.

122. Jones, *Teaching*, 85.

123. Ibid.; Hooker, *Laws of Ecclesiastical Polity*, 3.1.10 quoted.

124. See chapter 11 below.

125. Jones, *Teaching*, 86.

126. Ibid., 88.

127. Ibid.

128. Ibid., 89; against purgatory citing 2 Cor 5:8 and Rev 14:13; against indulgences Ps 99:7, Mark 2:7, I John 1:7; against the adoration of images and relics Exod 20:4, 5, 2 Kgs 18:4; against the invocation of the saints Acts 10: 25, 26, Rev 19:10.

Under Articles 23 and 34, on ministry in the church, Jones defended the principle of a regular ministry as against his Brethren friends' church order. But he was also careful to defend "preaching or teaching . . . in an unofficial capacity"[129] as having New Testament support.[130] Also, as with lay baptism, for a lay person to preside at the Lord's Supper was irregular but not therefore invalid.[131] For this Jones quoted Thomas Rogers, chaplain to the early High Church Archbishop of Canterbury (1604–1610), Richard Bancroft. Thus he hoisted some later High Churchmen on their own petard: "We think not (as some do) that the very being of the Sacraments dependeth on . . . whether the baptizer, or giver of the bread and wine, be a minister or no."[132] The New Testament gave no clear information on this, so Jones quoted the well-known New Testament commentator Henry Alford (not an Evangelical), who stated that the minister's acts of consecration were not by his own authority, "but only as the representative of the whole Christian congregation."[133] Jones's High Church Oxford professor, William Ince, had written to similar effect.[134]

If High Churchmen and Anglo-Catholics used Article 23 to support their claim for episcopal ordination as a *sine qua non* of valid ministry, Jones showed that it was only an in-house rule: the Church of England "refuses to judge other bodies of Christians."[135]

To Articles 25–31, on the sacraments, Jones gave almost a sixth of his whole exposition. He followed Moule[136] (after Daniel Waterland and Ussher) on the words "as by an instrument" in Article 27 "Of Baptism," quoting the *covenantal* or "deed of [property] conveyance analogy" of the Anglican anti-Deist theologian, Daniel Waterland. This clearly distinguished the "legal instrument" (i.e., the "sacrament") from the "real estate" (i.e., "the grace"). The latter was conveyed only to the person duly qualified to receive it, namely, the believer.[137] A later principal of the college, D. B. Knox (1916–1994), son

---

129. Ibid., 91.
130. Ibid., citing Acts 11:19, 20 and 18:26.
131. Ibid., 92.
132. Ibid., 91, quoting Rogers, *English Creede*.
133. Jones, ibid., 91–92, quoting Alford, *Greek Testament*, at 1 Cor 10:16.
134. Ince, *Scriptural and Anglican View*, 10.
135. Jones, *Teaching*, 92.
136. Moule, *Outlines of Christian Doctrine*, 238–41, 245–46.
137. Waterland, *Review of the Doctrine of the Eucharist*, 147; Jones, *Teaching*, 101, but not explicitly referencing Waterland.

of Jones's early Moore College student, D. J. Knox (1875–1960), adopted the same legal-instrument analogy.[138]

To the challenge of non-pedobaptist evangelical believers (Baptists, and Jones's Christian Brethren friends), and the High Church and Anglo-Catholic views of baptismal regeneration, Jones thus provided a clear and convincing treatment. Following Moule, Jones adopted the covenantal approach. He argued from the analogy of Jewish circumcision, and the whole-family baptism of proselytes into Judaism; from Peter's "the promise is to you and to your children" (Acts 2:39); from the baptism of whole households; from the inclusion of children in the exhortation passages to the church (Eph 6:1; Col 3:20); and from Christ's words about receiving little children (Matt 19:14). Critically (*contra* his High Church or Anglo-Catholic reader), the language "this child being regenerate" was that of "faith and charity," for "the whole Liturgy is constructed on this same model; those who profess and call themselves Christians, are treated as such."[139]

Articles 28–31 defined the second sacrament, the Lord's Supper ("Eucharist"). This involved not only the complete once-for-all nature of Christ's atoning work and of justification by faith, but also the very nature of a sacrament. The teaching of Article 28 had been critical for the English Reformation. Jones treated it under four heads: "The Meaning of the Lord's Supper," "The Conditions of Right Reception," "The Manner in Which Christ's Body and Blood are Given," and "Certain Superstitions and Errors Condemned."[140]

An important but incomplete view of its meaning was that the Lord's Supper was the sacrament of the unity of believers in Christ.[141] But its "more distinctive meaning," was "*a Sacrament of our Redemption by Christ's death*," for in it "we see . . . Christ dying as our substitute; we hear Him cry 'It is finished': and it brings assurance to our souls."[142] It "is a 'certain sure witness' (Article XXV)" that "stirs up and strengthens our faith," for it "appeals to the eye" just as the preached word "appeals to the ear."[143] Jones rehearsed the three grounds of the rejection of transubstantiation in Article 28: the words of Scripture, the nature of a sacrament, and the unscriptural ritual resultants of the error it rejected—the reservation, procession, elevation,

---

138. Knox, *Thirty-Nine Articles: The Historic Basis*, 37; ibid., in Knox, *Selected Works*, 2:134.

139. Jones, *Teaching*, 105–7.

140. Ibid., 108–13.

141. Ibid., 108.

142. Ibid.

143. Ibid.

and worshiping of the sacrament.[144] Similarly Article 30 rejected the denial of the cup to the laity.[145]

As for the meaning of Christ's words, "This is my body," "This is my blood" he noted "the common usage of Scripture" in phrases like "I am the door," and that Christ's words "Drink this" were quite intelligible from King David's words: "Shall I drink the blood of these men who have put their lives in jeopardy?" His men had "obtained [water] at the risk of their life-blood."[146] The article also excluded "the popular theory" (of Anglo-Catholics) that the consecrated elements conveyed "the present glorified body of Christ."[147] Rather, said Jones, "We feed on a crucified Saviour, when we can say in faith, 'He died for me.'"[148]

Article 31 "Of the one Oblation of Christ finished upon the Cross" (along with Articles 11 and 17 together) Jones thought especially important, for Article 31 "affirms the doctrine of the one oblation of Christ finished upon the cross," for which Jones listed the scriptural grounds.[149] It rightly condemned "the sacrifices of Masses," for they "did insult to the completeness of [Christ's] finished work" and "held out a hope of pardon" that had no scriptural warrant.[150] The scriptural doctrines, therefore—the finished sacrifice of Christ (Article 31), forgiveness by faith on this ground (Article 11), and the comfort in the assurance of God's predestinating love (Article 17)—together should remove division among Anglicans. The causes were unscriptural thinking: semi-Pelagianism and sacramentalism. Jones understood and embraced the Reformation teaching of the Thirty-nine Articles of Religion.

Conclusion

Nathaniel Jones thus spelled out an Evangelical interpretation, scholarly and accessible, of English Reformation doctrine. He retained, along with catholic Trinitarian and Christological orthodoxy, the Reformation emphases on the sole authority of Scripture, Christ's once-and-for-all atoning sacrifice,

144. See "Decree Concerning the Most Holy Sacrament of the Eucharist," chapters 4–6, in Schaff, *Creeds*, 130–33, and Canon 6, in Schaff, *Creeds*, 137–38.
145. Jones, *Teaching*, 113.
146. Ibid., 112, quoting 2 Sam 23:17.
147. Ibid., 111–12.
148. Ibid., 111–12. See Moule, *Outlines of Christian Doctrine*, 261–62; Litton, *Introduction to Dogmatic Theology*, 460–61.
149. Heb 9:28; 10:12, 17, 18.
150. Jones, *Teaching*, 113.

and the grace of God, namely the undeserved favor of his forgiveness, merited solely by Christ's once-and-for-all atoning work, appropriated only by "a sure trust" in him. Jones revealed his location on the extended spectrum of Evangelicalism adopted by many of his day by giving a premillennial meaning to "the last day" in Article 4. This was no Brethren skewing of his thought,[151] but only a view widely held among evangelical Protestants.

The Teaching of the Articles placed the tradition of Moore College well and truly back on the track laid down by its first three principals under Bishop Barker. Those who valued Jones's teaching indicated how important they believed it to be by reprinting his book forty years on.[152]

---

151. *Pace* Lawton, "Nathaniel Jones," 372–73.
152. Jones, *Teaching*.

6

Evangelicalism Maintained

SHINING THROUGH ALL OF Jones's efforts to apply biblical teaching to personal piety and daily living is his commitment to the Reformation's sole authority of Scripture and to the doctrinal system of the Thirty-nine Articles. Most notable in this second part of his *oeuvre* is the series of addresses he gave in the founding years of the Katoomba Christian Convention. His love for the Book of Common Prayer (1662), and his devotional and practical application of it is manifest in his three published expository studies of its liturgical riches. A number of his occasional addresses and sermons became pocket-sized tracts. In these his specific place in the Evangelical spectrum is evident—not prominently extended by eschatology, more by Keswick holiness, while remaining solidly Reformational.

Jones's Katoomba Addresses of 1904 and 1905

Marcus Loane wrote that Jones taught and lived "the true Keswick doctrine."[1] His nine early Katoomba Christian Convention studies, *A Handful of Corn Upon the Top of the Mountains*,[2] show consistent, exegetically careful scholarship, albeit lightly worn. On passages in the Epistle to the Hebrews, for example, his authority was Westcott's great commentary on the Greek text.[3]

Jones's application was always biblically grounded as well as practical and devotional. His doctrine of holiness was that of the careful,

---

1. Loane, *Centenary History*, 98.
2. Jones, *Handful of Corn*. The title refers to Ps 72:16.
3. Westcott, *Epistle to the Hebrews*.

Cambridge-trained exegete, H. C. G. Moule after 1884. In that year Moule had accepted the Keswick doctrine as expounded by Evan Hopkins—with some refinements.[4] In his standard doctrinal textbook, he consequently defined the sum of Christian ethics as: "a *total abstinence* in Christ's name from admitted sinning, of motive and act, and positively, a *true and entire dedication* of 'spirit, soul, and body' to the will of God."[5]

Moule drew a parallel between the role of faith in justification and its role in holiness: faith was also "the restored man's equipment, in Christ, for his holy purpose" of sanctification.[6] He contrasted this same faith—"this humble reliance on God"—with "a process of discipline and labour,"[7] while yet affirming that "the Scripture doctrine of Sanctification teaches no effortless passivity."[8]

A Handful of Corn Upon the Top of the Mountains is the mature expression of Jones's holiness teaching. It is noteworthy that he does not use the word "millennium" when speaking of the future hope. The first address was foundational: "The Christian's Ground of Glorying" (Rom 5:1-11). The Letter to the Romans, said Jones, excluded all self-glorying (Rom 3:27) since "salvation from beginning to end is of God." The believer glories in three things: the future hope (Rom 5:2) of the restored "glorious image of God stamped on man at his creation"; in tribulations and their resulting "patience" ("persistent spirit") and "probation" ("temper of the veteran"); and in the "hope" ("of final victory") (Rom 5:3, 4). Ultimately, the hope was grounded in "the great inspiring consciousness of the love of God" received from the Holy Spirit (v. 5). The Christian's boast is in "God Himself" (v. 11): "in the knowledge of the Father's [loving] heart" manifested in Christ's cross (v. 8), not just in his gift of justification (vv. 9, 10).[9]

In the second address, "On Working out our own Salvation" (Phil 2:12, 13) Jones ruled out any idea of "passivity," found later in so-called Keswick teaching at Oxford.[10] He sums up the theme of his text pithily with the aphorism "You work out, as He works in," reiterated at each major point. He argues, here, from the sovereign power of God to the believer's responsibility—not free will, but "man's response to God's ability." Let the Spirit "take

---

4. Moule, "Introduction," in Smellie, *Evan H. Hopkins*, 12–14.

5. Moule, *Outlines of Christian Doctrine*, 191.

6. Ibid. Moule gives as references Acts 15:9; Gal 2:20; Eph 6:16, and "probably" Acts 26:18.

7. Ibid.

8. Ibid., 193; so also Ryle, *Holiness*, 47–49, and his chapter 4 "The Fight," 50–65.

9. Jones, *Handful of Corn*, 10–13.

10. Packer, *Keep in Step*, 146, 147, 155–57.

full control; and then do you work out as He works in." A call to "a larger sphere," such as that of a missionary, may come but meanwhile "show God's power in you by living a life of holy contentment, of gentle forbearance, of watchful consistency and of faithful testimony just where you are."[11] The words "faithful testimony" *could* be read as urging all to be verbal evangelists, as some Keswick speakers did.

The third address, "St Peter's Call to Holiness" (1 Pet 1:13–21) was basically a call to the *moral* separation from the world that is entailed in consecration to God, who alone is holy. Holiness "belongs to men so far as they cleanse themselves from all defilement and come into harmony with His mind and will."[12] Holiness was God's work, but "we must see that we are in a right attitude before Him,"[13] the attitude of "*a controlled mind . . . of* (emotional) *sobriety . . . of a fixed hope*" in Christ's second coming, and "*of a new allegiance*—to God, and not the self-life."[14] The perfection required[15] was a "right adjustment of soul" as we trace Christ's "life of absolute surrender, spotless purity, and perfect trust" in "'every instance of behaviour'" (so the Greek of 1 Pet 1:15).[16] The motivation was the command of God's word, the nature of God's future judgment on his own children, and the cost of the believer's redemption, which was Christ's own blood.[17]

"The Life of Perfect Love" (1 Sam 18:1–4; 19:1–7, etc.), the fourth study, was an exemplarist use of the story of Jonathan's love for David. Jonathan "beautifully illustrates . . . the Christian who is taken up with the Person of the Saviour."[18] The Keswick phrase, "Higher Christian life,"[19] meant "the experience of the Christian who has looked beyond the gift to the Giver."[20]

Jones possibly came close to suggesting that every believer is obliged to be a verbal evangelist: like Jonathan of David, "when . . . full of love to Christ we are bound to overflow" in speaking of Christ.[21] But he went on to say that we will "rejoice if we are 'counted worthy to suffer shame for His Name,'" and "can look beyond this time of his rejection, and hail that

11. Jones, Handful of Corn, 14–20.
12. Ibid., 21.
13. Ibid., 24–25.
14. Ibid., 25–26.
15. Matt 5:48 (not given by Jones).
16. Jones, Handful of Corn, 24–27.
17. Ibid., 28.
18. Ibid., 31–32.
19. Boardman, Higher Christian Life.
20. Jones, Handful of Corn, 30–32.
21. Ibid., 33.

crowning day that is coming."[22] Jones looks to Christ's future advent: "Will [Christ] be able to bear the testimony to our great love for him that David bore to Jonathan?"[23]

The fifth study, "Three Aspects of Christ in His Own Nature," aimed to motivate the above "loving adoration" of Christ.[24] Jones began with the high Christology of Hebrews 1 and 2 on Christ's "eternal relation to God." He followed Westcott and the new Revised Version (1881).[25] On the believer's coming to Christ "crowned with Glory and Honour" that Hebrews 1:6 set forth he again provided a memorable aphorism: that "the dignity of man as God originally created him [was] . . . *not one remove above the apes, but one remove below the angels.*[26] Christ at the right hand of God was "the pattern and pledge of what we shall be."[27]

His sixth study, "The Rest of God" (Heb 3:7–4:11) spelled out that present salvation was "to be enjoyed day by day" through "our listening to His voice, and yielding to His will"[28] "Faith has linked us to the company of *obedient* hearers." The promised rest [that] the Israelites "failed to enter into"[29] was "a *spiritual rest now . . .* an experience of liberty, fellowship, and joy." There was no need to remain "fretted with worry and anxiety, overcome by temptation, burdened with sin," excusing yourself with "O wretched man that I am, who shall deliver me?"[30]

If some of Jones's former Moore College students were too preoccupied with the thought of the Lord's return and even its date,[31] the seventh study, "St Paul's View of the Future" (2 Cor 5:1–10), demonstrates that Jones himself was not. He understood that here Paul only thought it "probable" and subsequently, "possible" that "he [would] be alive at the Lord's return, when the first resurrection would take place."[32] Jones did value "this blessed hope of the Lord's return, and the putting on of the glorified body" as "a practical power in our lives" (2 Cor 5:1–5). But an immediate return of the Lord

22. Ibid., 34–35.
23. Ibid., 34–35 (2 Sam 1:26 not given by Jones).
24. Ibid., 45.
25. Westcott, *Epistle to the Hebrews*.
26. Jones, *Handful of Corn*, 43. Emphasis added.
27. Ibid., 44–45.
28. Ibid., 45–46.
29. Psalm 95:11.
30. Jones, *Handful of Corn*, 51–53, following Moule's exposition of Rom 7:24 in his *Epistle of St Paul to the Romans*.
31. For example, Howe, *Dawning of That Day*; see Braga, *Century of Preaching Christ*, 55.
32. Jones, *Handful of Corn*, 55. See also Jones, *Teaching*, 30–33.

being no certainty, it "does not call for us . . . to allow our earthly affairs to get into disorder, or to neglect making provision for those dependent upon us. We may have to pass through the dark valley of the Shadow of Death."[33] Moreover, the future judgment of Christians (1 Cor 5:9–10) *"will take account of their works,"* with degrees of reward for their service of Christ—"all we have ever done," even "the thoughts of our hearts."[34] So far from God's grace relieving Christians "of all sense of responsibility," the judgment "will make a very great difference in our lives if they are lived in the light of that coming day."[35]

Jones's penultimate study (Matt 19:3–12) was on the need to be reconciled with an offended neighbor before engaging in worship. The Christian believer should "look back to see whether some unkind word, or thoughtless action" had offended a Christian brother.[36] Believers should not "force on God an offering He does not want" or "still their conscience" by thinking (in typical Jones humor), "at all events I don't claim to be one of those 'higher life' people." Scripture promised fullness of joy if you rather "put the wrong right . . . and then come and offer your gift."[37]

The final study, "The Lord's Supper" (on 1 Cor 11:23–26)[38] exemplified Jones's piety—it was centered on Christ's cross. His audience knew "diversity of formal worship" in their various Protestant communions, so Jones drew their minds to the "one central doctrine from which all others radiate; and one central act of worship and fellowship."[39] The meeting place of God and sinner and "the meeting place of brethren of widely differing views,"[40] this "Central Ordinance of Worship" was "a silent witness to [the] central truth" of "the living Christ who was dead."[41]

Breaking the bread, Jones stated, "bears witness to the doctrine of *Christ for us*, the ground of our justification."[42] *Eating the broken bread* "bears witness to our identification with Christ in His death, the secret of our sanctification." "A dead man (Rom 6:2, 6, 7, 11) cannot respond to

---

33. Jones, *Handful of Corn*, 59.
34. Ibid., 62.
35. Ibid., 64.
36. Ibid., 67.
37. Ibid., 69.
38. Ibid., 71–78.
39. Ibid., 71–72.
40. Ibid.
41. Ibid., 73–74.
42. Ibid., 75. (Jones quoted here the hymn "I hear the words of love," by Horatio Bonar, a Free Church of Scotland minister.)

temptation... cannot feel a slight or resent an injury."[43] *Our attitude at the table*[44] should be that of "looking upward." In the text "until He come" (1 Cor 11:26) "we have the doctrine of the second coming of Christ, the hope of the Church."[45] Thus "the great truths of justification, sanctification, and future redemption are all set before us in this service."[46] The bread—one loaf or slice—he wrote, "represents many in one. Here we have the doctrine of the Church." He was reminded of the Keswick watchword, "All one in Christ Jesus."[47]

Finally, *our attitude toward the world* must be one of separation, for we could hardly "be looking and longing for [the Lord's] return and be identified with the ungodly in their tastes and pleasures."[48] The tenor of his "separation" holiness was nothing other than that of Handley Moule as noted in chapter 4 above—not withdrawal from society. Did "the world" of Sydney in 1904–1905 not manifest self-centered taste for reputation and the pleasures of wealth condemned in the gospels?[49]

Two of Jones's successors at Moore College, principals T. C. Hammond and Marcus Loane (principal 1954–1958), would become speakers at the Katoomba Convention over many years, and members of its council.[50] Former students of Jones on the council included Harry Howe (d. 1932), Herbert Begbie and R. B. Robinson. Archbishop Mowll would appoint both the latter archdeacons.[51]

Writings and Addresses Touching on Holiness in Society

Jones, the premillennial Keswick holiness preacher, was far from discouraging Christian participation in and exercise of influence in society. An address to tertiary students in 1899, "The Ideal Life and How to Live It" was reported in *The Victorian Churchman*.[52] The *ideal* was, like Christ, to do the

43. Ibid., 75–76.

44. The term "altar" was deliberately excluded from the Prayer Book order of the Lord's Supper from 1552 on.

45. Jones, *Handful of Corn*, 76.

46. Ibid., 77.

47. Ibid., 77–78.

48. Ibid., 79.

49. See Moule on "world" in chapter 4 above.

50. Braga, *Century of Preaching Christ*, 159.

51. Loane, *Mark These Men*, 40, 49.

52. Jones, "Ideal Life," 287–88.

will of God (Heb 13:21) in whatever "state of life into which it has pleased God to call me."[53] Jones explained the perfection required in the text (Heb 13:21): "Now the God of peace . . . make you perfect in every good work to do his will." This goal, perfection, "confronts us at the very beginning of the ideal life." Following Westcott's exegesis,[54] Jones concluded that "perfect" amounted to "right adjustment of soul" to God's will. Christians must "put right at once" any of their being "out of gear," or of their neglect of prayer or of the study of God's word (i.e., Scripture). They must put right the "harbouring of some secret sin" or allowing the rush of life to "hustle" them "out of their spirituality." [55] Such was holiness as applied by Jones to these future university graduates. Such he must surely have taught his Moore College students to minister to their future congregations.

Another example of Jones's attitude to social matters was his sermon preached in St Paul's Cathedral, Melbourne in 1907 at the consecration of his friend John Douse Langley to be the second Bishop of Bendigo. While rector of St Philip's, York Street, Sydney, Langley was stirred by the deep depression of the 1890s to establish his Church Labour Home to provide "simple work for the unemployed."[56] Jones now, however, insisted on the biblical focus required of a bishop for his special task. Quoting the first apostles (at Acts 6:4), "We will devote ourselves to prayer and the ministry of the word," he first highlighted what the rite for the Consecration of Bishops in the Prayer Book therefore stated. The bishop's task was primarily one of teaching and exhorting, *rather than* of being: "an ecclesiastical statesman, a good administrator, one who can finance his diocese well and who can organise all kinds of work in a successful way . . . [be] the man of business, the ideal chairman of committees, the social reformer."[57] The apostles had protested: "It is not reason" (*sic* AV) "that we should leave the word of God, and serve tables" (Acts 6:2). Jones, an experienced Sydney synodsman, did not exclude social concern from the *church's* task as distinct from the task of its chief pastors: "The church has to confront problems, political, social, educational and financial." He referred to the great educational controversy then still going on in England.[58] "This is the Church's work," and "it must be done, but not by our chief pastors." The bishop needed "to-day" was "the

---

53. Catechism, Book of Common Prayer. Being a product of the Reformation the Catechism attributed a real value to the professions as vocations and spheres for Christian holiness of life.

54. Westcott, *Epistle to the Hebrews* at Heb 13:21.

55. Jones, "Ideal Life," 288.

56. Cole, "Langley," 215.

57. Jones, "Consecration," 46.

58. See Knox, *Reminiscences*, 238–47.

man who realises that the great essential work of his office is the spiritual work, the man who will be the centre of all the spiritual force and spiritual fire in his diocese."[59]

This was no eschatologically or holiness-motivated unconcern for society by the church as the body of believers.[60] Jones here was entirely in tune with a sermon by him at a Moore College reunion in 1905, which he had cut out and kept a report of among his papers:

> The Principal of Moore College, preaching from the text John 1:42, "He brought him to Jesus," pointed out that "the various social methods adopted—the cricket club, the debating class, the church club," were absorbing the time of the clergy, taking them from their proper work, which was the ministry of the Word.[61]

Jones's view of the ministry was that Christians needed godly instruction from their bishops and clergy to be "separate" by way of godly contrast with "the world," as Handley Moule explained that idea.[62] That was their biblically grounded task as set out in "The Making, Ordaining and Consecrating of Bishops, Priests [Presbyters] and Deacons" in the Book of Common Prayer.

Jones's Publications on the 1662 Prayer Book Liturgical Year

Jones's friend since 1884, W. H. Griffith Thomas, wanted him to write a work on the Book of Common Prayer, presumably for Griffith Thomas to publish in the Anglican Church Handbooks series. Jones had a profound appreciation—theological, pastoral, devotional and even *aesthetic*—of and for the Reformation doctrine and piety of the book. Early in his Perry Hall work, Jones commended the devotional value of Prayer Book doctrine at the Church Congress of 1894 held in Hobart.[63] In 1897, shortly before moving to Moore College, he had presented a paper, "The Value of the Prayer Book as a Manual of Doctrine," to the quarterly meeting of the Evangelical Churchman's Association in Melbourne.[64]

59. Jones, ibid.
60. *Pace* Lawton, *Better Time to Be*, 70–79.
61. Jones, Sermon, 6.
62. Moule, "Christian's Relationship," 71.
63. Jones, "Devotional Value," 153–55.
64. Jones, "Value of the Prayer Book," 78–79.

Jones began by emphasizing the necessary conjunction of devotion with doctrine, for "Devotion without doctrine . . . is like a ship without a rudder." The Prayer Book "insists . . . that healthy devotion must spring from the root of sound doctrine." It not only recognized "the character of God"— "His holiness, His power, and His love"—but also had a "clear grasp of the work of Christ" as against "recent theology's emphasis on the Incarnation" (a Liberal Anglo-Catholic emphasis). Again, the Prayer Book assumed "a deep sense of our need of the help of the Holy Spirit." The collects especially stressed God's power and promise "to turn the sinner's 'I cannot,' into His 'I can.'" [65]

His second point was "the prominence [the Prayer Book] assigns to the reading of the Holy Scriptures. The devotional life needs food." For clergy to read most of the Old Testament once a year, the New Testament [three times] and the Psalter twelve times (as set down in the Prayer Book calendar) was no waste of time. Thirdly, the Prayer Book was adaptable, fitted "to every aspect and need of the devotional life," meeting the "very needs" which nonconformists tried to supply. The weekly Holy Communion, for example, was an ideal service for the purpose of personal consecration. [66]

Jones suggested that in Morning or Evening Prayer, the sermon would be better placed immediately following the New Testament reading. Services might be made "bright and full of life" by the singing of certain parts, since "what the Church of England needs to make her the glory of all the churches is the spirit of her own services."[67]

Jones's subsequent pocket pamphlet, *Our Daily Sacrifice*, was his beautifully crafted exposition of Morning and Evening Prayer, written "to help Church of England people to enter into the spirit" of the main forms of Sunday public worship.[68] As a Reformation Evangelical, Jones truly valued Prayer Book teaching. The very title, *Our Daily Sacrifice*, focused on the New Testament concept of worship as one's daily life before God. Reformation doctrine shone through his application to piety and holiness. He spelled this out in his five-fold analysis (three main divisions and two supplementary) of the two services.[69]

---

65. Ibid., 78.

66. Ibid., referring to "The Order how the Psalter is appointed to be read" and "The Order how the rest of Holy Scripture is appointed to be read" in the 1662 Book of Common Prayer.

67. Jones, "Value of the Prayer Book," 79.

68. Jones, *Our Daily Sacrifice*, 1 (alluding to Girdlestone, et al., *English Church Teaching*, 78).

69. Ibid., 3.

1. "Preparatory introduction—Confession of sin."[70] The "penitential introduction" was like the tuning of an instrument before playing it: "we seek to have our hearts put in tune," first by hearing the words "from God's own Book" concerning the proneness even of "regenerate man" to sin, and "the readiness of God to forgive." Secondly, therefore the Exhortation insisted on "the need of confession . . . especially when we meet" in "the Presence Chamber of the Holy One." Next, therefore, "we . . . cry out in the Confession 'there is no health in us . . . have mercy upon us . . . restore us, according to Thy promises.'" The fruit of indwelling sin made daily confession necessary. Fourthly, the absolution, "the assurance of pardon and peace" spoke both to those who have not yet repented and believed, and to those who "have been reconciled to God" (1 John 1:8). Finally, now we could "look up and say 'Our Father,' before . . . the service of praise which is to follow."[71] Jones's exposition continued on the note of heartfelt worship.

2. "First great part of Worship—Praise."[72] Having sought "*cleansed* lips . . . now we ask for *opened lips*" to praise, and to pray that they may also be "kept lips." Again Jones brought in his music motif: "Thus, with our hearts in tune, and our lips prepared . . . the music begins . . . First . . . we strike a few comprehensive chords of praise, which indicate the theme of the coming chorus—'Glory be to the Father, and to the Son, and to the Holy Ghost.'"[73] having "robes washed white in Christ's Blood" the congregation summons itself to praise with Psalm 95 at Morning Prayer, "invit[ing] us to praise God." The Psalms follow, which "in all ages have gladdened and comforted the hearts of God's people." Jones quotes the experience of Augustine and of Luther, extols the ministry of the Psalms as a comprehensive "treasure house" of devotion and concludes with a quotation from Hooker.[74]

Jones addressed the difficulty of the warlike Psalms. He thought that their "warlike tone" could be used "in the light of Eph vi. 12, 'Our wrestling is . . . against the principalities, against the powers . . . '"[75] On the imprecatory Psalms, the Psalms of "vindictive tone," Jones agreed with the former Bishop of Melbourne, James Moorhouse, and thought they were to be understood as "mementoes of that gradual

---

70. Ibid., 6.
71. Ibid., 6–11.
72. Ibid., 12–22.
73. Ibid., 13.
74. Ibid., 14–20, Hooker, *Laws of Ecclesiastical Polity* 5.37.2.
75. Ibid., 20–21.

and stately progress of revelation through which ... the Law was made 'our schoolmaster to bring us to Christ.'"[76] He missed Calvin's thought that the psalmist was speaking "not in his own cause but in that of God."[77] Finally, Jones found bright relief in singing the Gloria "to the God of love, redemption and grace" at the end of each Psalm.[78]

3. "Second great part of worship—Instruction."[79] "First, from the Old Testament ... God's love [was] foreshadowed in type and prophecy, or manifested in providential dealing with the old fathers."[80] Again Jones brought in the motif of music, as he expounded the congregation's response to the Old Testament reading of God's love with the *Te Deum*[81] "that glorious old hymn ... first ... of praise to Father, Son, and Holy Ghost... Secondly ... to our Lord Jesus Christ... Finally ... [we] pray [to] be kept daily from sin, and conclude with the shout of triumph, 'O Lord, in Thee have I trusted, I shall never be confounded.'"[82]

Jones likewise highlighted the theme of God's love in the New Testament reading, which told of "God's love fulfilled." The *Song of Zacharias*[83] (at Morning Prayer) thanked God for the arrival of his promised salvation. Similarly at Evening Prayer, Mary's and Simeon's "hymns of grateful thanksgiving" followed the Old and New Testament readings.[84]

4. "The Incentive to Worship—Confession of faith."[85] In the words of the Apostles' Creed we "take daily stock of our possession in Christ." Jones quotes a beautiful "daily act of faith" given by Handley Moule.[86] The Creed summed up "the great truths of the whole Bible."[87] The "I"-form of the Creed pointed to the "conscious relation of belief and trust towards God."[88] The catechism memorably summarized it: belief

---

76. Ibid., 23, quoting Moorhouse, "Charges on Church Work" (*Church Work*, 47). Moorhouse was the successor (1876–1886) of Bishop Charles Perry in Melbourne.

77. Calvin, *Commentary on the Book of Psalms*, Vol. II, 337.

78. Jones, *Our Daily Sacrifice*, 23–24.

79. Ibid., 24–27.

80. Ibid., 23–24.

81. Full title, *Te Deum Laudamus* ("We praise Thee, O God").

82. Jones, *Our Daily Sacrifice*, 25–26.

83. Luke 1:68–79, John the Baptist's father's song of praise after naming his son.

84. Jones, *Our Daily Sacrifice*, 26–27.

85. Ibid., 27–31.

86. Ibid., 28 (no reference).

87. Ibid., 29.

88. Ibid., citing Augustine, "Sermon to Catechumens on the Creed" (source not

"'in God the Father, Who hath made me . . . in God the Son, Who hath redeemed me . . . in God the Holy Ghost, Who sanctifieth me.'"[89]

5. "Third great part of Worship—Prayer," in which "the predominating element" of praise "appears again" in the General Thanksgiving. He concluded by quoting Heb 13:15: "By Him, therefore, let us offer the sacrifice of praise to God continually, that is the fruit of our lips, giving thanks to his Name."[90] This blend of warm feeling and clear mental understanding, this faith that was personal trust, characterizes Jones's exposition of 1662 Prayer Book worship. It harmonized with his commitment to the doctrine of justifying faith as enshrined in the Thirty-nine Articles.

Both his *Arise; Shine* and *Resurrection Life* display the same scholarly underlay of Jones's thought as found in *Our Daily Sacrifice*. *Arise; Shine* was a coat-pocket pamphlet study of the collects, epistles, and gospels (read at the Lord's Supper) for the Epiphany season; *Resurrection Life* studied those of Eastertide. Jones—the "preacher of righteousness" as Lawton so aptly called him[91]—was "struck with the connection between the facts of the gospel and the bearing of those facts upon the lives of Christians" to be found in the "Collects, Epistles, and Gospels in our Prayer-book."[92] In *Arise; Shine* he makes use of this connection in expounding "the teaching of the Epiphany and that of the Sundays that follow."[93] The Epiphany (January 6) itself "commemorates the fact of Christ's manifestation to us." The collect, epistle, and gospel set for each of the following Sundays strike the keynote, "How to Shine," showing "how they who shine for Jesus now, will shine with Him in the glory of the life to come."[94] Keswick teaching informed but did not limit his application. The starting point, "doing the will of God," began with "entire self-surrender" ("The First Sunday after the Epiphany").[95] On the following Sundays, there was "shin[ing] for Jesus in the home" with "practical holiness" (Second Sunday);[96] shining "in the midst of a hostile world . . . by living gentle, blameless, peaceable lives, while we commit our

---

given), and quoting "Bishop Moorhouse Charges," (Moorhouse, *Church Work*, 50).

89. Jones, *Our Daily Sacrifice*, 30–31.
90. Ibid., 32.
91. Lawton, "Nathaniel Jones," 361.
92. Jones, *Arise; Shine*, 1.
93. Ibid.
94. Ibid., 4. See Book of Common Prayer at "The Epiphany" (the manifestation of Christ to the Gentiles).
95. Jones, *Arise; Shine*, 6.
96. Ibid., 8.

cause to God" (Third Sunday);[97] and "shining as members of the Church" (the Fifth Sunday) by forbearing even with "mere professing believers."[98]

Most striking, in view of the widely adopted misperception of Jones, was his exposition of the Fourth Sunday—"Shining in our Relation to the State."[99] This is even further evidence that Jones did not exclude social responsibility from the Christian's obligation. His perspective remarkably anticipates Henry Wace's *Record* article, "The Gospel and Politics" (1910).[100] Jones explicitly rejects the notion of "many good people who think that the Christian should have nothing to do with politics" on the grounds that they are "passing through" a world at present "under Satan."[101] Rather, "Satan's authority is usurped, and as subjects of the rightful king we should not let him have all his own way." That we are pilgrims and strangers in the world "is no reason why we should not *try to make the world a better place*."[102] The state is the "divinely-appointed institution" by which God restrains evil through the governing authorities, who are "His ministers."[103] Christians, therefore, must "recognise their authority, and render to all their dues" (Rom 13:1–7). "Every Christian who has a vote is a little bit of the Emperor." Therefore, as well as praying for good governance "we must, by a wise exercise of the franchise, do what lies in our power for the furtherance of that object. The man who neglects to use his vote as a talent from God commits a sin of the same kind as a neglectful ruler."[104]

The voting franchise had been universal for adult males in New South Wales since 1858, and for women in the new Commonwealth of Australia since 1902. Positively, Jones insisted: "We have responsibilities as members of the State, and in so far as we exercise these for the glory of God, we shall shine for Jesus in our political life. . . . We must use the power we have to influence our rulers for righteousness."[105] At the same time, "we must also cry to the 'Only ruler of princes,' 'Save us, or we perish.'"[106] The individual's life of faith was not without its socio-political responsibility.

---

97. Ibid., 10.
98. Ibid., 13–14.
99. Ibid., 10–12.
100. Wace, "Gospel and the Political World," 88–98.
101. Jones, *Arise; Shine*, 10.
102. Ibid., 11. Emphasis added.
103. Ibid.
104. Ibid., 12.
105. Ibid., 11–12.
106. Ibid., 12.

Resurrection Life: A Prayer Book Study for Easter Tide was Jones's last publication in book form.[107] He expounds the holiness thrust of the sets of collect, epistle, and gospel appointed for the Lord's Supper on Easter Even, Easter Day, and the five Sundays After Easter, and points out their scriptural allusions. There are eight short studies.

The first was "Resurrection Life: Its Starting-point." The collect (alluding to Rom 6:4) indicated the starting-point of the life of sanctification—that Christians "died with [Christ] in order that we might rise with Him and walk in newness of life." We are therefore to "share the power of his resurrection."[108]

The second study, "Resurrection Life: Its Nature" (of Easter Day), he called the "present experience" of the risen life, defined by the collect as one "in which good desires are brought to good effect."[109] Jones elucidated the tension between the "good desires" and the bringing of them to "good effect" by the Moulean (Keswick) contrast between the "fruitless good desires" (Rom 7:19, 22, 24) and the "self" supplanted "by the indwelling Christ" (Rom 8).[110] The key to the victory "lies in the words 'in Christ Jesus'" (Rom 8:1). Therefore, "the resurrection life of the believer is a joyful, victorious, overcoming life."[111]

The Epistle for Easter Day (Col 3:1–7) described the resurrection life by its call *"for lofty aspirations."*[112] Jones quoted Moule: "[to] 'seek the things which are above is to go out in spirit towards a Christ triumphant and reigning.'"[113] In the command of "a decisive act" to "'mortify . . . your members,'"[114] namely "[their] 'carnal functions'" ("'fornication, uncleanness,' etc."), lay "the secret of walking in separation from sin."[115] Memorable if not exegetically convincing today was his striking illustration. He contrasted Jesus's laid-aside grave-clothes (Gospel for Easter Day, John 20:1–10) with those of Lazarus (John 11:44b): "Too many Christians are like Lazarus—bound hand and foot with grave-clothes."[116]

---

107. Jones, *Resurrection Life*.
108. Ibid., 9–11.
109. Ibid., 12.
110. Ibid., 13–14.
111. Ibid., 14.
112. Ibid.
113. Ibid., 14–15. (Reference for Moule not given.)
114. Ibid., 15, quoting Col 3:5 and correctly rendering the force of the Greek.
115. Ibid.
116. Ibid., 16.

The five Sundays after Easter spelled out the characteristics of this resurrection life. The "First Sunday: Purity" (the theme of the collect for the day being "pureness of living and truth"). Jones noted how the English Reformers safeguarded the devotional with doctrine, believing with Luther that "purity can only be the portion of those who have already found peace." The words in the collect, "Christ died for our sins, and rose again for our justification," referred to Romans 4:25, the inference of which "follows in the very next verse (Rom 5:1): 'Being therefore justified by faith, we have peace with God through our Lord Jesus Christ.'" Thus, "the foundation," namely "reconciliation with God" was the condition for trying to "raise the structure of a holy life."[117]

The collect referred back to the first of the Easter Day sentences: "put away the leaven of malice and wickedness" (1 Cor 5:7, 8). The Jews, wrote Jones, for a week after Passover, customarily searched their houses with a lighted candle to remove any food scraps that might contain leaven. This "furnishes a striking image" of thorough removal of moral corruption. We must prayerfully search "every secret corner of the heart" with "the candle of the Word."[118] Again Jones was characteristically Reformational and Evangelical, emphasizing the role of the word in the spiritual-moral growth of the Christian believer. To make clear the force of the Greek tense, he re-worded the Prayer Book Easter Day sentence "is sacrificed" to "*once for all* sacrificed" for us. Analogously, "sin is to be put away permanently."[119]

Jones saw the epistle (1 John 5:4–12) as "further enforcing" the theme of purity. He quoted Westcott's definition of the "world" that faith overcomes: "the sum of all the limited transitory powers opposed to God which make obedience difficult."[120] "Whatsoever is born of God" (v. 4) Jones saw as virtually equivalent to being raised with Christ, and so "as partakers of Christ's life victory is our portion." Faith—believing that Jesus is the Son of God—was the [pre]condition of victory.[121] The gospel for this First Sunday after Easter (John 20:19–23), he acknowledged, bore only indirectly on the theme of purity: Jesus's presence in the midst "carries with it the obligation of continual purity."[122]

For the "Second Sunday: Christ-likeness" was the resurrection-life characteristic. Jones carefully noted that the collect insisted on the priority

---

117. Ibid., 18–19; Moule, *Epistle of St. Paul to the Romans*, 141–42.
118. Jones, *Resurrection Life*, 19–20.
119. Ibid., 21. Emphasis added.
120. Ibid., 22; Westcott, *Commentary on the Epistles of St. John* at 1 John 5:4–5.
121. Jones, *Resurrection Life*, 23; Alford, *Greek Testament*, vol. 4, at 1 John 5:4.
122. Jones, *Resurrection Life*, 23.

of justifying faith—"that we most thankfully receive that His inestimable benefit," namely, that of the Son's sacrifice for sin—before attempting to follow his example of godly life.[123] Not passivity but "effort" or "time" and "trouble," a continuous "daily thing," was required.[124] Here again was his aphorism, "he works in—do you work out" noticed earlier.[125]

The epistle (1 Pet 2:19-25) was the source of the collect's language and clarified what Christlikeness meant. The Greek word translated "example" (*hypogrammon*) (v. 21) denoted a pencil-drawing provided by the teacher for the pupil to trace over in ink. Christ's life was for Christians "diligently to follow each detail"[126]—no guile in their speech, not reviling back when reviled. When unjustly punished, the believer should take sufferings to be the self dying daily on the cross, that we may "'live unto righteousness.'"[127]

The last verse of the gospel (John 10:11-16), "there shall be one fold (RV, "flock") and one shepherd," referred to "the Great Shepherd [in] his Resurrection . . . standing by our side . . . as we strive to plant our feet in the footprints of His life of patient suffering."[128] The believer "looks up at the Great Shepherd, and cries: "Though I walk through the valley of the shadow of death, I will fear no evil; thy rod and thy staff comfort me."[129] Griffith Thomas, though few other readers, surely knew of Jones and his wife's loss of four infant children while in Victoria, and his friend's present life-threatening frailty.

The "Third Sunday After Easter: Consistency"—of Christians' lives with their professed faith was the subject of the collect ("eschew those things . . . contrary to their profession, and follow such . . . as are agreeable to the same") and the theme of the epistle (1 Pet 2:11-17). Jones was no killjoy, but only wished to sensitize his readers to their responsibility and to motivate them to be "strangers and pilgrims in this world," as "citizens of heaven. . . . [who] soon must . . . hasten homewards."[130] He defended the bodily "appetites and desires implanted in us by a wise Creator." It was only "unlawful and inordinate gratification which converts them into lusts hostile to the soul."[131] Believers' "good works" would command admiration and esteem,

---

123. Ibid., 25.
124. Ibid., 26.
125. See above on *Handful of Corn*, second address.
126. Jones, *Resurrection Life*, 26-27.
127. Ibid., quoting 1 Peter 2:24.
128. Ibid., 29-30.
129. Ibid.
130. Ibid., 33.
131. Ibid., 34.

and constrain unbelievers "to acknowledge the worth of our religion."[132] On the gospel for the day (John 16:16–22) he quoted Westcott again to explain that Jesus's words "ye now therefore have sorrow" meant that their suffering was "the necessary condition and preparation for joy."[133]

For the "Fourth Sunday after Easter: Fixity of Heart," the theme came from the collect's words, "that . . . our hearts may surely there be fixed." Jones referred back to the epistle for Easter Day to explain how that might be: "set your affections on the things that are above."[134] He denies that this "would involve the neglect of practical duties," but given the collect's reference to "unruly wills and affections" and "sundry and manifold changes of the world," he asks how the heart could "be fixed in heaven."[135]

The epistle (Jas 1:17–21) and the gospel (John 16:5–15), he said, gave the answer. James brought before believers "the character of the God with whom we have to do," "the unchanging God" (Jas 1:11),[136] who was "*a God of unchanging grace.*"[137] That he gave the greatest gift of all (John 3:16) was proof that "[t]he God who changes not is love."[138] Moreover, "*Our regeneration is proof of His unchanging grace. 'Of His own will begat He us with the word of truth.'*"[139] This was Jones's biblicist, Thirty-nine Articles "Calvinism," as was also his quotation, "He which hath begun a good work in us, will perform it until the day of Jesus Christ."[140] Jones was pastorally encouraging. Change from prosperity to adversity, friends failing us, or a state of health "bring[ing] on physical depression" would never destroy spiritual serenity "if we could look away from them to our unchanging God whose face of love ever shines upon us and who will never leave us or forsake us."[141]

The gospel (John 16:5–15) told how God will "order our unruly wills" (the collect): through the indwelling Holy Spirit, which Jesus promised by pointing to Pentecost: "I will send the Comforter" (John 16:7). He "comes to control the will and re-create the heart," as God promised (Ezek 36:26).

---

132. Ibid., 35–36.
133. Ibid., 36, quoting Westcott, *Gospel According to St John*, 2:230.
134. Jones, *Resurrection Life*, 38.
135. Ibid., 40–41.
136. Ibid., 41.
137. Ibid., 42.
138. Ibid.
139. Ibid., 42–43, quoting Jas 1:18.
140. Ibid., 43 (Phil 1:6, but reference not given).
141. Jones, *Resurrection Life*.

"This is how God makes us love the thing which he commands, so that our hearts are fixed in Him,"[142] thus referring to the collect.

On the "Fifth Sunday: Reality" was the characteristic of resurrection life. Jones grounded "heavenly mindedness" in "earthly usefulness." The collect's words, "that by thy holy inspiration," inspiration which derived from "the heavenly atmosphere," was "with a view to action."[143] The epistle (Jas 1:22–27) emphasized action ("Be ye doers" v. 21), but that must "spring out of hearing" (vv. 19, 21). Many, however, "make no effort to break off their own besetting sins," like the love of money. Jones spelled out "reality" lists from the epistle: "The control of the tongue"; "sympathy with the afflicted"—that is to say, "relieving the wants of the poor" as opposed to religious ritual and sacrifices; and keeping oneself "unspotted from the world," for God was not served since Christ's resurrection "with elaborate vestments; the garb of purity is what we have to wear."[144] The gospel (John 16:23–33) gave "good encouragement" by telling us of "*the efficacy of prayer*" as well as of "*the Father's love for us*" and "*of Christ's victory over the world.*"[145]

Like *Arise; Shine*, Jones's *Resurrection Life* demonstrates both his concern for biblical devotion and his theological–pastoral insight into the riches of the liturgical year enshrined in the Book of Common Prayer. He always remained grounded in biblical Reformation doctrine, with which he integrated devotional application and elements of Keswick teaching. In all, he also "looked for . . . the life of the world to come,"[146] without tying this to a specifically premillennial expectation. Such was his piety.

Jones stayed for part of his time in England in 1908 in the home of his friend, W. H. Griffith Thomas, now principal of Wycliffe Hall. He must have taken the manuscript for *Resurrection Life* with him, for Griffith Thomas commended it warmly in his introductory note to Jones's book.[147] Together with *Our Daily Sacrifice*, the two late works *Arise; Shine* and *Resurrection Life* look like the beginnings of the work on the Prayer Book that Griffith Thomas had invited him to write. It seems a pity that he did not live longer and leave similar studies for the Sundays of Advent and for Whitsunday (Pentecost) and Trinity Sundays, also of Lent.

---

142. Ibid., 43–44.
143. Ibid., 45.
144. Ibid., 46–49.
145. Ibid., 49–50.
146. Niceno-Constantinopolitan ("Nicene") Creed (AD 381).
147. Jones, *Resurrection Life*, 5–6.

A Brief Overview of Some Pocket Tracts

Jones's tracts show something of the scope of his thinking. A few related to his concern for holiness as the fruit of justification by faith. Some applied to current issues in Sydney; others were for particular occasions and situations. They illustrate points of his position on the conservative part of the Evangelical spectrum of his day.

God's Way of Justification[148] was singled out for mention in "An Appreciation" published on his death. The writer remembered that Jones "loved the Church of the Reformation with its loyalty to the pure Word of God and the Sacraments ordained by Christ."[149] Thus, a sermon in Moore College Chapel, *"Touch Me Not." An Examination of a Popular Theory of the Sacraments*, critiqued as unbiblical the Anglo-Catholic notion that in the sacraments "'man in his double nature is put into . . . complete . . . contact with the Incarnate Glorified Lord.'"[150] At an anniversary of the Protestant Church of England Union (a Sydney organization opposed to ritualism founded by Mervyn Archdall in 1898),[151] Jones preached on *Our Priestly Privileges* (Heb 13:9–16).[152] He integrated the Reformation insight into God's grace and the believer's "altar" as the "crucified Saviour" with a "continuous experience" of its "power in our daily life."[153] His Protestantism, always firm and clear, was continually related to living trust in God. He criticized a sacerdotal view of the Christian ministry in his sermon on John 20:22–23, *The Church's Commission*.[154] Against sacerdotalist priestly claims, Roman as well as Anglo-Catholic, he stressed that only God could forgive sins.[155]

Jones was a strong supporter of missionary work. *Partners with the Holy Ghost* addressed the annual meeting of the Gleaners' Union, the youth organization of the Church Missionary Association of New South Wales.[156] He expected his young hearers to rise to the challenge of his bold argument

---

148. Jones, *God's Way of Justification*.

149. Anonymous, "The Rev. Canon Jones," 17. Very likely by S. J. Kirkby, formerly a student under Jones and at the time of his death teaching at the college and highly appreciative of him.

150. Jones, "Touch Me Not," 7 (here "His" corrected to "his"). Jones is quoting another unmentioned source.

151. Judd and Cable, *Sydney Anglicans*, 144, 166.

152. Jones, *Our Priestly Privileges*.

153. Ibid., 13.

154. Jones, *Church's Commission*.

155. Ibid., 14–15.

156. Jones, *Partners with the Holy Ghost*, 1.

for translating the Greek of Hebrews 6:4 as "partners with,"[157] not "partakers of" the Holy Spirit (AV).[158] He then highlighted the importance and "practical advantages" of that partnership in missionary work and missionary decision.[159]

His sermon, *The New Cart*, is interesting for its moralistic exposition by analogy of the compromised return of the ark of the covenant to the tabernacle in Jerusalem (1 Chr 15:13 [RV]). He criticized "going to the world to borrow methods" for church money-raising, thus "ignoring the rules laid down in Holy Scripture,"[160] which he cited from the Corinthian epistles.

In an address, *The Manifestation of God to those Who Keep His Word* (1903) to a Grubb mission-inspired "Annual Christian Conference," Jones defended Scripture against negative criticism.[161] He gave an intelligent exegetical and theological argument for the full authority of both the New Testament and the Old Testament. He applied this authority to the holiness purpose of the conference.[162]

"*He Is Ever the Same*" and *Jesus Only* were pastoral addresses, both applying to holiness of life. "*He Is Ever the Same*" expounded Psalm 23—here was the Good Shepherd's "all-sufficing presence," his "abundant provision" and "restoring guidance," whether in the dark of its last three verses or the light of the first three.[163] *Jesus Only* told how, after Christ's Transfiguration, the disciples saw "Jesus only" (Matt 17:8). He alone was "all sufficient" for "justification from my past sins," "power to meet present temptations," and "our prospect for the future."[164] Jones sounded no premillennial note.

Conclusion

Nathaniel Jones thus represented a position on the Evangelical spectrum of thought that cannot be characterized as "anxious"[165] or even *preeminently* one of premillennial hope. His sermons and addresses on various subjects proclaimed his sustained and scholarly commitment to basic Reformation themes: the sole authority of Scripture and the exclusive role of trust in

---

157. Probably based on Westcott, *Epistle to the Hebrews*, 73.
158. Jones, *Partners with the Holy Ghost*, 2–6.
159. Ibid., 6–11.
160. Jones, *New Cart*, 9.
161. Reported in *Sydney Morning Herald*, August 7, 1903, 6.
162. Jones, *Manifestation of God*, 12–15.
163. Jones, *"He is Ever the Same,"* 15.
164. Jones, *Jesus Only*, 13.
165. Dickey, "Jones, Nathaniel," 191–92.

Christ to receive God's forgiveness. To this, he added the Keswick doctrine of holiness as defined by Evan Hopkins and Handley Moule. This emphasis on a holiness of life empowered by living biblical faith shone out from all his devotional writings, not least from those on Prayer Book liturgy. It also characterized his life.[166]

Jones's thought was pietist by way of an *emphasis*: an emphasis on holiness of life and depth of devotion. Neither this nor his premillennial hope ever altered or diminished his commitment to the Reformation biblical foundation of the Church of England. The above confirms Loane's assessment: "he was . . . in the finest school of Evangelical thought."[167] Such was his legacy to Moore College, its students and its diocese.

---

166. Loane, *Centenary History*, 98–99.
167. Ibid., 111–12.

Figure 3: D. J. Davies

7

Liberal Evangelicalism Embraced
Formation of a Historian

Introduction

DAVID JOHN DAVIES, "BEN" as he was known to his students, was the personal choice of Archbishop John Charles Wright. The new principal brought to Moore College the broadening Liberal Evangelical spectrum of the Group Brotherhood.[1] It was to dominate the training of Sydney ministers for nearly a quarter of a century, and have definite impact on the diocese. Wright brought to Sydney another one of the Group Brotherhood to be dean of St Andrew's Cathedral, A. E. Talbot (1877–1936), who taught part-time at the college.

Davies's Youth 1879–1901

David John Davies was born on February 12, 1879, in Elerch, Cardiganshire, Wales—the first-born of Sarah Davies (née Pugh) and David Davies, both school teachers[2] and both Evangelicals possibly affected by the Moody missions of 1881–1883, which included Wales.[3] David Davies gained his BA from Trinity College, Dublin (TCD), in 1886. It was then a place of Evangelical influence, where the great George Salmon, Regius

---

1. See chapter 2 above.
2. West, "A Principal Embattled."
3. Orr, *Light of the Nations*, 193.

Professor of Divinity since 1866, was at the peak of his powers.[4] David Davies was ordained in the Church of England (and Wales) and served in Monmouthshire. In 1897 he moved to a parish just outside Bradford, which was in the Diocese of Ripon in Yorkshire.[5] The younger Davies thus initially had a Welsh upbringing (he spoke some Welsh), but was educated in English. He left school at age fourteen, being from a relatively poor though devout Evangelical clerical household. Marcus Loane remembered him as knowing long passages from the gospels off by heart.[6] He had outstanding musical gifts and played both the piano and the pipe organ. Living in Bradford from age eighteen, he witnessed the economic distress of urban industrial England.[7]

The Evangelical weekly *The Record* would almost certainly have come into his parents' home, and possibly also *The Churchman*, then a monthly journal. But we find no hint that R. A. Torrey's great British campaign of 1903–1905 touched him, or the revival in Wales in 1904–1905, which added so many to the churches.[8] The same is true for him of the premillennial hope of Christ's personal return, and of the Mildmay and Keswick holiness emphasis.

On leaving school Davies became a pupil-teacher. He studied for his matriculation and entered Trinity College, Cambridge, in September 1901, aged twenty-two. Since he received the Elland Society's Jetson Exhibition to assist those studying for the ministry, he identified as an Evangelical. The Reverend John Charles Wright was an active member of that Evangelical society at the time.[9]

The Cambridge Environment 1901–1911

Trinity College was by far the largest college in the university. Davies enrolled in the History Tripos. His tutor was Canon Reginald St John Parry (1858–1935), a classicist,[10] joint editor of the *Cambridge Greek Testament for Schools and Colleges*, and author of several of the commentaries.

Davies found himself in the midst of a galaxy of the famous or famous-to-be in the world of thought and science. Ideas and discoveries that would

4. Also a distinguished mathematician.
5. "Davies, David," *Crockford's*, 345.
6. Interview with Loane, June 5, 2001.
7. West, "A Principal Embattled."
8. Piggin, *Firestorm of the Lord*, 9.
9. Davies, "Our Late Archbishop," 9.
10. Smith, Jonathan, letter to the author, April 9, 2005.

influence the twentieth century were germinating and growing. Unlike the Oxford of Jones's student days, Cambridge did not have any theologically conservative professors and teachers of note by this time. Norrisian Professor of Divinity (1899–1901) Handley C. G. Moule had just left to be consecrated Bishop of Durham (on October 18, 1901). In philosophy and history, some of the outstanding figures were not professing Christians of any kind; those in theology were, at least to some degree, theologically liberal. The student Cambridge Intercollegiate Christian Union (CICCU) was strong in 1901, but would soon face a theological crisis arising from changes in the Student Christian Movement.[11] Ridley Hall was becoming less resistant to liberal theological thinking. Davies's new intellectual and spiritual environment strongly favored the formation of liberal theological convictions. The Group Brotherhood, formed in 1906—when Davies was a new curate under one of its founders—would later list its *liberal* "heredity": the modern world's "historical method, its philosophy of personality, and its scientific view of the universe."[12]

Philosophy and Mathematics

The brilliant coterie of publishing philosophers in Cambridge could hardly leave the young Davies unaffected. John McTaggart (1866–1925), fellow of Trinity since 1891, "eminent agnostic,"[13] personal idealist, and "hostile critic of Christianity,"[14] was author of *Studies in the Hegelian Dialectic* (1896) and had published his *Studies in Hegelian Cosmology* in the year Davies enrolled. His semi-popular *Some Dogmas of Religion* appeared the year Davies qualified for ordination. Early on in Davies's student days saw published the lectures of Trinity fellow and Knightbridge Professor of Moral Philosophy, Henry Sidgwick (1838–1900), on the ethics of Green, Spencer, and Martineau.[15] Other Trinity men included G. E. Moore (1873–1958) and Bertrand Russell (1872–1970). In the year Davies finished part 1 of the History Tripos (1903), Moore published his *Principia Ethica*: a "Prolegomena to any future Ethics that can pretend to be *scientific*."[16] In this same year, Bertrand Russell

---

11. Barclay, *Jesus Lane Lot*, 52–70.
12. Rogers, "Introduction," v.
13. Brooke, *History of the University of Cambridge*, 118.
14. Passmore, *Hundred Years of Philosophy*, 76n.
15. Sidgwick, *Lectures*.
16. Brooke, *History of the University of Cambridge*, 439, citing Moore, *Principia Ethica* (1903) ix, xii–xxvii. Emphasis added.

produced "probably his greatest work,"[17] *The Principles of Mathematics*, and his explicitly anti-Christian essay, "A Free Man's Worship."[18]

Since the days when T. R. Birks was Knightbridge Professor of Moral Philosophy (the 1870s) there had been no Evangelical among the Christian philosopher-theologians in Cambridge. Close to the Christian side, however, was James Ward (1843–1925), a fellow of Trinity College since 1875 and twice Gifford lecturer (1896–1898 and 1907–1910).[19] Against Herbert Spencer and company, Ward "was regarded as one of the most acute critics of naturalism and one of the most powerful defenders of theism."[20] Under him, in the year Davies left for Moore College, Bernard Muscio (1887–1926) began his postgraduate work.[21] Muscio, a graduate of the University of Sydney (1922–1926) and future professor of philosophy there, was known to Nathaniel Jones and his vice-principal, G. A. Chambers, and was probably a Christian believer. Another theist was W. R. Sorley (1855–1935), who came to Cambridge as Knightbridge Professor of Moral Philosophy in 1902. His point of departure was moral experience—a matter Davies would later emphasize. Both Ward and Sorley are likely to have appealed to the budding historian in Davies by their conception of history as a science *and* of its distinguishing mark as such: the taking into account of ethical value by investigating *persons*. The "experience of moral values was no less objective than our knowledge of natural facts."[22] History could therefore be scientific. The mathematician and future philosopher, Alfred North Whitehead (1861–1947) was, like Ward, a fellow of Davies's college (1884–1910). He had been Russell's tutor, was his collaborator in their joint *Principia Mathematica* (1910–1913), and a teacher of the famous astrophysicist A. S. Eddington.[23]

Philosophical idealism was part of the intellectual environment of Davies's student days. In a rectory near Oxford, John Illingworth (1848–1915), a contributor to *Lux Mundi*,[24] was putting out idealist philosophical theology, emphasizing personality, while conservative of the transcendental

---

17. Quinton, "Russell," 661–62.
18. Russell, "Free Man's Worship," 46–47.
19. Ward, *Naturalism and Agnosticism*; Ward, *Realm of Ends*.
20. Macquarrie, "Anglo-American Philosophies of Spirit," 64.
21. Grave, *History*, 37–38; O'Neill, "Muscio," 650–51.
22. Macquarrie, "Ethical Approach to Theism," 68–69. See Sorley, *Ethics of Naturalism*.
23. O'Connor and Robertson, "Arthur Stanley Eddington."
24. Illingworth, "Problem of Pain," 113–26.

Trinity.²⁵ Illingworth was widely read; some of his books saw cheap popular editions. At the University of Oxford itself, the neo-platonic William Ralph Inge (1860–1954) was Lady Margaret Professor of Divinity from 1907–1911. J. K. Mozley recorded in 1910: "[Inge] has asserted himself on the side of Protestantism" and was of only the slightest "sympathy with the Modernist revolt."²⁶

Christians in Cambridge included William Cunningham (1849–1919), a Broad Churchman, a fellow of Trinity, and the Archdeacon of Ely; he was Davies's mentor in Economic History (part 2 of the History Tripos). Cunningham looked on his friend, T. H. Green, as "my master in all that I care about in philosophy," and was a disciple of F. D. Maurice in theology and social questions,²⁷ a fact significant for Davies. Cunningham contributed the substantial first essay, "The Christian Standpoint" to the *Cambridge Theological Essays*,²⁸ which came out the year after Davies graduated. He affirmed the widely accepted Kantian doctrine of human autonomy: that "the personal religious consciousness refuses to submit to any intellectual authority outside itself."²⁹ This would be Davies's position, especially with regard to Scripture. Davies was "a Liberal in scholarship,"³⁰ however close he may have kept to catholic orthodoxy.

Theology

The young Davies would come into contact with the theologically distinguished and advanced, but, like Cunningham, all liberal to varying degrees. In Davies's time at Cambridge the philosophically-minded theologian, Frederick Robert Tennant (1866–1957), published works on God and science, and on the doctrine of sin.³¹ In 1907 he returned to Cambridge as a lecturer in the university and fellow of Trinity College. Tennant attempted to be strictly empirical in his method. His ethical theism took "the realization of personality and of moral values to be the *raison d'être* of the world,"³² a

---

25. Ramsey, *From Gore to Temple*, 24.
26. Mozley, "Religious Life," 28.
27. Cunningham, Audrey, *William Cunningham*, 22, 50.
28. Swete, *Essays on Some Theological Questions*.
29. Cunningham, "Christian Standpoint," 1–53.
30. Loane, *Centenary History*, 137.
31. Tennant, *Origin and Propagation of Sin*; Tennant, *Sources of the Doctrine of the Fall*; Tennant, "Being of God," 55–146.
32. Tennant, *Philosophical Theology*, 2:258.

notion that Davies would echo.³³ The chaplain of Trinity College, Edward Harrison Askwith, contributed "Sin, and the Need of Atonement" to *Cambridge Theological Essays*.³⁴ Davies's view largely followed that of the Trinity chaplain's non-propitiatory moral-influence *cum* governmental doctrine of the atonement.

Ernest William Barnes (1874–1953) was a brilliant graduate (second wrangler, 1896) and a London fellow of Trinity College.³⁵ Davies never forgot a kind personal touch Barnes showed him when sitting his entrance examination in 1901. To the surprise of many in the university, Barnes had professed Christian faith as an undergraduate and sought ordination in Davies's student days.³⁶ He was one of the contributors to *Liberal Evangelicalism* (1923),³⁷ but at the same time was also prominent in the Modern Churchmen's Union.³⁸ He exemplified the oneness *in principle* of theological outlook found between the Liberal Evangelicals and the Modern Churchmen.³⁹ As the new Bishop of Birmingham in 1924, he became notorious not only for suppressing ritualist extremism,⁴⁰ but also for his radical, modernist theological views.⁴¹

Biblical Studies

Old Testament studies were dominated by liberal scholars. H. E. Ryle, Hulsean Professor of Divinity (1888–1900), defended a liberal—albeit cautious—approach to the Old Testament.⁴² Robert Sinker (fellow and librarian of Trinity College), however, was a centrist Evangelical. His series in *The Record* came out as a book not long before Davies entered the college. He critiqued the negative criticism: "We are not prepared to be dragged at the wheel of those who would give us a discredited Old Testament, an emasculated New Testament, a fallible Christ."⁴³ Sinker published three

---

33. Davies, *Church and the Plain Man*.
34. Askwith, "Sin, and the Need of Atonement," 175–218.
35. Doctor of Science (1906) and Fellow of the Royal Society (1909).
36. Davies, "Bishop Barnes," 9.
37. Barnes, "Future of the Evangelical Movement," 287–304.
38. *ODCC*, "Modern Church People's Union," 1104.
39. Storr, *Freedom and Tradition*, 111–14.
40. Davies, "Bishop Barnes," 9.
41. Duffield, "Barnes," 106; Barnes, *Should Such a Faith Offend?*
42. Ryle, *On Holy Scripture*; Pollock, *Cambridge Movement*, 125.
43. Sinker, *"Higher Criticism,"* 184.

more books on the Old Testament,[44] but if they read him neither Davies nor Dean Talbot appears to have been persuaded.

Davies made a special study of the historicity of the gospels.[45] Cambridge provided plenty of background scholarship—some less, some more negatively critical. Frederic Henry Chase, Norrisian Professor of Divinity, contributed the essay on the New Testament gospels in *Cambridge Theological Essays*.[46] The three-volume *magnum opus* on the gospels of Vincent Henry Stanton (1846–1924), Ely Professor of Divinity, began to appear as Davies completed part 1 of the History Tripos.[47] The conservative Princeton New Testament scholar, J. Gresham Machen, found positive use for Stanton's work.[48] E. H. Askwith, wrote a work on the historical value of John.[49] Syriac scholar Francis Crawford Burkitt (1864–1935), Norrisian Professor of Divinity (from 1905), was a modernist pioneer of gospel form criticism. His work on gospel history came out in 1906;[50] and in 1909 appeared his essay, "The Eschatological Idea in the Gospel" in *Cambridge Biblical Essays*.[51]

Having ordination in view, during his History Tripos studies Davies attended three courses offered by professors of the Divinity School: F. H. Chase, "Acts of the Apostles"; H. M. Gwatkin, "Early Church History," and A. J. Mason, "I Peter 3:18–4:21." By May 1905, Davies could state that among a few other works and "many text-books used," he had read "wholly or in part" standard New Testament biblical commentaries: Alford's *Greek Testament*, Conybeare and Howson's *Life and Epistles of St. Paul*, and G. Salmon's *Introduction to the New Testament*. On the Old Testament, he mentioned only A. H. Sayce's *Early History of the Hebrews*, which was critical of the Wellhausen documentary hypothesis. For doctrine he had read Handley Moule's *Outlines of Christian Doctrine*; on the Thirty-nine Articles, Boultbee (Evangelical), Maclear and Williams (Anglo-Catholic); Richard Hooker's *Laws of Ecclesiastical Polity* (the critical Volume 5); and the sermons of both the reformation bishop, Hugh Latimer and the early High Church bishop, Jeremy Taylor. He had also read Illingworth's *Personality, Human and*

---

44. Sinker, *Essays and Studies*; Sinker, *Daniel and the Minor Prophets*; Sinker, *Saul and the Hebrew Monarchy*.

45. See chapter 9 below.

46. Chase, "Gospels," 371–419.

47. Stanton, *Gospels as Historical Documents*.

48. Machen, *Virgin Birth of Christ*, viii, 29, etc.

49. Askwith, *Historical Value*.

50. Burkitt, *Gospel History*.

51. Burkitt, "Eschatological Idea," 193–213.

Divine.⁵² Which of these mostly orthodox works he may have read in his father's library before going up to Cambridge or during university vacations we do not know. His Bible studies given at Holy Trinity Church, Cambridge in 1908 (see below) prove that he had accepted a liberal approach by then.

History: Davies's Tripos Subject

Cambridge was distinguished in its historians—both secular and ecclesiastical. This suggests Davies's approach to the Bible was that of the historical methodology he learned. Since the natural sciences dominated the Cambridge of 1890–1910,⁵³ it is not surprising that the empirical method was claimed widely across the disciplines, including history. Lord Acton (1834–1902), a liberal Roman Catholic, the second Regius Professor of History at Cambridge (1895–1902), "helped immeasurably to establish history as a serious academic discipline, and to make the Cambridge school a branch of European learning."⁵⁴ He believed that history was "the judgment seat, a source of moral understanding."⁵⁵

On January 26, 1903 (in Davies's second year) Acton's successor, J. B. Bury, an atheist, delivered his famous inaugural lecture "The Science of History."⁵⁶ Its main contention would remain a conviction of the budding Liberal Evangelical, David Davies—that history was "a science, no less and no more."⁵⁷ Aiming at "a scrupulously exact conformity to facts," it must bring "reason and critical doubt to bear on the material," and "the critical method was one of the means to secure it."⁵⁸ By critical method Bury must have meant this "bringing reason and critical doubt to bear,"⁵⁹ but he left unstated what his presumably naturalistic criteria would be. He went on to state that history that was true "can be ascertained only through the discovery, collection, classification, and interpretation of facts—through scientific research."⁶⁰ A key element in this was, Bury added, that the "idea of human development" enabled history "to define her scope."⁶¹

52. Davies, Answer to Question 9 lists all the above detail.
53. Brooke, *History of the University of Cambridge*, 155–157.
54. Ibid., 233.
55. Ibid., 422.
56. Bury, *Inaugural Lecture*.
57. Ibid., 7.
58. Ibid., 9–11.
59. Ibid., 9.
60. Ibid., 23–24.
61. Ibid., 17.

Of course, Bury's final center of reference for the acceptance and knowledge of the meaning of facts lay *a priori* implicitly in man, not in God as understood in Christian theism. But Davies would easily have related Bury's standpoint positively to the liberal notion of "progressive revelation" in the Old Testament and "critical doubt" to the criticism of the biblical books as historical sources.

Henry Melvill Gwatkin (1844–1916), Dixie professor of Ecclesiastical History was a fellow of St John's College and a recognized authority on Arianism,[62] whose lectures on Early Church history Davies attended. For Gwatkin, too, history was a scientific discipline. Gwatkin became equally well-known for his 1903–1905 Gifford Lectures.[63] Davies admired and used both Gwatkin's historical and theological work, and would have heard his oft-repeated stricture that the older Evangelicals had "abstained from learning like the beasts of the field."[64] This stricture did not apply to Davies or to Nathaniel Jones, and certainly not to T. C. Hammond.

Davies's director of studies for part 1 of his History Tripos was probably none other than George Macaulay Trevelyan (1876–1962),[65] assistant lecturer in Modern History. Trevelyan later succeeded Bury as Regius Professor of Modern History at Cambridge.

Davies's mentor in part 2 of the History Tripos, William Cunningham, was "the real founder of Economic History as a discipline,"[66] Cunningham had rooms in Whewell's Close (which is opposite the gate of Trinity College) and "took trouble to know his pupils personally."[67] His convictions in several respects are important for understanding Davies's outlook. For one thing, he (in his daughter's words) could not accept "the fundamental principle [of the Christian Social Union] that Christian law would be the ultimate authority on social practice."[68] His reason was that Christ's teaching had a different social context and aim—"a spiritual aim as supreme in earthly life," whereas "the growth of material prosperity did not necessarily promote virtue, nor did a high standard of living arouse the spirit of self-sacrifice."[69] Moreover, Cunningham followed F. D. Maurice's teaching "that it was not for the Church to direct the State in political or social affairs." But

---

62. Gwatkin, *Studies of Arianism*; Gwatkin, *Arian Controversy*.
63. Gwatkin, *Knowledge of God*.
64. Elliot-Binns, *Evangelical Movement*, 142.
65. Smith, Letter; cf. Trevelyan, Note to Davies.
66. Salter, "Preface," x.
67. Cunningham, *William Cunningham*, 78.
68. Holland, *Ground of Our Appeal*.
69. Cunningham, *William Cunningham*, 71–72.

it *was* "the definite duty of Christians as individual citizens to take their part in the good government of the realm,"[70] an emphasis of Nathaniel Jones noted above. Cunningham also pointed out (like his fellow Scot, James Denney) that socialism relied on compelling people by civil law to do what was right, whereas Christianity relied on moral suasion.[71]

Another important conviction of Cunningham's was his opposition to free trade: a conclusion he had come to in stages by 1903.[72] Davies followed him in these views and did not preach a gospel of social reform of society, but agreed with the common Kantian rejection of external intellectual (or moral) authority he saw in Cunningham. Also important for Davies's thought would be his mentor's conviction that the historian could not explain the facts of history deductively, that is by applying, in the case of economic history, the principles of economic theory.[73] Rather he must work inductively, producing a general explanation from the ascertained facts, which was the scientific method in history. Thus, one could not simply condemn socialism *a priori*, as did the laissez-faire theorists.[74]

Notable Fellow Students and Some Friends

John Maynard Keynes (1883–1946)—a brilliant mathematics graduate (BA 1904) tutored by A. N. Whitehead—was a member of the Cambridge Apostles,[75] along with Moore and Russell. He would later have world influence in the application of economics. Arthur Stanley Eddington (1882–1944), mentioned above, was a Christian (Society of Friends) and a future household name in the natural sciences. He entered Trinity College in 1902 and was senior wrangler in 1904. By 1913 he was Plumian Professor of Astronomy, and in 1927 he gave the Gifford Lectures.[76] He and Davies became good friends; Davies stayed with him in Cambridge during his final trip back to England in 1934.

Other outstanding students would feature in Davies's future life and work. Albert Edward Talbot (above) was another Trinity College man

---

70. Ibid., 99, citing *Times*, August 28, 1914.

71. Ibid., 21–22, 71, and Cunningham, *Socialism and Christianity*, 12–14; Denney, *Church and the Kingdom*.

72. Cunningham, *William Cunningham*, 98–99, citing *British Association Report*, 751; Cunningham, *Case Against Free Trade*, 135.

73. Ricardo, *On the Principles*.

74. Cunningham, *William Cunningham*, 52–80.

75. Brooke, *History of the University of Cambridge*, 128.

76. Eddington, *Nature of the Physical World*.

and gained double firsts in the Theology Tripos (1904, 1905). He served briefly under Bishop E. A. Knox in the Diocese of Manchester from 1907 to 1909, and thereby, presumably, became known to John Charles Wright. He taught at the CMS College in Islington, then followed Davies to Australia to be Dean of Sydney from 1912 to 1936. J. W. Hunkin, at Gonville and Caius, graduated twelfth wrangler in 1908. He became the vice-principal of Wycliffe Hall, Oxford, and was Archdeacon of Rugby when Davies and Talbot nominated him for Archbishop of Sydney in 1933 but he was not elected.[77] In 1935 he was consecrated Bishop of Truro, less than three weeks before Davies's death. Hunkin made his mark as a liberal biblical scholar, and, like E. W. Barnes, contributed an essay to *Liberal Evangelicalism*[78] and moved close to the Modern Churchmen's Union. Howard West Kilvinton Mowll (1890-1958), a future Archbishop of Sydney from 1933-1958, gained a Second Class in parts 1 and 2 of the History Tripos (1911, 1912) at King's College. He was president (Lent Term 1911 to May 1912)[79] of the CICCU after it disaffiliated from the SCM in March, 1910. Did Davies—a firm supporter of the SCM—personally encourage A. C. B. Bellerby, an Emmanuel College student and the president of the CICCU 1909-1910, to urge the CICCU to broaden its basis and remain with the SCM?[80]

Junior Cleric and Cambridge Don 1905–1911

In this period appear the basic historical, socio-economic, and theological ideas that characterized Davies as principal of Moore College, Sydney. His papers, Bible study series, and sermons fall within the now broadened, liberalized spectrum of Evangelicalism. They indicate a changed concept of the Christian message.

Following his study at Ridley Hall for the academic year 1904–1905, Davies was ordained deacon to be curate part-time under the vicar of Holy Trinity Church, H. L. C. V. de Candole. De Candole taught Pastoralia at Ridley Hall, was one of the foundation members of the Group Brotherhood, and had been also a Keswick speaker for a time. Davies preached and taught under him regularly from 1905 to 1911.[81]

Theologically, most revealing of Davies's broadened Evangelicalism were his three Wednesday evening "Studies in the Book of Isaiah" of January

77. See chapter 9 below.
78. Hunkin, "Kingdom of God," 174-93.
79. Loane, *Archbishop Mowll*, 45-46.
80. Pollock, *Cambridge Movement*, 170-74.
81. *Service Register*, June 18, 1905 to August 24, 1911.

1908, and his Sunday sermons expounding the Epistle to the Romans in September of that year. As it happened, both series were given in Holy Trinity Church during the build-up to the disaffiliation of the CICCU from the SCM.[82]

In the Romans series[83] he adumbrated themes that would appear in later work. In particular, on justification by faith, "one of the watchwords of the [Evangelical] party,"[84] he used not Handley Moule's commentaries[85] nor that by James Denney,[86] but the exposition by the liberal Anglo-Catholic, Charles Gore.[87] Gore was appreciated by all Evangelicals for his apologetic writings in the conflict with open modernists like H. D. A. Major. Gore's notion of justification, however, was that of the seventeenth century High Church theologian, Bishop George Bull (1634-1710):[88] that God imputes righteousness to the believer in Christ in *anticipation of what he will become.*

The death of Christ as atonement is a central doctrine of the Christian faith. For Davies the notion of Christ's death was first and foremost a motivating example. He combined this with the governmental view so as to link it with his view of justification. Justification was (ours), "in virtue of a new attachment under which our life has passed. . . . [But] of course this preliminary acquittal is provisional" (following Gore[89]). He explained further: "The law of God . . . must be acknowledged by the sinner before God can pardon the sinner *with beneficial moral effect."* The death of Christ "was a solemn and striking manifestation of God's justice, of the punishment which sin deserved (the governmental view).[90] Man "can share in the benefits of Christ's death by faith, by self-surrender to Christ, an act of the whole man, reason, heart, will." It is therefore, "no legal fiction."[91]

The historic forensic notion was rejected and characterized as "a fiction" by its critics, famously in a detached note, "The Righteousness of God."[92] This move was reminiscent of Immanuel Kant's thought and favored

---

82. For the process of disaffiliation see Pollock, *Cambridge Movement*, 159-74.

83. Davies, "Studies in Romans," was a series of nine expositions given in August and September, 1908.

84. Storr, *Development of English Theology*, 69.

85. Moule, *Epistle of Paul the Apostle to the Romans*; Moule, *Epistle of St. Paul to the Romans*.

86. Denney, *Paul's Epistle to the Romans*.

87. Gore, *Epistle to the Romans*.

88. Bull, *Harmonia*.

89. Gore, *Epistle to the Romans*, 1:26-30.

90. Davies, "Studies in Romans," 3. Emphasis added.

91. Ibid.

92. Sanday and Headlam, *Critical and Exegetical Commentary*, 36-39.

by T. H. Green, who had so influenced the *Lux Mundi* Anglo-Catholics led by Gore.[93] An assumption of human moral autonomy probably underlay this judgment. Davies's rejection of the historic doctrine is an index to his theological outlook. Both justification and the atonement were adjusted by liberals to accord with the commonly supposed growing moral consciousness of modern man.

Later, under the heading, "Being Justified by Faith," (on Rom 5:1–2), Davies argued that God pointed to "Calvary and the empty tomb, both historic facts" saying, "If you trust me I will for Christ's sake accept you as righteous. . . . I will by my Spirit make you righteous."[94] Quite ignoring Denney, Moule, and Litton[95] (to say nothing of Article 2 of the Thirty-nine Articles), here Davies followed with support from a sermon by H. M. Gwatkin. It was the human-oriented Ritschlian interpretation of "reconciliation," and was contrary to the New Testament concept that God was reconciling *himself* to accepting sinners: "Christ died for us while we were yet enemies of God. . . . This assurance *is* the atonement, which means *the reconciliation of our heart to God:* and there is *no other atonement* for sin."[96]

On the terms "atonement," "reconciliation," and "redemption," Davies used Sanday and Headlam's commentary on Romans, saying that the words "express ideas that spring from the death of Christ considered as a sacrifice for . . . the sin of mankind," the idea of sacrifice being integral to the religion of the New Testament.[97] "Sacrifice" was a prominent F. D. Maurice theme.[98] Terms such as "propitiation," being "inspired by the Holy Ghost" must be left "to Him to interpret."[99] On "propitiation" he quoted Sanday and Headlam again: "Sufficient for us to know that through the virtue of the One Sacrifice . . . there is a 'sprinkling' which makes us free to approach the throne of grace."[100] Davies himself concluded that "being declared righteous by faith" means "in the end the righteousness which was only potential in us at first becomes actual and our salvation is complete." Any listener who

---

93. Orr, *Christian View*, 466.

94. Davies, "Studies in Romans," 8.

95. Denney, *Death of Christ*, 143–47; Moule, *Epistle of Paul the Apostle to the Romans*, and Moule, *Epistle of St. Paul to the Romans*, both at Rom 5:10; Moule, *Outlines of Christian Doctrine*, 79–80; Litton, *Introduction to Dogmatic Theology*, 232.

96. Gwatkin, *Eye for Spiritual Things*, 237. Emphasis added. This was a Ritschlian idea of justification (see Orr, *Ritschlian Theology*, 150).

97. Davies, "Studies in Romans," 8. Quoting Sanday and Headlam, *Critical and Exegetical Commentary*, 92.

98. Maurice, *Doctrine of Sacrifice*.

99. Sanday and Headlam, *Critical and Exegetical Commentary*, 94.

100. Ibid.

turned to the back of the Prayer Book must have seen the discrepancy with Article 2 ("to reconcile his Father to us") and Article 11 ("accounted righteous . . . only for the merit of our Lord and Saviour"). Doctrinally, Davies was no Reformation Evangelical.

Was his notion of justification by faith known to Archbishop Wright? Did Wright care? His own copy of Gore's *Romans* is held in the Moore College Library, marked in places, but without comment where Gore discusses "propitiation" and rejects a substitutionary atonement. In 1912, Wright had Davies preach three Lenten sermons from the Epistle to the Romans at the morning service of St Andrew's Cathedral Sydney.[101] Davies must have used the above material.

His three "Studies in Isaiah" at Holy Trinity Church on winter Wednesday evenings in January, 1908, were based on the popular commentary by the "modernizing" (his own term) Presbyterian, George Adam Smith (1856–1942).[102] This book, "more than any other, [gave] currency in English-speaking lands to the idea that the second section of Isaiah is the product of [Israel's] exile."[103] Critics who fragmented the prophecy presupposed the nineteenth-century rejection of predictive prophecy—an issue of a Christian theistic worldview. Davies never made any reference to the works of either James Orr or Abraham Kuyper, though published by well-known British firms not long before Davies enrolled for his degree.[104] Smith, a firm adherent of the notion of "progressive revelation" (chapter 2 above), believed that "the battle of modern criticism with the traditional theories of the Old Testament had been fought and won."[105]

In his series on Romans, Davies had said, "Luther was a very advanced higher critic in some respects" (a view highly contested recently),[106] adding that while today "the whole Bible is subjected to merciless and often capricious criticism," yet, "we must not fear knowledge that is knowledge indeed."[107] Davies accepted George Adam Smith's higher critical approach. Upholding the traditional Protestant "right of private judgment"[108] he announced that he would state what seemed to him "the salient points in the prophet's message and so . . . allow you to exercise your own judgment,"

---

101. Davies, "Preachers for the Month," 3.
102. Riesen, "Smith," 780–81.
103. Young, *Studies in Isaiah*, 37.
104. Orr, *Christian View*; Kuyper, *Encyclopedia of Sacred Theology*.
105. Smith, *Modern Criticism*, 73.
106. Godfrey, "Biblical Authority," 227–30.
107. Davies, "Studies in Romans," at "Prolegomena II."
108. Ryle, *Knots Untied*, 34–47.

for "each of us is ultimately responsible for his or her position in matters religious."[109]

Socio-Economic Matters

Davies's Liberal Evangelical outlook on the Bible and the atonement was in the background of his socio-economic views.

On March 3, 1910, he gave a paper, "Socialism and Society," to the Cambridge University Adam Smith Club. The first decade of the century had seen much industrial strife and the rise of the Labour Party in Britain. Davies not only had first-hand knowledge of industrial workers' districts from his own penurious youth; he had also studied economic history under William Cunningham, its pioneer. His basic early diagnosis of the social problem was *poverty*—physical, mental and moral—and the desirable Christian social goal was for this world to be a kingdom of righteousness. The means of achieving it was by the moral persuasion of "the corporate consciousness," not by the enlightened self-interest of classical economic theory.[110]

He was not uninterested in the spread of Christianity abroad. A century of Protestant missionary enterprise had climaxed with the great World Missionary Conference, held in the summer of 1910 in Edinburgh. On November 18, 1910, Davies addressed the Cambridge and District Clergy Union on "The Need of India." His mentor, William Cunningham, had visited India in 1881–1882 and recorded his observations on Christian missions there.[111]

In Emmanuel College 1905–1911

Davies joined "Emma" in 1905 as Director of Studies in History. He was also appointed a university lecturer in history, and was surely amongst the Society of Junior Historians when they had their first formal meeting in January, 1911.[112] At Emmanuel, a future Archbishop of Melbourne, Frederick Waldgrave Head, having a first class in the History Tripos (1896), a fellow of the college (1900), dean and tutor from 1903, was now senior tutor and was to become chaplain in 1907. Was it Davies who put Head's name forward

109. Davies, "Studies in Isaiah."
110. Davies, "Socialism and Society," which he published separately and in *ACQR*.
111. Cunningham, *William Cunningham*, 38, 48–49.
112. Brooke, *History of the University of Cambridge*, 235.

for archbishop to his Anglican Church League friends in Melbourne when Harrington Lees died in 1929?

Within Emmanuel College in 1909 occurred the "Chawner Affair." The master, William Chawner, read a paper to the first meeting of the Religious Discussion Society of the college, which he then published and distributed widely as *Prove All Things*. In this he rejected "external authority": "The canons of criticism require us to abandon as unhistorical . . . the Virgin Birth, the Resurrection and Ascension." Likewise, he protested against the "*a priori* reasoning" of the traditional natural theology used to deduce the existence of "the infinite."[113] Davies would apply these same themes in a paper to "The Heretics" (founded 1916) of Sydney, but within a theistic framework. He did not deny miracle in principle, though other Heretics did, and never denied the virgin birth of Christ or his resurrection. *Prove All Things* caused a group of twelve undergraduates led by C. K. Ogden (1889–1957), later a well-known philosopher-linguist,[114] to form the Cambridge Society of Heretics (known as "The Heretics") on December 7, 1909.[115]

Another Emma undergraduate at this time was Leonard Elliott Binns (BA first class part 1 Theology Tripos, 1911, second class part 2, 1912). H. M. Gwatkin "laid his mark on" Binns when Davies was teaching there. Binns proceeded to Ridley Hall (1912–1913) which by then was under Principal Tait, and became his vice-principal (1913–1915). "[A] convinced Evangelical, but . . . also Liberal,"[116] Binns (later L. E. Elliott-Binns) became a published historian of English theological thought.[117]

Both Binns's and Tait's positions at Ridley Hall—and that of J. W. Hunkin at Wycliffe Hall, Oxford—exhibit the influence of the liberal, broadened shift in the Evangelical spectrum: a shift of which Davies was a part. In 1922, liberal thought would disturb even the great flagship of Evangelicalism, the Church Missionary Society,[118] and result in the formation of the Bible Churchmen's Missionary Society. The presence of J. W. Hunkin and E. W. Barnes within the Group Brotherhood (self-named "Anglican Evangelical Group Movement" from 1923) shows that within Liberal Evangelicalism itself, there was no clear line drawn between the Anglican Evangelical Group Movement and the Modern Churchmen's Union.

113. Bendall, Brooke, and Collinson, *History of Emmanuel College*, 432; Chawner, *Prove All Things*, 14. See also Pollock, *Cambridge Movement*, 177.

114. Ogden and Richards, *Meaning of Meaning*.

115. McNeile, "Religious Situation," 11; Fiske, *Heretical Hellenism*, 1.

116. Binns, *Evangelical Movement*, ix.

117. Ibid.; Elliott-Binns, *Religion in the Victorian Era*; Elliott-Binns, *Development of English Theology*; Elliott-Binns, *English Thought 1860–1900*.

118. Binns, *Evangelical Movement*, 70.

On March 1, 1910, Davies was initiated at Isaac Newton Lodge, Cambridge,[119] of which William Cunningham was also a member; he would be very active as a Mason in Sydney. In 1911 he was made a fellow of the Royal Historical Society, Cunningham then being president. These things—his appointment at Emmanuel, his election to the Royal Historical Society, and his initiation into Isaac Newton Lodge—all indicate a close connection with Cunningham, whom he also assisted with some research.[120]

Liberal Evangelical Convictions Embraced

By the time Davies arrived at Moore College in 1911, his convictions represented the broadened spectrum of the Group Brotherhood of Liberal Evangelicals. They were different from those of Nathaniel Jones and such as Handley C. G. Moule, Robert Sinker, Henry Wace, and E. A. Litton. The influence of his training in history undoubtedly played a role: the conviction that history was a science, together with the approach of the Cambridge philosophers, theologians, and biblical scholars mentioned above. Like most others, he did not question the presuppositions underlying much of this intellectual milieu, and his beliefs were now "liberal Evangelical." This was in accord with what he himself and some other Evangelicals in the Church of England were coming to believe they could hold and defend with intellectual integrity. Like Davies, they might stop short of rejecting Christ's virgin birth and his resurrection, but they were willing in principle to question the reliability of Scripture both historically and doctrinally. Thus, on liberal critical assumptions, Davies (and the others in the group) adopted a different doctrine of Christ's atoning death and of justification.

Conclusion

Davies was part of the new liberal trend among some of the younger Evangelicals in the Church of England. Only later did the Group Brotherhood's leaders announce the "Anglican Evangelical Group Movement" and define the principles of their position.[121] It never had strict boundaries. Davies may have joined the Group Brotherhood with de Candole, his vicar, from its inception. He appears in a mid-1909 photograph of a Brotherhood gathering.

---

119. St. Clair and St. Clair, "V. Wor. Bro. Ven. Archdeacon David John Davies," 10.
120. Davies, Answer to Question 9.
121. "Introduction," *Liberal Evangelicalism*, v–viii.

John Charles Wright, their first chairman, is there, and was already the archbishop-elect of Sydney.[122]

As Archbishop of Sydney, Wright quite deliberately called two early fellow Group Brothers to join him. One was Davies—to be principal of Moore College (1911), the other Edward Albert Talbot—to be dean of St Andrew's Cathedral (1912). Together they self-consciously brought to Sydney—its diocese, theological college, and cathedral—the outlook of the liberal broadening of the Evangelical spectrum within the Church of England occurring back in the mother-country.

122. Davies, "Our Late Archbishop," 8–10.

8

Liberal Evangelicalism Stated and Applied

IN MAY 1909, THE Reverend Canon Francis Bertie Boyce, a mover for social reform, succeeded in his campaign to persuade the Sydney synod to elect John Charles Wright as Archbishop of Sydney. In England, Wright had been the first chairman of the new Group Brotherhood in 1907, which had a "concern for pressing social and theological issues."[1] He took up office in November 1909, and with the passing of Nathaniel Jones in June 1911 he sought a principal who would share the outlook of the Group Brotherhood: an outlook they would later call "Liberal Evangelicalism."[2]

Wright's commissaries in England and the well-known Evangelical, Francis James Chavasse, recommended Davies. Chavasse, formerly principal of Wycliffe Hall, Oxford, had succeeded J. C. Ryle as Bishop of Liverpool. The difference of intellectual principle in the Group Brotherhood's broadening was not yet widely perceived, to judge by the theological mix of contributors to *Anglican Church Handbooks*, edited by W. H. Griffith Thomas.[3] Wright had met Davies at Group Brotherhood meetings and, presumably, before that in connection with the Elland Society's granting of assistance for his study at Cambridge.[4] Davies, now thirty-two, had just married Grace Augusta Lawe, a cousin of his vicar, H. L. C. V. ("Corrie") de

---

1. Judd and Cable, *Sydney Anglicans*, 160, 172n1.

2. See chapter 2 above.

3. Thomas, *Anglican Church Handbooks* (included works by C. F. d'Arcy, Guy Warman, and R. B. Girdlestone).

4. Davies, "Our Late Archbishop," 8–10, (included a photo identifying most in it, titled "'The Brothers'—Conference of Evangelical Clergy at St Aidan's College, Birkenhead, 15th, 16th, 17th July, 1909.") For the Elland Society see Balleine, *History of the Evangelical Party*, 64.

Candole. On November 11, 1911, their ship, the new *S. S. Aeneas*,[5] docked briefly in Melbourne. There Davies joined a garden party celebrating the first anniversary of Ridley College, founded to be the Evangelical institution for the training of Anglican ministers in Victoria.[6] The principal, George Ellis Aickin (1869–1937) was a fellow Liberal Evangelical. He had previously been teaching at St Aidan's College, Birkenhead, under A. C. Tait as principal.[7] David and Grace Davies arrived in Sydney five days later.[8]

Davies was to find significant intellectual company in Sydney. The Challis Professor of History at Sydney University was George Arnold Wood, Manchester (BA 1885) then Oxford-educated (BA 1888, MA 1890), "a reluctant agnostic."[9] Davies soon became Lecturer in History and Economics for the Extension Board of the university. At the Anglican St Paul's College, within the university and next door to Moore College, the warden was the scholarly Dr. Lewis Bostock Radford (1868–1937), a graduate of Cambridge, but not an Evangelical. He was founder-editor of the new *Australasian Church Quarterly Review* (1910), to which Davies was to contribute generously. Davies would preach at Radford's consecration as Bishop of Goulburn in 1915.[10] Arthur Garnsey MA (Sydney, Classics), "a liberal churchman of Catholic background,"[11] succeeded Radford at St Paul's College in 1916. Davies and Garnsey became friends and Davies was made a Fellow of St Paul's. In July 1912, Arthur Edward Talbot (1877–1936), fellow Cantabrian and member of the Group Brotherhood, arrived to be Dean of St Andrew's Cathedral. The Reverend H. N. Baker MA (Sydney, Philosophy)—earned under the idealist Francis Anderson, Challis Professor of Philosophy from 1890 to 1921—would be associated with Davies in work on "the social problem." Anderson's idealism was sympathetic with "a doctrinally deliquescent Christianity."[12] Davies probably found Baker's views supportive on economics and socialism, and on personal realization.[13]

Davies would have found a different affinity with the more conservative and Evangelical clergy of an intellectual cast of mind. In June 1912 Archbishop Wright appointed the Irishman, Dr. Everard Digges La Touche

---

5. Sunk in convoy by German bombers in July 1940.
6. *The Argus*, November 13, 1911, 11.
7. Cole, Keith, "Aickin," 2; Adam and Denholm, *Ridley College*, 23.
8. *SDM* 2, no. 9 (1911) 9; *SDM* 2, no. 12 (1911) 15.
9. Crawford, "Wood, George Arnold," 556–58.
10. Davies, *Pastoral Ideal*.
11. Garnsey, *Arthur Garnsey*, 72.
12. See Grave, *History*, 25.
13. Ibid., 20–21.

MA, LittD (TCD)[14] as Diocesan Missioner. He had been serving in a rural New South Wales diocese for a few months. Digges La Touche (1883–1915) had been converted from agnosticism when an undergraduate, through T. C. Hammond. Only recently he had given the prestigious Donnellan lectures,[15] and Davies used him at Moore College to teach the subject, Dogmatic Theology. Much older was the redoubtable Canon Mervyn Archdall (b. 1846), a friend of Nathaniel Jones and now rector of the then rural parish of Penrith. He would retire in 1913 and move back to suburban Sydney, where he became available to younger Sydney clergy who wished to consult him.[16] The scholarly Samuel M. Johnstone—an exact contemporary of Davies and a graduate of both TCD (1909) and Queen's College, Belfast (1915)—had "a philosophic turn of mind and a strong sense of historical values,"[17] and was the new rector of the important parish of Parramatta.

Davies found some affinity with Presbyterian, Congregational, and Methodist teachers of theology in Sydney—all liberal, or modernist. He became secretary of the Joint Board of Theological Studies that they set up in 1915. The Presbyterian Scots-Irishman, Samuel Angus (1881–1943), "essentially a Christian Unitarian in his theology,"[18] had arrived in that same year to be the professor of New Testament exegesis in the theological hall in St Andrew's College, like St Paul's, a college within the University of Sydney.[19] At his suggestion, in 1916 they formed a private dining club of ten members, "The Heretics," each of whom once a year must present a paper of mutual interest and intellectual stimulation.[20] Perhaps Davies suggested the name, remembering the society called "The Heretics" set up in Cambridge in 1910, which rejected "all appeal to authority in the discussion of religious questions."[21]

The new principal of Moore College was very active on a broad front outside the classroom and chapel. His Evangelical biblicism *cum* activism found expression in his being, for many years, part of the governance and advocacy of the work of the British and Foreign Bible Society in Australia.

---

14. TCD awarded the LittD to Digges La Touche for his *Christian Certitude*.
15. Digges La Touche, *Person of Christ*.
16. Archdall, *Mervyn Archdall*.
17. Loane, *Mark These Men*, 42, 43.
18. Ellis-Jones, "Relevance of Dr. Samuel Angus," 1; Dougan, *Backward Glance*, 12–14; Parer, *Australia's Last Heresy Hunt*, 24–25.
19. Dougan, *Backward Glance*, 7–8.
20. Ibid., 23; Cable, "First and Second Book of Chronicles," 2–3.
21. See chapter 7 above for the Chawner affair at Emmanuel College.

He was also twice elected President of the New South Wales Council of Churches (1931–1933).[22]

Davies pursued actively his Freemasonic membership initiated in Cambridge. He was a foundation member of three lodges: the Sydney Lodge of Research (1914) to whose journal he often contributed;[23] Lodge Enmore (Enmore being a suburb near the college); and Lodge University of Sydney, becoming its chaplain in 1924.[24] Fellow Freemasons included his second vice-principal,[25] G. C. Glanville (a Nathaniel Jones graduate), and W. G. Hilliard (former high school language teacher, self-read in theology, a parish clergyman who was also involved in the instruction of the college students and was later a bishop). Later, Freemasons included at least two clerical members of the college committee[26]—S. M. Johnstone and H. G. J. Howe. A number of prominent conservative Evangelical clergy in the Diocese of Sydney were lodge members,[27] not to mention laymen.

In the latter half of 1913, Davies participated in the series of Sydney diocesan parochial conferences. His paper at one of these (recounted below) resulted in a permanent break with those in a more conservative part of the Evangelical spectrum. Being a member of the Sydney Diocesan Social Problem Committee set up in 1913, he lectured and published papers touching on the problem (defined essentially as poverty), its causes, effects, and remedy. He made it the subject of his Moorhouse Lectures,[28] delivered at the height of the Great War in 1917. He published them as *The Church and the Plain Man*,[29] his one book, for which he was awarded the coveted Cambridge Bachelor of Divinity degree in 1920.[30] He was active in the discussions of the Anglican General Synod committee for a national constitution, and that on Prayer Book revision. He published thoughtful and well-informed articles on these two matters in the *Sydney Diocesan Magazine*[31] (an initiative of Archbishop Wright) and in *The Australian Church Record*. The latter was

---

22. Not the later Council of Churches in New South Wales, which is linked with the World Council of Churches.

23. *Transactions of the Sydney Lodge of Research* (*TSLR*), most volumes from 3 (1916) to 19 (1932).

24. St Clair, "V. Wor, Bro.," 10–11.

25. Loane, *Centenary History*, 119.

26. The committee was set up in late 1919. See below in this chapter.

27. West, *Innings of Grace*, 64.

28. In memory of Bishop James Moorhouse (1826–1915), Bishop of Melbourne, 1876–1886.

29. Davies, *Church and the Plain Man*.

30. A published work of quality being the basis for the degree.

31. See under Abbreviations: *SDM*.

essentially the voice of the Anglican Church League in both Sydney and Melbourne, representing those opposed to Anglo-Catholic doctrinal and, especially, ritualist pressure. In view of Anglo-Catholic plans to celebrate the centenary of Keble's historic Assize sermon of July 1833,[32] in June 1933 Davies was guest of the Anglican Church League in Melbourne for a special lecture on the Thirty-nine Articles.[33]

Davies's First Moore College Period: Christian Scholar, Social Thinker, and Freemason

Davies began in January 1912. There were twenty-three students, many from the last year of Jones (the college still followed the northern hemisphere academic year). Throughout all of 1911, Moore College had been effectively under the acting principal and admirer of Jones, the able Sydney J. Kirkby. By the academic year 1913–1914 Davies could rejoice in a distinguished and inclusive group of teachers at the college, even if most were part-time. They included J. V. Patton (vice-principal), Kirkby (tutor, now BA, Durham), Dean Talbot, Dr. E. Digges La Touche and H. N. Baker (rector of a parish) as visiting lecturers. Digges La Touche, now openly disagreeing with Davies, finished at the end of 1914, and Kirkby resigned to become the rector of the parish of St Anne's, Ryde. Davies seems to have lectured on doctrine after Digges La Touche left, as well as on church history, and at least when Marcus Loane was a student in the early 1930s, also on the Greek text of John's gospel. He gave the sermon in the daily college morning chapel services.

The new principal immediately introduced significant changes. He enrolled the students automatically in the Student Christian Movement and in the Church of England Men's Society of New South Wales, which he formed in 1912. To raise the academic standing of the college, he required first-year students to study for the university matriculation and second-year students "to attend at least one course of lectures at the university."[34] The curriculum of the college now changed from the Preliminary Theological Examination to that of the Licentiate of Theology (ThL) of the Australian College of Theology. In 1916 this body elected him a fellow (ThSoc), its equivalent of an honorary doctorate. In the later 1920s, presumably on Davies's recommendation, the *Manual of the Australian College of Theology* put the much reprinted work of the American evangelical liberal Baptist, W. N. Clarke

32. Keble, "National Apostasy," 129–48.
33. Examined in chapter 9 below.
34. Loane, *Centenary History*, 114.

(1841–1912), *An Outline of Christian Theology*, in the "List of Suggested Books" for ThL under "Doctrine." Multiple copies of Clarke's book, each one numbered, were kept at Moore College in the care of the vice-principal for the use of students.[35]

Davies's published *oeuvre* for this roughly twenty-year period was wide-ranging. Apart from *The Church and the Plain Man*, and besides his published lectures on socio-economic issues, he wrote a number of contributions to the new journal edited by Dr. Radford, and to the journal of the Sydney Lodge of Research,[36] reviews for the *Sydney Diocesan Magazine* and many pieces for Australian Anglican church newspapers. Unpublished materials include (not examined in this study): a number of fully written-out lectures for his Sydney University Extension Board teaching of history and economics; full lectures on the personalities and ministry—though not their doctrines—of some early Evangelical leaders; lectures on Scripture; some Bible exposition; a fully written-out sermon; and many sermon outlines. Some of the papers he gave at meetings of The Heretics are also extant.

Early Statements of Davies's View of Holy Scripture

All Davies's statements on Scripture reveal his liberal outlook, and his view of Holy Scripture soon became an issue in Sydney. It was already apparent in September 1912, in his review of fellow Cantabrian E. C. Dewick's 1908 Hulsean Prize Essay on New Testament eschatology.[37] Dewick, a graduate of St John's College, had passed through Ridley Hall under Principal T. W. Drury in 1905–1906, the year following Davies's study there. Dewick himself claimed orthodoxy, that is, to hold the catholic doctrine of the person of Christ.[38] He was in principle liberal in his view of Scripture, including the gospels.[39] Like Davies, Dewick bore out what J. K. Mozley, then part of the Group Movement,[40] had recently observed of W. R. Inge and F. C. Burkitt: "the combination of even the most advanced cases of criticism with at least an appearance of strenuous orthodoxy is no impossibility."[41] Dewick, of course, was not as advanced a critic as Mozley's examples.

35. See Moore College Library catalogue, under "Clarke, William Newton."
36. *ACQR* and *TSLR*.
37. Dewick, *Primitive Christian Eschatology*. Davies, "Review of *Primitive Christian Eschatology*," 372–76.
38. Dewick, *Primitive Christian Eschatology*, 377.
39. Ibid., 179.
40. Davies, "Our Late Archbishop," 15.
41. Mozley, "Religious Life," 28.

Dewick completely ignored the premillennial eschatology already held widely in his day by Evangelicals, some of scholarly caliber. He referred only to the liberal discussion. He even stated that "during the latter part of the nineteenth century, the Doctrine of the Last Things seemed to be receding into the background of Christian teaching."[42] Davies was glad, of course, that the author had countered the damage to Christianity from the "Consistent Eschatologist," Albert Schweitzer, and the Roman Catholic modernist, Father George Tyrrell.[43] Dewick had "clearly shown" that Albert Schweitzer and others' view that Christ "expected an immediate and catastrophic end of all things," simply "[did] not fit the facts of the case."[44] But Davies marked without demurral in his review copy Dewick's view that Jesus claimed authority (e.g., in Matt 5:21, 22, 28, 32, 44, "but I say to you")[45] to "alter" the "teaching of the Old Testament where necessary." On the other hand, he praised Dewick's presentation of Christ's eschatological teaching in the gospels that "at its basis [was] a sublime optimism, a perfect faith in the final victory of good over evil." Such was "substantially the witness of the Gospel records."[46]

Digges La Touche had devoted more than fifty pages of his Donnellan lectures to the "consistent eschatologists" such as Schweitzer and the Roman Catholic modernists.[47] He must have had his own thoughts when he saw Davies's review in September 1912.

Relations were initially positive between Digges La Touche and the principal. Davies had invited his new lecturer in doctrine to speak at the beginning of the new academic year of 1912-1913. He wrote that Digges La Touche had given "helpful and outspoken messages at the opening services of the term" (Michaelmas, 1912). "The discussion on 'Inspiration' . . . had aroused keen interest."[48] Towards the end of the academic year, on May 22, 1913, the British Admiral Sir George King-Hall, Commander of the Royal Navy's Australia Station, had chaired the annual Moore College Commemoration. Digges La Touche was present and surely must have noticed how Dean Talbot and Principal Davies were "rather taken aback" when the admiral "spoke very strongly on the accuracy of the Bible and held forth

---

42. Dewick, *Primitive Christian Eschatology*, 1.

43. Schweitzer, *Quest of the Historical Jesus*; Tyrrell, *Christianity at the Crossroads*. See "Tyrrell, George," in *ODCC*, 1661-62 and Vidler, *Variety of Catholic Modernists*, 109-33.

44. Davies, "Review of *Primitive Christian Eschatology*," 375.

45. Dewick, *Primitive Christian Eschatology*, 138.

46. Davies, "Review of *Primitive Christian Eschatology*," 374.

47. Digges La Touche, *Person of Christ*, 151-205.

48. Davies, "Moore College Notes," *SDM* 4, no. 7 (1913) 21.

... showing how ignorant" were some of the "so-called Higher Critics." The students applauded the admiral "very much."[49]

In the latter half of 1913, out of concern about "the present intellectual atmosphere," a committee under Everard Digges La Touche organized the above-mentioned series of parochial conferences. The intention was to entirely change the intellectual atmosphere of Sydney from the present unfaith to that of rational conviction and belief in the Lord Jesus Christ.[50]

Held at St Andrew's Church, Summer Hill, the theme of the second conference was "Progressive Revelation." On the evening of August 7, 1913, Davies read his paper, "The Certainty of Christ," while on the following evening, Canon Mervyn Archdall and S. M. Johnstone read their papers, "The Authority of Christ," and "The Authority of the Bible."[51]

The background to Davies's treatment of the topic and its choice was most likely the recent volume *Foundations*,[52] particularly B. H. Streeter's view that at least with regard to Christ's teaching, there was "a strong presumption in favour of the substantial reliability of the general impression given by [Matthew, Mark, and Luke] of the life and teaching of our Lord."[53]

Davies's paper appears to have moved Digges La Touche and others listening to ask him how the authority of Christ's teaching was regarded in Moore College. Near the beginning of his manuscript, Davies distinguished "the aim of modern constructive criticism" from "the destructive sort." Defining neither, he had defended the former as "necessary," seeking to understand and not to destroy. He noted that "an increasing number of men of learning . . . are criticising the Church, the Bible, our Lord Himself, in a spirit of reverent yet searching inquiry."

Davies, "[trying] to put a few facts" before his audience, went on to affirm that Scripture "is the documentary evidence" of both the "history and human experience" that attest "the fact of progressive revelation" (undefined) and "contains the substance of God's message to man."[54]

Warning bells may have been ringing in the ears of Digges La Touche, Mervyn Archdall and S. M. Johnstone at this point as they listened. Davies had not defined his term "progressive revelation," and had said only that Scripture "contains" the "substance" of God's message to man. More positively, he then referred to the multitude "whose lives have been shaped

---

49. King-Hall, Diaries, May 22, 1913, September 12, 1913.
50. *SDM* 5, no. 9 (1913) 19, 22.
51. Ibid., 20. Archdall and Johnstone's papers not located.
52. Streeter, "Historic Christ," 83.
53. Ibid., 83–84.
54. Davies, "Certainty of Christ."

and transformed and renewed and glorified by what the Bible has taught them."[55]

Digges La Touche may have been somewhat reassured by Davies's use of "the experimental proof," which he himself used,[56] when Davies said: "The Christian faith . . . is the religion of a Person." That person "is, not was, Christ." He is "our God, my God . . . a part of my own life, He has entered into my experience."[57] In this, Davies brought in the idealist theme of personality, emphasized by the philosopher T. H. Green and more lately by William Temple,[58] as well as by Illingworth.[59] Davies claimed that the highest revelation of God was not in nature, history, or the Bible, but in personality. Our certainty was to be found in the "Personality of Christ."[60]

Evangelicals present at this conference such as S. J. Kirkby, Mervyn Archdall, S. M. Johnstone and Everard Digges La Touche were also Christ-centered Evangelicals,[61] but they made no such dichotomy between the revelation of God in the person of Christ and the revelation of Christ as recorded in Holy Scripture. Reassuring, on the other hand, was Davies's affirmation of Christ's deity: "Christ is the perfect revelation of God to men, because He was himself both."

The remainder of Davies's paper, "The Certainty of Christ," defended the "historic Christ" against any skeptics present. He was sure, as a historian trained in and "using the recognised methods of historical science," that Christ lived and died and rose again. And the oral tradition preserved in the gospels, said Davies, "is reasonably unchanged and consistent." The "documentary sources, especially the gospels" were "very soon written down from the reports of eyewitnesses and hearers and in some cases by the eyewitnesses themselves." He added his own testimony: that he "tries to be a scientific historian" and had "for years carefully studied the documents of the New Testament" and found them to be first-class historical authorities; out of their "agreements we can construct the portrait of a Personality such as Christ claimed to be and such as Christians have believed Him to be." He was "a Personality, such as no human genius could invent . . . who stands out unique in history." Davies's certainty of Christ was "attested by a cumulative

55. Cf. Orr, *Problem of the Old Testament*, 467–78.

56. Digges La Touche, *Christian Certitude*, 288–92; Digges La Touche, *Is Christianity Scientific?*, 19–20.

57. Davies, "Certainty of Christ."

58. Temple, *Nature of Personality*.

59. See chapter 7 above.

60. Davies, "Certainty of Christ."

61. Loane, interview, 2004; Archdall, Mervyn, "Hymns," 1–3 and 8–12, in Archdall, Henry, *Archdall*, 126–28, 133–37.

probability."62 This was the traditional apologetic stemming from Butler's *Analogy of Religion*.

Davies was aware of the role of naturalistic assumptions in the negative higher criticism with regard to the miracles, the virgin birth and the resurrection.63 Digges La Touche's own writing was explicit as to the role of the broadly Hegelian presuppositions underlying the *negative* assessment of the gospel data.64 A liberal approach to Scripture, albeit in Davies's case not radical, would meet with a resistance that entailed the election of a conservative Archbishop of Sydney two decades later.

Davies, Digges La Touche, and others had already been in discussion on the matter of the gospels' witness to Christ. Shortly after the conference of early August 1913, E. H. B. Claydon, the Rector of St Luke's, Concord and Burwood, wrote to remind Davies and the other members of "our Evangelical Group"65—that they were to meet at Moore College on the first of September.66 He referred to "the Cambridge Statement" (which this writer could not trace). This may have been connected with a recent letter of the examining chaplains residing at Cambridge to the Archbishop of Canterbury, on the question in the Book of Common Prayer at the ordination of Deacons: "Do you unfeignedly believe all the Canonical Scriptures of the Old and New Testaments?" The *Cambridge Magazine* even included letters on the issue from Bertrand Russell!67

Whatever "the Cambridge Statement" was, at its coming meeting, the "Group" would discuss "Digges La Touche's proposed amendment" to their "Cl. 2 Sect. II." It included a strong statement: "THE DEFINITIVE AND AUTHORITATIVE RECORD OF [CHRIST'S] INERRANT TEACHING IS PRESERVED FOR US IN THE SACRED SCRIPTURES OF THE OLD AND NEW COVENANTS."68 On September 12, 1913 Claydon sent Davies a revised form of Davies's own previous amendment, to be considered in October:

> While the mind and will of God have been, and are revealed through individual experience as also in history and nature, they are made known to us chiefly in Holy Scripture, which is

---

62. Davies, "Certainty of Christ." See also Digges La Touche, *Christian Certitude*, 269–92.
63. See chapter 9 below on his Heretics Club paper, "Modern Scholastics."
64. See Digges La Touche, *Christian Certitude*, 293–300.
65. Had Davies initiated a Sydney "Group Brotherhood"?
66. Claydon, Letter August 25, 1913.
67. Reported in "Cambridge Notes," *Comment and Criticism*, 1:87.
68. Claydon, Letter August 25, 1913 (upper case typescript original).

the authoritative record of the final Self-revelation of God in the Person and Work of our Lord Jesus Christ, the absolutely inerrant Teacher. The presence of this divine element in Holy Scripture gives to it final authority in all matters of religious belief and conduct.[69]

This limited the absence of error in Scripture to Christ's teaching (as far as that could be established), but did not make Holy Scripture the basis for interpreting the other source of revelation, namely that of nature.

There is no documentary record of further "Evangelical Group" meetings in the Davies papers. Several key Evangelicals (members of the "Group"?) wrote to Davies to seek assurance about his teaching at the college. In May 1914 Mervyn Archdall, E. Digges La Touche, J. Young, H. S. Begbie, S. M. Johnstone, and S. E. Langford Smith met with Davies at Moore College in response to his invitation. They had let him know of three "leading questions which the brethren intend[ed] to ask":

> First, did he believe that Christ, being God and man, was absolutely inerrant, before and after his resurrection, when he spoke on any subject? Secondly, did he believe that the Bible, Old and New Testaments, was so inspired of God as to be truthful and finally authoritative for the knowledge of God's will and for saving faith in Christ? Thirdly, did he believe that the Holy Scriptures, as interpreted by the Holy Spirit in the believer and in the Church are the absolute and final authority in matters of faith and practice?[70]

Davies wrote out his response in full on Moore College letterhead: "Memoranda, Disputation of brethren, May 21/14" and summarized it in penciled notes done that morning. First, he would assure them, "If it can be proved from Scripture that our Lord made a definite statement to a certain effect that statement would be accepted as final." Secondly, with regard to the "attitude towards Holy Scripture," he simply noted "Article VI" (Thirty-nine Articles, "On the Sufficiency of Holy Scripture"). Thirdly, as to the authority of the Scriptures, they, "as interpreted by the Holy Spirit in the believer and in the Church, constituted the supreme authority in matters of faith and practice."[71]

Davies's "Memoranda" begged the question: on what critical assumptions might something be "proved"? Moreover, what would the meaning of

---

69. Claydon, Letter, September 12, 1913.
70. Smith, S. E. Langford, Letter to Davies, May 18, 1914.
71. Davies, "Memoranda."

"as interpreted by the Holy Spirit" be? Later in 1914, at an Anglican Church League function at St Andrew's Church, Summer Hill, Digges La Touche publicly expressed concern about the principal's doctrine of Scripture.[72] The next year, against Archbishop Wright's express wish, Digges La Touche left with the Anzacs in 1915 as a sublieutenant and was killed not long after he landed at Gallipoli.

A Protestant in Churchmanship

Davies's basic Protestant stance was quite apparent. He reviewed very favorably the new Evangelical work, *The Tutorial Prayer Book*.[73] Its individual contributors included some well-known scholarly Evangelicals, including F. S. Guy Warman, later prominent amongst Liberal Evangelicals. The text was still used in Moore College half a century later. Davies thought well of Sydney Carter's contribution on the Reformation in the *Anglican Church Handbooks* series,[74] and of G. R. Balleine's pioneer history of the Evangelical party.[75] He continued to contribute to church newspapers on the constitutional "nexus" between the Church of England in Australia and the parent body in England, and on the rising assertiveness of Anglo-Catholicism. His opposition to Anglo-Catholic ritualism must have eased the tension between him and the conservative Evangelicals in the Diocese.

Davies also contributed to the *Australian Church Record* (*ACR*), which was virtually the organ of the anti-ritualist Anglican Church League (ACL), of which he became a vice-president. His contributions in other Australian Anglican papers such as the more High Church and Anglo-Catholic leaning *The Church Standard* elucidate his Protestant outlook.

Two early articles on Puritanism in *The Australasian Church Quarterly Review*, while not uncritical of the movement, rebutted the prejudice of both the influential Anglo-Catholic writer, W. H. Frere, and the conservative High Church historian, W. H. Hutton.[76] A more distinctly Evangelical article followed, describing the spiritual-moral deadness of eighteenth-century England and the great benefits of the revival under the Wesleys.[77]

---

72. Personal interview with Donald Robinson, February 3, 2005, recounting his father, R. B. Robinson's memory of the event.

73. Davies, "Review of *The Tutorial Prayer Book*," 27–28.

74. Davies, "Review of Carter," 24–26.

75. Balleine, *History of the Evangelical Party*.

76. Davies, "Some Historical Aspects," 242–58, 324–36, referencing Frere, *English Church in the Reigns* and Hutton, *English Church from the Accession*.

77. Davies, "English Church," 217–33.

Statements such as these give some idea of the Protestant tone of his church history teaching in Moore College.

Continuing Statements on Scripture

From 1916, Davies contributed to the journal of the Sydney Lodge of Research.[78] Two lectures on Scripture (called the "Volume of the Sacred Law" or V.S.L. in Freemasonry) clarify the nature of Davies's Liberal Evangelical biblicism. He confined himself to the Old Testament, for Freemasonry included all theists, and thus Jews, within its potential membership.

His very first lecture set out "The Literary History of the V.S.L.,"[79] "one of the greater lights of Masonry."[80] His approach was that of the inductive, would-be neutral historian: examine "the actual text" in order that "it tell its own story" rather than "fit it into preconceived ideas."[81] He explained that much of the "enormous accumulation of materials" discovered in modern times had "brought positive gains" while necessitating the giving up of "certain traditional ideas."[82] He defended "Higher Criticism" as "merely the attempt to determine the date, authorship, meaning and purpose of a book . . . where no external evidence is available."[83] On the historical side, it "tries to value the contribution" to history of the biblical books' narratives of events, or "by their valuation as indicating processes of development either in progress or decay."[84] As before, he did not raise the question of the choice of prior assumptions which a historian might use in higher criticism.

Davies emphasized that "the one purpose of the V.S.L. is a *religious* purpose, to serve as the record of revealed truth—the record of the Most High making Himself known to men."[85] He also set forth a notion of progressive revelation in the V.S.L.: "the picture of progress on the whole," that is, of "moral development from a lower to a higher stage," as in the "vast step between the atmosphere of Judges and that of Isaiah 53, or even of Ezekiel."[86] His conception of progressive revelation was still not clearly

78. *Transactions of the Sydney Lodge of Research* (1914–1956).

79. Davies, "Literary History," 5–21.

80. Ibid., 5. The three greater lights of Freemasonry are the V.S.L., the square, and the compass (geometrical instruments).

81. Ibid., 6.

82. Ibid., 13.

83. Ibid., 16.

84. Ibid., 17.

85. Ibid., 18.

86. Ibid., 19.

spelled out. He also reassured his audience of the V.S.L.'s "exceeding great riches as literature, as a repository of moral guidance, and as the inspiration of all true progress."[87]

Davies's Social Thought and Publications

Even as the first Labor government in New South Wales was elected in 1910, similar developments in society to those in Britain were also occurring in Australia. The new premier was J. S. T. McGowen, an Evangelical layman[88] very active in the inner-suburban parish of Redfern, where Francis Bertie Boyce, a clerical social-reform campaigner, was rector.

During the Sydney Diocesan Synod of 1912 (September 30 to October 4), but incidental to it, Archbishop Wright had presided over a "Conference of Churchmen" which "discussed at length," *inter alia*, "the growth of socialism, the estrangement of the masses from the Church, the unequal distribution of wealth, and the various panaceas for the industrial evils."[89] Davies was among those presenting papers, his being on "the stages of the social system." He became one of the ten members of the Social Problem Committee then set up; its purpose was "to educate a 'Church conscience' on the subject, to secure an enlightened Christian opinion," promote industrial peace and "a recognition of the truths of Christianity" among "the masses."[90] Early in the next year, 1913, Davies read an adapted version of his Cambridge paper, "Socialism and Society" to the Junior Clerical Society of Sydney.[91] A series of seven evening lectures in the Chapter House of St Andrew's Cathedral commenced with Davies on "the historical facts of the development of capitalism (29 July, 1913)."[92] As noted above, he published a number of related articles and gave public lectures.[93]

---

87. Ibid.
88. Linder, "'Honest Jim' McGowen," 44–59; Linder, "McGowen," 234–35; Nairn, "McGowen," 273–74.
89. Davies, "Social Question," 21.
90. Ibid., 21–22.
91. Davies, *Socialism and Society*, also published in *ACQR*, "Socialism and Society," 304–21.
92. Davies, "Social Problem Committee," 7–8.
93. Davies, *Labour Problem, Wages System,* and other titles.

The Moorhouse Lectures of 1917

In 1917 Davies spelled out most fully his own socio-theological position in his Moorhouse Lectures, published after the Great War as *The Church and the Plain Man*—essentially an essay in practical theology. All the themes of the Chapter House meeting during the 1912 synod appear. He sought, in principle, a remedy for the social problem in Australia, broadly considered. Perhaps through his Cambridge mentor William Cunningham, T. H. Green's idea that "I cannot realise good for myself without promoting the good of others in some degree," underlay Davies's whole appeal to cooperation, to which selfishness and competition were both opposed.[94]

In Lecture 1 "Things as They Are," among the "broad facts" that Davies saw as giving shape to the problem for the churches was a prevailing indifference to "organized religion."[95] He analyzed the causes—a wide range of factors, including the materialism that bred selfishness and the antisocial effects of city life. He praised positive evangelical social achievements but criticized the "mistake of exclusive pietism" (undefined) and the failure of both liberal and sacerdotal presentations of Christianity. In short, human-centered selfishness had led to religion being "centred in man rather than in God."[96]

The modern prevalence of "Organized Selfishness" (Lecture 3) had originated in the Industrial Revolution, and had led to the dominance of the economic interest in politics. "Organized selfishness was not concerned with spiritual interests." There had been material progress, but (Lecture 2) relative poverty had increased. The Great War had exemplified the outcome of the principle of mammon, which was organized selfishness.[97] In Lecture 4 "The Progress of Labour" Davies's expertise in economic history explained the origins of trade unionism, the wider movement of socialism, and the still wider then topical movement called syndicalism.[98] All three, whatever their positive achievements, manifested organized selfishness. Labour had a religious aspect: it was a sacred cause and gave scope for personal expression. Here was the church's opportunity to proclaim the life most worth living in the gospel of Jesus Christ and the kingdom of heaven, here and now, as the ideal state of society. Those who refused to enter it were mak-

---

94. Sidgwick, *Lectures on the Ethics of T. H. Green*, 56–57. See Audrey Cunningham, *William Cunningham*, 57.

95. Davies, *Church and the Plain Man*, 1–33.

96. Ibid., 34–109.

97. Ibid., 110–51.

98. Syndicalism was an early twentieth-century movement to have the trades unions control the means of production.

ing "the Great Refusal." The way into it was "the Great Surrender" to the power of the cross.[99] Such was Davies's Liberal Evangelical crucicentrism and conversionism.

Lecture 5, "A Study in Personality. The Plain Man in His Environment,"[100] rejected both the "rationalist" statement that people were outgrowing religion and the "obscurantist" view that the world could not be won for Christ, so just "sit and wait for the consummation." Such an obscurantist view, of course, was not what Nathaniel Jones had taught.

Davies analyzed six aspects of the plain man's environment. "1. The Plain Man's Education": the state school system dominated by "the secular" interest had several benefits but depreciated religious factors. Economic interest dominated its successful human products.[101] "2. The Plain Man's Home Life": modern industrialism disintegrated "family solidarity." The atmosphere of dominant self-interest tended also to "the secularization of marriage."[102] In "3. External Social Intercourse" self-interest led often to indulgence in the "grosser vices," as well as to "respectable self-indulgence."[103] "4. Fundamental Difficulties" lying between the plain man and the church were his personal moral deficiencies and his intellectual-moral environment.[104] "5. What the Plain Man Responds To" were "visible success" and "the personal touch" (a point of personal idealism),[105] which are a guide to "6. What the Plain Man Wants [i.e., lacks]": this included a "moral lever," namely, Christ's cross.[106] His "wants" were the very things that the church could provide.

The last two lectures, "6. The Strength of the Church. The Available Resources"[107] and "7. Moving Forward"[108] spelled out Davies's convictions about the church's message, the men and machinery, and his proposals for reaching the plain man. These were, in effect, his manifesto for his labors as principal of the college, his work on the Sydney diocesan Social Problem

---

99. Davies, *Church and the Plain Man*, 152–95.
100. Ibid., 196–228.
101. Ibid., 198–205.
102. Ibid., 205–13.
103. Ibid., 213–16.
104. Ibid., 216–25.
105. Ibid., 225–26.
106. The liberal view of the atonement as exemplary only, not as objective accomplishment first of all.
107. Davies, *Church and the Plain Man*, 229–76.
108. Ibid., 277–324.

Committee, indirectly for his Masonic lodge activity, and his involvement in the Australian branch of the British and Foreign Bible Society.

As for the church's message, it was dependent on the Bible, the church being the "'witness and keeper of Holy Writ'[109] and not its creator." But Davies makes no statement at all regarding what the message is, namely, its content. Instead, he provides seventeen pages of a position statement on the Bible and its impact.[110] This biblicism was explicitly Christo-centric: "Jesus Christ . . . is the final authority behind both Bible and church." Davies's overall very positive example of liberal statement made a number of important points and gave an impression of a high, fairly conservative, appreciation of the Bible. He explicitly aimed to exclude not only the "obscurantist" approach and the "irresponsible" liberal criticism of Scripture, but also the Anglo-Catholic placing of the church's authority above it.

In principle, however, his position had not changed since the clash with Everard Digges La Touche and the others in 1913–1914. He would speak of the authority of Scripture as the documentary record of God's self-revelation; the Bible "contained" "the substance of [the Church's] message," without which "the Church has to rest on the shifting sands of uncertain tradition."[111] Davies was a historian to the core: "No documents, no history, is the modern position."[112] But he completely overlooks the effect of naturalistic *a priori* assumptions on assessing the documentary evidence. Also, his "authoritative Word of God" contained so-called "double narratives" of events that sometimes "violently disagree"—for instance the creation narratives of Genesis 1 and 2—as if there were no other explanation for the literary facts.

On the other hand, Davies wished to be thoroughly Christ-centered in his reading of Scripture, and, unlike more left-wing theological liberals, he was not anti-doctrinal in principle: "The fact of Christ [is] a fact both historical and eternal. . . . Holy Scripture is the authoritative statement of the authoritative interpretation of the Person and Work of Christ."[113] At the same time, he spoke only of the merely "*substantial* agreement of the different writers" on "the fact of Christ . . . the nature of His Person and the scope and meaning of His Work for man and in man unto God."[114]

---

109. Thirty-nine Articles, Article 20 "Of the Authority of the Church."
110. Davies, *Church and the Plain Man*, 230–46.
111. Ibid., 230.
112. Ibid., 231.
113. Ibid., 233.
114. Ibid., 234. Emphasis added.

Davies lacked a first-hand grasp of the best scholarly conservative approaches. Following a liberal on the matter of inspiration, Marcus Dods (1834–1909), he identified the doctrine of verbal inspiration with "the mechanical or dictation theory,"[115] which had never been the church's position. He believed that adherents of verbal inspiration regarded Scripture as "a collection of oracles and proof texts."[116] Certainly, those premillennialists who were also dispensationalists (Nathaniel Jones was not one) had a literalistic worked-out schema of progressive revelation.[117] Davies's liberal approach would acknowledge "the human element" in Scripture and, as he thought, "grasp the principle of progressive revelation."[118] "Progressive revelation" in liberal theological usage meant not the unfolding of God's revelation to Israel over time, including his temporary commands required for the cultural context, but the progressively leaving behind of much error—moral and doctrinal—claiming to be revelation.[119]

No one denied that literary analysis had brought many new facts to light and thus illuminated the meaning of the text. Davies seemed to believe that when he conjoined such analysis with "critical investigation" he was religiously neutral.[120] He cited no obscurantist example. Neither conservative scholars like Handley C. G. Moule, nor the others that Principal Nathaniel Jones had relied on, fell into either the "rationalist" or the "obscurantist" camp. Nothing Davies ever wrote compares with Everard Digges La Touche for scholarly critical awareness.[121]

Davies focused on the gospel witness to Christ: "If doubt is cast upon the record [of Christ in the gospels], that doubt falls upon the facts." The church's message then loses "its note of certainty." The church's "roots are set in historical facts," he rightly insisted. "Modern historical science" required "documentary testimony"; as "the general veracity of Holy Scripture"[122] is authenticated, Scripture either verified or corrected tradition.[123] Davies

---

115. Dods, *Bible*, 107–18. See also Clarke, *Use of the Scriptures*, 46–47.

116. Davies, *Church and the Plain Man*, 235; for which see, for example, Seeberg, *Text-book of the History*, 395–96. See also chapter 1 above.

117. The Exclusive Brethren founder, J. N. Darby (1800–1882), systematized a concept of successive dispensations in the history of God's dealings with humankind. The *Scofield Reference Bible* (1909) gave it wide circulation.

118. Davies, *Church and the Plain Man*, 236.

119. He appears to have ignored, for example, Orr, *Problem of the Old Testament*, 465–78, and Orr, *Bible Under Trial*, 227–43.

120. Davies, *Church and the Plain Man*, 236.

121. See Digges La Touche, *Christian Certitude,* and *Person of Christ.*

122. Davies, *Church and the Plain Man*, 230–31.

123. Ibid., 231.

therefore rejected the Roman Catholic and Anglo-Catholic appeal to tradition as an independent source of revelation. "The facts set forth in Holy Scripture" set limits to the church's authority, for the supreme authority behind both Bible and church was Jesus Christ. "The terms of [the Church's] witness are recorded in the Bible, which the Church acknowledges and uses as the Word of God." Nowhere else does Davies so nearly identify "Word of God" with the Bible. The "fragmentary memoirs" of the first three gospels were sufficient "to show what manner of man [Christ] was."[124]

Specifically on biblical criticism, Davies stated here that "modern scholarship has confirmed" the church's "general position" that the biblical writings are "a true and trustworthy account of the deposit entrusted to the Church." Criticism, by bringing out more clearly the human element in the sacred writings, had also brought out the divine element more clearly.[125]

This last position was typical among those who favored the negative critical approach of supposedly neutral historical science. The representatives of Davies's day included Marcus Dods and (especially) William Newton Clarke, whose books on the Bible denying its infallibility were published in the year Davies completed Ridley Hall.[126] Yet Dods seemed more confident than Davies of the reliability of the gospel records, for he included "all four accounts" as giving "a consistent image of Christ,"[127] whereas Davies spoke only of the three synoptic gospels, Matthew, Mark, and Luke. T. C. Hammond in Dublin very probably saw Warfield's review of Dods's book and read there: "Which Christ of the fallible Scriptures shall we be ultimately forced to put up with?"[128] In Sydney, the admirers of Digges La Touche may well have asked whether Davies had ever even seen the late Irishman's own published treatment of modern Christology.[129]

Davies's paragraphs in *The Church and the Plain Man* on the right use of the Bible and the function of its "honest critical study"[130] seem to reflect the views of Clarke and Dods. First, on the right use of Scripture, reverence was to be emphasized more than intelligence, although Davies would reject the notion of "oracles," "proof texts" and "a hard literalism and a grotesque realism," while also not allowing subjectivism to run riot and

---

124. Ibid., 233.
125. Ibid., 234.
126. Dods, *Bible*; Clarke, *Use of the Scriptures*, especially 127-70.
127. Dods, *Bible*, 153.
128 .Warfield, Review of *The Bible*, 109-15; republished in Warfield, *Critical Reviews*, 111-27.
129. Digges La Touche, *Person of Christ*.
130. Davies, *Church and the Plain Man*, 235-41.

strange heresies and schisms to arise.[131] Nathaniel Jones's published work certainly indicates that he encouraged nothing like such reading of Scripture at Moore College.

Davies's paragraphs reveal verbal and notional similarities to W. N. Clarke, who wrote against the supposed "dictation theory" as being still influential, saying that it was "high time to give an intelligent answer" to questions like, "Are we at liberty to dissent from biblical statements? Are we in any true sense judges of the value of biblical statements?"[132] The term "oracles," which Davies used, is certainly reminiscent of Dods, who identified the traditional idea of inspiration with the oracular possession-states of ancient Greco-Roman culture.[133]

The Liberal Evangelical Davies sounded most like a traditional Evangelical when discussing the devotional inspiration afforded to the student of Scripture. "It is the Spirit working through the word" as "but the instrument" that brought the soul to God.[134] The Bible was "an efficient instrument of communication between God and man" in one's "personal seeking after God and the personal appropriation of the Holy Spirit's ever abiding presence." That was the "personal touch" aspect of the study of Holy Scripture.[135]

Davies concluded this chapter with a social apologetic: the history of what the Bible had done in the world justified the claim he had made for its authority and benefit. Negatively, enemies of the church had attempted to impugn its authority; positively, its great power was traceable in the sixteenth-century Reformation, the Evangelical revival of the eighteenth century, and the great missionary expansion of the nineteenth century.[136]

Davies's summary of the strength of the church in using the Bible's authority reflects his own integration of both the phenomenon of personality and the importance of documentary historical witness. These were Liberal Evangelical themes, as already observed.[137] He concluded a summing up of his salient points by saying: "The true final authority for Christians is Jesus

---

131. Ibid., 235–36.
132. Clarke, *Use of the Scriptures*, 46–47.
133. Dods, *Bible*, 107–10; Davies, *Church and the Plain Man*, 236.
134. Davies, ibid., 241.
135. Ibid., 241–42.
136. Ibid., 242–45.
137. Rogers, "Introduction," v.

Christ."[138] It was Dods's book that explicitly emphasized that Christ, not the Bible, was the ultimate authority.[139]

The 1919 Moore College Committee

Highly significant for the ongoing task of the principal in the life of the college was the Moore Theological College Ordinance of the 1919 Sydney Diocesan Synod, which set up the Moore College Committee. This took over the managerial role of the trustees and resulted in some loss of independence for Davies.[140] A remarkable feature of the committee was the identity of the men elected to it by the Standing Committee of Synod.[141] We must assume some strength of conservative forces on this committee. It seems likely that Standing Committee chose them in the light of Davies's theological reputation earned in his very first years, and confirmed to fellow Masons by his Sydney Lodge of Research statements (1916), possibly also by his Moorhouse Lectures published as *The Church and the Plain Man* (1919). Four of the five clergy were conservative Evangelicals. Three of those four were older graduates of Moore College under Jones: G. A. Chambers, also vice-principal under Jones though theologically somewhat broader,[142] H. G. J. Howe more emphatically premillennial than Jones, and S. E. Langford Smith recently appointed Canon. The fourth was S. M. Johnstone, who with Langford Smith, Archdall, and Digges La Touche, had confronted Davies over his view of Scripture in 1914. Of the clergy, at least Johnstone and Howe were fellow Masons. Sydney Langford Smith, "much more tolerant towards men who were more liberal in their outlook than was commonly recognized," would become a force in synod, and was "more than any other single person . . . responsible for the election of Bishop Mowll of West China" as archbishop in 1933.[143] S. M. Johnstone was later a chief counselor to Archbishop Mowll.[144] Of the five laymen elected, Mr. H. L. Tress—a lawyer prominent in synod and a committed Evangelical—was one of the founders of St Paul's, Chatswood and its Sunday school superintendent from 1914. H. G. J. Howe had been the first minister (1901–1914), followed later by two others trained by Jones—D. J. Knox (1924–1932) and R. B. Robinson

138. Davies, *Church and the Plain Man*, 245–46.
139. Dods, *Bible*, 59.
140. Loane, *Centenary History*, 122–23.
141. *Sydney Diocesan Directory . . . 1920*, 447.
142. Sibtain with Chambers, *Dare to Look Up*, 7.
143. Loane, *Mark These Men*, 25.
144. Ibid., 43, 44.

(1933–1935). Tress became a trustee of the college (1928–1942) and would be strongly in favor of inviting T. C. Hammond to succeed Davies. Two other laymen the Standing Committee elected were W. J. G. Mann, a future chancellor of the diocese, and C. R. Walsh: both members of the first Federal Council of the Church Missionary Society of Australia.[145] One may assume that both were conservatively Evangelical.

The big issue with Davies was the inspiration and authority of Scripture. Clergy and laity of Jones, Archdall, and Digges La Touche's cast of mind had not been persuaded to accept his liberal broadening of the Evangelical spectrum. It is hardly surprising that "there was always some degree of friction between Archdeacon (appointed without territorial jurisdiction in 1917) Davies and the college committee."[146] Davies was indeed, from 1919, "A Principal Embattled."[147] John Charles Wright had introduced a Liberal Evangelicalism into a key institution for the ongoing character of the diocese. Over Davies's twenty-four years, the college students would experience teaching mostly from those in the liberal part of the Evangelical spectrum, including Vice-Principal Glanville (possibly) and the part-time assistants.[148] Probably his Protestant overlap with other Evangelicals against ritualism, as well as his shared Masonic membership with some, made relations workable between Davies and the Moore College Committee.

---

145. "First Federal Council of CMS," in Cole, *History of the Church Missionary Society*, photo facing page 84.

146. Loane, *Centenary History*, 133; pace West, "A Principal Embattled," for, given that there were several Masons on the committee, it seems unlikely that his being a Mason as such was a factor.

147. West, "A Principal Embattled."

148. Glanville, the vice-principal, also a Freemason, is said to have denied agreeing with Davies in doctrine, but the writer has seen no documentary evidence to confirm or refute this.

9

Liberal Evangelicalism Maintained

FROM 1920 ON, DAVIES's health declined, which became more obvious in the early 1930s. He felt it a blow when Archbishop Wright died suddenly in late February, 1933, and a bitter disappointment when the synod elected Howard Mowll on April 7 of that same year.[1] Even so, he continued an active speaking program throughout the period. This chapter surveys Davies's thinking in these further addresses: on the interpretation and authority of Scripture, the meaning of Christ's death, the Reformation, and the Thirty-nine Articles. A brief look at his defense of the Christian faith concludes the chapter.

A Position Statement on Appeal to Authority to Fellow Heretics

Davies's earliest extant Heretics Club paper spells out a controlling element in his thought as a professed Liberal Evangelical. The "most important rule" of the Cambridge Heretics was the "rejection of all appeal to authority in the discussion of religious questions."[2] Davies's paper to the Sydney Heretics, "Modern Scholastics,"[3]—given on the eve of his departure to Cambridge for leave in 1920—reiterates this principle while exhibiting an important limit to his liberal outlook.

---

1. Loane, Letter to author, March 1994.
2. McNeile, "Religious Situation," 11.
3. Davies, "Modern Scholastics." See McIntosh, "'External Prop' or 'Divine Fiat'?," 67–91. Title of Davies's paper taken from Briggs, *Bible, the Church and the Reason*, 97, 104, 284.

The original objective of the Sydney Heretics was "the sharing of their research in theological scholarship."[4] In "Modern Scholastics," Davies shared his thinking as a proponent of history as scientific. Shrewdly, he chose to critique two thinkers on the same grounds—a Christian bishop, the Liberal Anglo-Catholic Charles Gore, and an arch-agnostic natural scientist, Thomas Henry Huxley (d. 1895). Both were "obscurantists":[5] Gore "the Conservative Scholastic," and Huxley "the Natural Science Scholastic." Methodologically, each supported himself on an *a priori*: "an Infallible authority," "a prop to their faith," as he would put it again later.[6]

Davies argued that by "critical examination of the documents," the "scientific method of investigation" in historical study aimed to tell "what actually happened without considering whether the facts as they occurred are for or against a particular point of view."[7] Such "searching investigation" "generally confirmed" J. B. Lightfoot's historical account of the origin of bishops as a separate order of ministry.[8]

Gore had published his essay, "The Holy Spirit and Inspiration" in *Lux Mundi*[9] to "succour a distressed faith" in the context of "modern knowledge, scientific, historical, critical,"[10] especially with regard to the criticism of the Old Testament at that time. Gore, "one of the most favorable examples" of the conservative modern scholastic, had unscientifically adopted an *a priori* fixed idea "that Christ *must* have laid down some plan or method of church organization" and an "external guarantee" of its continuity and infallible authority.[11] Protestant obscurantists looked for the same guarantee in Scripture. Moreover, his book on the ministry failed as scientific history because he had noticed only events which suited his purpose.[12]

In an aside, Davies stated that the notion of scientific history not only excluded the *a priori* method, but also the goal of "complete certainty." In the "old search for infallibility, the mistaking of cocksureness for reasonable certainty," he said, the obscurantists "spend their time mainly in trying to save discredited ideas and traditions from the rubbish heap and in abusing

---

4. Emilsen, "Heretics," 75, quoting G. W. Thatcher, a charter member.

5. Davies, "Modern Scholastics," 11.

6. Davies, "Communion Addresses."

7. Davies, "Modern Scholastics," 4.

8. Ibid., 6–9 (as opposed to the Roman/Anglo-Catholic and Greek Orthodox theory of tactual succession of bishops from those ordained by Christ's apostles).

9. Gore, "Holy Spirit and Inspiration," 315–62.

10. Gore, "Preface," xi.

11. Davies, "Modern Scholastics," 6–7.

12. Gore, *Ministry*.

people who differ from them." Such were the conservative scholastics.[13] Davies may have been alluding to certain fellow Sydney Anglicans on the Moore Theological College Committee, recently appointed by synod in 1919.

T. H. Huxley, the famous defender of Darwin's theory of natural selection, was also a "scholastic"! Davies had in mind Huxley's *Science and the Christian Tradition*, arguing that Huxley "dabbles in theology," taking for granted "the rigid uniformity of nature" and forgetting that "the subject matter of theology includes many things that were outside the ordinary scientific category." Huxley also forgets, argues Davies, that in theology the scientist "is not dealing with dead matter or hypothetical abstractions but with human beings."[14]

Davies critiqued Huxley's rejection of miracle (his agnostic worldview presupposed that the observed laws of nature were inviolable): a "particular branch of science is not omniscience," and though the uniformity of nature could not be proved, "we can generally reckon upon it." But finally, argues Davies, we do not "know all the conditions" and have not "tried all the combination of events that are possible." While the leading thinkers did not hold "the idea of nature as a closed mechanical system," he claimed, its "residual effect" constituted the real but "purely scholastic objection to the virgin birth and the resurrection of Jesus Christ."[15]

Although not arguing on the basis of a Christian theistic worldview as necessary for science, on this point the Liberal Evangelical Davies was orthodox with regard to key doctrines, and challenged fellow Heretics like Samuel Angus, and such as Ernst Troeltsch and J. B. Bury, who excluded all miracles in principle. Huxley's *Science and Christian Tradition* concluded (as summarized by Davies) that miracles were incredible on any historical evidence,[16] while yet conceding that "the position that miracles are 'impossible' cannot be sustained."[17] Davies then quoted Henry Gwatkin's Gifford Lectures: "There is no reason why [miracles] should not be decided on historical evidence like other historical questions, for we have found nothing of weight in the a priori assumption so often brought against it."[18]

Davies put forward the familiar argument that the principle of uniformity was disturbed by humans when they modified their environment

---

13. Davies, "Modern Scholastics," 11–12.
14. Davies, "Modern Scholastics," 12.
15. Ibid., 12–13.
16. Ibid., 4, 18.
17. Huxley, *Science and Christian Tradition*, 204, 207.
18. Gwatkin, *Knowledge of God*, 1:196.

and did so with purpose. *A fortiori*, then, "cannot God, the Creator and Sustainer . . . control nature to suit His purpose," such as the incarnation and "the moral reformation of the world?" Christ's divinity was attested in documents that were "first class authorities." If you established miracles like his Incarnation and Resurrection, Davies argued, Jesus's own miracles "are easily credible."[19] He went on to recall a paper given at Cambridge by Professor Silvanus P. Thompson, a Quaker and a famous physicist of his day.[20] With regard to Christ's resurrection, Thompson had "laid great stress on the transformation in the character and outlook of the apostles." [21] Davies was saying that current objections to Christ's miracles were due to scholastic "method and mental habits," and therefore, investigators needed to examine their presuppositions.[22] The minutes do not report the discussion.[23]

Thus, the Liberal Evangelical Davies never denied any articles of the Apostles Creed.[24] In the words of a modern writer, he insisted on "approaching miracles within a framework of belief about God. . . . [an] implicit attack on the rationality of the *secular view* of the uniformity of nature."[25] Digges La Touche's argument from his manual *Is Christianity Scientific?*[26] was possibly in his mind. His Evangelical conversionism closed this long paper with a revealing paragraph: "The real objection to receiving the gospel story as true" was its claim "upon the heart's allegiance." The evidence justified "the venture of faith" and had never disappointed those who had made it honestly.[27] This argument resembled that of Digges La Touche and others in the conservative end of the Evangelical spectrum of that day,[28] but Davies did not say on what grounds he confidently regarded elements of the gospel story as evidence.

19. Davies, "Modern Scholastics," 19.
20. See Smeal and Thompson, *Life and Letters*.
21. See Thompson, "Resurrection."
22. Davies, "Modern Scholastics," 21.
23. "Minute Book," vol. 1, April 1920.
24. Loane, Interview, June 5, 2001.
25. Brown, *Miracles*, 167–68. Emphasis added.
26. Digges La Touche, *Is Christianity Scientific?*
27. Davies, "Modern Scholastics," 21.
28. Digges La Touche, *Christian Certitude*, 291–92; Digges La Touche, *Is Christianity Scientific?*, 19–20.

Interpretation of Scripture and Premillennialism

On May 16, 1922, a fellow Mason, Brother H. G. J. Howe, a respected Evangelical clergyman and a member of the Moore College Committee, read a lecture to the Sydney Lodge of Research. He took it directly from his forthcoming book, *The Dawning of That Day*. His title was "The Plans of the GAOTU [Great Architect of the Universe] and their Approaching Consummation."[29] Howe, by then rector of the large suburban parish of All Souls, Leichhardt, was among the more enthusiastic premillennialist graduates of Moore College under Jones. He was sure, in view of the great crisis just past, the Great War, coinciding with the fulfilment of prophecy perceived in the surrender of Jerusalem to General Allenby in 1917, that "the Day of the Lord" had already dawned.[30] In the vigorous discussion afterwards, Davies questioned Howe's historical points, his view of history, and his hermeneutic of biblical prophecy. He took care to make some positive comment as well.[31]

A month later, in June 1922, Davies addressed the King's Birthday Convention at St Paul's, Chatswood. H. G. J. Howe had been the first incumbent (1902–1914) of the parish[32] and Mr. H. L. Tress, a lawyer, also a member of the Moore College Committee, had been an active parishioner from the beginning and still was. Davies's topic was "The Interpretation of Scripture."[33] He reiterated his usual points, among them that the Bible "contained" (not that it was) "the record of the progressive revelation of God,"[34] and that the Bible was to be studied like any other literature.[35] So, if studied according to the historical method, which Davies illustrated by applying it to Revelation,[36] then the Bible "yields to us the true secret of the only life really worth living," which was the "life of *personal consecration* ... a life of service ... [through which] God chooses to extend His kingdom and build it up."[37] Davies had applied his method—perhaps pointedly—to a key source of premillennial expectation: the New Testament book of Revelation. Stating much of the standard historico-grammatical exegesis, he

---

29. Howe, "Plans of the GAOTU," 9–22; Howe, *Dawning of That Day*.

30. Howe, "Plans of the GAOTU," 21–22.

31. Davies, "Discussion," 23–26.

32. One of several long-weekend Keswick-type conventions held at certain Anglican parish churches for decades into the twentieth century.

33. "Convention," 4; Davies, "Interpretation of Scripture," 1.

34. Davies, Ibid., 6.

35. So Jowett, "Interpretation," 330–433.

36. Davies, "Interpretation of Scripture," 10–12

37. Ibid., 16.

had condemned the method of surveying "a patchwork of proof-texts."[38] A not-too-merely-implicit critique of Howe's reading of Scripture was clear.

Five years later, on June 21, 1927 Davies gave a second lecture on Scripture to the Sydney Lodge of Research: "The Interpretation of the V.S.L."[39] He was keen to get lodge members to read it profitably. The V.S.L., he said, "teaches us, as no other book does, to know God."[40] It also had the "power of moral uplift and ethical inspiration." Quoting S. T. Coleridge's phrase, Davies said the Bible "'finds' us" and shows: "how absolutely necessary it is for us *to know God*. We learn in the V.S.L. what God has done for us, what he will do for us, and what he expects from us."[41] What he had done and would do for us in Christ, Davies must pass over in the context of theism as defined in Freemasonry. He could and did mention that the purpose of Freemasonry was moral improvement.[42]

The main use of the Bible, "to teach us about God," entailed methods of study that would promote the best interpretation. The "patchwork of proof-texts" method, Davies said, ignored "the great fact of progressive revelation."[43] Of the three (valid) methods of interpretation, the "literalist method"[44] and the allegorical method were appropriate for some parts of Scripture.[45] But *the historical method*, which aimed to place the student in the original context, would "help us to realize what the author . . . tried to say."[46]

Howe would bring out a third edition of *The Dawning of that Day* in 1925, issue a revised and enlarged edition three years later, and finally an English edition. For applying the historical method, Davies instanced the New Testament Apocalypse (Revelation) and the Old Testament book of Daniel, both being sources of key texts for premillennial expectation. Davies urged that both Daniel and Revelation were "tracts for hard times," not, he implied, sources of information about future history, to be obtained by "the frequent practice of picking bits here and there" put together to form "an incontrovertible proof." To read the Bible profitably, Davies wanted his fellow Freemasons to "distinguish . . . the eternal [moral] truth from

38. Ibid., 15.
39. Davies, "Interpretation of the V.S.L.," 31–42.
40. Ibid., 32.
41. Ibid., 33.
42. Ibid.
43. Ibid., 35.
44. Ibid., 36.
45. Ibid., 37–38.
46. Ibid., 38.

its circumstantial expression," and "thus . . . to apply to ourselves the truth . . . and test ourselves thereby."[47] Davies's final emphasis here accorded well with the personal moral improvement aims of Freemasonic meetings.

The Atonement: Chapel Talks of Michaelmas 1924[48]

Three years after his return from Cambridge, Davies gave eight chapel Communion addresses to his students. While on leave, he probably met up again with former Group Brotherhood member, J. K. Mozley. Davies had reviewed Mozley's well-known work, *The Doctrine of the Atonement*, finding the final chapter "suggestive."[49] He would also have re-associated with other old Group Brotherhood friends. Their intended manifesto, *Liberal Evangelicalism*, was very likely already in the wind, for collaboration and mutual reading of the essays had preceded its publication in February, 1923. Davies was probably its unnamed reviewer in the *Sydney Diocesan Magazine*.[50]

The Group Brotherhood's manifesto had not only adopted a strong moral influence view of the atonement, but also repudiated the church's historic stance. The Liberal Evangelical sought to explore, as in personal idealism, "the impact of the Cross upon personality," namely its moral influence.[51] Indeed, R. T. Howard's Essay 6 "The Work of Christ"[52] provides some immediate background for interpreting Davies's expressed thought in 1924 and later. Howard claimed that his "Liberal Evangelical" stance, was "true to the *deepest teachings*" of Scripture, indeed: "true to the facts of human experience as we understand them in these modern days, continuous in the line of development with the theories of the past."[53] The autonomous, supposedly growing moral consciousness or "human experience" was the liberal court of appeal. The Liberal Evangelicals were writing as if E. A. Litton and H. C. G. Moule were simply *passé*, to say nothing of James Denney's treatment of the New Testament evidence.[54] Howard, moreover, defined God in pure Ritschlian or modernist terms: "Our starting point is the nature of God. God is Love (Jn 6:63, 65). . . . We must go further, and say

47. Ibid., 41–42.
48. Davies, "Communion Addresses."
49. Davies, Review of *Doctrine of the Atonement*, 14–15.
50. Davies, Review of *Liberal Evangelicalism*, 14–16.
51. Rogers, "Introduction," *Evangelical*, vii.
52. Howard, "Work of Christ," 121–46.
53. Ibid., 121. Emphasis added.
54. See chapter 2 above.

that God is only Love; all His attributes and activities are simply functions of his love."[55] The notion of Christ's death being the "propitiation" for our sins[56] was therefore true only in the subjective sense, that: "as a matter of actual experience the vision of the Cross does deal with the guilt [i.e., guilt-feeling] of sin and assure men that they have been forgiven."[57]

R. T. Howard's exposition was dominant in Davies's 1924 chapel communion addresses, which he presumably repeated in following years. Thus, "propitiation" meant that Christ's death, his blood, symbolized by the wine, was "assurance of free forgiveness and the power to live the godly life.... Here is the *moral leverage* to make the world a better place to live in."[58] This was only subjective, and Davies gave no objective explanation. Later in the series[59] he discussed the Prayer Book and biblical term "sacrifice" together with "propitiation" (at 1 John 2:1) and "expiation,"[60] perhaps hinting at an objective meaning. Thus, on "expiation," he stated that "this involves the idea of penalty, or satisfaction" for gaining forgiveness, that Christ's death removed some obstacle in God. He went on: "In some way we cannot adequately describe, He made expiation for our sins, doing for us what we could not do for ourselves."[61]

On "propitiation" he was, of course, at pains to deny it was as found in "the cruder forms of heathenism," namely "to persuade or even compel a malevolent deity to go away." He also rejected the "less ignoble idea ... that a god ... may require an offering to appease his wrath" as found in "many places in the Old Testament." But in the New Testament, and here his "progressive revelation" is revealed, the expression "the wrath of God" was borrowed from the Old Testament "to express the hatefulness of sin in the sight of God. God as a moral Being cannot condone evil doing." As "the Moral Governor of the Universe," he "is responsible for the maintenance and vindication of the moral order."[62]

---

55. Howard, "Work of Christ," 122–23. See Ritschl, *Christian Doctrine of Justification*, 273; Orr, *Ritschlian Theology*, 112–119, 254–58; and Vos, "Scriptural Doctrine of the Love of God," 1–37, reprint, 425–57.

56. Book of Common Prayer, "Order of the Administration of the Lord's Supper," quoting 1 John 2:2 (AV).

57. Howard, "Work of Christ," 137 and 137n1.

58. Davies, "Communion Addresses," 5–6. Emphasis added.

59. Ibid., 1–26.

60. Mozley, *Doctrine of the Atonement*, 14.

61. Davies, "Communion Addresses," 24.

62. Ibid.

Such wording, like his language earlier at Holy Trinity, Cambridge, fits a governmental view of the atonement like that of R. W. Dale (1829–1895),[63] or of J. K. Mozley on propitiation: "God's attitude to sin is made perfectly plain."[64] One presumes that Davies, like Mozley, found "morally disquieting" the view of the great dogmaticians Hodge, Shedd, and Strong: the view grounded (so Mozley) in their method and their "premises as to the inspiration of Scripture."[65] Davies's modern, improved moral consciousness overruled what the sixteenth-century Reformers enshrined in the Prayer Book as God's "holy indignation." Not so T. C. Hammond.[66] The governmental view allowed "no real satisfaction of justice, no real substitution, and no real enduring of the penalty of the law."[67] Yet Davies adopts beautiful language to describe it: "The Holy Communion is the memorial of that one redemptive act on Calvary, the Trysting place where perfect love and perfect justice meet."[68]

Davies's concluding and applicatory words are reminiscent of F. D. Maurice's doctrine of sacrifice[69] and display his ultimate focus as his moral and social interest: "FOR HERE IS A GREAT PRINCIPLE AT WORK. Sacrifice is the price of progress.... The Son of God yielded up his body to the cross to open up the highway for the spiritual progress of mankind.... We shall find ourselves up against the world spirit that measures success by personal gain."[70]

The college students knew well the only use of the word "sacrifice" in the Prayer Book order of Holy Communion, which used the words from Romans 12:1–2: "Here we offer and present unto thee ... ourselves, our souls and bodies, to be a reasonable, holy, and lively sacrifice unto thee." Ignoring Christ's objective redemptive accomplishment at the foundation of his personal sacrifice, Davies derived from it only the "Great Principle": that sacrifice was the price of the spiritual progress of mankind out of selfishness. This Liberal Evangelical, social-motivational focus on the cross of

---

63. Dale, *Atonement*.

64. Mozley, *Doctrine of the Atonement*, 79.

65. Ibid., 177. Presbyterian Charles Hodge's *Systematic Theology* (1872–1873), William G. T. Shedd's *Dogmatic Theology* (1889–1894), and Baptist Augustus Hopkins Strong's *Systematic Theology* (seven editions 1883–1902, at least before 1894) all held to the Reformation view of Christ dying in the place of sinners.

66. Hammond, "Significance of Christ's Death," 39–49.

67. Hodge, *Systematic Theology*, 2:573.

68. Davies, "Communion Addresses," 25.

69. Christensen, *Divine Order*, 204–6.

70. Davies, "Communion Addresses," 26. Upper case and emphasis is original.

Christ, broadly applied, would stand out in his public sermon seven years later.

"Good Friday Meditation" of April 3, 1931

In this same thoroughly moralistic, Liberal Evangelical key, Davies spoke at a united service in the prominent Congregational Church in Pitt Street, Sydney. His text was "Jesus of Nazareth, King of the Jews" (John 19:19).[71] He did not even mention the forgiveness of sins, but described sin eloquently as "the hideous tragedy . . . of racial and religious animosity . . . pride . . . hatred and contempt," and "worldliness"—the essence of which was "the selfish view of life." "Selfishness" was the widely adopted liberal definition of sin.[72] W. R. Inge found selfishness as the root of sin to be "the leading conception" in the New Testament.[73] In his meditation, Davies said Jesus's "acceptance of the Cross was the true way out," for "the Cross tells us" what was true generally in history: "that the world is made better by sacrifice." History was one of the sources of revelation. Perhaps with modernists and fellow Freemasons in the congregations in mind, Davies stopped short even of alluding to Christ's deity: "The great Master Builder Himself gave His life for the world. The power of Jesus over the hearts and wills of men is derived from His sacrifice on their behalf."[74] This "power of Jesus" led into Davies's climactic point: the world's need of "the moral leverage of the Cross"; "If God so loved, nay still loves us, we ought to love one another. The Cross of Jesus is the one moral lever that can lift a man out of himself."[75] The "worldliness," that is, "the selfish view of life," was why "the moral leverage of the Cross is needed," first of all to cast worldliness out of our own hearts and out of the church and then we can begin that spring cleaning of our community which is so long overdue. Davies attacked the Australian "Protective Tariff" of the time as un-Christian and "rotten economics and worse morals."[76] Here, Davies preached unalloyed the centrality of the cross in the one-sided liberal sense, which excluded the *objective* ground of the forgiveness of sins, namely Christ's death. On this Good Friday, his overriding

---

71. Davies, "Good Friday Meditation," 1.

72. Askwith, "Sin, and the Need of Atonement," 175–218; Moberly, "Atonement," 313.

73. Inge, *Personal Idealism*, 173. (Moore College Library copy was purchased by D. J. Davies at Angus and Robertson, Sydney.)

74. Davies, "Good Friday Meditation," 4.

75. Ibid., 5.

76. Ibid., 7.

concern was to apply Jesus's obedient sacrifice of himself as a behavioral motive for the improvement of the life of human society.

Conclusion on Davies's View of the Atonement

One might summarize Davies's convictions by quoting the American conservative evangelical scholar J. Gresham Machen (1881–1936), almost his exact contemporary: "The essence of [the modern conception] is that the death of Christ had an effect not upon God but only upon man."[77] Students at Moore College and people in the pew could only have felt unclear about how they should understand the words in the Prayer Book's "Order for the Administration of the Lord's Supper": "Who made there by his one oblation of himself once offered. . . ." Immanuel Kant, filtered through S. T. Coleridge and F. D. Maurice, reinforced by Albrecht Ritschl (and the reading of W. N. Clarke)[78] reigned over Christ's cross within and outside the college in the teaching of the principal.

Papers on the Reformation

Davies's Protestantism was quite explicit. He brought his historical scholarship and method of the interpretation of Scripture to bear, testing Roman Catholic claims in a pamphlet he wrote for the New South Wales Council of Churches.[79] In August 1926 he read a paper to his fellow Heretics on R. H. Tawney's *Religion and the Rise of Capitalism*.[80] It was almost certainly the anonymous review just published in the July *Sydney Diocesan Magazine*. He expressed satisfaction in Tawney's refutation of the "partisan fallacy" that the Protestant Reformation was responsible for "the abuses of modern commercialism."[81]

"Protestant"

In 1929, the year following the second rejection by the House of Commons of the proposed revised Prayer Book, a motion before the Sydney Diocesan Synod of 1929 moved that Sunday, November 3 of that year be observed as

---

77. Machen, *Christianity and Liberalism*, 118.
78. Clarke, *Outline*, 342–49.
79. Davies, *Roman Catholic Claims*.
80. "Minute Book," August 1926.
81. Davies, Review of *Religion and the Rise of Capitalism*, 12–14.

"Reformation Sunday" to commemorate Luther's nailing of his "Ninety-five Theses" to the door of the Castle Church in Wittenberg.[82] Davies wrote a paper pointing out, however, that 1929 was "A Notable Quatercentenary"—namely, of the second Diet of Speier and its ensuing "Protest" (April, 1529), from which the term "Protestant" had come. These original Protestants had "rejected the absolute sovereignty claimed [by] the Pope" over both state and church, and "appealed to God and to conscience" as transcending "man-made laws and institutions." Against Anglo-Catholic objections, Davies gave the historical evidence for the valid use of the term by the Church of England.[83] Valid points, yet surely the main concern of the movers for a Reformation Sunday in the diocese was the authority of Scripture and God's gracious forgiveness of sins.

Liberal Appraisal of the Reformation

Davies's other papers on Reformation documents and themes also passed over doctrines central to that movement. We may presume the liberal note they sounded was like that heard in Davies's college church history lectures on the subject. In mid-1926, T. C. Hammond had presented public lectures in Sydney on the Reformation's various positive outcomes.[84] Now to the Heretics in July 1929, Davies read "Gains and Losses of the Great Reformation."[85] The Reformation "was not . . . a breach of Catholicity," not an Erastian "reduction of the Church into a Department of the State," nor "the despotic imposition of a new system upon an unwilling people." Positively, it was "a great movement" that "had to make headway against a system claiming the Divine right of prescription" and against a "vast mass of vested interest, buttressed by superstition."[86] So much for the gains.

Davies then turned to the losses. He listed first, "the breach in the unity of Christendom," then the "extravagances of reaction" against medievalism, "a bewildering variety of doctrine and practice," and also "much *odium theologicum*"—for it was intolerant. "A more permanent limit . . . was the tendency to treat the imperfect beginnings as final solutions," which

---

82. Sunday November 3 was the Sunday next after the eve of All Souls Day, October 30, 1934.

83. Davies, "Notable Quatercentenary" was apparently prepared also for publication (no place found).

84. Hammond, *Reformation and Modern Ideals*.

85. "Minute Book," July 1929.

86. Davies, "Gains and Losses," 13–14.

became "as finally authoritative as any papacy ever claimed to be."[87] The doctrinal "fixed formulae" of the Reformation created a tension between "an absolute supremacy of Scripture" and "liberty of interpretation."[88] He recurred to the main, Kantian theme of his "Modern Scholastics" paper, "external authority": "The Reformation was worshiped as a fetish by large numbers . . . who were looking for the kind of infallibility that the Reformation had really discredited."[89] Davies regretted that "liberal views"—for example, Luther's comments on whether the Epistles of James and Jude were truly canonical[90]—were exchanged for "a stiff, mechanical theory of inspiration . . . to set an infallible book against an infallible Pope."[91] He went on to make his staple accusation that later writers use the Bible as a "repository of proof texts for previously conceived dogmas, without regard to the context."[92] He mentioned no particular writer.

But, he argued, "solid gains . . . far outweigh the losses." The "open Bible" influenced "the ideals and conduct of the people." The Reformation "also brought a purer faith": "Above all it swept away all the satellites who had crowded out the figure of Jesus . . . as Saviour and Lord . . . to whom every individual had the right of direct approach."[93]

Was Davies dismissing the rich work of doctrinal formulation from the Augsburg Confession (1530), the Thirty-nine Articles (1552–1571) and many other confessions to the mid-seventeenth-century Westminster Confession of Faith (1646) as vitiated by proof-texting? In any case, he refocused on the person of Christ from a liberal point of view: "The Reformation was a return to the real unity of Christendom to be found in personal devotion to Jesus Christ." Samuel Angus professed such devotion, but was it to the biblical Christ?[94] Nothing in Davies's paper reflected an Evangelical satisfaction in the recovery of the biblical gospel.[95]

The last but "by no means least" of the gains of the Reformation was that of a more personal and ethical religion, and "less a demonstration of external" state power. Here, Davies joined the Liberal Evangelical's idealist

---

87. Ibid., 16–17.

88. Ibid., 18.

89. Ibid.

90. Luther did not believe that the New Testament Scripture was fallible, but that the church was.

91. Contrast Thompson, *Sure Ground*, especially 283–87.

92. So Farrar, *History of Interpretation*, 357–94; and Gwatkin, *Knowledge of God*, 2:237–40.

93. Davies, "Gains and Losses," 19–20.

94. Compare Machen, *Liberalism*, 80–116.

95. As in Girdlestone et al., *English Church Teaching*, 260.

themes of "personal" and "personality" with his appreciation of the church's recovery of its "proper spiritual function." As a Liberal Evangelical historian, Davies noted with satisfaction that the Reformation had promoted political liberty and national development.[96]

The paper contained not even an implicit focus on the cross of Christ, yet that was bound up with the Reformation watchwords *sola gratia, sola fide, sola scriptura*, which entailed the *solus Christus*, and justification through faith in him. Those in the coming 1929 synod who had imbibed Jones's appreciation or were inspired by Hammond's teaching in 1926 had such a focus. Davies shared, however, their satisfaction with the failure of the 1928 Prayer Book.[97]

Liberal Perspective on Luther's Thought

Despite the low point his health had reached by 1933, Davies could presumably draw on much of his past material for his engagements outside the college. Shortly after Mowll's election, he read a second paper on the Reformation to his fellow Heretics—"Martin Luther's Contribution to the Religious Thought of the Sixteenth Century."[98] Davies examined the four historic documents: Luther's "Ninety-five Theses" (1517) and his "Three Great Reformation Treatises" of 1520. Though an excellent historian, Davies seems to have ignored the sympathetic analysis by Henry Wace (1836–1924), published in the very same volume he used for his treatment of these documents.[99] The contrast between Wace and Davies's presentation is revealing.[100]

Wace had begun by placing Luther in the context of the medieval Western Church's moral and religious power derived from the terror and dread of hell,[101] and the attendant abuses. The preaching of indulgences violated the "deepest principles which the church had taught [Luther]" namely, "the inexorable character of the Divine law, the necessity and blessedness of the Divine discipline of punishment and suffering and that the law of Christian

---

96. "Gains and Losses," 21.

97. See chapter 11 below.

98. Davies, "Religious Thought in the Sixteenth Century"; this wording of title "Martin Luther's Contribution" above from "Minute Book," April 24, 1933.

99. Wace, "On the Primary Principles," [ix–xxxvi (1883)]; 425–48 (1896). (The page references to the 1883 edition are shown within square brackets here and in the following footnotes.)

100. Davies, "Religious Thought," 1–21.

101. Dante, *Inferno*.

life is that of lifelong penitence."[102] Having found the answer to these in God's merciful offer of righteousness, Luther published his "Ninety-five Theses" for public disputation on October 31, 1517. Davies did not mention Luther's climactic reference to Christ and his cross.[103] Wace had noted that Anselm's doctrine of Christ's atoning death—a doctrine Davies did not accept—did away with the notion of the Mass as an offering for sin.[104] On Luther's treatise *On Christian Liberty*, Wace himself did not realize that Luther always assumed a double nature of justification, derived from Augustine, *The Spirit and the Letter*: both the objective status of being forgiven *and* inward change.[105] This point aside, however, Davies's exposition did not otherwise clarify Luther's treatise, which Luther himself regarded as "a summary of the Christian Life in small compass";[106] nor did he attempt to draw its teaching together in a synthetic statement.[107] Wace did both at some length, bringing out the role of faith in embracing the promises of God.[108]

In commenting on the *Appeal to the German Nobility*, Wace had made the important historical point that Luther asserted "the central principles" of "equal rights of laity and clergy" and "the soul's independence of all human power, by virtue of the truth of justification by faith."[109] Davies's exposition of this treatise was fuller than that of *On Christian Liberty*. He noted that in the *Appeal*, Luther had described three "paper walls" of Romanist claims: (1) that the spiritual estate is above the temporal; (2) that no one may interpret the Scriptures but the Pope; (3) that no one can call a council but the Pope.[110] Here Davies left Luther's text largely without explanation, whereas Wace had provided some historical and doctrinal context, including "the truth of justification by faith."[111]

In the third treatise, *On the Babylonish Captivity of the Church*,[112] Luther applied the principle of the authority of Scripture to critique the Roman system of seven sacraments. Wace had reminded his readers that Luther

---

102. Wace, "On the Primary Principles," [xiv-xv]; 429-30.
103. Theses 92-95. Davies, "Religious Thought," 1.
104. Wace, "On the Primary Principles," [xx-xxi], 434-35.
105. Seeberg, *Text-Book*, 2:233, 235, 260-61.
106. Wace, "On the Primary Principles," [xxi], 435; citing Luther's introductory letter to Pope Leo X.
107. Davies, "Religious Thought," 11-15.
108. Wace, "On the Primary Principles," [xxi-xxix], 435-43.
109. Ibid., [xxx], 442.
110. Davies, "Religious Thought," 11-15.
111. Wace, "On the Primary Principles," [xxx], 442.
112. Wace and Buchheim, *Luther's Primary Works*, [141-245], 294-410.

was appealing "to laity and clergy alike, on the ground of their spiritual freedom, to abolish the abuses of the Roman Church." Luther's "primary principle" was faith, that is, "a response to the word and promise of God." In distinction from the Anabaptist claim to their own inspiration and the Romanist appeal to the authority of the Church, Luther upheld the "rule of faith," namely, "the due authority of the Scriptures."[113]

Davies, however, did not explain this, but did point out that Luther "goes back to the original Institution" of the Lord's Supper to assert "that the mass is neither a work nor a sacrifice but a promise of Christ, 'the testament of Christ . . . to those who believe in Him.'"[114] Therefore, not to utter the words of institution openly—as the ritualists failed to do—deprived the people of a promise for them to believe, rendering the supper useless for God dealt with men only by promise. Davies correctly interpreted Luther's position here as "assert[ing] direct dealing between God and individual human beings."[115]

Both Wace and Davies added a coda to their exposition of this document, revealing their differing positions on the spectrum of the day's Evangelicalism. Wace drew attention to the fact that "the general effect of Luther's teaching upon the condition of the world" was to restore to "clergy and laity alike, complete independence of the existing ecclesiastical system, *within the limits of the revelation contained in the Holy Scriptures.*" Moreover, "it established *Christian Liberty* . . . [though not] absolute liberty." Only Christian liberty "is really free."[116] Davies's coda showed his Liberal Evangelical emphasis on personality, religious experience, a critical approach to Scripture, and "truth." The personality of Martin Luther "typified and concentrated" the "elements of [the] revolt" of the Italian Renaissance, only in a positive form: "the spirit of criticism" and the means for its effectiveness. These included the study of the Scriptures in their original languages, and their translation and publication, so that the people were able to challenge church authorities. Citing *The Babylonish Captivity*[117] Davies wrote: "Luther had imbibed sufficient of the spirit of the New Learning to appreciate the self-evidencing power of truth."[118] Thus he found the claim for the authority

---

113. Wace, "On the Primary Principles," [xxxi], 443–44.

114. Davies, "Religious Thought," 17; Wace and Buchheim, *Luther's Primary Works*, [163], 319.

115. Ibid., 15–19.

116. Wace, "On the Primary Principles," [xxxv-xxxvi], 447–48.

117. Ibid., [228–29], 391–92.

118. Davies, "Religious Thought," 22.

of autonomous reason in Luther: a finding his liberal fellow Heretics were likely comfortable with.

An interesting statement of Davies confirms this reading of him: "This is a remarkable anticipation of the function of intuition in the perception of truth, and it expresses a cardinal principle of the Reformation as a movement of thought."[119] "Intuition" presumably referred to the epistemology of philosophical idealism dominant at Cambridge in his day, to which his personal friend, the astronomer Arthur Eddington, also adhered.[120] Davies was not talking of the Holy Spirit's internal testimony to the truth of the scriptural message.[121]

Although Davies gave a fair summary of *The Babylonish Captivity*, his inadequate treatment of Luther's doctrine of Scripture and its authority revealed his liberalism.[122] His view of justification and the atonement, earlier described, also affected his grasp of Luther's contribution in these classic Reformation documents. The contrast is marked—not only with Wace, but also with his predecessor at Moore College, Nathaniel Jones, and his own successors, T. C. Hammond, Marcus Loane, and David Broughton Knox. Even if "not an Evangelical *pur sang*,"[123] Wace shared the same appreciation of the Reformation watchwords.

Melbourne ACL June 12, 1933— The Thirty-nine Articles

Less than two months after the election of Howard Mowll, so disappointing to him, Davies went to Melbourne to speak on the subject, "The Thirty-nine Articles." The local Anglican Church League had organized a meeting in the Chapter House of St Paul's Cathedral in view of a coming worldwide Anglo-Catholic celebration of Keble's Assize sermon, "National Apostasy," given July 14, 1833.[124] The strong Freemason and Chairman of Ridley College's Council, Dr. George Bearham, presided.[125] Frederick Waldegrave Head,

---

119. Ibid., 23.

120. Passmore, *Hundred Years of Philosophy*, 332, 334.

121. For the internal testimony of the Holy Spirit to the truth of Scripture see Calvin, *Institutes*, 1.7.5.

122. Cf. Godfrey, "Biblical Authority," 227–30, and Thompson, *Sure Ground*.

123. Mozley, *Some Tendencies*, 26.

124. Davies, "Thirty-nine Articles," 1.

125. *ACR*, July 20, 1933, 6. Despite his frail health, Davies also wrote several other historical pieces occasioned by this centenary, including "Some Points Concerning the Oxford Movement" (Heretics Club paper, 1932) and "From 1841 to 1845."

a fellow Liberal Evangelical and historian, and friend of Davies from Emmanuel College days, had become Archbishop of Melbourne in 1929.

At every point that evening Davies was the careful historian and Protestant. He indicated several things that made it necessary to study the Articles: that they were "the official confession of the faith of the Church of England,"[126] "the proposal to celebrate the centenary of the Oxford movement,"[127] and the ongoing attempt "to frame a comprehensive constitution for the Church of England throughout Australia."[128] Yet another reason was the "variety of interpretations put on them."[129] Some Anglo-Catholic views were hostile towards the Articles; others tried to give them a "Catholic" interpretation, like Newman in his *Tract XC* (1841). Others still alleged they were an "*eirenicon* or *henotikon* between Catholic and Protestant."[130]

Davies moved straight to Article 6 "Of the Sufficiency of the Holy Scriptures for Salvation," which he saw as "the heart of the Protestant position." He explained it by way of contrast with the Council of Trent, which had earlier insisted that the historically unreliable "unwritten traditions" from Christ through the apostles must play a role. From this, Trent inferred the authority of the Apostles' successors to interpret Scripture.[131] The Oxford or Tractarian Movement had attached "great importance to the tradition" and to the authority of the church's ministry. This was contrary not only to Article 6, but also to Article 20 "Of the Authority of the Church."

Davies's second criticism of Tractarianism was "one of the key principles of the Protestant Reformation . . . namely 'Justification by Faith'" (Article 10). But here Davies engaged neither with Trent nor with Newman's view as set out in his *Tract XC*, which was that "Faith, as being the beginning of perfect or justifying righteousness . . . is said by anticipation to be that which it promises,"[132] essentially the same as Davies's own view.[133] Rather, he cited the parable of the prodigal son (Luke 15:11–32) as containing "the heart of it," that "Personal trust in God is the only possible basis for a right relation with God."[134] Avoiding the Pauline concept of "justification," which

---

126. Davies, "Thirty-nine Articles," 1.
127. Ibid., 2.
128. Ibid., 3.
129. Ibid.
130. Ibid., 3–5.
131. Ibid., 6–7.
132. Newman, *Tract XC*, 12–14.
133. See chapter 7 above.
134. Davies, "Thirty-nine Articles," 11.

Article 10 adopts, Davies used "The Prodigal Son" as his own "proof text" for the old liberal or modernist view, held by the Ritschlians like Samuel Angus.[135] On the other hand, Davies did remind his hearers that on Article 13 "Of Works before Justification," Newman and the Tractarians confused justification and sanctification.[136]

On Article 17 "Of Predestination and Election," he chose the "non-committal" interpretation: that the article was "merely affirming the idea without elaborating it." This liberal outlook permitted Davies to claim that there was "no inherent conflict between Arminianism and Evangelicalism."[137] On Articles 19–36 (*On the Church*) Davies's Protestant, anti-Roman Catholic stance was just as firm as that of Jones and T. C. Hammond: "It is here that the cleavage was most apparent between the Reformers and the Romanists," and so also "that the Tractarians were most severely criticized."[138] Davies's lecture now engaged in a kind of running debate with Newman's *Tract XC*. As an historian, he could confidently and correctly conclude that the Articles did not, *contra* Newman, define the Church of England as a *via media* between Protestantism and Romanism: "An examination of the official documents has convinced me that the Church settlement under Elizabeth was definitely Protestant and not in any way a compromise between two extremes."[139]

The lecture bears out the summation of Marcus Loane, a student under him in his last years of teaching, that Davies was "a Protestant in churchmanship, a liberal in scholarship."[140] Davies's exposition was consistent with the evidence above from his Cambridge days—that he had embraced the liberal broadening of the Evangelical spectrum that had emerged in the early twentieth century.

Davies's Apologetic Approach

On the Sunday scarcely more than three weeks after Archbishop Wright's sudden death on February 24, 1933, Davies gave the very first Gunther Memorial Lecture in St Andrew's Cathedral, Sydney. The subject was the

---

135. Ritschl, *Christian Doctrine of Justification*, 94–95, 535; Angus, *Forgiveness and Life*.
136. Davies, "Thirty-nine Articles," 11.
137. Ibid., 11–12.
138. Ibid., 12.
139. Ibid., 27. If a *via media*, the English Reformation was such between Wittenberg (liturgically) and Geneva (doctrinally).
140. Loane, *Centenary History*, 137.

evidence for Christianity, treated so as to appeal to the ordinary person of the community.[141]

Davies addressed first the creedal phrase, "I believe in God," an issue possibly made more acute for Christians in Sydney by the appointment in 1927 of the Scotsman, John Anderson, to the University's Challis Chair of Philosophy. Anderson rejected all religion, including Christianity:[142] a position noticeably different from the tenuously Christian idealism of his earlier predecessor, Francis Anderson. Davies said he had found the substance of his lecture effective "in more than one 'teaching mission.'"[143] His text was: "For in Him we live and move and have our being" (Acts 17:28). Davies believed in God—"I put my whole trust in God"—and had a "definite sense of personal dependence on" and "recognition of obligation and responsibility towards Him."[144]

His approach was the traditional evidentialism with current reference as well as pointing to the fact that presuppositions were necessary for every field of knowledge, and that we necessarily assumed "the reality of ourselves and of the world." Similarly, "we take for granted the fact of God and . . . it works out to be true."[145] This did not necessarily define God as the self-existent creator, over and against idealism. Davies adduced also "the evidence of consciousness"[146] (the *sensus deitatis*?) and "the moral argument," the one "proof" that Kant allowed.[147] Davies defended the sensitive human conscience as a thing not derivable by the evolutionary notion of a self-protective instinct.[148] Evolution described the *process* of cause and effect in the natural order; the sense of guilt belonged to another order.[149]

Davies then outlined the evidence of "God's Three Books: Nature, History, and the Bible."[150] The Book of Nature demanded a first cause, but required further revelation. The Book of History supplemented it, seeming "to indicate . . . a Power at work which makes for righteousness," for "despite periods of decay and corruption," history was "a tonic for drooping

---

141. Davies, *Gunther Memorial Lecture*, 6.

142. Passmore, "Philosophy," 153–54.

143. Davies, *Gunther Memorial Lecture*, 6. These missions would have included those undertaken for the Student Christian Movement.

144. Ibid., 12.

145. Ibid., 9–12.

146. Ibid., 13–14.

147. Kant had critiqued and denied all but this one of the five traditional proofs for the existence of God.

148. Ibid., 14–17.

149. Ibid., 16, citing Gwatkin, *Knowledge of God*, 1:19.

150. Ibid., 17–23.

spirits."[151] But it was from the Bible that "most plainly and directly" we learn about God. In it "we have the record of what earnest men have learned and felt and known and believed about God"—a "progressive revelation . . . recorded in the Old Testament" and climaxing in "the New Testament which records the life of Jesus Christ and the Gospel." The Bible was a world "bestseller": its own best witness. It had earned the title "'The Word of God' . . . by its influence on human hearts and lives." Belief in God enables us to read the Bible profitably, Davies said, and helps us read the other two books: nature and history.[152] His was a liberalized form of the traditional apologetic.

Davies's Passing

When in April 1933 the Sydney synod met to elect an archbishop "the Diocese was split from top to bottom over questions of Modernism": a fact which must also have affected the attitude of the college committee towards Davies.[153] The pronounced modernism of Davies's fellow Heretic, Samuel Angus had been coming to the fore since 1929. In 1933 it was in the daily newspapers as well as on the agenda of the coming General Assembly of the Presbyterian Church in New South Wales, to be held in May.[154] This high profile of modernism amongst the Presbyterians no doubt strengthened the conservative Evangelicals' resolve and widened their appeal in the election synod of April, 1933. Howard Mowll was elected on April 7.[155] Davies "was very upset," Marcus Loane recalled from his second year as a student in the college, "for Davies badly wanted Archdeacon Hunkin of Rugby . . . a Liberal like himself."[156]

But the charge of "modernism" had been leveled with effect against Hunkin—probably not unjustifiably, for his "standpoint was markedly liberal."[157] The Anglican Evangelical Group Movement theological leader and historian of English theology, V. F. Storr,[158] agreed that "Modernism, as represented by the Modern Churchmen's Union, and Liberal Evangelical-

---

151. Ibid., 20–22.
152. Ibid., 22–23.
153. Loane, letter March 1994, alluding to West, "A Principal Embattled."
154. Dougan, *Backward Glance*, 10–17.
155. Loane, *Archbishop Mowll*, 126.
156. Loane, Letter, March 1994.
157. Williams, Editorial, 349–50 (on Hunkin's passing); Dunstan and Peart-Binns, *Cornish Bishop*, 146–48. See Hunkin, *Gospel for Tomorrow* for a sample of Hunkin's outlook.
158. Storr, *Development of English Theology*.

ism, as represented by the Anglican Evangelical Group Movement" stood for the same thing "in broad aim and ideal," although they were different in emphasis.[159] It is not clear whether Davies and Talbot, in nominating him, or indeed other synodsmen were fully aware of how liberal Hunkin was. The synod elected Howard West Kilvinton Mowll, a conservative Evangelical, not premillennial in conviction but embracing the Keswick extension.

Consequent upon the synod result, Dean Talbot, the President, and Davies, the Vice-President, both resigned from the Anglican Church League, whose activities under Jones-educated clergy and lay leadership had effected Mowll's election. Together with Arthur Garnsey and others, the two formed "The Anglican Fellowship," which then arranged for Garnsey to give a series of lectures in the Chapter House of the Cathedral on the relatively new form-criticism of the gospels. Mowll's ship docked on March 1. Whether intentionally or not, Garnsey's first two lectures (February 27 and March 6, 1934)[160] fell on either side of Mowll's arrival, and the third was postponed to March 19, presumably by Mowll's installation on March 13.[161]

Davies had become quite ill in late 1933. After he had undergone surgery the college committee, acting on his doctors' advice, in February 1934 granted him six months' leave to visit England. Mowll arrived on March 1, in time to attend a farewell to the principal before he sailed. On June 29, 1935, less than a year after his return from leave, Davies died, aged fifty-six. Although he had been "a principal embattled" and his years as a Liberal Evangelical principal had not been without their tensions with the college committee,[162] his funeral service in St Andrew's Cathedral was packed with friends and former students. Students of all views remembered their principal's "fatherly interest and great kindness."[163] The committee acted with kind consideration towards his family's needs, recommending to the Trustees that Mrs. Davies be paid the principal's full salary to the end of September. The family continued in the residence until February 1936.[164] Hammond's arrival was due in April.

159. Storr, *Freedom and Tradition*, 111.
160. Garnsey, *How the Gospels Grew* (each lecture carries its date on the title page.)
161. Loane, *Archbishop Mowll*, 132.
162. West, "A Principal Embattled."
163. Loane, *Archbishop Mowll*, 137–38.
164. Loane, *Centenary History*, 138.

Conclusion

Davies's liberalism, of course, was nothing like the extreme modernism of E. W. Barnes, Bishop of Birmingham, or that of Samuel Angus. Davies had maintained an attempt to broaden the Evangelicalism of the college and the diocese to a liberal position—on Scripture especially, and on Christ's atoning work. He had done so out of a sense of scholarly integrity—on his assumptions. Some were persuaded, and liberal opinion did not die out in Sydney after him. But a consequence of the Liberal Evangelical era in the diocese was that leading Evangelicals taught under Jones were determined to see that it did not continue.

Of those students unpersuaded by Davies, Reginald Langshaw (1911–2001), a student in 1932–1934, remembered that he himself "still held Reformation principles and that sort of thing" but had become more open to seeing the truth that Anglo-Catholics and others might hold.[165] Another, and the most important for the future of the college and the diocese, was the young Marcus Loane, whose student years overlapped with the first two of Langshaw. He remembered that the few who came in as conservative Evangelicals "didn't lose their Evangelical spirit at all but they never developed the steel or the strength that one might have seen in them, because they didn't get it in the college."[166]

Archbishop Mowll appointed Loane resident tutor and chaplain of the college upon his being made deacon in March 1935.[167] Loane was afterwards Vice-Principal (1938-1953), Principal (1954-1957), Co-adjutor Bishop (1958-1966) and finally Archbishop of Sydney (1966-1983). In him, the Reformation and Keswick Evangelical tradition of Nathaniel Jones (without his premillennialism) continued and grew stronger both in the college and the diocese.

---

165. Langshaw, interview late 2000 (day and month not recorded). Langshaw was Eleanor Abbot Scholar and Senior Student in 1934.

166. Loane, interview June 5, 2001.

167. Loane, *Centenary History*, 135.

Figure 4: T. C. Hammond

10

Reformation Evangelicalism Embraced
Formation of an Apologist-Pastor

Introduction

T. C. HAMMOND WAS an outstanding exception to the generalization that the energies and abilities of conservative Evangelicals were directed to pastoral ministries and evangelism rather than to basic intellectual challenges. His was a theologically penetrating and historically informed mind. With the right academic appointment, Hammond might well have developed into the next guiding Evangelical theologian after Henry Wace. Instead, after spending 1903 to 1919 in parish work, he took on the role of superintendent of the Irish Church Missions (ICM) until 1936. Following that, he was principal of a small theological college in the Antipodes for another seventeen years: Moore Theological College. This role in combination with that of Mowll as Archbishop of Sydney from 1934 turned out to be of historic importance for the Anglican Diocese of Sydney as well as for the college. Not only was the use of the Book of Common Prayer—that is, English Reformation liturgical practice—consolidated in the diocese, the caliber of Evangelical theology in the college was also more finely honed under Hammond. Sydney Evangelical pulpits were more confident and distinctively Evangelical and their services firmly resistant to ritualist tendencies.

Hammond had not been theologically unproductive before his move to Sydney. In the Church of Ireland, he had constantly faced a growing High Church and Anglo-Catholic thrust, as well as the challenges of liberal theology. The status of the Roman Catholic Church after Irish independence came as a third challenge, coinciding with his ICM work. As a result of his engagement on all three fronts, Hammond became a kind of "compleat theologian":[1] a master of historical and theological issues and a centrist Evangelical, stamped by the doctrinal outlook of the English Reformation, now brought wholly up-to-date.

Family, YMCA, Street Evangelism[2]

Hammond was not formed merely by his context in Roman Catholic Ireland, important though that was. His formative environment was both more complex and complete. Born in County Cork, Ireland, on February 20, 1877, his father, Colman Hammond, was an Evangelical layman from an old Anglo-Irish Cork family. For a few years in the early 1850s, Colman Hammond served with the Church Missionary Society in Sierra Leone, where his first wife died. He became a master in the Royal Navy, but had to take early retirement.[3] He then took up farming some distance out from the city of Cork, remarried, but died when young Thomas was only six years of age. Mrs. Hammond sold the farm, and Thomas and two sisters moved with her into "a succession of modest houses in the city."[4] The majority of Church of Ireland people were not wealthy; at thirteen, Thomas necessarily left school for employment on the Irish railways. About that time, he joined the newly inaugurated Cork branch of the Young Men's Christian Association where he became very active, even organizing a debating club. He met and heard visiting prominent evangelical Christians of the day. John McNay, a young Scottish Presbyterian and businessman in the city, led the youth work of the Cork YMCA. Under him, Hammond experienced a Christian conversion that involved "three miserable months."[5]

No doubt a factor in Hammond's concern for Roman Catholics was the death of his older brother, James Henry Hammond, at age twenty-seven. James had become a teacher in the order of the Christian Brothers. Probably another factor was that in Cork, his Roman Catholic aunt on his mother's side and her agnostic husband were both fond of discussion and debate. From ten years of age, Thomas was learning to defend himself from their attacks.[6] Taking part in the YMCA street preaching in Cork—addressed

---

1. Cf. Izaak Walton, *The Compleat Angler* (1653).
2. Nelson, *T. C. Hammond*, 27–51.
3. Ibid., 13.
4. Ibid., 30.
5. Ibid., 37.
6. Ibid., 45.

primarily to the majority Roman Catholics—he became the notorious "Boy Hammond."[7]

ICM College, TCD, Dublin Parish, YMCA Addresses 1907, Early Apologetic Engagement

It is not surprising that in 1895, aged eighteen, Hammond enrolled in the three-year training course for the Society for Irish Church Missions at their college in Dublin.[8] This voluntary society had been founded by English Evangelicals in 1849, and Hammond "gained a thorough grounding in Scripture and Anglican theology": the Old and New Testaments, the Thirty-nine Articles of Religion and the Book of Common Prayer.[9] He also learned "the intricacies of Roman Controversy" and an early exposition of "The One Hundred Texts."[10] He was "trained to know, quote, and always verify your references."[11]

"The One Hundred Texts" had been selected as early as 1862 for the Christian religious education ministry of the ICM and for Scripture memorization in the Sunday schools of churches in England and Ireland that supported the society. All from the New Testament, the texts provided a grounding in Christian doctrine, with which Roman Catholic doctrines touching on salvation were compared. After he came to Sydney, Hammond's own expanded edition with its learned notes was used in a number of the parishes.[12]

On the Articles, he may have been taught at the college from T. P. Boultbee's pioneering Evangelical *Commentary*, or from the more comprehensive H. C. G. Moule's *Outlines*.[13] Hammond's own copy of the latter, marked characteristically with blue pencil, survives in the library of Moore College. During and following his training, he engaged in itinerant evangelism with the ICM. By 1899, however, now intending for ordination, he undertook independent study by which Trinity College, Dublin, allowed

---

7. Ibid., citing Hammond, *Memories*.
8. Ibid., 46–51.
9. Ibid., 50.
10. Cheetham, *One Hundred Texts*; Fishe, *Questions and Answers on the One Hundred Texts*.
11. Nelson, *T. C. Hammond*, 47, 50.
12. Ibid., 47; Brine, "Foreword," v–vi.
13. Boultbee, *Commentary*; Moule, *Outlines of Christian Doctrine*.

non-attending students to sit the first-year examinations.[14] Hammond entered the university in January 1900.

Hammond's TCD Education

Trinity College was no intellectual backwater.[15] The provost, George Salmon (1819–1904) had a European reputation for his mathematical work[16] and was famous for his study of the gospels, and for his critique of the Church of Rome's claims.[17] The Professor of Modern History and Regius Professor of Greek, was J. B. Bury, an atheist. In 1902, he would succeed Lord Acton (d. June 1902) as Regius Professor of History at Cambridge, where D. J. Davies was reading that subject. Hammond himself started in history before moving into philosophy.[18]

Like Salmon and Bury, other TCD men were also polymaths, and like Salmon, ordained clergy of the Church of Ireland: John Pentland Mahaffy, the Professor of Ancient History, and J. H. Bernard, the Archbishop King's Lecturer in Divinity, both published in philosophy. Together they had translated Kant's *Prolegomena* (1889) and published a paraphrase and commentary on his *Critique of Pure Reason*.[19] Bernard himself had published his first edition of Kant's *Critique of Judgment* (1892),[20] and recently his own edition of Joseph Butler's *Analogy* and *Sermons*.[21] The biblical scholar, Thomas Kingsmill Abbott, had recently translated Kant's *Critique of Practical Reason* (1898), which became the standard English version. Henry S. Macran, a Hegelian, was elected Professor of Moral Philosophy in 1901. Thus, as philosophical idealism reigned at Cambridge for D. J. Davies, so also in TCD for T. C. Hammond—through Plato, Kant, Hegel, and T. H. Green. We have seen in chapter 1 that many public challenges to the historic Christian faith in the pre-World War I era were grounded in idealism (particularly absolute idealism) and a naturalistic understanding of new scientific knowledge. C. F. d'Arcy (1859–1938) was a brilliant TCD graduate and a future primate of all Ireland. His Donnellan Lectures of 1897–1898, *Idealism and Theology*, were published shortly before Hammond enrolled. D'Arcy's lectures sought

14. Nelson, *T. C. Hammond*, 52.
15. McDowell and Webb, *Trinity College Dublin*, 283.
16. Salmon, *Properties of Surfaces*.
17. Salmon, *Infallibility of the Church*.
18. Nelson, *T. C. Hammond*, 54.
19. Mahaffy and Bernard, *Kant's Critical Philosophy*.
20. Kant, *Kant's Kritik*; Kant, *Kant's Critique*; Kant, *Kant's Introduction*.
21. Bernard, *Works of Bishop Butler*.

to answer absolute idealism's rejection of the Christian doctrine of God.[22] Even as Hammond finished his BA, F. W. Macran's Donnellan Lectures usefully surveyed English Christian apologetic approaches from the era of Butler and eighteenth-century deism to that of the late nineteenth century and Darwinian evolution.[23]

Hammond's education in philosophy and theology included his own early attention to the rationalist philosophical approach.[24] As an undergraduate, he was active in the Student Theological Society, and in May 1903 read "The Creeds and Modern Thought" (now lost?), which very likely included comment on the recent volume by Oxford idealists, *Contentio Veritatis*.[25] The society report praised Hammond for "a profound and judicious paper" of "weighty tone" and an eloquence comparable with that of J. H. Bernard's famed divinity lectures.[26] In November 1903 the Theological Society awarded him its Special Certificate and Silver Medal for Composition.[27]

Late in 1902, the year that James Denney published his definitive *Death of Christ*,[28] G. T. Manley, then a Church Missionary Society teacher of theological students in India, urged the Christian Union to have "well-grounded and settled convictions on the central fact of the Atonement of Christ."[29] Such would remain a central feature of Hammond's thought.

Hammond and other alert Evangelical students of Trinity College would not have missed the fact that earlier in May 1903, the London University College Christian Association had held a course of lectures defending Christianity. The main speakers included some Evangelicals: Dean of Canterbury Henry Wace, Laudian Professor of Arabic at Oxford D. S. Margoliouth, and G. T. Manley. Lively correspondence was generated in *The Times* over a response by the admired physicist and mathematician of the day, Lord Kelvin: "Science positively affirms Creative Power."[30]

---

22. D'Arcy, *Idealism and Theology*, 143–45.
23. Macran, *English Apologetic Theology*.
24. See Digges La Touche, *Need for an Evangelical Revival*, 2–3.
25. *Contentio Veritatis*.
26. *Trinity College Dublin* 9 (1903), 100.
27. Ibid., 139.
28. Denney, *Death of Christ*.
29. *Trinity College Dublin* 8 (1902), 168. Manley was Senior Wrangler 1893 and formerly Fellow of Christ's College, Cambridge.
30. Seton, *Christian Apologetics*, xi, 25; also Orr, *Bible Under Trial*, 20.

Hammond won the prestigious Wray Prize for the best dissertation at the honors graduation examination in philosophy, the gold medal in Logic and Ethics, and the Downes Prize for Extempore Speaking.

In accordance with the dovetail arrangement for future ordinands with the undergraduate Arts School, Hammond had started some of the divinity classes before graduating BA.[31] He continued with them to complete the Divinity Testimonium of the TCD Divinity School,[32] which shared both some faculty and a distinguished reputation with Arts. As well, the "largely Evangelical nature of the nineteenth century Church of Ireland," at least "low church" if not openly Evangelical, was "well represented" among both students and professors.[33]

Hammond was exposed to liberal, although not necessarily radically liberal, biblical scholarship in the persons of T. K. Abbott[34] and the young A. H. McNeile (1871–1933), afterwards Fellow and Dean of Sidney Sussex College, Cambridge. J. H. Bernard, later Archbishop of Dublin and author of a well-known commentary on the Gospel according to John,[35] represented the High Church tradition. For books on the Reformation and Evangelical side, H. C. G. Moule's *Outlines of Christian Doctrine* was still in print, while a new edition of Litton's *Introduction to Dogmatic Theology*, enriched with Henry Wace's introductory remarks, came out while Hammond was still doing Arts. Litton's reprinted *The Church of Christ*, useful for High Church and Anglo-Catholic issues as well as specifically for some controversy with Rome, had recently appeared. For biblical studies, the provost, George Salmon, though he "tended toward a liberal Evangelicalism" with regard to authority was known in Cambridge as the "hammer of the Germans," [36] having famously refuted the skeptical Tübingen approach to the New Testament gospels. His substantial New Testament *Introduction*, was still in use.[37] His last work, a study of the gospels, was published posthumously, only three years after Hammond finished his formal divinity studies.[38] Salmon's famous lectures to divinity students on the controversy with Rome, *The Infallibility of the Church*, remained in print and unrefuted.

---

31. Nelson, *T. C. Hammond*, 5.
32. The postgraduate diploma in theology.
33. Nelson, ibid., 53. See also Acheson, *History of the Church of Ireland*.
34. Abbott, *Critical and Exegetical Commentary*.
35. Bernard, *Critical and Exegetical Commentary*.
36. Bailey, *History of Trinity College, Dublin*, 229, reporting J. H. Bernard (as recorded in Robert H. Murray, *Archbishop Bernard*, 66).
37. Salmon, *Historical Introduction*, xxxi and 643.
38. Salmon, *Human Element*.

In Old Testament studies, the works of C. H. H. Wright (1836–1909) were current. Wright, like other conservatives such as Henry Wace, for example, accepted criticism in principle, but not an *a priori* naturalistic approach. His *Introduction to the Old Testament* had seen its fifth edition in 1900, and his commentary on Daniel, a focus of Old Testament criticism at the time,[39] would be published the year after Hammond finished his Divinity Testimonium in 1905. One must assume that S. R. Driver's *Introduction*, which Wright himself called "indispensable for all real students,"[40] was also read. While Hammond was still finishing his divinity studies, Wright, with Charles Neil, published the first edition of *The Protestant Dictionary*, which defended the Reformation character of the Church of England and Church of Ireland.[41] It seems significant for his Reformation Evangelicalism that Hammond purchased, presumably in these years, the last two volumes of the *Presbyterian and Reformed Review*, and received its replacement, the *Princeton Theological Review*.[42] Both journals were edited by B. B. Warfield of Princeton Theological Seminary.

Made deacon on December 20, 1903, Hammond began busy parish work as the curate assisting at St Kevin's, Dublin, while completing the Divinity Testimonium, gaining second-class honors (not firsts, probably because he had not included Hebrew). He was ordained presbyter on March 26, 1905, aged twenty-eight. W. H. Griffith Thomas's Oxford Doctor of Divinity thesis on the Lord's Supper[43] was published even as Hammond concluded his formal studies. Two years later, a new edition of Cranmer's classic study on the Lord's Supper came out.[44] Hammond would master it and expound Cranmer's doctrine at Moore College as the authentic Anglican doctrine.

In January 1906, aged nearly twenty-nine, Thomas Chatterton Hammond married John McNay's younger sister, Margaret, by whom he would have four children. In 1910, he became the incumbent at St Kevin's. In a majority Roman Catholic environment, his was a clear voice expounding a biblicist, crucicentric, conversionist message conforming to the biblical and

---

39. Wright, *Daniel*.

40. Wright, *Introduction*, 227.

41. Wright and Neil, *Protestant Dictionary*. See "English Church," "Thirty-nine Articles," etc.

42. Hammond's personal sets of these journals are in Moore College Library.

43. Thomas, "*Sacrament of our Redemption.*"

44. Wright, *Archbishop Cranmer*.

Reformation tenor of the Thirty-nine Articles of Religion and the Book of Common Prayer.[45]

First Apologetic Theology

Though busy with parish work, Hammond undertook *Modern Religious Developments*: a series of three public lectures for the Dublin YMCA from February to May, 1907. The first lecture makes a pre-emptive critique of a forthcoming radical book, *The New Theology*,[46] based on the author R. J. Campbell's own recent lengthy pre-publication account in the *Daily Mail*.[47] Attempting to achieve relevance for the church among modern intellectuals, Campbell had begun with a non-Christian concept of God's immanence—that of absolute idealism—and some viewed his approach sympathetically.[48] Rejecting the doctrines of original sin, expiatory atonement and the deity of Christ, he looked for the revival of the church through social reform and moral action. Hammond's treatment is a signpost pointing to his Evangelical approach. His tone is charitable, but his argument trenchant: Campbell's divine immanence excluded any "real distinction between humanity and deity."[49] Spinozist but inferior to Spinoza, Campbell's doctrine of divine immanence did "not carry with it the possibility of a Divine Transcendence in any sense."[50]

Hammond's critique touched on the underlying worldview, thus gaining depth and penetration. He did not make explicit, however, that Campbell's monistic outlook, with its desire for autonomy—human independence of God—must compromise the modern pursuit of truth. At the same time, the high quality of Hammond's argument and his scholarly mastery of the issues well and truly holds its own beside the critique of the distinguished Oxford professor A. C. Headlam, published soon after the book itself came out.[51] Hammond's depth of reading was evident: Spinoza's distinction between humanity and God,[52] T. K. Abbott's edition of Immanuel Kant on eth-

---

45. See Nelson, *T. C. Hammond*, 57–60.
46. Campbell, *New Theology*.
47. Hammond, "New Theology," 5.
48. See Langford, *In Search*, 33–38.
49. Hammond, "New Theology," 4.
50. Ibid., 10. Benedict de Spinoza was, in translation, much republished in the latter part of the nineteenth century.
51. Headlam, "New Theology," 79–109. Headlam was by then professor of dogmatic theology at King's College, London.
52. Hammond, "New Theology," 9–10.

ics and the theory of religion,[53] Joseph Butler's *Analogy of Religion*,[54] James Orr's much published *Christian View of God and the World*,[55] Alexander Campbell Fraser (a Scottish ethical theist who was also a specialist on Bishop Berkeley),[56] Edward H. Griffin (an American Christian philosopher),[57] the Anglican Handley C. G. Moule,[58] and the Scottish Presbyterian James Denney.[59] Hammond's 1907 lecture was a foretaste of his future apologetic writing, which continued well into his Moore College years. The final lecture of this YMCA series, an assessment of Christian Science, likewise exhibited his TCD education in both philosophy and theology.[60]

Continued Defense Against Idealism

Books on the immanence of God kept appearing in these years—some closer to, others more distant from historic Christianity.[61] Charles d'Arcy commented that the "idea of Immanence" had "dominated the minds of many schools"[62] in the theological wrestling with the doctrine of Christ in these years.[63] The Donnellan Lectures of Hammond's friend Everard Digges La Touche would speak of T. H. Green's "almost, if not quite, pantheistic basis" for treating the incarnation.[64] Hammond contributed a substantial appendix, "Consciousness and the Sub-conscious," to his friend's book. It exhibited his competence in the work of William James and the psychological speculation connected with the personality of Christ.[65]

---

53. Kant, *Kant's Critique*, vi, 347–52; Hammond, "New Theology," 15, 16.

54. Bernard, *Works of Bishop Butler*; Hammond, "New Theology," 16–17, 25.

55. Orr, *Christian View*, 169, 182; Hammond, "New Theology," 17–18, 19.

56. Probably Fraser, *Philosophy of Theism*. See Passmore, *Hundred Years of Philosophy*, 539; Hammond, "New Theology," 16.

57. Griffin, "Personality," 518; Hammond, "New Theology," 12.

58. Moule, *Outlines of Christian Doctrine*, 82; Hammond, "New Theology," 27.

59. Denney, *Death of Christ*.

60. *Christian Science*.

61. D'Arcy, *Christianity and the Supernatural*; Warschauer, *Problems of Immanence*.

62. D'Arcy, *Christianity and the Supernatural*, v.

63. Langford, *In Search*, 66–67, 186–88.

64. Digges La Touche, *Person of Christ*, 122–23.

65. Hammond, "Consciousness and the Sub-conscious," 403–415, referencing James, *Principles* and *Varieties* and the theological discussion that had ensued.

On Immanence and Transcendence

The year before he wrote "Consciousness and the Sub-conscious" and about the time D. J. Davies was receiving Archbishop Wright's invitation to be principal of Moore College, Hammond published an article on God's immanence and transcendence.[66] He noted that, being influenced probably by the evolutionary school of philosophy, "most modern writers seem to take it for granted" that the admission of a process in nature completed "the argument . . . which asserts a wholly immanent process."[67] Hammond had in his sights the influence of the agnostic T. H. Huxley's Kantian idea that the power behind nature is unknowable, and Herbert Spencer's materialist notion that reality is matter and motion. His concern was to establish that pure immanentism is impossible and at the same time to rule out either the need for or the propriety of a "God of the gaps" defense of miracle.[68] The pure immanentist position failed to explain fully "the mental element in man," to account for the interpreter. He cited Arthur James Balfour in support of the view that (in his own words) "knowledge is in the last analysis a transcendent fact."[69]

Hammond argued from the analogy of humanity to God, who must be assumed to be personal. Like Bishop Joseph Butler, he is assuming the Creator-creature distinction without overtly starting with it. Thus the (human) mind is indisputably transcendent in relation to everyday facts. In pure thought, "the knower remains distinct from the known even while all that is known is traceable to the activity of the knower."[70] "In the region of personal experience," Hammond was arguing, "there can be no true doctrine of immanence without a doctrine of transcendence."[71] Since this test "responds to all the features of rationality" in man, it must "exhibit . . . its [same] essential characteristic" when applied to "the Greater Spirit." He argues for a natural theology from natural revelation: "So it seems just . . . to regard [nature] as the expression of an intelligence, and hence as the immanent manifestation of a Transcendent Self."[72]

He concluded that in this way God's immanence and transcendence combine as one and have a moral end: "So while all the truths associated

---

66. Hammond, "Immanence and Transcendence," 198–215.
67. Ibid., 200.
68. Ibid., 211–21.
69. Ibid., 207 (referencing "a recent meeting at the British Association").
70. Ibid., 213.
71. Ibid., 214.
72. Ibid.

with immanence may still be profitably maintained, it is possible to call back again morality, revelation, and hell."[73]

In this his initial constructive apologetic essay attempting a neutral approach, Hammond was establishing himself as an articulate Evangelical theologian in the prevailing fashion. The essay grappled with one of the major issues impinging on Christian faith, Roman Catholic and Protestant. Hammond worked towards a contemporary intellectual defense and exposition of an historic Reformation Evangelicalism. He brought to bear his education in philosophical and theological enquiry against contemporary liberal restatement on one hand, and against the Anglo-Catholic renewal of pre-Reformation doctrine on the other hand. *Liberal* Evangelicals, taking idealism for granted and feeling constrained to embrace a liberal position, could not so clearly do this.

On his visit to Sydney in 1926, Hammond would have learned of Francis Anderson (1858–1941), the not-long retired Hegelian idealist professor of philosophy at the University of Sydney. Anderson was sympathetic to "Christianity."[74] But to a monist, the historic Christian notion of God as creator, ontologically distinct from his creation (transcendent), was inadmissible. Ten years later in 1936, when Hammond arrived at Moore College, a new professor of philosophy, John Anderson, also a Scot, no idealist but also a monist, had been in the chair since 1927.[75] Hammond's introductory lecture at Moore College in 1936 was, according to an unnamed former student's recollection, "the transcendence of God."[76]

Authority in Religion

Hammond knew, of course, the nineteenth-century discussion on the issue of authority. His two articles addressing this subject were published in World War I Ireland, following the Easter Rising of 1916. "Authority in Religion," and "Authority in Religion II: The Place of Dogma"[77] are as intellectually impressive as they were important. They provided the basis for Hammond's statement on the authority of Scripture that the Inter-Varsity Fellowship of Evangelical Unions would adopt as its own.[78]

73. Ibid., 215.
74. See also chapter 8 above for Francis Anderson.
75. See Grave, *History*, 18–21, 24.
76. Nelson, *T. C. Hammond*, 101. Loane, not trained in philosophy, remembered it as on "Transcendentalism" (*Centenary History*, 140) which seems less likely.
77. Hammond, "Authority in Religion," 287–99; "Authority in Religion II," 25–39.
78. Hammond, "Fiat of Authority," 156–206; republished as Hammond, *Inspiration*

As noted in the case of D. J. Davies, a Kantian rejection of "external authority" entailed and sustained a liberal orientation with regard to Scripture as revelation. Hammond securely remained on his conservative Evangelical—indeed his Reformed—base. He noted that the problem of authority in religion was one amongst many "suggested by the present war"[79] (of 1914–1918), which was itself an effect of the impact of idealist immanentism, an older contemporary would later add.[80] Hammond considered that the "exacting task" of inquiry into the grounds of authority was never more necessary.[81] He alluded clearly to the Liberal Anglo-Catholic, A. E. J. Rawlinson's essay, "The Principle of Authority" in the volume *Foundations*;[82] nor had he missed B. B. Warfield's critical review of that book.[83] He alluded less clearly to R. Brook's essay rejecting the external authority of an infallible Bible.[84] He argued that while history showed that humanity's progress required both submission to authoritative leaders and revolt from outward forms, the solution was not in anarchistic individualism, but in "a truer apprehension of basal principles,"[85] in "laying afresh the foundations."[86] How then could individualism and authority be reconciled?

Hammond introduced an argument for the right of private judgment—properly understood—which is important for his future writing on religious authority. It was "not private in the sense of being mere individual eccentricity," but "in the sense that it represents the spiritual answer to the individual's need."[87] Thus, "the assent of the individual" to "formal enunciations of belief" (the Creeds) could be won by evidence that they "represent facts which must . . . evoke his acknowledgment . . . and also represent satisfaction of the inner craving of his immortal nature."[88]

One reason why submission to such a higher authority had "never in fact become universal" was that "a rational being is capable of

---

and Authority.

79. Hammond, "Authority in Religion," 287.
80. Webb, *Study*, 141–49.
81. Hammond, "Authority in Religion," 287.
82. Rawlinson, "Principle of Authority," 361–422; Hammond, "Authority in Religion," 292.
83. Warfield, Review of *Foundations*, 526–38 and 320–34.
84. Brook, "The Bible," 29–30.
85. Hammond, "Authority in Religion," 287.
86. Ibid., 292. See Rawlinson, "Principal of Authority," 375–77.
87. Hammond, "Authority in Religion," 293.
88. Ibid., 294 (*contra* Rawlinson, "Principle of Authority," 375).

development."⁸⁹ A second was that there were "differences in mental and moral insight." A third was "the fact of degeneration" in the individual or nation, which might prevent development.⁹⁰ Thinking probably of the Council of Trent, Hammond cited "half-reformations"⁹¹ that "retard the advent of purer doctrine."⁹² He did not mention the creature's sinful desire for independence from the Creator—the craving for autonomy.

His fourth and final major point, the authority of Scripture, exhibited his commitment to Reformation principles. G. E. Lessing (1729–1781) "ha[d] his sneer at Bibliolatry," which Lessing defined as: "that veneration . . . claimed for the books of the Bible, particularly the books of the New Testament."⁹³ That sneer, writes Hammond, had ignored the claim of the book to contain the thoughts of God: supremely the communication of God manifested in the flesh. The "unforced submission of the will" came when Holy Scripture was "recognised as the message of God to the soul."⁹⁴ Hammond capped off his discussion by quoting the Westminster Confession of Faith on the internal testimony of the Holy Spirit to the authority of Scripture.⁹⁵ He appreciated the Confession, which was chiefly the work of Church of England clergy and depended considerably on the work of the Irish archbishop, James Ussher. Hammond was an Anglican Reformation theologian as he addressed the liberal challenges of his day.

His sequel article, "Authority in Religion: II. The Place of Dogma,"⁹⁶ again recalled the Great War, and the liberal claim that the old must go and be replaced by a "Realism" that disliked to be called "New."⁹⁷ In 1915, the Scottish Presbyterian theologian teaching in Cambridge, John Wood Oman (1860–1930), had said, "war is ever a kind of apocalyptic. . . . Ideas that men had thought eternal are discovered to be only the fashion of a departing time."⁹⁸ The Dean of Durham, Herbert Hensley Henson, had forecast that "men must face again the old questions," for "the traditional theology" would again be "seen to be plainly inadequate to express the truth of religion

89. Ibid.
90. Ibid., 295.
91. Cf. the Puritan expression "but halfly reformed," (which I owe to Professor John Gascoigne).
92. Hammond, "Authority in Religion," 295–96.
93. Hammond is alluding to Lessing, "Bibliolatry," xxxix–xl.
94. Hammond, "Authority in Religion," 298.
95. Ibid., 298–99, quoting Westminster Confession of Faith, chapter 1 "Of the Holy Scripture," 5.
96. Hammond, "Authority in Religion: 2," 25–39.
97. Ibid., 37.
98. Langford, *In Search*, 251, citing Oman, *War*, 4–5.

as they must need perceive it."⁹⁹ Hammond thought differently: "It is very doubtful if the war will change much . . . The old answers will frequently arrest attention and dogma will come to its own again."¹⁰⁰ The reason was that "sin and redemption move in a region inaccessible to modern artillery." Indeed, the dogmas of "a faith as wide as the world" were "formulated amid the birth-pangs of modern Europe" and will not go under.¹⁰¹

Hammond later saw his confidence justified—with the rise of the Inter-Varsity Fellowship in Britain after the Great War, again later with the reestablishing of Frederic Barker's ideal for a predominantly Evangelical diocese in Sydney. Both of these developments would owe much to Hammond: the articulate defender of his authentic Anglican—that is to say, his English Reformation—heritage.

The essence of Hammond's defense of dogma in the second article was Biblicist: that while the authority of creeds was limited and provisional (not his term), they represented the fruit of the church's role as the keeper and interpreter of Holy Writ.¹⁰² "A Romanist and an intelligent member of the Brethren could equally, in good faith, subscribe to 'the three ancient creeds.'"¹⁰³ This is worth remembering with regard to a notion that Jones's connection with the Christian Brethren was in conflict with his own theological position. The Reformers did not, as "so-called liberal theologians represent," "cast away the authority of the Church and substitute the authority of the Bible."¹⁰⁴ They "merely professed to set in bold relief the revelation of God [in the Bible] and to control tradition by its explicit teaching."¹⁰⁵ It was "the ground on which [authority] is based" that the Reformers changed.¹⁰⁶ They were "the men of insight" who contributed to historical development.¹⁰⁷ "Reformed Theology," Hammond claimed, "wields a powerful influence" which stems with "very definite content" from a "coherence . . . due to its necessary deductions from certain established principles" of its period. "Freedom from dogma can only mean, therefore, freedom from thought."¹⁰⁸ Hammond drew parallels between science and Christian

---

99. Henson, "Church After the War," 256, cited in Langford, *In Search*, 252.
100. Hammond, "Authority in Religion: 2," 30.
101. Ibid.
102. Ibid., 32.
103. Ibid., 33.
104. Ibid., 31.
105. Ibid.
106. Ibid., 31–32.
107. Ibid., 33.
108. Ibid.

dogma. Science had "built up its creed slowly and admitted new articles or modified old ones with obvious reluctance," building it up "in precisely the same manner" as Christianity. And science, like Christianity, had made rapid "advances in [its] application to practical life."[109]

Hammond saw a further parallel between Christian dogma and science. As true science "must subject itself to nature," which "as an article of faith" it holds to be one, so "revelation is the quarry from which [Christian] dogma comes." In science "subsequent research may modify to some extent the terms in which older truth was expressed, but can never invalidate that which is true." Likewise, "whatever has been truly extracted" from the quarry of revelation has abiding value. "Subsequent labour may fit and shape and polish as well as increase the store. But the substance must remain unaltered." Hence in both science and religion, there are "buildings that require completion," but "it is no longer possible to lay afresh the foundations."[110] Re-statement of doctrine must therefore apply to "but a small proportion of the whole credal content."[111] The church's ministry was "to appeal to . . . hearts and consciences," seeking "to give [the dogmatic] decisions" of the past "their true value in relation to existing conditions."[112] Such was Hammond's reassurance to both the High Churchman and the Evangelical in the Church of Ireland in the face of liberal questioning.

So, did the right of private judgment "sweep away the true teaching office of the Church?" Rather, he affirmed, it based itself "upon the lessons of antiquity, indeed, but ever checking them" by "fearless and independent study of God's Word."[113] Dogma, "like any scientific formulation of experience," Hammond maintained, "remains undisturbed." It could be restated because it was approximation, but restatement is not ever "likely to negative the attainments of the past"; to assert that would be a repudiation of "the very notion of progress."[114]

Hammond concluded with the proposition that "authority is the compulsion of truth itself. Dogma is the expression of its binding force as truth," as spoken in the past. But "the message of past and present must awaken an intelligent response in the individual soul." In his next words, the reader finds a solution to external authority that escaped Liberal Evangelicals such as D. J. Davies: "It is through such a response that that which was formerly

---

109. Ibid., 34.
110. Ibid., 34–35.
111. Ibid., 35.
112. Ibid.
113. Ibid., 36.
114. Ibid., 38.

external becomes internal... the deepest conviction of our own heart....
Ever upon such rocks does [the Son of God] build His Church."[115]

Hammond's First Published Paper on Roman Catholicism

Hammond was already known as a "sound Protestant" at St Kevin's, his Church of Ireland parish in Dublin. He was also an activist Evangelical who wrote to the newspapers to defend those "wronged on account of their faith" (presumably Protestants) or other injustices.[116]

In January 1915 Hammond published his second *Irish Church Quarterly* article, "The Fascination of the Church of Rome: A Reply,"[117] provoked by a previous article pleading for Anglo-Catholic ritualist introductions.[118] It throws light on Hammond's Protestant Anglican—his Reformation Evangelical—case against ritualism and Rome. The previous article had argued that an unstable minority within the Church of Ireland had a Romeward instinct and sought to explain that this was for reasons of "temperament and feeling." The implicit demand was for the Church of Ireland to recognize "certain so-called Catholic developments."[119] To do so would be to hinder the drift of Roman Catholics towards the Church of Ireland. "Our fathers ... disregarded 'temperament' when it conflicted with truth."[120]

Hammond pointed to errors arising from the seeking of a psychological explanation for everything. First, that of "wide generalization," one example in this case being the claim that Protestants more easily "sacrifice ... their convictions upon the marriage altar." In fact, the statistics proved that after the Pope's *Ne temere* decree of 1907 concerning marriage of Roman Catholics to non-Roman Catholics, in Dublin, at least, the number of Roman Catholic conversions to Protestantism was larger than the reverse. It was a similar case in England.[121] Hammond also pointed to the failure of the Price article to define its terms, such as "objective," which it used for "the palpable," such as "the tangible Mass."[122]

---

115. Ibid., 38–39.
116. Nelson, *T. C. Hammond*, 59.
117. Hammond, "Fascination," 60–69.
118. Price, "Fascination," 316–26.
119. Hammond, "Fascination," 60.
120. Ibid., 61.
121. Ibid., 62.
122. Ibid., 63.

The article by the Anglo-Catholic ritualist was also guilty of the "tacit assumption that temperament creates facts," which was "the second error of the average psychological method of enquiry."[123] Thus "our burial service is bare and cold because it permits the mourner to do nothing for the deceased. But suppose he can do nothing." Hammond thought "he must be strangely irresponsive who is not moved by the ringing note of triumph in the fifteenth chapter of First Corinthians."[124]

"Temperament," Hammond argued finally, was "a product of training." He cites the "dubbing" of "every resuscitated medieval superstition as 'Catholic' by a particular party within the Anglican communion."[125] "To say that the reality of worship is foreign to Protestant principle is the reverse of the truth."[126]

To the argument that the Bible was wanting because it was reticent—as in fact it was—on "Episcopal government, Confirmation and Infant Baptism," Hammond replied that history was likewise reticent. But Rome defiantly solved this (double) problem "by creating her own standard."[127] The Evangelical dogmatician E. A. Litton had argued similarly.[128]

Resistance to Ritualism and Associated Doctrine

Hammond was at one with both Nathaniel Jones and D. J. Davies on this matter, and this was evident while he was the incumbent of St Kevin's from 1910. As in the article just examined, he repeatedly demonstrated his commitment to the Reformation character of the Church of England and Church of Ireland. He spoke for the Anti-Ritualist Society and wrote to the press to correct even the Archbishop King's Professor of Divinity, J. H. Bernard, on a point of liturgical use. He took determined action against a move by a Church of Ireland bishop to provide prayers for the dead.[129]

Hammond's Evangelical biblicism also lay behind his public attempt to recall the TCD Divinity School to "adequate Protestant and Evangelical

---

123. Ibid., 65.
124. Ibid., 66.
125. Ibid., 68.
126. Ibid.
127. Ibid., 69.
128. Litton, *Church of Christ*, 186-200 (on episcopacy), 144-49 (on infant baptism).
129. Nelson, *T. C. Hammond*, 59-60. There were horrendous war casualties on the Continent in 1915.

instruction."[130] As a convinced Reformation theologian bound by his ordination vows, Hammond opposed the innovations of those pressing for a closer conformity of the Church of Ireland with Roman Catholicism, or for a reversion to pre-Reformation times.

There was no weakening of Evangelical emphasis on the cross of Christ in his address (1917) to the Irish Church Union of Down, Connor, and Dromore in Belfast. Rather, *The Cross on the Communion Table* was his Reformation biblicism in crucicentric and activist mode. A Church of Ireland bishop had been proposing, in the midst of sentiment aroused by the war, to have Canon 36, which forbade placing a cross on the communion table, deleted from the Church of Ireland constitution.[131] Hammond argued that the Church of Ireland had gained, not lost, spiritual power and missionary zeal since 1871,[132] when the canon had been passed by a full and unanimous house of the General Synod. The canon was a statement against "the Ritualist movement across the water," which had by then succeeded in "rendering the English Church Services in some centres more Roman than the Romish Service itself."[133] In England in 1876, the Judicial Committee of the Privy Council had "declared that a cross erected behind the Communion Table was forbidden by law."[134]

Hammond, who had begun his studies at TCD in history, was always historically rigorous. He further pointed out that the "sign of the Cross" came early in the third century, and that Eusebius of Caesarea had made much of it after Constantine's conversion, around the year 312. But it was not until 423 that the Christian historian Sozomen mentioned the cross being actually placed on the table. At that time "sacerdotalism had gripped the imagination of the ministry."[135] He reminded his audience: "You are invited to reverse the mature judgment of the Reformation." The Reformers, who "were opposed by the keenest intellects of the Roman Communion," were themselves "really studied" men. Crosses were removed by "the deliberate injunctions of the Council in Edward VI's time, and later . . . [by] Queen Elizabeth supported by the whole Bench of Bishops."[136]

Moreover, the newly proposed move now invited them "to break with God's Word, which declares 'Thou shalt not make to thyself any graven

---

130. Ibid., 60, citing Minute Book of St Kevin's Parish.
131. Hammond, *Cross on the Communion Table*, 2.
132. Ibid., 4.
133. Ibid., 6.
134. Ibid., 8.
135. Ibid., 9.
136. Ibid., 10.

image.'"[137] More than once, Hammond referred to "the outraged feelings of humble parishioners."[138] Later, when in Sydney, the Red Book Case[139] would similarly resonate with him. Hammond, married to a Presbyterian, appealed to the fact that the existing canons had "permitted the son of the Puritan to join in worship with his less pronounced brother."[140] Unity in a common understanding of the gospel would always override denominational divide for this Reformation Evangelical. His resistance to Anglo-Catholic ritual innovation was principled and informed, no mere mindless prejudice.

Conclusion

Hammond's Evangelicalism included both a Reformation stance toward the ecclesiastical challenge of his day and a cogent critique of theological liberalism. If the shrinking Protestantism and growing liberalism of the Church of Ireland hierarchy did not favor his preferment, the Irish Church Missions would soon be keen to re-employ him—this time as a leader. Later, Hammond would have a profound influence on the course of Anglican Evangelicalism in Sydney and beyond. He was also to play a key role in the final framing of a constitution for the Church of England in all of Australia.

---

137. Ibid., 11.
138. Ibid., 1, 3, 12.
139. See chapter 12 below.
140. Hammond, ibid., 12.

11

Reformation Evangelicalism Defended and Expounded

Introduction

EARLY IN 1919, SOON after the armistice of World War I, T. C. Hammond was appointed Superintendent of the Irish Church Missions in Dublin, and his first years were those of the civil troubles.[1] The Easter Rising (1916), the Irish War of Independence, and the ensuing Civil War (1922–1923) issued ultimately in the establishment of the Irish Free State, in which the Roman Catholic Church in Ireland would have a new status. One of his main tasks was to instruct future workers of the Irish Church Missions. He was now also the editor of the ICM monthly, *The Catholic*. As an Evangelical theologian and a presbyter of the Church of Ireland, he challenged the Anglo-Catholic and liberal trends within Anglicanism as well as Roman Catholicism.

Hammond nowhere stated that it was impossible for Roman Catholics to be saved as such, only that certain unbiblical Roman Catholic doctrines, together with Rome's discipline, hindered apprehension of saving faith. His Reformation Evangelicalism was evident in all his publications. His pamphlet *How the Roman Church Treats the Bible*,[2] produced not long after he became superintendent, is not extant in Australia. The title of the ICM newspaper, *The Catholic*, appropriately claimed the historic orthodoxy of

---

1. Nelson, *T. C. Hammond*, 65–66.
2. See Nelson, ibid., 161.

Reformation Protestantism. His editorials would be interesting to research, but are not treated here.

The Caxton Hall Discussion (1922)

In London, in October 1922, Hammond replaced the speaker (who had fallen ill) in an advertised "discussion" with a Mr. Hand, a member of the Catholic Evidence Guild, but not himself a trained theologian. The agreed subject was: "There is only one Church founded by Christ, and on earth the head of that Church is the Pope, the Vicar of Christ."[3] Hand's opening statement had been fully approved by the Cardinal Archbishop of Westminster, Francis Adolphus Bourne (1861–1934).[4] He argued that Christ founded this society "with divine authority to teach Supernatural truth, and has imposed upon the human race the obligation to hear and believe its teaching under pain of eternal damnation."[5] God, he continued, "through the relationship that Christ established between Himself and Peter . . . has actually appointed for all ages One who when He speaks, can, with the authority of Christ, bid the storms of controversy abate."[6] Hand's concern was "that the Church must be infallible in its expression of God's laws in the supernatural order."[7] In the background were the decrees of the first Vatican Council (1870), which included the dogma of the infallibility of the Pope when speaking *ex cathedra*.[8] Hand stated: "The Holy Spirit dwells in the Church, so that when the Church speaks through the mouth of the Pope, the Holy Spirit guards him from error."[9]

Hammond acknowledged his "cordial agreement" with much that Hand had said, but was careful to distinguish the proposition "that our Lord founded one Church" from the proposition that "on earth the head of that Church is the Pope, the Vicar of Christ." His argument comprehended dogma, history, the witness of Scripture (the basic concern), "the judicious Hooker," theologian of the late sixteenth-century Church of England, and the Roman Catholic "Coryphaeus of controversialists," Robert Bellarmine (1542–1621). He questioned the validity of papal claims by putting them in

3. *Church of Christ*, title page.
4. Caithness, "Prefatory Note," 4.
5. Hand, "Address," 13.
6. Ibid.
7. Hand, "Addenda," 37.
8. "Dogmatic Decrees," chapter 4 "Concerning the Infallible Teaching," in Schaff, *Creeds*, 266–71.
9. Hand, "Addenda," 41.

the context of church history.¹⁰ Hammond concluded courteously by thanking Hand "for the manner in which he has conducted himself," and the audience for "demeanor worthy of a great occasion." He hoped that as a result of the meeting all present might "be united in closer and deeper devotion to ... the Lord who loved us and washed us from our sins in his own blood."¹¹ Hand replied in like kind.¹²

To the record of what had been said, each speaker was permitted to publish his own addenda. Against Hand's "Addenda"—on the authority of the Pope—Hammond argued the case against papal supremacy from his careful reading of ancient and modern primary sources, including Cardinal John Henry Newman.¹³ Hammond also published a small booklet, *Comments on the Discussion*, again citing Newman on the Vatican Council. He rebutted factually each of Hand's points, and brought to bear much evidence from Irish Roman Catholic history on the claim of the Pope's *personal* infallibility.¹⁴ The whole was Hammond at his learned Reformation Evangelical best.

Doubts of the Sons

As part of his ICM superintendent duties Hammond addressed "a defence of Romanism" that was being "used largely to interest those whose feet are tending towards Rome."¹⁵ *Faith of Our Fathers*, by Cardinal Gibbons (1834–1921) of Boston, USA, had seen many editions and reprints and its circulation was enormous.¹⁶ Claiming careful revision, it had been reissued in 1920 (again in 1927).¹⁷ Hammond's critique was therefore important and his title was pointed—*Doubts of the Sons*.

Hammond brought to bear the early Fathers, medieval theology (especially Thomas Aquinas), and that of Roman Catholic theologians since the Reformation, notably Robert Bellarmine (1542–1621). Hammond had read many sources of intra-Roman discussion and "the authorised formularies and systematic defences of the Church of Rome."¹⁸ He had checked standard

10. Hammond, "Address," 19–28.
11. Hammond, "Reply," 37.
12. Hand, "Mr. Hand's Reply," 37–38.
13. Hammond, "Addenda," 45–50.
14. Hammond, *Comments*, 16–24.
15. Hammond, *Doubts of the Sons*, 1.
16. Ibid., 49.
17. Gibbons, *Faith of Our Fathers*, title page.
18. Hammond, *Doubts of the Sons*, 49.

encyclopedic reference works and official government publications for accurate statistics. He did not overlook any questionable assertion of the cardinal's defense of Rome, or any unfavorable comparison of Protestant fruits with Roman Catholic.[19]

Hammond emerged from a "closely reasoned examination" with a verdict that represented his anti-Roman polemic at its sharpest. The cardinal's book was so "plausible [a] case" that it might tempt a Protestant reader "to imagine that the Roman system has been grievously misrepresented."[20] But the more than 400 pages of *Faith of Our Fathers* were "all written in the same vein of rhetorical inaccuracy."[21] Hammond found it to be a "specious defence of Roman doctrines and practice" whose author "persistently minimises the effect of certain Roman tenets." The cardinal's list of "Roman resemblances to New Testament doctrine" could be "easily and most effectively retorted upon him." Instances of the cardinal's special pleading included: "parading admitted examples" of papal sanctity while "ignor[ing] the evidences of scandal"; contradicting Cardinal Newman on "the relation between Apostolic and Papal guidance" (a point in the Caxton Hall discussion); "pervert[ing] the criminal statistics ... to support his theory" that Roman Catholicism is morally superior in its results; and minimizing prayer to "the Blessed Virgin Mary" and "the extravagant language" used of her.[22] Against Cardinal Gibbons's claim that chapter 6 of the Gospel of John supported a literal eating of Christ's flesh in the Mass, Hammond provided quotations from Jerome, Tertullian, and Athanasius, among "many more" that he "could append," "to show the slender basis even in the Fathers for the more startling innovations which Cardinal Gibbons seeks to impose as veritable and ancient truths."[23]

There was an eloquent indignation in his tone.

Concerning Penal Laws

History remained a love for Hammond, which is evident in "these studies written popularly"[24] for *The Church of Ireland Gazette* in the centenary year of the Roman Catholic Relief Act of 1829. They are both an anti-Roman polemic and a Protestant apologetic by a Reformation Evangelical.

19. Ibid., 49.
20. Ibid., 49.
21. Ibid., 41.
22. Ibid., 49–50.
23. Ibid., 51.
24. Hammond, *Concerning Penal Laws*, 6.

Under the Irish Free State since 1922, Hammond was attempting "to supply fruitful lines of investigation" into the history of the old Penal Laws of Ireland, which imposed "penal disabilities on account of religion."[25] This awakened strong feelings grounded in "convictions, which, on examination, prove[d] to be very remotely related to the actual facts of the situation."[26] He desired to lend a historical perspective: "The vacillation of great and good men in relation to . . . toleration indicates that as a matter of civil jurisprudence the problem presented perplexing situations."[27] Thomas Aquinas, Lord Acton, Gibbon, Elizabeth I, and Archbishop Whitgift (1530–1604) all justified persecution under particular historical circumstances. Therefore, Hammond wrote, "it strains credulity to believe that such varied minds . . . were alike governed by uncontrollable vindictiveness."[28] Hammond liked to think here, tentatively, that "the milder temper of to-day is . . . partly at any rate," a result of past experience of suffering. "The study of history [did] reveal a progress."[29] This reminds one of the Liberal Evangelical historian D. J. Davies. Despite the impact of the Great War, the "Whig interpretation" of history as progress was dominant for many at that time.[30]

One hundred years on from the Emancipation Act of 1829, Hammond thought it was "abundantly evident that the leaders of the destiny of English and Irish Roman Catholics had no small share in retarding their followers from entering on an inheritance of freedom."[31] It was "the pressure of events" that "forced a changed attitude on religious questions as they affected those outside the pale of the Roman communion."[32] He viewed "developments of ages" as "the outworking of a Divine Providence."[33]

Chapter 1 of "Penal Laws: Meaning and Early Christian History" defined them as laws against religious ceremonies and beliefs, and traced their origin in Christendom to the inheritance of the Roman system of jurisprudence. Constantine the Great's penalties for the dissentients from the Nicene Creed and enactments for the observance of Sunday "laid the foundation for . . . subsequent developments."[34] Both sides at the time of Ni-

25. Ibid., 1.
26. Ibid.
27. Ibid., 2.
28. Ibid., 2–3.
29. Ibid., 4.
30. Bebbington, *Patterns*, 85–89.
31. Hammond, *Penal Laws*, 5.
32. Ibid.
33. Ibid.
34. Ibid., 11.

caea subsequently consented to the policy.[35] His reference was the standard work, Gwatkin's *Early Church History*.

The select episodes Hammond recounted included the "Donatist Dispute" (chapter 2), "The Lateran Council" (chapter 4), the "Elizabethan Legislation" (chapter 7), "Ireland and the Reformation" (chapter 9), the "Penal Code of William and Mary" (chapter 11), and the "Internal Dissension amongst Roman Catholics" (chapter 14) after the Relief Act of 1778. The act had granted English Roman Catholics "a liberal toleration of their religion and a security and free disposal of their property."[36] In that same year the Protestant-dominated Irish Parliament passed a similar measure for Irish Roman Catholics, in 1782 conceded a measure of independence, and in 1793 "placed [them] in a more favorable position than [their] English or Scotch co-religionists or," except for a seat in Parliament, "than the Protestant Dissenter in England."[37] However soon afterwards support rose in Ireland, North and South, for a French invasion of England, and by 1798 the North was ranged against the South in "the outer darkness of civil strife."[38] Hammond concluded his chapter, "The Position in Ireland," with the alliterative eloquence of deep sadness for his country:

> And so the dreams of philosophers, the intrigues of politicians, the perorations of patriots, the efforts of statesmen and the genuine struggles of seekers after a full and more Christ-like comprehension seemed destined to combine to work ruin for Ireland. . . . As often before her own sons hounded her to suicide.[39]

In hope of the relaxation of the Penal Laws, the Roman Catholic bishops welcomed the Union (1800) "with outstretched arms."[40] But relief did not come until 1829.

How, then, did this Reformation Evangelical respond to the "the common criticism made by Roman Catholic controversialists that the Reformers were themselves intolerant"?[41] Simply by noting that "the . . . theology of the sixteenth century reflects in this matter the teaching that prevailed in the Catholic Church . . . from the beginning of the fifth century."[42] More-

35. Ibid., 12.
36. Ibid., 133.
37. Ibid., 161.
38. Ibid., 164.
39. Ibid.
40. Ibid.
41. Ibid., 37.
42. Ibid., 37-38.

over, not only was it usually undesirable suddenly to abandon "age-long traditions," but also that the people "would be likely to construe complete relaxation [of penalties] . . . in a most unfavourable manner."[43] Hammond also notes that "the germs of a wider tolerance" lay in Hooker's position that the "supreme power" of Christian rulers "in ecclesiastical affairs" was not "a principle of Divine Law" but of "human right"[44] (implying that it was not immutable).

Again Hammond insisted on an historical perspective: "the new [Protestant] States . . . found themselves compelled to fight for their very existence." He listed the "counter Reformation" in Hungary, Spain's attempt "to purge the Netherlands of the stain of dissent," the massacre of Huguenots on St Bartholomew's Day, the revocation of the Edict of Nantes and the bull against Henry of Navarre.[45] "On the one hand, while the reformed bodies still retained" compulsory conformity to the state's ecclesiastical system,[46] they administered this with "a measure of leniency."[47] Thus, in Ireland the fine for non-attendance at the parish church was "seldom exacted . . . and perfect toleration and political equality existed . . . previous to the rebellion of 1641."[48] But Pope Paul IV's bull *Cum ex Apostolatus Officio* (of February 15, 1559), which deposed schismatic or heretical rulers, complicated things.[49] Hammond knew the history, and was convinced that "parliamentary repression [was] neither a safe or desirable way of checking erroneous beliefs."[50]

Resisting Anglo-Catholic Pressures: Reaffirming Reformation and Biblical Doctrine

Hammond's involvement in resisting ritual (and doctrinal) innovations tending to reverse the Reformation character of the Church of Ireland was to entail some pressured historical research in the midst of his Irish Church Missions work.

---

43. Ibid., 42.
44. Ibid., 46–47, citing Hooker, *Laws of Ecclesiastical Polity*, 8.2.5.
45. Hammond, *Penal Laws*, 49.
46. Ibid., 51.
47. Ibid.
48. Ibid., 52.
49. Ibid., 52–53.
50. Hammond, "Emancipation," 217.

Authority in the Church

It was the final year of World War I when Hammond began to be involved in a Church of Ireland synodical dispute that closely touched Reformation theology. The Divinity School at TCD was using Procter and Frere's history of the Prayer Book,[51] which promoted Anglo-Catholic views such as that "God is localized in the Chancel for the purposes of worship."[52] At the Church of Ireland General Synod of May 1918 Primate John Crozier (1858–1920) had ruled against a proposal that the synod have "a direct voice in the nature of the teaching given to intending candidates for Holy Orders in that Church,"[53] instead of allowing each local diocesan bishop to determine autonomously the syllabus and textbooks for study. Archbishop of Dublin, J. H. Bernard, had so determined at TCD. Hammond prepared an impressive historical study for counsel for an appeal in the General Synod against the late primate's ruling.

In his brief Hammond explained that he had "endeavoured to confine [his] enquiry to the single issue regarding the authority of an individual Bishop, and the various limitations upon it which are revealed in the course of history."[54] Granting that the current regulations for the theological requirements of candidates were unsatisfactory (chapter 1), Hammond then outlined (chapter 2) the history of the reconstruction of the Church of Ireland after its disestablishment in 1869, and the powers of its General Synod. The consequences of the late primate's ruling favored High Anglicanism. He adduced E. A. Litton's "thoughtful testimony" to the "exaltation of the order of Bishops at the expense of the others." In the disestablished Irish Church there had been "cordial co-operation of the different orders of clergy, and of the clergy and laity, each with recognized powers and duties."[55] He traced the "Checks upon Episcopal Authority" (chapter 3) from the earliest times: the community was always involved. Having implications for "the whole conditions surrounding ordination," the evidence "established . . . beyond doubt that Bishops exercised from the first their important duties under the authority and by the control of the community at large."[56]

The testimony of the Reformation bishops Parker and Grindal, supported by the evidence of the early councils, made it "impossible to

---

51. Frere, *New History*.
52. Hammond, *Cross on the Communion Table*, 6.
53. Hammond, *Authority in the Church*, 1.
54. Ibid., iii,
55. Ibid., 19.
56. Ibid., 30.

assent wholly to the opinion of Dr Bernard that no one except a Bishop had a vote or a share in the decision that was the outcome of the conciliar deliberations."[57]

After a study of the theory of Cyprian of Carthage (chapter 5) in context, he traced the "Gradual Encroachments of Episcopacy" (chapter 6) to the pre-Reformation era. With the advent of the Reformed church (chapter 7 "The Reformation Break"), "the introduction of new methods [was] of real significance"—the downfall of the "Spiritual" courts and the reserving of all judicial power to the crown. He quoted the conservative High Churchman Bishop Christopher Wordsworth, who in 1877 wrote that while bishops and clergy "*derive* their authority to preach or minister the sacraments . . . from Christ alone," yet "the *places*" where it is "*exercised and applied*" and "the *external* jurisdiction by which [it] is supported, are from the laws of the realm."[58] In chapter 8 "Problems in Jurisdiction," Hammond carefully defined terms like *jurisdiction* as he traced the position of the Church of Ireland.

Although *Authority in the Church* was "a masterly argument," as Nelson says, the appeal was lost. Also, Nelson seems to imply, this study was long held against Hammond.[59] *The Churchman*, however, called it "enlightening" and "deserv[ing] careful study" for "its bearing on the whole future of the National Church,"[60] that is, the Church of England. It formed a probable background to Hammond's role in the future "Red Book" case (1943–1948), and it was a useful preparation for his final achievement in Sydney—formulating the successful version of a constitution for the whole Church of England in Australia in 1955.[61]

The Prayer Book Debate in Parliament

After the House of Commons rejected the proposed "Deposited Prayer Book" in December 1927, a modified version came before parliament again in June 1928. An Anglo-Catholic representation propagated the idea that the Thirty-nine Articles did not condemn "the philosophically grounded and attested teaching" of the Church of Rome on transubstantiation.

---

57. Ibid., 40.

58. Ibid., 84, citing Wordsworth, *Miscellanies* 3:143–44. Hammond did not give volume number; the italics are Wordsworth's.

59. Nelson, *T. C. Hammond*, 61.

60. Editor, "Church Book Room Notes," 221.

61. See next chapter for both matters.

Hammond gave "a carefully reasoned account of the real meaning of the Scholastic doctrine."[62]

He showed by examining the intricacies of scholastic philosophy that the Council of Trent had adopted the metaphysical view of the Lateran Council (1215), defended by Thomas Aquinas. This was incontrovertibly what Article 28 "Of the Lord's Supper" rejected.[63] Hammond was one of the many Evangelical clergy, including Bishop E. A. Knox, who contributed to the success of its Evangelical members in persuading the Commons to reject the proposed new book.

On The Thirty-nine Articles and 1933

Anglo-Catholic pressure continued to rise, however, as the centenary approached of Keble's July 14, 1833 historic Oxford Assize sermon, "National Apostasy." In 1931 Hammond contributed to a pamphlet series on the Thirty-nine Articles the evidence that they were intentionally framed against certain Roman Catholic positions.[64] He was concerned to authenticate "the real significance of the Reformation note so clearly sounded in this confession of faith."[65] Even in Article 2 "Of the Word, or Son of God, Which was Made Very Man," Hammond traced "the earliest note of opposition to the Roman position" concerning Christ's sacrifice in the phrase, "also for all actual sins of men." Hammond added this to Article 31 "Of the Oblation of Christ Finished upon the Cross" and compared it with Trent to make clear the reference to the Roman pronouncements on *justification* in 1547, *penance* in 1551, *the Mass* in 1562, and *purgatory* in 1563.[66] These "unite[d] in declaring" that through "the Mass, Penance and Purgatory" a degree of "satisfaction for actual sins" can supplement "the one offering of Christ once made" (Article 31). The phrase "for all actual sins of men" was "the acid test by which systems of theology were appraised in the sixteenth century."[67]

In the same way, on "justification," "good works," "the Church," "the Sacraments," and "the Sacrifice of the Mass" Hammond compared the

---

62. Knox, "Foreword," 4.
63. Hammond, *Does the Doctrine of Transubstantiation . . . ?*, 6–7, 41.
64. Hammond, *Thirty-nine Articles*.
65. Ibid., 3.
66. "Decree on Justification, Decree concerning . . . the Eucharist, on . . . Penance and Extreme Unction, Decree concerning Purgatory," in Schaff, *Creeds*, 89–110, 126–39, 139– 58, 198–99.
67. Hammond, *Thirty-nine Articles*, 7.

specific references in the Latin version of the Articles with the Latin of the Canons and Decrees of Trent. The Articles were "that formulated system that exhibits the genius of the Reformed Creed."[68] Hammond, as a Reformation Evangelical theologian, was motivated and able to achieve what the Keswick and premillennial Evangelical Nathaniel Jones, not quite so well equipped, also did well. D. J. Davies's lecture on the Articles showed he, a Liberal Evangelical, did not value them quite like that.[69]

On the Oxford Movement Claimed as Revival[70]

Davies the historian did not examine the Oxford Movement's claim of continuity with Evangelicalism. Hammond did so, shortly before the centenary celebrations of Keble's Assize sermon. In answer to "voices... declaring that the Oxford Movement was 'the completion' of the Evangelical Revival,"[71] Hammond contrasted the two movements.

The Evangelicals, in speaking of "sin, redemption, regeneration, justification and sanctification" as "realities in personal experience," brought "new motive-power" into the moralist focus of "Low Churchism"—which was mere "behaving well for the future."[72] They had "revived much of the essential teaching of the Reformers" but only "after a piecemeal fashion." Most of those who did not separate from the Church of England, as did the Evangelical Arminian Methodists, "accepted the tenets of Calvinism," but only Charles Simeon, and later Dean Goode and Nathaniel Dimock, attempted theological formulation of their Reformation heritage.[73] The Evangelicals, Hammond wrote, "while strong Biblicists, were, so far as Bible study permitted, undogmatic,"[74] meaning they were not dogmaticians. A comparison might be made with D. W. B. Robinson, who inspired many Moore College students to achieve fine biblical scholarship over the years,[75] but was emphatic that he had never studied systematic theology.[76]

The Oxford Movement, on the other hand, Hammond viewed as "the outcome of incoherence," something which he found in its leading

68. Ibid., 16.
69. See chapters 6 and 9 above.
70. Hammond, "Evangelical Revival," 1–12.
71. Ibid., 2.
72. Ibid., 2, 4, citing Butler, *Analogy*, part 2, chapter 5, section 9.
73. Hammond, "Evangelical Revival," 6.
74. Ibid.
75. See Shiner, "Appreciation," 9–62.
76. Robinson, Interview.

promoters: J. H. Newman (later Cardinal Newman), the Anglo-Catholic "political star" William Gladstone, Hurrell Froude, and John Keble.[77] The influence of Charles Gore had brought in the very "Liberalism against which Pusey fulminated."[78] Tractarians had "weakened the witness of the Church of England."[79] In sum, the Oxford Movement had "not completed the Evangelical Revival," and Hammond thanked God "they ha[d] not finished it."[80] Evangelicals . . . should therefore take heart and patiently "build more securely" than their early forefathers.[81]

So Hammond wrote in 1931 and 1933. Three years later this Reformation Evangelical would be principal of Moore Theological College in the Diocese of Sydney. Veterans of the Nathaniel Jones era, who had got to know him in 1926, would welcome him with open arms, and Hammond would train the college's Evangelical students to "build more securely."

Hammond and Protestant Liberalism

In the years of his ICM work Hammond's mind continued to engage with basic issues that arose from the side of Evangelical Liberalism. His awareness of theologically liberal writers and grasp of the issues enabled him to speak to a wide audience, including Evangelicals generally.

"The Fiat of Authority" (1925)[82]

This essay would become a landmark statement and be republished by the IVF as representing its own position. It originated as a contribution to a centrist Evangelical group representing scholarship that resisted the liberal accommodation of the Anglican Evangelical Group Movement.

By late 1917 the theological liberalism of the Group Brotherhood had come to dominate the governing body of Evangelicalism's flagship, the Church Missionary Society. The General Secretary from 1910 to 1923, C. C. B. Bardsley, was of this outlook, and some on the society's general committee presented a memorial urging a liberal broadening of the society's

---

77. Hammond, "Evangelical Revival," 8.
78. Ibid., 10.
79. Ibid., 12.
80. Ibid.
81. Ibid.
82. Hammond, "Fiat of Authority," 156–206. See McIntosh, "'External Prop' or 'Divine Fiat,'" 67–91.

position on "revelation and inspiration." In response to this the Fellowship of Evangelical Churchmen was formed on November 22, 1917. Their central concern was "the essential deity" of Christ and "the infallibility of all his utterances as recorded in Holy Scripture"[83]—not a particularly stringent requirement. The second half of it voiced the very same issue that Digges La Touche and others had raised with Principal Davies in Sydney only a few years before.

The new Fellowship of Evangelical Churchmen (FEC), whose members included Henry Wace, dean of Canterbury, presented its counter-memorial. The CMS General Committee adopted a concordat in February 1918,[84] but it had proved unsatisfactory. From March to November 1922 the FEC members of the CMS General Committee attempted to return the society to its original principles. Eventually the CMS committee refused to accept an amendment formulated by Wace, Bishop E. A. Knox and others, an amendment that would have bound the CMS to "belief in the absolute truth of [Christ's] teaching and utterances, and [belief] that His authority is final." Anticipating that the CMS General Committee would reject this, the FEC committee had provisionally "called into existence the Bible Churchmen's Missionary Society." Immediately after their amendment was lost they announced the new society's formation.[85] Today that society is called "Crosslinks."

In that same November the Group Brotherhood was about to publish its coming-out volume, *Liberal Evangelicalism* (February 1923), announcing itself as the "Anglican Evangelical Group Movement."[86] The work was clearly in the mind of the FEC men as they planned their own statement, *Evangelicalism* (1925), which included Hammond's contribution—"The Fiat of Authority."[87] His essay was abreast of the most advanced contemporary thinking, including that of Liberal Anglo-Catholic A. E. Rawlinson's forthcoming appeal for a new policy.[88] Hammond's very title alluded to a recent essay by his archbishop, Charles d'Arcy, insisting: "no controversy can be

---

83. Scales, "Illustrations of Compromise," 229, 229n56.

84. Ibid., 229.

85. Ibid., 228–233; also Knox, *Reminiscences*, 329. See Hewitt, *Problem of Success*, 461–73.

86. Rogers, *Liberal Evangelicalism*.

87. Hammond, "Fiat of Authority," 156–206; cf. Rogers, "Religious Authority," 28–50, and Storr, "The Bible and its Value," 80–100. A fellow contributor with Hammond to *Evangelicalism* was the well-known Canadian Evangelical, Dyson Hague (1857–1935), with "Justification," 79–109.

88. Burroughs, "Evangelicalism," 54n2; Rawlinson, "Authority," 83–97.

settled by the *fiat* of any man . . . or by the authority of any tradition."[89] Hammond's reading, we assume, also included the *Presbyterian and Reformed Review* and *Princeton Theological Review* with their critical reviews by Benjamin Warfield and others, and James Orr's *International Standard Bible Encyclopedia* (1915), for which Warfield had written the articles "Revelation" and "Inspiration."[90]

In part 1 of his essay, "The Character of Inspiration," Hammond aimed to clear away "much of the objection to verbal inspiration" which arose "from a wrong employment of words,"[91] and to adduce evidence that demonstrated the strength of his case. Explicitly, he wrote for those (like Bishop E. A. Knox, no doubt) who with him assumed a personal God who has revealed himself in Scripture, "in so far as [it] is regarded as a human utterance under divine influence."[92] He argued that it was not completely correct to say (as had D. J. Davies) that the church had never defined inspiration, but rather that it had not done so fully. Against the popular position that "the men were inspired, not their words" Hammond offered a definition: "Inspiration must be regarded as the expression of the Divine will in human thought, to the extent that human thought can express it."[93] The "fundamental thought embodied in the word 'inspiration'" was that God communicated his will through the medium of language. "It is eloquent of [the Divine] grace," he wrote, "that He should control the medium he employs."[94]

Perhaps for the benefit of Evangelicals like Bishop E. A. Knox, who had recently disowned "verbal inspiration,"[95] Hammond explained that it implied neither the *ipsissima verba*[96] quotation of the Old Testament in the New, nor the mechanical transmission of the Divine thought "like a gramophone record."[97] No doubt with Farrar's Bampton Lectures of 1885 in mind,[98] he said that "verbal inspiration" meant simply that the language in which the Divine thought was "produced by normal rational processes" was "an adequate vehicle for its communication," a view "as remote from

---

89. D'Arcy, "Christian Liberty," 13. Emphasis added. D'Arcy was appointed Archbishop of Armagh and Primate of All Ireland from 1920 until his death in 1938.

90. Warfield, "Inspiration," 1473–83, and "Revelation," 2573–82.

91. Hammond, "Foreword," iii.

92. Hammond, "Fiat of Authority," 156–57. See Knox, *On What Authority?* and *Reminiscences*, 327–28.

93. Ibid., 167.

94. Hammond, *Inspiration*, iii.

95. Knox, *On What Authority*, 180–225.

96. (Latin) "identical words."

97. Hammond, "Fiat of Authority," 168–69.

98. Farrar, *History*.

a mechanical theory as it can be."⁹⁹ Hammond's immediate predecessor at Moore College, D. J. Davies, assumed a mechanical notion in the term.

Hammond rebutted the critical theories: that of "degrees of inspiration as between," (for example) "the sayings of Christ and prosaic details of Old Testament history."¹⁰⁰ He also rejected Wellhausen's Hegelian reconstruction of Israel's history (often the liberal referent of "progressive revelation"). That made the Old Testament a book containing a verifiably "wholly erroneous view of national development with hopeless anachronisms discoverable by the wit of man."¹⁰¹ Hammond allowed, of course, for *forms* of literature: fiction and parable "may be admitted" to "teach Divine truth," but not if they seemed to be "masquerading as facts."¹⁰² In support he cited a scholar who, while rejecting this view of inspiration, conceded that the aggregate of "errors of history and knowledge and defects in the text and its transmission" was "so slight as to be practically negligible."¹⁰³

As for the variations between the gospel accounts of Christ's words, the Synoptists (Matthew, Mark, and Luke) exhibited "sufficient agreement to show that the records ultimately depend upon some common source" and "enough difference to show that . . . the operating intelligence of the [writers] was not passive but active."¹⁰⁴ Hence "those who begin by denying verbal inspiration end by involving themselves in a hopelessly mechanical form of word warfare"!¹⁰⁵ He suggested several reasons for the distinctive character of the Gospel of John.¹⁰⁶ The theory of original documents without minor discrepancies such as "possible misreading of numbers, misplacing of names and, in a few instances, the order of events . . . lacks complete cogency."¹⁰⁷ Nevertheless, "the phenomenon of inspiration appears as the activity of God upon men clothing the Divine ideas in human language."

The notion of progressive revelation in the sense of divinely guided stages in men's ascent to "the full apprehension of truth" was correct, he argued.¹⁰⁸ But Divine control had lovingly restrained "the intrusion" of any

---

99. Hammond, "Fiat of Authority," 171; cf. Knox, "Propositional Revelation," 1–9, republished in Knox, *Selected Works*, 2:307–17.

100. Hammond, "Fiat of Authority," 173.

101. Ibid., 178.

102. Ibid.

103. Curtis, "Infallibility," 262–63. Quoted in Hammond, "Fiat of Authority," 179.

104. Hammond, "Fiat of Authority," 181.

105. Ibid., 182.

106. Ibid.

107. Ibid., 184.

108. Ibid., 185.

"residual effect of sin" into "the area of vital concern." The dual nature of Christ, he adds, "establishes once and for all the possibility of a perfectly human thought exhibiting absolute harmony with the Divine purpose."[109]

In part 2 "Problems of Authority" Hammond grounded in the character of inspiration thus defined. He explained that the two forms of this remaining question must not be confused: "How has the authority [of Scripture] *demonstrated* itself?" and "What are the historic conditions under which the decision concerning inspiration *manifests* itself?"[110]

He first defused Immanuel Kant's critical "abstract problem of authority"[111] (to which D. J. Davies anchored his "external prop" criticism). Neither the state nor the church actually exerted a "purely external authority on the individual as such." In the case of the church, there was the common basis of revelation and the indwelling of the Holy Spirit "in every true member."[112] Since the church had not reached perfection, however, to suppress individual liberty of conscience was "the error of spurious Catholicity"; but to disregard the community was "the error of so-called Modernism."[113] Hence, Holy Scripture's authority as the Word of God "is of that ultimate nature which can indeed be made manifest to conscience ... but cannot be made the subject of formal propositions, or supported by superior external attestation."[114] He seems to be implying, in different words, the testimony of the Holy Spirit to Scripture, something that conscience can recognize, once regenerate.[115]

"That certain utterances are inspired is finally determined by the appeal to the conscience and its moral influence,"[116] he continued. The conscience of the individual absorbed its morality "from institutions and customs" that were themselves the product of "precedent moral consciousnesses."[117] But no individual could impose his stage of attainment on God[118] (as the modernist imposed his supposedly growing moral consciousness, one might add). Christ's teaching with authority was not that of an external "ecclesiastical

---

109. Ibid., 185–86.
110. Ibid., 186–87. Emphasis added.
111. Kant, *Religion*.
112. Hammond, "Fiat of Authority," 187–89.
113. Ibid., 189–90.
114. Ibid., 190–92.
115. As Calvin, *Institutes*, 1.7.4–5; Warfield, "Calvin's Doctrine," 219–325 (reprint, 29–130).
116. Hammond, "Fiat of Authority," 192.
117. Ibid., 193–94.
118. Ibid., 193.

imprimatur," but appealed to his word and his works and its "consonance with" Moses, for example. The epistles indicated the work of the Spirit to create "a spiritual capacity for spiritual reception."[119]

What of "that school of interpreters" which asserted that "the Church was before the Bible"? (One thinks of the Liberal Anglo-Catholic, Charles Gore, whom Davies criticized for leaning on this "external prop."[120]) Hammond answered that the church only "recognised the Sacred Scriptures as being God's message to man and published abroad its conviction" based soundly on "the inherent power of the Scriptures themselves."[121]

The second question was, why was the scope of inspiration "limited to the circle of canonical Scripture?"[122] Hammond sought "to determine the principle under the guidance of which the Canon has been formed." One element "persistently ignored," he wrote, but "prominent in the ancient discussions" was the authority of Christ. It was therefore the authority of his words, of the apostle Paul and of his writings, and of the first recipients who had personal acquaintance with the authors. The same was true for Moses and hence the authority of the Old Testament.[123] Hammond argued that, rightly interpreted, the facts supported "the theory of immediate personal authority" in the formation of the canon. Thus, in place of initial "more or less imperfect gospel narratives," "God supplied the Church" with the present fuller narratives.[124] The Old Testament canon had been determined in the Jewish church before Christ and it was Jesus's Bible, and that of the early church. Writings excluded from the New Testament finally did not attract "the reverence attached to the genuine writings of the apostolic age."[125]

Moreover, the canon, closely considered, exhibited "an inner principle of unity clearly revealed in the New Testament books." It seemed "ill-advised . . . to revise the labours committed to the glowing period" of "immediate contact with the Son of God," or recent contact.[126]

The above is only a synopsis of Hammond's eloquent and carefully crafted essay. It was in part the fruit of his thinking on authority published in the *Irish Church Quarterly Review*.

---

119. Ibid., 195–96.
120. Davies, "Modern Scholastics," 5.
121. Hammond, "Fiat of Authority," 199.
122. Ibid., 199.
123. Ibid., 200–201.
124. Ibid; cf. Luke 1:1–4.
125. Ibid., 201–3.
126. Ibid., 204–6.

"The Significance of the Death of Christ" (1935)

The Christian student world of the day faced the dismissal by liberal thinkers not only of the inspiration of Scripture but also of the historic Reformation view of the cross of Christ. Warfield called this "the established church-doctrine of satisfaction."[127] In the Prayer Book service of the Lord's Supper the Anglican communicant always heard a summary of the doctrine of Christ's death: "Who made there by his one oblation of himself once-offered a full, perfect and sufficient sacrifice, oblation and satisfaction for the sins of the whole world."[128]

This deliberately excluded the late medieval scholastic doctrine expressed in the Roman Catholic Mass, while retaining the biblical notion of Christ's death in the place of sinful human beings for their forgiveness. Liberal thinkers, as noted in chapter 1, were troubled by what their consciences saw as a moral problem in this very idea.

Hammond wrote his defense of the historic doctrine in a chapter, "The Significance of the Death of Christ," for the small Inter-Varsity Fellowship book, *From the Manger to the Throne: Outstanding Events in the Life of Our Lord*.[129] We remember that in 1902, the year of James Denney's classic treatment of the New Testament evidence, Hammond had heard G. T. Manley emphasize the importance of settled conviction on the doctrine of the atonement.[130] There were quite different and influential treatments about, then and in the following decades. In 1901 R. C. Moberly had published his "great book," *Atonement and Personality*.[131] Its central thesis was "Christ the Perfect Penitent."[132] Hammond had probably seen B. B. Warfield's verdict, that it was a high version of the moral suasion or governmental view, in which Christ performed a work "terminating immediately on God" and secondarily on man.[133]

Far from the First World War leading to a deepened Anglican reflection on the cross,[134] by that time many liberal writers thought of Christ's death as terminating purely on man: it could persuade a person of the need to repent, and thus receive forgiveness by God, defined only as love.

---

127. Warfield, "Chief Theories," 351–69.
128. *Prayer of Consecration*.
129. Hammond, "Significance of Christ's Death," 39–49.
130. Trinity College Dublin 8 (1902), 168; Denney, *Death of Christ*.
131. Ramsey, *Gore to Temple*, 46, referring to Moberly's *Atonement and Personality*.
132. Ibid., 46–47.
133. Warfield, "Chief Theories," 366–67.
134. Pace Ramsey, *Gore to Temple*, 44.

This was true of R. T. Howard's chapter "The Work of Christ" in *Liberal Evangelicalism* (1923).[135] Dean Hastings Rashdall wrote from the standpoint of those "who feel how deeply the traditional views have libeled the view of God's character."[136] K. E. Kirk's essay "Atonement" (1926), argued that (in Ramsey's words) "only the slenderest basis, if any, can be found for substitutionism in St Paul and that the New Testament doctrine may be best summed up in the admittedly non-Biblical word 'reparation.'"[137] The Liberal Evangelical L. W. Grensted (one of those nominated for Archbishop of Sydney in 1933) also published on the subject.[138] The earlier (1901) and more popular presentation of the Australian-born Patrick Carnegie Simpson was supportive of the historic doctrine.[139]

Hammond responded to the objections like those of Rashdall indirectly: the apostle Paul had met objections which, like those of modern theology, were "the issue of highly reflective minds" trained in Greek philosophy. But Paul was conscious of a "real Divine intervention" in the cross for the "eternal salvation of men."[140] His preaching was "reproducing the thought of his Master" who, when Peter objected to Jesus's prediction of coming betrayal, rebuked him with the words, "Thou savourest not of the things that be of God."[141] Together with Jesus's other utterances foreshadowing his death, the rebuke indicated that he "regarded Himself as [one] whose earthly mission terminated in a sacrifice, conditioned by a special relation to sin."[142] It was his resurrection, "directly correlated to the crucifixion," that "charged with profound meaning" these utterances. Hence Peter's interpretation of the events of Good Friday and Easter: forgiveness, "the primary need," "now becomes possible."[143] This understanding pervaded the New Testament.[144]

Liberals might dismiss the New Testament writers as "steeped in Old Testament ideas of propitiatory sacrifice," but Hammond replied: "The Man Christ Jesus was strongly imbued with the sacrificial doctrine of His

---

135. Howard, "Work of Christ," 121–46.

136. Rashdall, *Idea of the Atonement*, 438n1. See Sellers, "Rashdall, Hastings," 825–26.

137. Ramsey, *Gore to Temple*, 55; Kirk, "Atonement," 262–70.

138. Grensted, *Short History*; Grensted, *Atonement in History and in Life*.

139. Simpson, *Fact of Christ*.

140. Hammond, "The Significance of the Death of Christ," 39.

141. Ibid., 40, quoting AV.

142. Ibid.

143. Ibid., citing Acts 2:38.

144. Ibid., 42.

people."¹⁴⁵ Hence the liberals' very objection to the New Testament witness only argued in support of it: that "without shedding of blood there is no remission."¹⁴⁶ This was "no mere excrescence" of the Christian message. "Round it cluster all the great words of the Gospel: Remission, Atonement, Justification, Access to God, Eternal Life. . . . And the 'covering' of the unclean is sacrificial."¹⁴⁷ No other elaboration of the significance of Jesus's death lay open to his disciples. His death "had to do with sin. . . . [and] sin by way of forgiveness."¹⁴⁸ Hammond underlined this by multiple gospel references showing that such was Jesus's own understanding—of himself and his task. To his followers the risen Lord gave this message of repentance and forgiveness of sins secured by his death. To interpret it they unlocked "the very treasures of Greek thought and of Roman jurisprudence . . . to unfold for us something of the glory and the majesty of this sacrifice of the Eternal Son for the sons of men."¹⁴⁹

Other objections to the historic doctrine from the New Testament needed to be met—the matter of Greek prepositions used to defend it and some of the "great words." Hammond reminded his reader that it was the message that mattered, and that the prepositions connected words to give meaning, namely, a message. The great words "Propitiation," "Offering," "The Just for the Unjust," "Sin-bearing," "The obedience of One" all had "a very definite content." Thus *propitiation* compelled us to picture "outraged Justice and the great need of securing mercy."¹⁵⁰ Unifying "these amazing messages of love and grace" was our union with Christ "adumbrated" by such figures as the bride and the bridegroom.¹⁵¹ Hammond concluded on the biblical note of triumph that links the cross to justification by faith: "There is therefore no condemnation to them who are in Christ Jesus."¹⁵² A few years later as principal of Moore College, Hammond would stimulate theologically a young science teacher, Leon Morris, who was preparing himself for the ordained ministry.¹⁵³ Morris later gained his Cambridge PhD (1951) for a thesis definitive on some of the same "great theological words," as he called

---

145. Ibid., 40.

146. Ibid., 44–45, citing Heb 9:22 (AV).

147. Ibid., 45. "Covering" alludes to the term "propitiation"—an atonement word repugnant to the liberal conscience.

148. Ibid., 45–46.

149. Ibid., 47.

150. Ibid., 49.

151. Ibid.

152. Ibid., citing Rom 8:1.

153. Morris, "Foreword," xiv.

them.[154] He became an internationally respected New Testament scholar and authority on the biblical doctrine of Christ's atoning death.[155]

Hammond's Appreciation of his Reformation Tradition

Hammond was invited to contribute to a conference of the Church of Ireland held in October 1932 commemorating the 1500th anniversary of the landing of Patrick in Ireland. In his presentation he brilliantly surveyed things truly valuable in his own church's tradition. In a crowded evening session following another's paper on the Irish church's theological witness before the Reformation, Hammond rose to give his on "Post-Reformation Theology in the Church of Ireland."[156] With condensed eloquence he led his audience to gaze through a window into a room crowded with the great Irish theologians of the past. He brought them into view, one by one. His personal reading of their works illuminates them all, and he lost no opportunity to challenge High Church and Anglo-Catholic as well as liberal digressions.

He first brought before them "the incomparable Ussher," whose masterful historical study of the Church Fathers in answer to the Jesuit challenge was a "salutary admonition to those who would talk glibly of 'Catholic consent.'" As a theologian Ussher "command[ed] the respect of all time."[157] He "modelled his outlook upon the great questions on the Reformed interpretation of the sage of Hippo." For Ussher the regenerate person only was "alive unto God," the unregenerate being unable to please God.[158] In distinction from all human writings, "the Scriptures of God . . . [were] the proper object of faith," and "justifying faith fixe[d] itself solely on Jesus Christ and him crucified."[159] Hammond also brought Ussher's thought on the church, the sacraments, episcopal authority, and his contribution to the Westminster Assembly (1643–1649) to his audience's attention.

---

154. Morris, "Preface," 7. Morris's thesis was the basis of his book, *Apostolic Preaching of the Cross*.

155. See Banks, *Reconciliation and Hope*, a *Festschrift* presented to Morris on his 60th birthday, containing contributions from twenty-one New Testament scholars—British, American, Canadian, Dutch and Australian.

156. Hammond, "Post-Reformation Theology," 97–105.

157. James Ussher (1581–1656), Archbishop of Armagh (1625), a Calvinist theologian and a historian "of vast learning." *ODCC*, 1684.

158. Hammond, "Post-Reformation Theology," 98, citing Ussher, *Answer to a Jesuit*, 448.

159. Hammond, "Post-Reformation Theology," 98, citing Ussher, *Answer to a Jesuit*, 702, 721.

Hammond brought next before the window the High Churchman, Jeremy Taylor (1613–1667), who "crowded great truths into the concentration of a sentence," such as, "Christ's Body is eaten only sacramentally by the body, but really and effectively only by faith, which is the mouth of the soul."[160] Then came William Magee (1766–1831), who on the atonement defended "the vicarious sacrifice and substitution in a masterly fashion."[161] Next appeared James Thomas O'Brien (1792–1874), who showed by his Greek scholarship that "faith signifie[d] 'a reliance on Christ, not blind or careless, but intelligent and cordial,'" and "that justification means 'a judicial act by which the innocence of the person justified is established or declared.'"[162] Hammond also brought C. H. H. Wright (1836–1909) into view,[163] followed climactically by the great George Salmon (1819–1904), whose *Introduction to the New Testament* was "still indispensable," and his *Infallibility of the Church* "so complete."[164] To conclude, Hammond brought back to their minds James Ussher, "greatest of the sons" of the Church of Ireland, who borrowed from "the greatest son of another such house," Augustine, the common "Rule of Faith,"[165] namely, Holy Scripture.

Hammond here demonstrated again his high estimate of the Reformation and characteristic Evangelical focus on Scripture's authority, Christ's cross as atoning death, and justification by faith. Such was his place in the Evangelical spectrum. Nathaniel Jones would have warmed to his presentation. D. J. Davies, Liberal Evangelical, would not have.

Contributions to the New Edition of The Protestant Dictionary of 1933

Such was Hammond's standing among the editors of a new edition (1933) of *The Protestant Dictionary* (1st ed. 1904) that he contributed five considerable additional articles, updated one long existing article, and wrote substantial

---

160. Hammond, "Post-Reformation Theology," 100, citing Taylor, *Real Presence*, 593.

161. Hammond, "Post-Reformation Theology," 101–102, citing Magee, *Discourses and Dissertations*.

162. Hammond, "Post-Reformation Theology," 102–103, citing O'Brien, *Attempt to Explain*, 44, 61.

163. Hammond, "Post-Reformation Theology," 103, citing Wright, *Intermediate State and Prayers for the Dead*.

164. Hammond, "Post-Reformation Theology," 104.

165. Ibid., 105.

supplementary notes for two other existing articles.[166] These all reflect the learned biblical and Reformation commitment shown in this chapter.

Conclusion

By mid-1935 Hammond's ministry and intellectual journey reached a penultimate and important fruition: in answer to the IVF's request that he produce a new handbook of Christian doctrine he was just started on dictating *In Understanding Be Men* when there came the invitation to head Moore College in the Diocese of Sydney. He was already probably the most accomplished dogmatician of his day in the Evangelical school. Meeting the challenges above had confirmed in him the conviction that all that was central to Reformation doctrine was also agreeable to God's word. He had addressed the philosophical issues underlying the "New Theology" as well as the importance of God's being as both transcendent and immanent. He could contend for his authority as expressed in Holy Scripture and for the meaning of Christ's death and other key Reformation doctrinal positions over against liberal re-statements. He knew and understood the Patristic theology and that of the medieval scholastics as well.[167] He had studied first-hand the Latin formulations of the Council of Trent, and was up-to-date with the challenges of High Church and Anglo-Catholic doctrines and their views of authority in the church. He could show the discrepancy of ritualism with the intentions of the 1662 Prayer Book. He understood the history and theology that gave context to these things. In all these areas he could communicate with the student, informed layperson, and scholarly graduate. He came to Sydney in 1936 as one fully prepared for the task of theological guide to a synod and archbishop returning a diocese to its Evangelical roots, and for the task of chief instructor of its future clergy.

---

166. Carter and Alison, *Protestant Dictionary*. New articles by Hammond were "Conversations, Malines," "Emancipation, Catholic," "Maynooth, the College of St Patrick," and "Unam Sanctam." He updated "Irish Church," and wrote supplementary notes to "Moral Theology" and "Purgatory."

167. For example, Hammond, "Schoolmen of the Later Middle Ages," 118–48.

12

Reformation Evangelicalism Maintained

FROM RECEIVING HIS CALL to Moore College in mid-1935 until his retirement as principal in 1953 T. C. Hammond published five major works. They confirm his place in the spectrum of Evangelicalism as a centrist, Reformation Evangelical of the day. His learned exposition of 100 single Scripture verses for children to memorize, *The One Hundred Texts*[1] (not analyzed below) in itself presents succinctly "an extensive body of divinity."[2] *In Understanding Be Men* (*IUBM*) became a best-seller handbook of Christian doctrine and has had the widest and longest influence. It was the first (1936) of an Inter-Varsity Fellowship trilogy that included *Perfect Freedom* (1938) and *Reasoning Faith* (1943). The latter two and *The New Creation* (1953) he wrote while principal of Moore College.

Lesser works from his Moore College period include *Pivot Points in Revelation*[3] (addresses to evangelical undergraduates), *Fading Light*[4] (early World War II talks on the spiritual roots of German aggression), and *Age-long Questions*[5] (addresses on the philosophy of religion). These will be treated below.

Not examined in detail for space reasons are the collections of his addresses to the Christian conventions at Katoomba in New South Wales,

---

1. Hammond, *One Hundred Texts* (1938). He completed the main text, which he had taught for many years, between finishing *IUBM* and leaving for Australia in March 1936; others then carried out the considerable editorial process needed for publication.
2. Ibid., xi.
3. Hammond, *Pivot Points in Revelation*.
4. Hammond, *Fading Light*.
5. Hammond, *Age-long Questions*.

Upwey in Victoria, and in Adelaide, South Australia.[6] Nor are his many journal articles, articles in the *Australian Church Record*, pamphlets on various subjects, nor his "Case for Protestantism" radio broadcasts (dealing with Roman Catholic doctrines).[7] Remaining unpublished are a fifty-page typescript, "The Church"[8] and a full typewritten analysis of Thomas Cranmer's treatise of 1550 on the Lord's Supper that he gave to the recently ordained deacons in their weekly class with him.[9]

In Understanding Be Men (1936)

It was "shortly after consenting to produce this volume" that Hammond was "induced to undertake a new task in Australia"[10]—the principalship of Moore College, Sydney. Douglas Johnson, general secretary of the IVF, came over from London in the summer of 1935 to assist Hammond in preparing the book, which was to be available at a mission to London University students early in 1936. Hammond dictated material between daily ICM commitments,[11] while Johnson worked on the typescript. He thus became a virtual co-author.[12] The second edition incorporated "one or two" clarified expressions and "a few additional notes" by Hammond.[13] Subsequent editorial changes were minimal.[14]

Intended for inquiring "Arts, Science and Medical Students," the volume was an up-to-date and succinct introduction to "the main fields of theological study and the magnificent productions of some of the great theological writers."[15] University students studied in an atmosphere of doubt of God's existence, the shades of liberal Christianity, as well as Roman Catholic and Protestant beliefs. Hence Hammond's approach was "such as

---

6. Hammond, "Five Addresses," 1–57; Hammond, *Light and Life*; Hammond, *Way of Holiness*.

7. Hammond, Preface, *Case for Protestantism*, 3.

8. See Edwards, "Developments in the Evangelical Anglican Doctrine of the Church."

9. Hammond, "Cranmer on the Lord's Supper."

10. Hammond, *IUBM*, (1936), v.

11. Nelson, *T. C. Hammond*, 88–89.

12. Hammond, *IUBM*, (1936), v; Johnson, Letters; cf. Goodhew, "Johnson, Douglas," in *BDE*, 333.

13. Hammond, *IUBM*, (2nd ed., 1936), v. A copy of the first edition, held in Moore College Library (now, Donald Robinson Library) contains Hammond's handwritten notes for inclusion in the second edition (published October, 1936),

14. Hammond, *IUBM*, (1951), v–vi.

15. Hammond, *IUBM*, (1936), v.

to include, as far as possible, different attitudes on controverted points while preserving the main outline of Evangelical thought."[16] The following account concentrates on his treatment of the chief questions that have come to the fore in the chapters above on Jones and Davies.

The Introduction laid some groundwork. First "The Supreme Importance of Christian Doctrine," a duty, for "truth produces its proper result and error always take revenge."[17] Then under "Classifications" Hammond urged accuracy in defining and describing "the great cardinal doctrines," to grasp clearly the chief theological systems and issues, such as "the so-called *Antinomies*" or "apparent contradictions."[18] He defined some important terms—revelation, faith and "the Faith," religion and theology, biblical and dogmatic theology. Under "Historical Considerations" he explained the general councils, the creeds and confessions and the chief theological divisions in the history of the Western European churches. These include the Protestant-Roman Catholic divide, the chief Protestant divisions, and "Principles Underlying the Divisions."[19] Seven main chapters called "parts" follow.[20]

Part 1 "Final Authority in Matters of Faith" affirmed that "I. Sources" of "our knowledge of theological matters" were chiefly (a) the traditional natural theology as derived from philosophy, science, and history independently of and supplementing (b) the Christian revelation recorded in Scripture.[21] Hammond made no note of the need of a regenerate Christian mind and of presupposing the existence of God as revealed in Scripture for a true handling of natural revelation. The Christian revelation recorded in the Holy Scriptures was pre-eminently "the life, character and teachings of Christ." Hammond usefully cautioned the student against "the search for the historical Jesus,"[22] a search which wrongly implied that it was safe to ignore either the Old Testament revelation foreshadowing Christ or the "amplification" afforded in the New Testament as a whole.[23] He made no

---

16. Hammond, *IUBM*, (2nd ed., 1936), vi. All further references are to the 5th edition (1954).

17. Hammond, *IUBM*, 13.

18. Ibid., 11–15.

19. Ibid., 16–23.

20. A potentially illuminating study of the changes in the bibliographies throughout the book cannot be followed here.

21. Ibid., 24–25.

22. Presumably alluding to Schweitzer, *Quest for the Historical Jesus* and the liberal quests he documented and which followed.

23. Hammond, *IUBM*, 24–25.

mention of the basic assumptions about God and the world underlying the liberal search.

Useful explanations of "The Canon of Holy Scripture" followed. "Canon" meant "'Rule of Faith' by which all doctrine must be tested." Scripture was "a collection of authorized books" accepted as "inspired and authoritative in matters of faith." Most important in determining their canonicity was that they possessed "the authority and inspiration of the Holy Spirit"[24]—in other words, that they were self-attesting. Hammond succinctly outlined the history of the New Testament canon.[25]

To the authority of Scripture, the major issue as between Evangelicals and liberals, Hammond gave considerable space.[26] He followed his substantial IVF pamphlet, *The Inspiration and Authority of Scripture*. On the mode of inspiration and its extent, he carefully removed common misunderstandings such as the notion that the Holy Spirit "*dictated* each word mechanically"[27] and the objections based on these. He was at one with Nathaniel Jones and distinct from D. J. Davies. He also insisted on the Reformation doctrine of the clarity (perspicuity) of Scripture as against the need (as according to Rome) of some authority external to it,[28] and "the Bible as its own interpreter."[29] Later Inter-Varsity Fellowship works spelled out clearly the necessary conditions of sound private interpretation, and recommended systematic study with guidance.[30] Contrary to Roman Catholic thought, Holy Scripture was wholly sufficient for things necessary for salvation (Article 6 of the Thirty-nine Articles).[31]

In part 2 "The Godhead," the doctrine of the Father, the Son and the Holy Spirit, Hammond laid out the common creedal heritage of the Roman Catholic, Orthodox, and Protestant creeds and confessions.[32] There was no hint of unorthodoxy with regard to the Trinity and the relation of the persons so mistakenly alleged by the Anglican archbishop of Perth in 2005.[33] On "The Being of God" Hammond followed the traditional Roman Catholic

---

24. Ibid., 27.
25. Ibid., 28–29.
26. Ibid., 30–40.
27. Ibid., 32.
28. Ibid., 34.
29. Ibid., 35–36.
30. Manley, *Search the Scriptures*, 11; Manley, *New Bible Handbook*, xi–xii.
31. Hammond, *IUBM*, 35.
32. Ibid., 53–58.
33. Carnley, "T. C. Hammond and the Theological Roots of Sydney Arianism," 5–11. See also Carnley, *Reflections in Glass*, 234–35.

and Protestant apologetic approach[34] of Thomas Aquinas and Joseph Butler. But he listed the five theistic proofs for the existence of God while warning that they "tell us nothing about God."[35] This seems problematic, for one would think that "we must first ask what kind of God Christianity believes in."[36] And Hammond surely knew that James Orr had written: "Proof in Theism . . . [consists] in showing that God's existence is itself the . . . ultimate basis on which all other knowledge, all other belief rests."[37] He also neglected the fact that the unregenerate person suppresses the true knowledge of God evidenced by the creation (Rom 1).

Under "The Nature of God"[38] he guided the student succinctly through God's *infinity, transcendence and immanence, personality and freedom* ("God is "free Personal Spirit"), *immutability and eternity*, the [self-] *manifestations of God*, and *some rivals of monotheism* (including atheism and agnosticism).[39] But in treating the divine *omniscience*, Hammond appears to have struggled with his own "moderate Calvinism." Or perhaps it was the fact that his evangelical readership included Methodists and those Baptists who were not Calvinists. He virtually equated human *responsibility* with human freedom when he categorized God's sovereignty and human freedom of choice (rather than human responsibility) as "so-called *Antinomies*" or "apparently opposing sets of ideas," whose harmonization—for example in the sinner's conversion—God alone knew.[40]

In part 3 "Man and Sin," on "God's Eternal Purpose and Human Free Will," he concluded that only the Augustinian (or Calvinist) view did "real justice to the grace of God," while there remained "a mystery connected with human freedom."[41] But then: Scripture clearly taught "human responsibility" (now instead of freedom) "alongside the clear statement that salvation is from start to finish solely upon the basis of divine grace."[42] Here the antinomy was better stated—as between human *responsibility* and

---

34. Namely, that "apologetics must deal neutrally with such questions as the existence of God," Van Til, *Defense of the Faith*, 360.

35. Hammond, *IUBM*, 41–43. For more on his apologetic method see below on his *Reasoning Faith*.

36. Van Til, *Defense of the Faith*, 30.

37. Orr, *Christian View*, 94.

38. *IUBM*, 41–69.

39. Ibid., 43–46.

40. Ibid., 15.

41. Ibid., 96–97.

42. Ibid. The latter is the Reformation *sola gratia*, clearly stated in Article 10 of the Thirty-nine Articles.

divine sovereignty.⁴³ Consistently he elsewhere stated: "the evil heart of unbelief in departing from the living God affects the whole nature of man; his reason, affections, and will are blinded."⁴⁴

In part 4 "The Person and Work of Christ" he rebutted the *"Kenosis"* notion of Christ's "emptying" himself of his deity and added: "It will be a great day for Christianity when its devotees rediscover the actual grandeur of the Person they dimly worship."⁴⁵ On Christ's physical resurrection he listed the usual evidential proofs, without noting first that the all-sufficient triune God of Scripture was "the ultimate basis on which . . . all other belief rests."⁴⁶

Christ's Atoning Death

Hammond added a seven-part appendix, "The Doctrine of the Atonement,"⁴⁷ the second major issue in the overt conflicts of Evangelicalism with various forms of liberal theology. It was a fuller presentation of his "The Significance of the Death of Christ."⁴⁸ In the modern period, he noted, "some have sought to explain away" the necessity for an expiatory or substitutionary view.⁴⁹ He urged "a careful examination of the actual words of Scripture," before "any theorising." He warned: "much confusion exists concerning the nature of divine justice and the ethics of the redemptive act" (the problem for liberals), and regretted the inaccurate phraseology of "many enthusiasts."⁵⁰

He considered the "Theology of the Doctrine."⁵¹ First was "The *'God-ward* Aspect,'" especially Christ's perfect obedience—a demonstration of God's righteousness and love, and "a satisfactory basis for the remission of sins."⁵² Christ's work was "not merely a substitute for an equivalent unfulfilled work of the sinner." It also had "an intrinsic value" consisting in "the infinite worth of his own Person." The "pivot point of the Roman Catholic system of teaching" and of "much modern Protestant teaching" was in prac-

---

43. As Packer, *Evangelism*, 22–24.
44. Hammond, *Bible Truths and Modern Fancies*, 11.
45. Hammond, *IUBM*, 108.
46. Ibid., 112–14.
47. Ibid., 121–33.
48. See in chapter 10 above.
49. Hammond, *IUBM*, 132.
50. Ibid., 121.
51. Ibid., 124–27.
52. Ibid., 125.

tice the incarnation. But the space Scripture gave to cardinal doctrines was conclusive: "It is unassailable that the Death of Christ is the very heart of Christianity."[53]

"The Manward Aspect" of the atonement, usually approached (in the liberal view) as the demonstration of God's love (as D. J. Davies thought), did not "begin to explain" the data of Scripture. God's love should lead us to realize "the intense loathing" his holy nature has for sin.[54] Hammond addressed the three categories of objections. First, that alleging the immorality of the doctrine as "the innocent suffering for the guilty" and designating it a "legal fiction" ignored the double scriptural connection: between the sufferer (Christ is also God) and God (the Father), and between the sinner and the sufferer.[55] He did not point to assumed growing human moral standards that resulted in the critics' "confusion." But he did point out that they overlooked "the element of the necessary connection between the innocent and the guilty," which the term "legal fiction" ignored.[56]

Secondly, the scientific objection, based on man's insignificance in a vast universe, Hammond dismissed—as if size, instead of "the Christian Revelation," were "a final criterion of value." Thirdly, the category of evolutionary hypotheses allegedly excluded "the guilt of sin necessitating an atonement." But even if supported by accurate observations, these hypotheses would not exclude God's interposition of an absolute standard at some point in human development.[57]

"Some Further Problems" had to do with misunderstanding words like "Penal Suffering," with having a false notion—the "*quantitative*" equivalence of Christ's suffering—and with the differing views of the divinely intended scope of Christ's vicarious atonement (whether universal or particular).

In part 5 "The Holy Spirit," he set forth the personality and deity of the Spirit, neglected as well as misunderstood, he said, in the theological writing of his day.[58] He explained the key terms in the Nicene Creed, a subordinate standard to Scripture of catholic orthodoxy. He stressed the need "to adhere closely to Scripture in all thought and discussion concerning the Persons of the Trinity."[59] He added a Reformation note: "The rediscovery of the unique

---

53. Ibid., 128.
54. Ibid., 126–27, citing Hodge, *Systematic Theology*, 2:495–527.
55. Hammond, *IUBM*, 128.
56. Ibid.
57. Ibid., 129.
58. Ibid., 134.
59. Ibid., 137.

and essential work of the Holy Spirit in the Church and the individual was one of the greatest bequests of the Reformation Divines."[60]

In the "Modern Period," however, "the more liberal school of thought" had regarded the Spirit as "impersonal, 'the Christian Consciousness' or Arbiter, in spiritual matters." "On the conservative side," there was a re-emphasis on the Spirit's personality and particularly "his work . . . of sanctification."[61]

Under the heading, "The Work of the Holy Spirit" after "I. The Divine Executor," that is, "of the counsels and purposes of the Godhead,"[62] Hammond included what were key doctrines for Evangelicals. Thus "God's Approach to the Sinner" included the topic "The Need of Grace," in which Hammond strove to make clear the bondage of the unregenerate person's will to the nature of the person[63] and hence the need of both "Prevenient Grace" and "The Effectual Call." He was sensitive to the objections of past controversy (Pelagians and Semi-Pelagians).[64] He explained "Repentance" and "Conversion, Regeneration and New Birth," discussed more fully in his final book, *The New Creation*. Puzzlingly, he did not touch on sin's noetic effects (effects on human knowing), which hinder correct acknowledgment of the revelation of God in nature as well as in Scripture.[65]

The second key doctrine for Evangelicals under "The Work of the Holy Spirit" was "The Remission of Sins and Justification," "the grand discovery and genius of the Reformation and Protestant theology." Hammond showed very clearly the fault in the Liberal Evangelical view of such as D. J. Davies (chapter 7 above): that "justification implies and rests upon the beginning of the new divine life in man."[66] For Hammond, on the contrary, the "unequivocal claim" of the Bible was "that the remission of sins and the justification of the soul before God" rested "entirely on the basis of our Lord's atoning sacrifice."[67] He rejected as contrary to the Scriptures "the modern plea" (of Liberal Evangelicals and other liberals)[68] that God overlooked sin "because [he is] a God of love."

---

60. Ibid., 138.

61. Ibid., 139. He alluded to "unbalanced extremes," probably having perfectionism in mind.

62. Ibid., 140.

63. Ibid., 143.

64. Ibid., 142–45.

65. Cf. Hodge, *Systematic Theology*, 2:99–102.

66. As also Clarke, *Outline of Christian Theology*, 407.

67. Hammond, *IUBM*, 148.

68. Howard, "The Work of Christ," in *Liberal Evangelicalism*, 122–23.

He also established the scriptural, Reformation position over against the Roman Catholic, which "confused justification and sanctification."[69] The biblical doctrine of justification was "the ground of our assurance of acceptance with God and . . . the source of all true spiritual liberty."[70] The taunt that Evangelical Christians "belittle the value of good works and moral effort" could be shown by "empirical test" to be false in "any true Evangelical community."[71]

Hammond devoted good space to the next key doctrine—"Union with Christ and Sanctification."[72] Though doubtless sharpened by Warfield's critiques of holiness schools, Hammond's thought was not at all contrary to that of Jones earlier: the Christian might and should know freedom from "the habitual practice of sin": "constant victory, yes; but inability to sin, no."[73] Neither "eradication" of sin nor its "suppression" was biblical, but "counteraction": "sin is no longer inevitable." And "if he should fall," the believer had a "Helper to plead his cause . . . (1 Jn 2:2)."[74]

In Australia, Archbishop Mowll had joined the council of the Katoomba Christian Convention in 1934. They included men trained under Nathaniel Jones—Herbert Begbie, from 1929, and R. B. Robinson, from 1931. Hammond gave the Bible expositions in January 1937, and often afterwards.[75] His subsequent series *So Great Salvation* became the semi-official clarification of the convention's doctrinal statement.[76] He greatly assisted in resisting the sinless perfectionist movement that arose amongst some within the Sydney University Evangelical Union in the 1940s.[77]

By contrast, the Liberal Evangelicals had sought "to think out anew what is called 'the Keswick message' in the light of scientific facts and in terms of modern psychology." They were looking "for a satisfying sense of the presence and power of God in their daily lives."[78] Davies was never

---

69. Hammond, ibid., 150–51.

70. Ibid., 151.

71. Ibid.

72. Ibid., 152–57. (A recent Moore College trained scholar has published a highly regarded full study of this topic: Campbell, *Paul and Union with Christ*).

73. Ibid., 156.

74. Ibid., 157.

75. Braga, *Century of Preaching Christ*, 67–69; Hammond, "Five Addresses," 5–46.

76. Braga, *Century of Preaching Christ*, 72, 105.

77. Lake, *Proclaiming Jesus Christ*, 24.

78. Rogers, "Introduction," viii–ix.

a speaker at the Katoomba Convention, though he spoke once at the Chatswood convention.[79]

IUBM has two final main chapters, part 6 "The Corporate Life of the Christian," and part 7 "The Last Things." The former, under 1. "The Church," cautioned Christians not to separate from a given community of the "visible Church of Christ" unless compelled by conscience guided by Scripture, and also not to assume that one way is "the *only* true way."[80] Hammond warned against "extreme forms of sacerdotalism and other perversions of the Apostolic tradition,"[81] still a topic of concern among Moore College students in the mid-1950s.[82] Hammond stressed that Scripture placed the emphasis on the Christian's direct relation to Christ, which "gives a dignity to the individual's judgment in matters of faith which no theory of Church discipline should lightly override." On the other hand, scripturally speaking, there is "the risk of serious loss" for the Christian who neglects "a spiritual 'home' in a local community of Christian[s]."[83] Perhaps with an eye to the kind of ecumenism promoted by the Student Christian Movement and the World Council of Churches, Hammond preferred "a Fellowship of the Spirit . . . in Conventions and elsewhere . . . based on their loyalty to the one true Head of the Church."[84] His Evangelical (Anglican) heritage put no denominational barriers in the way of believers sharing in Holy Communion.

Further, under "The Corporate Life of the Christian," as well as "The Ministry," Hammond treated "The Means of Grace" with a distinctly Reformation and Evangelical presentation. The latter consisted of prayer, Bible reading, the ministry of the word of God, corporate worship, the sacraments (the two ordained by Christ, visible tokens of God's grace) and their efficacy. Their efficacy was neither the Roman Catholic *ex opere operato* ("by the performance of the rite"), nor the "Zwinglian" (mere external pledges of loyalty to God) view, but "the Calvinistic view, with which the Anglican agrees."[85] Not that the High Churchman or Anglo-Catholic would have agreed!

Fittingly, Hammond's last topic was "The Last Things." A premillennial expectation of Christ's return was still influential in the Inter-Varsity

---

79. See chapter 9 above.
80. Hammond, *IUBM*, 160.
81. Ibid.
82. Bates, a University of Sydney student living at Moore College in 1955, in personal conversation with author in 2012.
83. Hammond, *IUBM*, 164.
84. Ibid., 166.
85. Ibid., 179.

Fellowship and among conservative Evangelicals.[86] In Sydney it was believed firmly all their lives by former students of Nathaniel Jones such as the leading Sydney figure Herbert Begbie, but it had not stood in the way of Hammond's acceptance.

He himself urged the utmost caution and care in interpreting "isolated texts" of Scripture where "dogmatism is impossible,"[87] while underlining the importance of Christ's return from the many references in Scripture to the fact.[88] One needed to be clear, however, that Scripture teaches "a coming in Person," and not, for example, that "Christ comes at death." The point of the doctrine was not to satisfy curiosity but to provide an incentive to righteous conduct and joyous anticipation.[89] The important truth was the "literal Personal Return of Christ," the "final glorification of the Church" and "irretrievable loss of the Christ-rejecters."[90]

On "Human Destiny" he found no warrant in the Bible for "annihilation" (complete cessation of being) of those condemned at the Last Judgment.[91] The *resurrection* of the Christian dead was the result of Christ's atoning death, of his (resurrection) authority, and of the Christian's union with Christ. Christ's resurrection body was "the pattern for our resurrection" and his glorified body the pattern for ours. Hammond neglected to connect remembering that "it is a spiritual body" with the Holy Spirit, only cautioning the reader not to "over-spiritualize" it.[92]

For the Christian, since the guilt of sin had already been "removed by the Atoning Sacrifice," judgment day was "chiefly in the nature of rewards for stewardship." Scripture warned, nevertheless, of serious loss for the careless Christian.[93] On the "Judgment of Non-Christians" Hammond excluded both universalism (finally all will be saved) and annihilationism.[94] He recommended a famous book by one of the greats of TCD,[95] which D. J. Davies also owned.[96]

---

86. E.g., the Anglican, Manley's *Return of Jesus Christ*.
87. Hammond, *IUBM*, 188.
88. Ibid., 189.
89. Ibid., 189–90.
90. Ibid., 192.
91. The tentative view of John Stott in Edwards, *Essentials*, 313–20.
92. Hammond, *IUBM*, 198–99.
93. Ibid., 199.
94. Ibid., 200.
95. Salmond, *Christian Doctrine of Immortality*.
96. Copy in Moore College Library stamped "D. J. Davies."

The final subject of *IUBM*, "The Consummation of All Things," simply states that the scriptural references "imply not annihilation" of the universe, but "a complete destruction of all links with an old and sinful world and the conversion . . . of the old into a new world, never to know sin and corruption."[97] Hammond concluded this last chapter with an exhortation to his "student friends" to study "the unfailing fulfilment of God's eternal purposes and covenants with man" from "Paradise lost in Genesis to Paradise regained in [the book of] Revelation."[98] He might have headed it, "In Praise of the Study of the History of Salvation." As a Reformation theologian, Hammond was biblicist from first to last.

For some fifty years *IUBM* was the textbook for the introduction to doctrine in Moore College. Interested members of some local Anglican parish youth fellowships in Sydney also studied it. One such was later Principal of Moore College, then Archbishop of Sydney.[99] Evangelical Union students purchased it at their conferences. Hammond's Reformation thought, related to contemporary theological debate, left its stamp on the college, on parishioners in the diocese and on many students in the English-speaking world.

Hammond's Wider Contribution in Australia

Hammond was a frequent speaker at conferences, such as those of the Inter-Varsity Fellowship of Australia and local Evangelical Union meetings.[100] A defining early contribution was at the Inter-Varsity Fellowship conference at Healesville, Victoria, over the new year of 1936–1937—his *Pivot Points in Revelation*.[101]

Hammond's addresses began by exhorting students to "speak of the things of God with the same depth and penetration as you speak of the things of the world."[102] This was the purpose behind *IUBM*. Modernists like Samuel Angus in Sydney and in Melbourne, Angus's fellow (Cairdian) Hegelian idealist[103] friend and ex-Presbyterian minister Charles Strong (1844–1942), were still influential. So Hammond warned: "the great danger

---

97. Hammond, *IUBM*, 201.

98. Ibid. Many students might still recognize the allusion to Milton's epic poems, *Paradise Lost* and *Paradise Regained*.

99. Peter Jensen, principal 1985–2001, archbishop 2001–2013.

100. Lake, *Proclaiming Jesus Christ*, 18, 21–27, 68–69.

101. Hammond, *Pivot Points in Revelation*.

102. Ibid.

103. See Passmore, *Hundred Years of Philosophy*, 54–56.

confronting the Evangelical Cause at the present time, particularly in Australia, is Modernism." The modernist

> feels that the advance of knowledge has made it impossible to accept the statements of the Old and New Testaments in the form in which they have come down to us. The thorough-going Modernist may attach . . . the right meaning to a saying of our Lord or of the Apostles, and then . . . reject the saying.[104]

By 1936, if not in 1926, Hammond must have learned of The Heretics club in Sydney, of which Angus was a member, as well as the Anglican, Arthur Garnsey at St Paul's College next door to Moore College, whose public lectures of 1934 at St Andrew's Cathedral had a modernist ring.[105] But Hammond also cautioned students against assuming that the higher critic of the Bible was necessarily also a modernist.

He addressed three main "pivot-points": "The Fact of Revelation; The Mode of Revelation; and The Character of Revelation."[106] He pointed out that the modernist's answer to the question, "Did God really speak?" was in accord with the philosophy which gave modernism birth, namely Hegelian Idealism. Thus, D. F. Strauss's *Life of Jesus*[107] had assumed that the "highest manifestation" of God's immanence in the world was man, through whose reason God (the idealist absolute) "expressed himself." The Old Testament therefore became "an account of the religious experience of man, slowly growing in volume of wealth of idea till it finds its culmination in Jesus Christ who is the last word in spiritual experience."[108] Hence Modernism's "fundamental principle" was revealed in its "immense amount of talk about the religion of experience. . . . We say [that revelation] is the direct voice of God. They say it is God making Himself known through the medium of our natural conscience."[109]

Hammond also cautioned them: if they met a modernist who denied that he held to the Hegelian philosophic root of it all, then to "be thankful that men and women are inconsistent."[110] This talk seems to have been Hammond's clearest and most helpfully penetrating criticism of the modernist's underlying principle. Hegelian Idealism had until recently been dominant

---

104. Hammond, *Pivot Points*, 3–4.

105. Garnsey, *Arthur Garnsey*, 180–94. See above in chapter 9, on Arthur Garnsey, *How the Gospels Grew*, 60–68.

106. Hammond, *Pivot Points*, 4–18.

107. Translated (1846) anonymously by Mary Ann Evans, the novelist "George Eliot."

108. Hammond, *Pivot Points*, 5.

109. Ibid., 6.

110. Ibid., 10.

in the philosophy department at Melbourne University and elsewhere in Australia,[111] and it underlay the thought of Angus and Strong.

His remaining four discourses in *Pivot Points* expounded the mode of revelation and its character and content. He explained more of the intellectual history behind the naturalistic, simple-development view of the Christian religion—that it was like that of other religions. He provided evidence to the contrary. In fact, the character and content of biblical revelation, a revelation of redemption, took into account the sinfulness of human beings. It isolated the people of Israel amongst the nations until they were ready to receive the gospel, "another pivot point of revelation."[112]

Contrary to what students of dispensationalist background may have thought, Hammond stated (as had Jones) that we are responsible "to make the world a better place for people to live in," but not to assume "that movements and processes will perfect mankind in the course of time."[113] He concluded his five addresses with the thought that by the study of the Old Testament "you can look at the processes of God through the ages and say, 'We have a good land and a goodly heritage.'"[114] The series was an important foundational statement for the new Inter-Varsity Christian Fellowship of Australia. It saw a second edition.[115]

Fading Light and Age-long Questions[116]

As the Second World War was looming and scarcely two years after he had arrived at Moore College, Hammond's learning and power of defending the Christian faith potentially reached a wider local public and readership. His five Gunther Memorial Lectures, entitled *Age-long Questions*, delivered in St Andrew's Cathedral, Sydney, elaborated on what he had set out in his recent bicentennial commemorative article on Bishop Joseph Butler's thought in *The Evangelical Quarterly*.[117] He dealt now with five great problems in Christianity—namely, immortality, sin, progress, salvation, and evidence for its truth. He treated the last problem using Butler's approach.

111. Grave, *History*, 24–46.
112. Hammond, *Pivot Points*, 24.
113. Ibid., 22.
114. Ibid., 25.
115. Ibid., title page.
116. Hammond, *Fading Light*, and Hammond, *Age-long Questions*. The lectures were given weekly on Mondays at 1.15pm, March 7 to April 4, 1938 (see *Sydney Morning Herald*, March 8, 1938, 10), thus leading up to Easter of that year.
117. Hammond, "Butler's Analogy," 337–55.

Early in the war Hammond gave a series of lunch-hour addresses in his church in Sydney, published as *Fading Light: The Tragedy of Spiritual Decline in Germany*. He attributed the neo-paganism that had motivated Germany's aggression to the effect of the same destructive criticism of Scripture as explained in *Pivot Points* above:[118] the criticism assumed human intellectual and moral autonomy.

IVF writing resumed: Perfect Freedom: An Introduction to Christian Ethics (1938)

This second and largest volume in his IVF trilogy was quite comprehensive and is held in a number of university libraries. There seems to have been no such British presentation by an Evangelical before 1938, yet according to one who was an Evangelical theological student in England at the time it "made little impact."[119] The same student, however, remembered being at once taken by Reinhold Niebuhr, *An Interpretation of Christian Ethics*,[120] which *Perfect Freedom* does not mention. On the other hand Hammond was no ivory tower thinker. In the build-up to World War II he warned: "If the leaders of the so-called Christian West pursue certain courses of action in the present crisis the very existence of modern civilization may be threatened."[121] Now was a "time of weakness and peril," in which the biblical injunctions for human conduct (here quoting Albert Einstein) "have lost their firmness. Nations that once ranked high bow down before tyrants who dare openly to assert: Right is that which serves us!"[122]

Hammond suggested that "the general reader," might read the introductory chapters then go straight to section C ("The Distinctive Claims of Christian Ethics") and section D ("The Moral Christian Life").[123] The rest he presumably intended for the university student of ethics.

The book declared his Calvinist point of view: "the focal point and controlling principle in all approach to the study of either Theology, or of Ethics, is the Sovereignty of God, Who has revealed His will to man."[124] He

118. Hammond, *Fading Light*, especially chapter 3 "The Division of Mansoul."
119. Babbage, personal letter.
120. Babbage, personal letter; Niebuhr, *Interpretation of Christian Ethics*.
121. Hammond, *Perfect Freedom*, 12.
122. Ibid., 13. Einstein's words, spoken "recently in New York." Quotation not referenced.
123. Ibid., viii. The introductory chapters (section A "Some Basic Problems," section B "Natural Ethics") comprise some 100 pages of nearly 400 for the whole book).
124. Ibid., vi.

defined "the Sovereign Trinity" as creating and "redeeming, regenerating and sanctifying."[125] He encouraged this high claim in the face of "the ill-digested influences of modern scientific teaching" and "an increasing revolt against specifically Christian Ethics." The disciple of Christ should know that "no representative of the world's philosophers bears any close comparison with the matchless Christ or even with the best of His followers."[126]

Hammond's basic acceptance of Butler's apologetic in the *Analogy of Religion* he now qualifies, saying that as Christian Theology transcended Natural Theology and "brings to the enlightened a totally new world view," so did Christian ethics transcend natural ethics.[127] He referenced 1 Corinthians 2:1–16 for the difference. Yet natural ethics provided "the scientific analytical test of the truth of Christian Ethics"![128] Later he claimed explicitly that "Christian ethics does not destroy, but on the contrary builds upon, Natural Ethics."[129] What one might call his "blockhouse methodology"[130] seems at odds with his stated controlling principle—God's sovereignty and revelation of his will to humanity in Christ.

It was in the clearly revealed will of God in the Scriptures that "the Christian system demonstrates its superiority"[131] to natural ethics, but he seemed to suggest that the issue went deeper. Because of "revolutionary concepts as the Divine sovereignty, Revelation, Depravation, Incarnation, Propitiation, Regeneration and Final Consummation,"[132] a "*distinctively Christian* Ethics" as a "Life System" transcended "Natural Ethics."[133] He spelled out the distinctives, but did not explain how Christian Ethics could build on the various schools of Natural Ethics, which all presupposed a worldview radically different from the "totally new world view" of Christian theism.

Hammond defended natural ethics as containing considerable elements in common with the Christian Ethics,[134] a statement consistent with New Testament data. He supported this with a long quotation from Calvin on

---

125. Ibid.
126. Ibid., 14.
127. Ibid., 16.
128. Ibid.
129. Ibid., 261.
130. Van Til, *Christian Apologetics*, 148–49.
131. Hammond, *Perfect Freedom*, 133.
132. Ibid., 17. Emphasis original.
133. Ibid., 150.
134. Ibid., 152.

the light of truth that shines in secular writers on many subjects[135] (Calvin's notion of common grace restraining sin). But the Christian student should guard against preferring "the dicta of ethical students" (i.e., "thinkers") "to the declaration of God's will revealed in His Word."[136] For Hammond the problem of natural ethics was only that of limitation—that it "can deal only with man as it finds him"—rather than a wrong starting point. He granted that Plato and Aristotle took morally for granted things that no Christian could approve.[137] Deeper, however, was his verdict that the "cardinal defect" of natural ethics was "that it reckons without the supernatural."[138] Moreover, while drawing on Christ's example and teaching, "more frequently than not," it left wholly "out of account" his "redemptive death and resurrection."[139] Hence it could not "combine fully the external standard of the will of God with that internal response due to the working of the Divine Spirit."[140] The Christian revelation in the Holy Scriptures was "a complete life-system which has no need to borrow material to supplement its main features from any pagan source."[141]

Perhaps Hammond's Calvinism here struggled to emerge fully from the waters of the rationalism that he clearly recognized in T. H. Green.[142] He appreciated and quoted Abraham Kuyper's *The Holy Spirit*; but had he accepted the full implications of Kuyper's *Encyclopedia of Sacred Theology*? On the other hand, he stated later: "If the Fall be admitted as a fact, it demands that we should receive with great caution the findings of Natural Ethics."[143] He also commented on the disabling effect of the fall on human moral thought and freedom.[144] It is also hard to read Hammond as fully consistent in the matter of the freedom of the will in this work. The fall "explains man's inability" to will and to do what is right,[145] and "the warping tendency" of sin revealed by Scripture, "inasmuch as this inherent warp is ours . . . [it makes us] responsible for its display in conscious choice."[146] But

---

135. Ibid., 150-51, quoting Calvin, *Institutes*, 2.2.15 (dependent on Rom 2:14-16).
136. Hammond, *Perfect Freedom*, 152.
137. Ibid., 153.
138. Ibid.
139. Ibid., 154.
140. Ibid.
141. Ibid., 41.
142. Ibid., 86, 94.
143. Ibid., 188-89.
144. Ibid.
145. Ibid., 190-91.
146. Ibid., 191.

he added: "responsibility depends on the concept of freedom."[147] Perhaps, by the will's freedom he meant "free to act in accordance with the person's moral nature," as he said in *IUBM*. But how is the person responsible for this nature? He does not seem to have addressed this question.

Hammond's rigorous education in philosophy at Trinity College, Dublin had brought him under the influence of Kant's theory of ethics, so appreciated by Professor T. K. Abbott,[148] and of the work of T. H. Green.[149] Nevertheless he classified Green's ethics critically, as "English Rationalistic Ethics."[150] Of course, there were true insights in Green,[151] which Hammond could and did quite properly use, as also those of other thinkers.

His wide-ranging chapters on "The Moral (Christian) Life" were full of cautions and advice to the young Christian student,[152] such as: "There is a great temptation that the Christian may slip into the trap of looking to the Church . . . for a detailed list of special duties and necessary abstentions."[153] There were pithy observations, too: "The word 'broadminded' . . . has been sadly overworked."[154] And, "the obligation 'to think through' is more frequently disregarded than any other."[155]

Only the merest sketch of his wide-ranging discussion under section D "The Moral and Christian Life" is possible here. He began with "Christian Duty and Christian Virtue" and "The Personal Life of the Christian" (chapters 19 and 20). A consideration of "The Christian and the Community" (chapter 21) included the duties of justice, veracity, sympathy, or active compassion, forgiveness, and of example and influence. Under "The Christian and Moral Institutions" (chapter 22) he explicitly urged the Christian to be "the buttress of all true moral institutions and the upholder of man's rights" such as the elements of the sacredness of human life, freedom, the right to hold property, the right to education, and not to separate "'secular' sciences" from "the truths of the gospel."[156]

---

147. Ibid., 190. Emphasis added.

148. Kant, *Kant's Critique*.

149. Hammond, *Perfect Freedom*, 417 (listing Green, *Prolegomena to Ethics,* under "Natural Ethics").

150. Hammond, *Perfect Freedom*, 94.

151. E.g., Hammond, *Perfect Freedom*, 67.

152. Ibid., 257–388.

153. Ibid., 257.

154. Ibid., 257.

155. Ibid., 278.

156. Ibid., 311.

He discerned "Five Social Institutions ordained by God":[157] the communities of sex (marriage and the family), culture, work, worship, and the state. Each "derives a new significance when . . . related to the governing idea of the call of God." Divine calling was not restricted to the ministries of the church[158] (a Reformation doctrine). He added chapter 29 "The Christian and Those of Other Race."[159]

A view also dear to Principal D. J. Davies and Dean E. A. Talbot was the notion that Christians were *obliged* to work. So also Hammond (writing towards the end of the Great Depression): "Times of general suffering" stood in the way of the ideal of "the right to work," but the Christian ought "to strive . . . to make conditions tolerable for all men, and there was an ethical duty in avoiding recklessness of speculation that might engender depression as a consequence."[160] Some of T. H. Green's secularized Christian thought here echoed in Hammond's mind as valid insights—moments of truth for one neither an ideological socialist nor ideological capitalist, but who strove to be Christian.[161]

In his chapter on the Christian and culture[162] he reflected on the education of children, the freedom of science, the claims of art, and the right of free speech. His guidelines included, with regard to education, "the enthronement of Christ as Lord of the home" as "one of the crying needs of the present time." This entailed the provision for every child to "know the essential truths of Scripture and have a real acquaintance with the revelation of God."[163] He added: "No education is worth the name that does not insist upon the individual's dependence on God and upon the absolute necessity of grace."[164] He spoke briefly of a Christian perspective on science:[165] its "theological presupposition" was the unity of God, implying the "complete harmony" of the universe, which the scientist looked for. As for the theory of evolution "as a scientific working hypothesis," for example, "the Christian is left a wide freedom as to the precise manner of the Divine formation."[166]

---

157. Ibid., 312.
158. Ibid., 315–82.
159. Ibid., 383–88.
160. ibid., 336.
161. Ibid., 342, 343.
162. Ibid., 374–82.
163. Ibid., 374–75.
164. Ibid., 375. See also below on his pamphlet *Abolishing God* of 1943.
165. Hammond, *Perfect Freedom*, 375–76.
166. Ibid., 376–78.

What of "limits to freedom of speech?" There needed to be "a delicate balance" between the liberty of the individual to state the dictates of his conscience and "the sacred right of the community to prevent disintegration and dissension."[167] On "The Christian and Those of Other Race" (chapter 29) he is anti-racist, and provides a judicious double summary statement: "It is the duty of the Christian . . . to give to all peoples the right and opportunity to exercise their [God-given] gifts to the fullest advantage . . . It is the supreme sin against an undeveloped people to withhold from them the gospel of the grace of God."[168]

He continues to bring a biblical and Reformational perspective in chapter 30 "Christianity, Progress, and the Ultimate Future." Christianity would sympathize with "many of the features of Humanism," with the secular confidence in the moral reformation and "golden age" of culture and "the final emancipation of man" in a "reconstruction of industrial life," and with Communism.[169] But "they fail to get at the root of the problem, human sin."[170] Even as D. J. Davies had talked of universal "selfishness," Hammond points out that the gospel had been confirmed repeatedly in history: "The true development of human life is conditioned by an inward operation of God the Holy Ghost commencing with the individual heart . . . [and] extending . . . to an inward regeneration of the whole nation."[171]

Jones would have agreed with him that "the ideal of a golden age" could only "be fulfilled under God's guidance and finally by His Personal intervention." This was not clear in Davies. As for the "Ultimate Future" of the world, Hammond thought that "only in the hope of personal immortality . . . can we look for . . . our share in the development of [God's] complete order."[172] Meanwhile, cultural progress both in the natural sciences and in social amelioration had been greatest, however imperfect, in the Christian nations.[173] Hammond reassured his reader of several final things: that no power could (ultimately) prevail against the church of God, that Christ's ethics were *absolute*, *permanent* "while capable of adjustment to various conditions," and *universal*, because they "deal directly with . . . God and man."[174]

---

167. Ibid., 379.
168. Ibid., 387. He was writing in the days of German anti-Jewish fascism.
169. Ibid., 389–90.
170. Ibid., 390.
171. Ibid., 391.
172. Ibid., 390–91.
173. Ibid., 394.
174. Ibid., 395.

He concluded this work with the source of its title in the ancient prayer: "O God ... *Whose service is perfect freedom.*"[175] Was it an unintellectual ethos among Evangelical students that limited the book's influence?[176] At least one Sydney layperson, an accountant, read it thoroughly—Wilfred Hutchison, Diocesan Secretary (1959-1973) and Lay Secretary of Synod.[177]

Reasoning Faith: An Introduction to Christian Apologetics (1943)

Completion of this, Hammond's final work in his IVF trilogy, was delayed by other tasks.[178] Apart from his being both incumbent of St Philip's, York Street, Sydney, Principal of Moore College, Gunther Memorial Lecturer, and giver of lunch-hour talks on Germany's "fading light," Archbishop Mowll required his assistance in many matters.[179] One such constraint[180] on Hammond's time arose from an action by liberal (largely) clergy formerly used to important roles in the diocese under Archbishop John Charles Wright's more comprehensive policy.

Hammond's Gunther Memorial Lectures, *Age-long Questions*, of March to April 1938 had hardly begun when Canon Arthur Garnsey, warden of St Paul's College in the university, sent the archbishop a lengthy "Memorial" later titled *A Plea for Liberty*.[181] Fifty of the senior clergy in the diocese signed this request for an audience with the archbishop.[182] They complained of finding themselves marginalized in favor of "conservative Evangelicals."[183] They also expressed "fear lest [Moore College's] students should be trained on narrow lines."[184] A recent sympathetic observer has

---

175. Ibid., quoting the *Second Collect, for Peace* (based on John 8:31-36; Rom 6:15-23) in "Order for Morning Prayer," Book of Common Prayer, 1549-1662.

176. Barclay, *Evangelicalism in Britain*, 15-45.

177. Wilfred Hutchison (1907-1973), given a copy in June 1941, marked it up right through the whole work. (His copy is in the possession of the writer).

178. Hammond, *Reasoning Faith*, 7.

179. Nelson, *T. C. Hammond*, 103-4. He also found it hard to decline invitations to speak and write (Babbage, personal letter).

180. Another was the "Red Book" case. See Nelson, *T. C. Hammond*, chapters 6 and 7 for the above demands.

181. Garnsey, *Plea for Liberty*, 4. The letter accompanying the Memorial was dated March 10, 1938, which was in the week of Hammond's first Gunther lecture on March 7.

182. See Garnsey, *Arthur Garnsey*, 153-63.

183. Loane, *Archbishop Mowll*, 143-49. See also Cable, "Memorialists," 10-24.

184. Arthur Garnsey, letter to his son, David, in Garnsey, *Arthur Garnsey*, 153.

found "a somewhat naively confrontational tone" in the Memorial.[185] Mowll called on Hammond, who formulated fourteen questions on the issues and statements in the Memorial. Mowll sent them to the signatories, requiring of each their individual answers before he would see them. They balked at this and the matter was never formally resolved.[186]

Some have unnecessarily assumed that Hammond's strong linking of arms with Mowll in the matter was colored by his Irish Church Missions controversy with Roman Catholicism. Sufficient explanation lies in this study's record of Hammond opposing liberal theological forces in ecclesiastical and student circles from his undergraduate days on. Mowll himself could hardly have forgotten the CICCU's departure from the Student Christian Movement in 1910 over liberalism[187] and both were aware of a broad liberal triumph in the Church of England.[188] Garnsey's liberal lectures on form criticism at his cathedral, already noted,[189] had framed the archbishop's arrival four years earlier.

Reasoning Faith had specifically the theological student in view as well as undergraduates generally.[190] It was a compact work, dealing in turn with "objections to the Christian system"—philosophical (atheism, agnosticism, pantheism, and various theistic positions), scientific (evolution versus creation), and historical (criticism of the New Testament gospels as revelation). Hammond had learned from the Scottish logician Alexander Bain (1818–1903), teacher of precision in thinking,[191] that "it is the duty of the apologist to counter contradictories" (objections), rather than to establish the contrary.[192] Broadly, that was Hammond's procedure in all three parts of this book. His approach also assumed the validity in principle of natural theology, as also of natural ethics in *Perfect Freedom*.

Hammond countered "Philosophical Objections" with some telling points. He was on the verge of a presuppositional approach when he wrote that the "Material Monist," follower of Ernst Haeckel, could not explain "how it is that concepts framed in the human mind obtain objective reality in an external world which is independent of that mind." He quoted T. H.

185. Armitage, "Memorialists," 21.

186. Garnsey, *Arthur Garnsey*, 153–63.

187. See chapter 3 above.

188. Judd and Cable, *Sydney Anglicans*, 240. They seem unaware that from his undergraduate days Hammond had learnedly defended a conservative and Evangelical theology against liberalism.

189. See "Conclusion" of chapter 9 above.

190. Hammond, *Reasoning Faith*, 9, 13, 14.

191. Sorley, *History of British Philosophy*, 293.

192. Hammond, *Reasoning Faith*, 10.

Green on John Locke: "A consistent sensationalism would be speechless."[193] He gave almost twenty pages to agnosticism (T. H. Huxley and Herbert Spencer). In its "popular developments," he noted, "there is an undue readiness to regard all mental deductions as figments."[194]

Having concluded that "the discursive reason cannot effectively deny [God]," he now had room for "the presumptions in favour of Theism," "a full presentation of the Divine."[195] His argument now may well have been helpful to Christians whose notion of God was that of historic Christianity, even as set out in the Apostles' Creed. Perhaps the same lent strength to the traditional apologetic, whether of Thomas Aquinas or of Joseph Butler, or of a James Orr, or of C. S. Lewis. But like them Hammond did not expose the assumption of human autonomy lying unspoken beneath all non-Christian systems of thought. His critique of Bertrand Russell's epistemology, though "a brilliant chapter" in the estimate of the senior wrangler to Russell in 1893,[196] illustrates this very lack.[197] It surprises that he did not point out that Russell admitted to "begging the question" (Russell's words) of the "inductive [causal] principle" (raised by David Hume),[198] but which the inner coherence of the Christian worldview justifies.[199] Hammond himself had previously said the "theological presupposition" of science was the unity of God, which implied the "complete harmony" of the universe.[200]

In part 2 "Scientific Objections to the Christian System" he focused chiefly on the theory of evolution. He enlisted the help of the young Dr. Harvey Carey, Demonstrator in Physiology in the University of Sydney, later to have a distinguished career as a professor of gynecology and obstetrics both in New Zealand and in Australia.[201] At the time it was popularly claimed that Darwin's *Origin of Species* had rendered "our old theologies and our old evidential treatises" of no weight.[202] Hammond addressed "the method of evolution," inorganic and organic. The theory could not explain origins. He concluded, on "evolution generally," that "pressed to its farthest

193. Ibid., 22, 23.
194. Ibid., 43.
195. Ibid., 59.
196. Manley, Review of *Reasoning Faith*, 186.
197. Hammond, *Reasoning Faith*, 92–106.
198. Hume, *Inquiry Concerning Human Understanding*, book 1, part 3, section 6.
199. Bahnsen, *Van Til's Apologetic*, 619, citing Russell, "On Induction," 107, 106 (69, 68 in 1959 reprint used by Bahnsen).
200. Hammond, *Perfect Freedom*, 376.
201. Harvey Carey (1917–1989), at Auckland University from 1953, the University of New South Wales from 1962.
202. Hammond, *Reasoning Faith*, 110.

limit of actual observation" it "does not preclude the idea of creation."²⁰³ He was following Alexander Bain's lead, rebutting a "contradictory."

He called the first chapter of Genesis "a poem of creation," and noted its orderly progression. He granted the notion that the word *day* represented God's acts under a figure of human acts.²⁰⁴ On the evidence for organic evolution and of paleontology and the problems in mutation and embryology,²⁰⁵ he concluded: "nothing . . . has yet been discovered that can be used legitimately to establish the notion of a mechanistic or materialistic view of the universe."²⁰⁶ It is of some interest today that he defended design: "Critics of Huxley had little difficulty in showing . . . that design . . . had by no means disappeared from the scheme of things."²⁰⁷ Why, he asked, "should it be necessary . . . to reject the working hypothesis [of] an ordering Mind?" Only this gave results.²⁰⁸

Reasoning Faith in part 3 treated "Historical Objections to the Christian System,"²⁰⁹ specifically to the claim that God has spoken. The contents of his message, his direct revelation, were embodied in "the religious books of the Jews" (the Hebrew Bible and the Greek New Testament).²¹⁰ The Deists, of course, had long ago rejected this theory of revelation—on their presumed view of God and the world. A recent revival of Deism's doctrine of transcendence (as opposed to the Christian) had reinforced modern Deism's denial of "the special messages of the Bible."²¹¹ Hammond stated that there was "nothing in any way improbable in the use of a *book* to record God's revelations of Himself."²¹²

The modern dogmatically advanced objection (or "contradictory") to special revelation by God asserted that revelation was a natural process of the human mind arising from a sense of wonder. This assumed that the religious writers made God in their own image.²¹³ Hammond did not challenge the silent assumption here that human reason was ultimate and au-

---

203. Ibid., 116.

204. Ibid., 123 (from Turton, *Truth of Christianity*, 133, 134).

205. Hammond, *Reasoning Faith*, chapters 16–19.

206. Ibid., 183.

207. Ibid., 125.

208. Ibid., 185. Similar in principle, with detail from modern discovery, is Andrews, *Who Made God?*

209. Hammond, *Reasoning Faith*, 186–270.

210. Ibid., 186 (my interpretation).

211. Ibid., 188.

212. Ibid., 189–90, quoting Kennedy, *Popular Handbook* (citing the title as *Christian Evidences*), 271–72.

213. Hammond, *Reasoning Faith*, 190. See also Feuerbach, *Essence of Christianity*.

tonomous, or reiterate his point in answer to the Deists on their "theory of God and the world."[214] He concluded only: "There is no convincing *a priori* reason against the idea of revelation."[215] The *possibility* (emphasis added) being established "it becomes a matter of evidence." This fulfills, of course, the "proper task" of apologetics that he had adopted, namely, to "counter contradictories," not to establish the contrary. On the other hand, a presuppositional apologetic aims also to achieve the latter. Similarly, when Hammond engaged with the recent negative form criticism of the gospels by Martin Dibelius (1883–1947),[216] he did not inform the students of Dibelius's underlying "presuppose[d] Kantian theory of reality and of knowledge." This "from beginning to end" determined what he found acceptable as fact in the gospel record.[217]

Hammond's acute and learned observations, however, and his use of "the older and more objective manner of dealing with the evidence," were doubtless persuasive to the convinced believer against Dibelius's "paradigms, tales and legends."[218] But did this approach challenge the skeptic below the surface, or leave the Christian believer exposed on one flank? The familiar, "let the facts speak for themselves," presupposed the religious neutrality of thought.[219] On the other hand, as one who had learned from the works of George Salmon, Hammond scored many a hit on the negative criticism of the gospel accounts.[220] He quoted from a phalanx of prominent New Testament and other scholars to argue his case. On the resurrection of Christ, he quoted tellingly from the book that earned Everard Digges La Touche his Doctor of Letters (on the testimony of the women in the gospels).[221]

Abolishing God (1943)

A published signpost of Hammond's thinking was his rebuttal of Challis Professor of Philosophy John Anderson's address to the New Education

---

214. Hammond, *Reasoning Faith*, 187–88.
215. Ibid., 190.
216. Ibid., 250–54, on Dibelius, *Fresh Approach*, and *Gospel Criticism*.
217. Stonehouse, "Martin Dibelius," 105–39, reprint in Stonehouse, *Paul Before the Areopagus*, 151–85. See especially 175–80 in the latter work.
218. E.g., Manley, Review of *Reasoning Faith*; Hammond, *Reasoning Faith*, 254.
219. Cf. Clouser, *Myth of Religious Neutrality*, 2–3 (on theories).
220. Salmon, *Historical Introduction* and *Human Element in the Gospels*.
221. Hammond, *Reasoning Faith*, 268, cites Digges La Touche, *Christian Certitude*, 199–200.

Fellowship (NSW) on religion in schools.[222] Anderson had argued that "religion and education are opposed" in principle because religion accepted "certain matters as dogma or on authority." This excluded them from enquiry, the object of education.[223] Hammond never published any critical analysis of Anderson's realist empiricism.[224] Yet Anderson's philosophy, though local, was very influential in Sydney and beyond in Australia.[225] Hammond appears never to have accepted that philosophical idealism was by 1943 already in eclipse.[226] Did he remain confident in a basically Kantian view of knowledge?[227]

In any case, it was the historian in Hammond who replied to Anderson's argument that scientific dogmas, the Ptolemaic system of astronomy, for example, had also held things back. But they had also "made the beginnings of astronomical science."[228] Similarly, "the possession of Christian dogma is as much a condition of development as the possession of scientific dogma."[229] And since no stem other than religion had been found on which to graft "sound moral principles," it was a great injustice to "shut out the child mind from this great area of . . . 'moral helpfulness.'"[230] The professor had failed to see that "religion and morality are alike pointers to the road that leads to fullness of human desires and the satisfaction of human needs."[231] Hammond did not seek out the basic underlying assumptions of Anderson's self-defined "empiricism."[232]

Two years later, however, writing on Karl Barth, Hammond returned to the noetic effect of sin and of the restraining role of common grace.[233] He was much clearer in this article than in his books and would seem to have

---

222. Anderson, "Address," 25–32; 203–13.

223. Ibid., 25, 203.

224. See Passmore, "Philosophy," 148–55.

225. Ibid., 155.

226. Hammond, *Reasoning Faith*, 92–106; cf. Passmore, *Hundred Years of Philosophy*, 174–200, 201–39.

227. See Van Til, *Introduction to Systematic Theology*, 304–7.

228. So also Chapman, *Stargazers*, 3: "the firm foundations of . . . science on which Copernicus and Galileo built."

229. Hammond, *Abolishing God*, 3–4 (reply to Anderson's address as reported in the student newspaper, *Honi Soit*, May 6, 1943).

230. Ibid., 5–6, citing James, *Varieties*.

231. Ibid., 15–16.

232. Passmore, "John Anderson," x–xxiv.

233. Hammond, "Barthianism and Natural Theology," 5–11.

become more consistent with his Reformation Evangelicalism in apologetic approach.[234]

The New Creation (1953)

Hammond's last book was possibly his crowning achievement in Evangelical systematic theology. The young J. I. Packer praised it as "standing in a direct line of succession from the great 'practical and experimental' expositions" of the Puritans.[235] Marcus Loane thought that the book, "based on careful exegesis" (and not so affected by philosophy), "was more welcome to Sydney readers" than *Perfect Freedom* and *Reasoning Faith*.[236] It was recommended reading at Moore College at least during Loane's time as principal (1954–1958).[237] Here was a full discussion of the application of redemption—from regeneration to glorification—for evangelicals across the Protestant denominations, an undertaking fully consistent with his Reformation Evangelicalism. Hammond referred to a range of nearly sixty important past works. He encouraged the reader to consider the interpretations of the passages of Scripture of the different schools of thought, including Roman Catholic, Anglo-Catholic, and liberal. He aimed not only to instruct his readers in the biblical teaching, but also to alert them to the various views, Evangelical perfectionism included.

Treating the sequence of the *ordo salutis* (order of the individual's salvation),[238] he begins with an analysis of the biblical teaching on regeneration, then treats the relation of regeneration to faith and baptism, as well as to perseverance and the faith that perseveres. Justification, the issue of the fruit of faith in the life of the believer, and the relation of saving faith to revelation all came into view.[239] In the second half of the work, featuring other aspects of the order of salvation, he expounds the status of all Christians as "sons" (adoption),[240] which he follows by four chapters on personal holiness (sanctification). Two chapters on the destiny of believers (glorification, and the resurrection body) conclude the work.[241]

---

234. See McIntosh, "How T. C. Hammond Defended the Faith," forthcoming in *Lucas*.

235. Packer, review of Hammond, *New Creation*, 22–23.

236. Loane, *Mark These Men*, 75.

237. Several former students of the college at a Retired Clergy Association meeting in Sydney (November 29, 2011).

238. See also his booklet *So Great Salvation*.

239. Hammond, *New Creation*, chapters 1–3 (11–65).

240. Ibid., chapter 8 (114–120).

241. Ibid., chapters 13 and 14 (166–192).

Hammond was always biblically grounded and Reformational in treating controverted matters under the various heads of doctrine. On the relation between the initial divine implanting of new life (regeneration) and justification he explained both the Roman Catholic and the Laudian (seventeenth-century High Church) contrary views. The Evangelical understanding was that regeneration was "the direct operation of the Holy Spirit," and not tied to baptism.[242] This "pure Augustinianism" had "strong scriptural support."[243] "The scriptural presentation of repentance" (an outcome of regeneration) indicated "a change of mind that penetrates to the very roots of the individual's life."[244] New Testament faith required that a conviction of mind must proceed to personal confidence in the divine truths, and so to the consent of the will, which was expressed in conduct.[245]

On the interpretation of the phrase in the Anglican rite of the Baptism of Children, "this child is regenerate"[246] Hammond thought that the "federal theory" of Calvin and Ussher was "the best way of combining the scriptural evidence in a coherent whole."[247] A later vice-principal of the college recommended Hammond's book, especially the chapter on "Regeneration, Faith and Baptism" (chapter 2), but did not discuss the federal theory.[248]

In chapters 4 to 7, on the central Reformation doctrine of justification, Hammond warned of the "very bad" moral effect of the "vials of wrath poured on 'legalistic ideas'" by liberals, who claimed to transcend law by "the higher principle of love."[249] The view of the modernists "transforms Christ into an ideal Example."[250] He corrected "a Protestant misconception" that Rome taught that we are saved by works—it taught that the "new life communicated . . . by baptism is not earned. It is the direct application of the merits of Christ."[251] He faults, however, the Roman Catholic interpretation of the word "faith" in Galatians 5:6 as "simple assent," for the apostle meant that "faith being confidence in the One who loved us and gave Himself

---

242. Ibid., 17.
243. Ibid., 18–20.
244. Ibid., 22.
245. Ibid., 25.
246. Book of Common Prayer (1662), "Ministration of the Publick Baptism of Children."
247. Hammond, *New Creation*, 39–47.
248. Robinson, *Meaning of Baptism*.
249. Hammond, *New Creation*, 68.
250. Ibid., 72.
251. Ibid., 70.

for us must express itself by means of love."[252] More categorically, he condemned the liberal or modernist view of justification, that "we must find room for some kind of legal fiction." It was "a gross absurdity to describe it as a fiction."[253]

In a later chapter Hammond recurred to natural theology,[254] which previously he had commended within certain limits.[255] He now cited Kuyper's seminal *Encyclopedia*, which reflected Calvin, and wrote that without the assistance of the book of special revelation (Scripture) the book of natural revelation "remains illegible."[256] Was he now rejecting an autonomous natural theology?

The New Creation set out his thought on sanctification and holiness in chapters 9–12. His doctrine, as he drew it from Scripture, was not different from that of Nathaniel Jones, and it was the background of his Christian convention expositions.[257] In chapter 11 he accepted Moule's post-Keswick (1884) exegesis of Romans 7, that it referred to the apostle's own normal experience when he did not meet temptation in the strength of "the definitely sought power of the Holy Ghost."[258] In chapter 12 "Factors in the Life of Holiness," on the sacraments, Hammond reached into his treasure-store from the Reformation. He quoted from the classic Calvinist *Heidelberg Catechism* (by Olevianus, 1563): "[The sacraments] are holy visible signs and seals ordained by God . . . that He may more fully declare and seal . . . the promise of His gospel unto us . . ."[259] Hammond did not confine his learning on the Reformation to that of the British Isles.

On the believer's hope, namely, the completion of the new creation, he argued against liberal and other views for a real resurrection of the body, but glorified, that is to say, transmuted (chapter 13).[260] On the future of the cosmos (chapter 14): "We would venture to declare that the New Testament looks to a final restoration of the world . . . the solemn enthronement of

252. Ibid., 105.

253. Ibid., 90. See Sanday and Headlam, *Critical and Exegetical Commentary*, 36, 94. Hammond nevertheless appreciated the overall greatness of the work.

254. Hammond, *New Creation*, 119–20.

255. Hammond, *IUBM*, 24–25; Hammond, *Reasoning Faith*, 60–91.

256. Hammond, *New Creation*, 119–20, quoting Kuyper, *Encyclopedia*, 309 (paraphrase of Calvin, *Institutes*, 1.5.14).

257. In addition to "Five Addresses" of 1937 and *So Great Salvation* above, was his *Way of Holiness*.

258. Hammond, *New Creation*, 146, quoting Moule, *Epistle of St. Paul to the Romans*, 195.

259. Hammond, *New Creation*, 161; *Heidelberg Catechism*, question 66.

260. Hammond, *New Creation*, 178.

our Lord as King of kings and Lord of lords. It will be accompanied by a manifest declaration to all men of God's righteous dealings in all ages."[261]

Principal of Moore College

Most of the college's students loved his Irish humor and sense of fun, exhibited inside and outside the classroom.[262] He would ask applicants to the college a key diagnostic question: "Are you sure your sins are forgiven?"[263] There was an emphasis on the student's knowledge of the text of Scripture. His main teaching subject was Christian doctrine, for which *IUBM* was used as an introduction to outline its whole range. He taught the Thirty-nine Articles in dialogue with their best liberal Anglo-Catholic scholarly exposition.[264] He critiqued at some points the textbook he assigned, written by W. H. Griffith Thomas, Nathaniel Jones's theological soul-mate.[265] Bishop Ken Short represented many who were taught by Hammond: "Again and again the point was, What did the Scriptures say?"[266] He also taught the subject Prayer Book, impressing the students with his encyclopedic knowledge of it.[267] The conservative Evangelical was really the only Anglican allowed by the Thirty-nine Articles and the Prayer Book.[268]

His assistants in the college heard his daily, learned chapel sermons. They included future scholars and leaders of note. His vice-principal from 1939, Marcus Loane, succeeded him as principal in 1954, became Mowll's coadjutor bishop in 1958, and was elected Archbishop of Sydney in 1966. A. W. Morton (1911–1973) studied and taught under him, and later gained the Oxford DPhil; his last six years of ministry were as Dean of St Andrew's Cathedral. E. K. (Keith) Cole (1919–2012), one of Hammond's graduates who also taught Old Testament under him, became a CMS missionary in Kenya, where he headed St Paul's United Theological College, Limuru. Cole later gained his ThD (Australian College of Theology), became vice-principal of

---

261. Ibid., 188.

262. Gerber, *Memoirs*, 3, 129, 144–45.

263. Informal personal conversation with David Hewetson, who was a Moore College student in 1952.

264. Bicknell, *Theological Introduction*.

265. Thomas, *Principles of Theology*.

266. Personal interview with K. H. Short, January 18, 2010, at his home in Kiama, NSW.

267. Gerber, *Memoirs*, 144.

268. Personal interview with K. H. Short, January 18, 2010, at his home in Kiama, NSW.

Ridley College, Melbourne, then founding principal of Nungalinya College (for Aboriginals) in Darwin, Australia.

David Broughton Knox, a son of Jones graduate D. J. Knox, never a student of Hammond's, joined the staff in 1947, taught generations of first year students using *IUBM*, became vice-principal under Loane and succeeded him as principal in 1959.[269] Donald Robinson, son of another Jones graduate, R. B. Robinson, also never a student in the college, studied at Cambridge 1948-1950 (Theology Tripos parts 1a and 3), joined the staff in 1952, was vice-principal from 1959, regional Bishop of Parramatta from 1973, then Archbishop of Sydney 1982-93. Robinson and Knox heard Hammond's daily chapel sermons; Robinson, Hammond's Sunday preaching at St Philip's, York Street while his curate there during the first two years on the staff. Other significant members of the teaching staff (more latterly called faculty) included Bruce Smith, who studied at the college in Hammond's last years as principal and was later a faculty member under D. B. Knox. Smith was greatly influenced by Hammond, and as a theologian was much admired by Knox. Another, inspired as a youth reading *IUBM*, later became principal of the college, 1985-2001, then Archbishop of Sydney, 2000-2013.[270]

Not all the many outstanding college graduates who thoroughly embraced Hammond's teaching can be mentioned. They also included Kenneth Short (mentioned above), who was regional Bishop of Wollongong from 1975, Anglican Bishop to the Australian Defence Force from 1979, and finally Dean of Sydney, 1989-1992. Harry Goodhew (b. 1931), regional Bishop of Wollongong from 1982, then Archbishop of Sydney 1993-2001, remembered the profound impact of Hammond's classes in 1958 to deacons on Thomas Cranmer's doctrine of the Lord's Supper.[271] Many others directly influenced by Hammond's teaching also had distinguished ministries in Sydney, other dioceses, and abroad with (mainly) the Church Missionary Society. His importance for Leon Morris's atonement scholarship has already been noted.

---

269. Knox studied at the London College of Divinity (London BD, 1941), several terms at Cambridge (1942-1943). While teaching at Moore College he gained the London MTh (1949), then studied at Oxford (DPhil, 1953).

270. Peter Jensen (BD London, 1970, MA Sydney, 1976), also studied at Oxford (DPhil, 1980).

271. Hammond, T. C., "Cranmer on the Lord's Supper." Casual interview with Goodhew, January 2016.

Conclusion

Hammond was a Calvinist Reformation Evangelical, fully convinced of the conformity to Scripture of the doctrine of the Thirty-nine Articles and to the 1662 Book of Common Prayer, which derived not much altered from the 1552 book. With that, he was abreast of all the important contrary discussion, old High Church, Tractarian, liberal and secular, to say nothing of his mastery of Roman Catholic doctrinal formulation. If his embrace of natural theology and natural ethics broadly followed that of leading systematic theologians before him, in his last works he may have increasingly realized how a full Christian theism was a necessary framework for every field of knowledge.

Hammond was an Evangelical of outstanding intellectual caliber and influence. He locates as a wide-ranging centrist Reformation theologian in the spectrum of twentieth-century Evangelicalism. Hardly inappropriate is the final comment on him of Marcus Loane: "a great man, whose like we may not soon see again."[272]

---

272. Loane, *Mark These Men*, 76.

13

Conclusion

FROM THE LAST YEARS of the nineteenth century to the mid-twentieth century the Evangelicalism taught in Moore Theological College, as well as that exhibited by the Diocese of Sydney, went through three broad phases exhibited in the persons of the three principals of the period. The above study has attempted to fill in some of the gaps in our knowledge of these three principals, each very able and learned. It has also questioned, in some cases corrected, certain widely accepted statements about their views—statements sometimes based on inadequate acquaintance with their literary remains, sometimes influenced by the perspective and standpoint of the writer. Light has been shed on the impact of their teaching on the diocese and on the community in which the college was located.

Moore College, and with it the Diocese of Sydney, had undergone theological variation before the arrival of Nathaniel Jones in 1897. Bishop Barker founded the college to prepare Evangelically minded clergy, resistant to both "rationalism and ritualism." From 1856 to 1884 the college principals always attempted to do this, while also receiving historic High Church students as from an accepted school within the Church of England. Barker's successor, the Broad Church Bishop Barry, appointed a principal in 1885 who turned out to be a cryptic ritualist and soon had to go. Barry's Evangelical successor, Bishop William Saumarez Smith, first appointed Bernard Schleicher, an old school High Churchman (thus not a ritualist) who was also firmly anti-rationalist with regard to the criticism of Scripture. When he died in 1897, the now Archbishop Smith appointed Nathaniel Jones, an Evangelical. On his death in 1911, Archbishop Wright, a Liberal Evangelical, appointed D. J. Davies. Wright died in 1933 and a conservative Evangelical, Howard Mowll succeeded him. With the passing of Principal Davies in 1935, Archbishop Mowll called T. C. Hammond, who took office in April 1936.

This succession closely reflected the shifts then occurring in England, where most Anglican clergy in Australia had been educated. In part (that is to say, aside from the millennial and holiness extensions) the changes reflected the responses of the Evangelical school in the home Church of England to the challenges, chiefly intellectual and ecclesiastical, of their day. As a result, premillennial and Keswick holiness extensions to a basically Reformation Evangelicalism (Nathaniel Jones, 1897–1911) gave way to a broadened self-designated Liberal Evangelicalism (D. J. Davies, 1911–1935), followed by a Reformation, centrist Evangelicalism (T. C. Hammond, 1936–1953) that retained the holiness extension. Consequently, among those clergy who were graduates and students of the college there came to be a clear discrepancy between the Evangelical schools represented in the diocese by the Moore College men. It was a tense synod in 1933 that elected Howard Mowll as archbishop. This study has attempted to clarify the varying positions on the Evangelical theological spectrum taught in the college and reflected in the diocese from the late 1890s until the early 1950s.

All three principals tried to be "valiant for truth" as they understood it. Jones's conservative, premillennial and Keswick but firmly Reformational section of the extended Evangelical spectrum was replaced by the rising Liberal Evangelical broadening with which Davies identified. Hammond represented a return to the distinctly Reformational conservative part of the Evangelical spectrum. The difference between the Evangelicalism of Jones and that of Hammond proved to be mostly a matter of emphasis and style. Except for the question of a millennium, the basic doctrinal outlook of both closely coincided. Between these two and Davies, however, the theological difference was one of principle, for it touched what Bishop Barker would have called rationalism. Davies's biblicism and crucicentrism was of a genus other than that of Jones and Hammond. But he and the other two principals were as one in rejecting ritualism, though not all Liberal Evangelicals were as firm in this last respect.

One assumes, of course, that as in any teaching institution, not all students who entered the college would have accepted without question the outlook of the principal and his assistants. Most were of Evangelical, some of High Church or even Anglo-Catholic background, before entering. Some perhaps changed their views while in college, some certainly did over the years of their ministry. But whether in whole or in part, they carried the influence of their principal into their activities as clergy—in parish, on committees, in synod, and in parachurch organizations.

The evidence shows that Nathaniel Jones's emphasis was neither that of an ardently this-world-denying kind of pre-millennialism, nor of an exclusive focus on the inner life of believers. His theological position was like that of Handley C. G. Moule, who himself also adopted a premillennial hope late in life. True, Jones did not urge his potentially future clergy to work directly for society's reform. But he was far from restricting the activity of Christian believers to some narrowly circumscribed "little flock" awaiting the imminent return of their Lord. His addresses to the Katoomba Convention and that to university students rather encouraged believers to be dedicated Christians in their callings, secular or spiritual, and in their responsibilities as enfranchised citizens. Jones's teaching, with that of his assistants in the college, was directed mainly towards developing in his students and other Christian believers a serious while joyful piety of living faith in Christ, trusting in him for both personal forgiveness and holiness of life. Clergy were to be examples to their flock and committed to promoting the gospel in parish and in diocese. In the long term, clergy and laity alike must resist some things and promote others. Jones's was a biblicist emphasis, similar to that found in the Book of Common Prayer. In doctrine Jones held closely to that of the Thirty-nine Articles of Religion. And though he seemed to have been weak on the bondage of the will he can correctly be thought of as Calvinist, albeit mildly so, in expression. Jones's convictions did indeed also embrace a premillennial hope, but he did not press this as essential for the Christian's piety. He loved Prayer Book devotion and doctrine. By his teaching and published sermons, he encouraged and enabled his students and other Christian believers to be solidly convinced of scriptural authority against liberal criticism and of the scriptural doctrines of salvation and the sacraments against ritualism. Academically, he and his few assistants prepared the college's students for outstanding results in the external theological examinations. He continued in the college what his predecessors appointed by Bishop Barker had striven to achieve.

Hence, with the advent of a Liberal Evangelical archbishop, John Charles Wright, and consequently a college principal of similar outlook (Davies, 1911), key Jones men bided their time until they could effect change through synod. Certain of them gave time and energy to the ACL and the *ACR*, and organized T. C. Hammond's visit in 1926. They welcomed a "moderate Calvinist" like T. C. Hammond to Sydney then, and to Moore College ten years later. It seemed to matter little, if at all, that he did not share the premillennial views that some of them held dear. Under Wright, a number of Jones men became energetically involved in the diocesan synod—its concerns (such as a constitution for the Church of England in Australia) and its committees, including the Moore College Committee set up by synod in 1919. They were active in evangelism and in parachurch organizations such as the Church Missionary Society (a few becoming its missionaries), the Bush Church Aid Society, the Katoomba Christian Convention, and the Scripture Union.

Archbishop Wright had known Jones briefly and admired him for his theological learning. Possibly he did not perceive how deep was the fissure between Liberal Evangelicalism and the Evangelicalism of Jones. In any case, the emergent theological tension within the broadening Evangelical spectrum in England was not initially clear to all. When Jones died, Wright called David John Davies, a member of the Group Brotherhood, a fellow Liberal Evangelical to succeed him. Wright's immediate Evangelical concern was with ritualism. The new archbishop wished to remove from his diocese what were now, especially since 1904, clearly unconstitutional liturgical practices and vestments. This was the high-profile side of his Evangelical activism. Principal Davies, was of one mind with him in the matter, as were most other clergy in the diocese, among them also those trained at Moore College under Jones. Wright was also interested in addressing "the social problem," namely poverty, and this interest was a main factor in his election. Davies actively spoke to and wrote on "the social problem," and his thought saw print in a number of publications. He worked on the new Social Problem Committee set up by the synod under Wright. It continues today as the Social Issues Committee.

The conversionist side to Davies's Evangelicalism was clearly evident in his bid to reach the non-church-attending man-in-the-street. This goal was set out in his book, *The Church and the Plain Man*, the fullest statement of his overall position. The church's message as he presented it there, however, was not the historic church doctrine of the atonement and justification by faith. Christ's cross was scarcely brought in as an objective accomplishment for the forgiveness of sin. It was, rather, chiefly the Lord's example of willing sacrifice, to be a moral lever against selfishness, which he saw manifest both in trade union and business. Although Davies emphasized the role of the Bible in conversion and spiritual growth, his liberal version of scriptural authority was predicated upon the assumed autonomy of human moral-doctrinal thought. So also was his view of Christ's saving death and man's forgiveness. In this respect Davies's Liberal Evangelical thought points up what divided him in principle from the men taught by Jones as well as from others who shared their more conservative and Reformational convictions. His book, however, merits praise for his analysis of the practical problems preventing the church from reaching and convincing "the plain man." It is very informative of the attitudes of both labor and capitalism at the time.

CONCLUSION

Even-handedly he showed both sides to be guilty of selfishness, his root concept of sin. Both sides needed to cooperate, not compete.

In Davies's years, the college student body included a number from an Evangelical background close to that of Jones. Some were parishioners of Jones's leading students, a few were even sons of these same men, or their daughters training in Deaconess House next door. Under Davies as principal, the conservative among his students could feel very much out of tune with the liberalism of the college teaching. In reaction they had recourse to classically Evangelical or Reformation sources for their own study and encouragement.[1] From an Evangelical point of view, the preaching of some was blunted by the college's instruction. However, both they and most of the liberals remained firmly Protestant with regard to ritualism.

For the history of Moore College and the Diocese of Sydney, Davies's predecessor had the most significant influence, which lay in the activism of Jones's students (and convinced laymen) noted above.[2] As Anglicans in the tradition of the English Reformation, convinced that its Prayer Book and Articles of Religion were firmly grounded in Scripture, they were conservatively biblicist, crucicentric, and conversionist, as well as anti-ritualist. So taught at the college and confirmed through Hammond's visit in 1926, leading Jones graduates worked to achieve the election of Howard Mowll as archbishop in 1933. Although Protestant in the sense of being opposed to the ritualist changes to the Prayer Book that Anglo-Catholics were pressing for along with their doctrines, it is not clear whether Davies associated himself with Hammond's 1926 visit. Davies's view of justification was shaped by his liberal outlook, with the consequence that the centrality of Reformation themes for authentic Anglicanism did not emerge clearly in his writing. Davies was deeply disappointed by the election of Howard Mowll as archbishop in 1933. Many of those who signed the Memorial protest to Mowll in 1938 were Davies's former students, although the fact that a proportion of the signatories comprised Jones's former students proves that the latter were not all a solid phalanx. Davies's liberal influence, which had proved insufficient in 1933, continued on for many years after. But it could not outweigh the historic Evangelical tradition of the diocese, reinforced by Jones and so strongly defended by T. C. Hammond in 1926, and uncompromisingly promoted by Mowll together with Hammond, once he arrived at the college. The leading Jones graduates gladly continued to exercise their ministry under and in close association with their archbishop. Thus, they extended to

---

1. Such as J. C. Ryle's works.

2. Detailed evidence for the latter is harder to establish and lies outside the scope of this study.

over a half-century from his election the influence of their principal on the Evangelicalism of the Diocese of Sydney.

Mowll's own Evangelicalism, having been fired in the CICCU controversy of 1910–1911, meant that he was staunchly opposed to liberalism. He was as firmly opposed as Wright to ritualism and the doctrine it stood for. But Mowll was more conservatively biblicist. He was also centered on the Reformation doctrine of justification by faith with its implications for conversion. When Davies died in 1935, Mowll's closest advisors, who included Bishop Sydney Kirkby (a graduate under Jones) and one or two others of like views, not to forget lay synodsmen like H. L. Tress, persuaded him to call T. C. Hammond, whose education at Trinity College, Dublin (1900–1905) happened to coincide very nearly with that of Davies at Trinity College, Cambridge, then Ridley Hall (1901–1905).

Even as a student Hammond was emerging as a budding theologian able to address leading theological trends. Within the Evangelical spectrum, his was a Reformation centrist position, conservative, and very close to that of Handley C. G. Moule, including the latter's view of holiness, and so not unlike that of Jones. His resistance to ritualism and Tractarian doctrines was both historically and theologically grounded. His appreciation of the Reformation had been sharpened also by his knowledge and direct experience of Roman Catholic doctrine and practice in Ireland. He knew well the scholastic theology of Trent and before. With regard to Anglo-Catholicism, he also knew its history and had argued powerfully against its view of episcopal authority. He had argued powerfully from the early Fathers to establish its limits before he came to Sydney and Moore College. He had also been an Evangelical leader in rebutting liberal theological argument and doctrinal statement of whatever degree. He had argued that for the regenerate Christian believer Scripture was in fact no mere "external authority." Under his name had appeared perhaps the only early-twentieth-century handbook to set forth a learned evangelical systematic theology for the non-theological student. *In Understanding Be Men* saw five editions and multiple reprints over more than thirty years.

Beginning with his principalship, this book set the doctrinal tone of Moore Theological College for the next fifty years. Hammond also took the students through the Thirty-nine Articles in dialogue with E. J. Bicknell's scholarly Anglo-Catholic exposition. He left students in no doubt concerning the biblical and Reformation doctrine of justification. He endeavored to ensure their confidence in the authority and inspiration of Scripture. He was ably assisted from the beginning by Marcus Loane, who became his vice-principal, later his successor. Hammond employed others of like conservative conviction to assist in the college. Premillennialism disappeared.

W. H. Griffith Thomas's *Principles of Theology* was read for ThL doctrine. For Prayer Book the college used Neil and Willoughby's *Tutorial Prayer Book* of 1913. Hammond was himself expert historically and theologically in the key areas of disputed churchmanship, both liturgical and doctrinal. Towards the end of his time as principal he lectured once a week to those recently ordained, on Archbishop Cranmer's classic *A Defence of the True and Catholic Doctrine of the Sacrament*. Hammond's lectures expounded the theology which underlay the service of the Lord's Supper in the Book of Common Prayer.

The books of his Moore College era on Christian ethics and apologetics for tertiary students did not sell as well as he had hoped. Perhaps that was in part because only a few evangelical students and graduates of all denominations felt strongly the intellectual challenges of their environment. In these scholarly works he did make a point, though not consistently, of the difference that the believer's regeneration should make to his or her thinking in every field of knowledge. Of wider appeal than these two works, apparently, was his last book, *The New Creation* (1953), which focused more on the biblical data than issues of soteriology.

Graduates of the college still living in the twenty-first century remembered the impact of Hammond's teaching. The authority of the Bible was basic: students were challenged with "What does the Bible say?" They especially appreciated his book, *In Understanding Be Men*. Parish evangelism and the sending of missionaries, together with resistance to the national challenge within the Anglican Church of Anglo-Catholic doctrine and ritual, appear to have gained most interest and attention at the college of his day—more than Keswick holiness teaching.

A number of his activities in Sydney contributed to Hammond's name as a controversialist. They include his formulation of the questionnaire Mowll sent in reply to the Memorialists of 1938, his prosecuting (for Mowll) of the long court case against the Bishop of Bathurst's "Red Book," his power of debate in synod, and his broadcast series, "The Case for Protestantism." But the historian needs to take care not to distort the centrist Reformational content and emphasis of his teaching, both inside and outside the college. Hammond conscientiously promoted the Anglicanism of the Thirty-nine Articles and the Prayer Book, and did so with great learning, salted with not a little incidental humor. One should remember also that it was Hammond who, with his friend, Bishop Hilliard (Mowll's co-adjutor bishop), finally succeeded in negotiating an acceptable constitution for the very mixed Church of England in Australia.

There were two spheres outside the college and the diocesan organization in which Hammond's thought was also important and gratefully remembered. He was called upon by the new Inter-Varsity Fellowship of Australia to bolster its theologically evangelical stand as opposed to the liberal approach of the Australian Student Christian Movement. He spoke frequently for the Evangelical Unions. The Christian Convention movement also enlisted him to expound biblical teaching on personal holiness. His ministry proved effective against the sinless perfectionists active among students both in Sydney and Melbourne.

Such has been the succession of conviction and piety taught in the college under Jones (1897–1911), Davies (1911–1935), and Hammond (1936–1953), in tandem with that of their respective archbishops who had called them. With the coming of Hammond, the Evangelical character of college and diocese became more distinctly Reformational and centrist. It addressed salient issues of the mid-twentieth-century context. Archbishop Wright's determined and Anglican constitutional exclusion of ritualism from his diocese was consistent with this. It was confirmed in the era of Hammond and Mowll, though the diocese did not become nearly as monochrome as some have assumed to be the case. As under Jones, the college itself hewed an exclusively Evangelical course in its teaching, while not rejecting the High Church or even Anglo-Catholic student. The swing back from a liberal to a more conservative stance under Mowll and Hammond makes Moore College, as well as the character of the Diocese of Sydney, an unusual phenomenon in the history of evangelical theological and ecclesiastical institutions.

The central question of this research has been to establish more clearly the nature and scope of the shifts in the spectrum of Anglican Evangelicalism in Sydney, both within Moore College and the Diocese of Sydney—always two closely related institutions, since the archbishop must license the principal. The doctrinal positions and emphases embodied in the Evangelical spectrum, as broadened by liberalism or as extended by a premillennial hope (for a time) and Keswick holiness teaching, left an abiding legacy within Sydney Anglicanism. Understanding the thought and influence of the successive principals is essential for a sound view of the history of the college, and of the diocese whose clergy it mostly provides. Light has also been cast on the larger issue of "the chasm" in Australian Anglicanism in a period of major intellectual and social changes—changes that were also shaping the character of global Evangelical Anglicanism of that time. Perhaps the light cast on such matters in this book will allow a better understanding of the significant role that Moore College and the Diocese of Sydney continue to play on the global Anglican stage.

Bibliography

Abbott, Thomas Kingsmill. *A Critical and Exegetical Commentary on the Epistles to the Ephesians and to the Colossians*. Edinburgh: T & T Clark, 1897.
Acheson, Alan. *A History of the Church of Ireland 1691–2000*. 2nd ed. Dublin: Columba and APCK, 2002.
Acton, John Emerich Edward Dalbert. *Lectures on Modern History*. Reprint, with an introduction by Hugh Trevor-Roper. London: Collins, 1960.
Adam, Peter, and Gina Denholm, eds. *Proclaiming Christ: Ridley College, Melbourne 1910–2010*. Parkville, Australia: Ridley Melbourne, 2010.
Alcock, Deborah. *Walking with God: A Memoir of the Venerable John Alcock, Late Archdeacon of Waterford*. London: Hodder and Stoughton, 1887.
Alford, Henry. *The Greek Testament: With a Critically Revised Text: A Digest of Various Readings: Marginal References to Verbal and Idiomatic Usage: Prolegomena: And a Critical and Exegetical Commentary*. Cambridge: Deighton, Bell, 1874.
A. L. O. E. [Charlotte Maria Tucker]. *Pride and His Prisoners*. London: Nelson and Sons, 1871.
Anderson, John. "Address." In *Religion in Education: Five Addresses Delivered Before the New Education Fellowship (N.S.W.)*, 25–32. N.p.: n.p., 1943. Reprinted in *Education and Inquiry*, edited by D. Z. Phillips, 203–13. Oxford: Blackwell, 1980.
Andrews, Edgar H. *Who Made God? Searching for a Theory of Everything*. Darlington, UK: Evangelical, 2009.
Anglican Church of Australia. *A Prayer Book for Australia: For Use Together With the Book of Common Prayer (1662) and An Australian Prayer Book (1978)*. Alexandria, Australia: Broughton, 1995.
Angus, Samuel. *Forgiveness and Life: Chapters from an Uncompleted Book, The Historical Approach to Jesus*. Sydney, Australia: Angus and Robertson, 1962.
Anonymous. "The Rev. Canon Jones, M.A., An Appreciation." *SDM* 2, no. 6 (1911) 17.
Archdall, Henry Kingsley, ed. *Mervyn Archdall: A Memorial of the Late Reverend Canon Mervyn Archdall, M.A.* Sydney, Australia: Angus and Robertson, 1922.
Archdall, Mervyn. *The Analytical Higher Criticism*. Sydney, Australia: W. M. Madgwick and Sons, 1903.

———. "Doctrine of the Church." 1912. Reprinted in *Mervyn Archdall: A Memorial of the Late Reverend Canon Mervyn Archdall, M.A.*, edited by Henry Kingsley Archdall, 46–47. Sydney, Australia: Angus and Robertson, 1922.

———. *Liturgical Right and National Wrong: A Vindication of the Rights of the Church. And a Criticism of Wakeman's History and other Books Approved by Bishops, and by the Fellows of the "Australian College of Theology."* London: Church Association, 1900.

Armitage, Chris. "The Memorialists." *The Anglican Historical Society, Diocese of Sydney, Journal* 55, no. 2 (2010) 18–25.

Askwith, E. H. *The Historical Value of the Fourth Gospel.* London: Hodder and Stoughton, 1910.

———. "Sin, and the Need of Atonement." In *Essays on Some Theological Questions of the Day: By Members of the University of Cambridge*, 175–218. London: Macmillan, 1905.

Atherstone, Andrew. "Benjamin Jowett's Pauline Commentary: An Atonement Controversy." *Journal of Theological Studies* 54, no. 1 (2003) 139–53.

———. "Wace, Henry." In *BDE* 688–90.

Auberlen, Carl August. *The Divine Revelation: An Essay in Defence of the Faith.* Edinburgh: T & T Clark, 1874.

Augustine. *De Spiritu et Littera.* In *Augustine: The Later Works*, edited by John Burnaby, 195–249. London: SCM, 1953.

Babbage, Stuart Barton. "Archbishop Mowll and Some Personal Reminiscences." Paper read to The Heretics Club (supplied to the author, undated).

———. *Memoirs of a Loose Canon.* Brunswick East, Australia: Acorn, 2005.

———. Personal letter to author, October 1, 2010.

Bahnsen, Greg L. *Van Til's Apologetic: Readings and Analysis.* Phillipsburg, NJ: Presbyterian and Reformed, 1998.

Bailey, Kenneth C. *A History of Trinity College Dublin, 1892–1945.* Dublin: The University Press, 1947.

Baker, D. W. A. "Archdall, Mervyn." In *ADB* 7:85–86.

Bale, Colin. "The Commonwealth Celebrations of 1901: Sectarianism and the Symbolic Unity of Federation." *Lucas* 27 and 28 (2000) 90–107.

Balfour, A. J. *Theism and Humanism.* The Gifford Lectures 1914. London: Hodder and Stoughton, 1915.

Ballantine-Jones, Bruce. *Inside Sydney: An Insider's View of the Changes and Politics in the Anglican Diocese of Sydney, 1996–2013.* Sydney, Australia: Ballantine-Jones, 2016.

Balleine, G. R. *A History of the Evangelical Party in the Church of England.* New ed. London: Church Book Room, 1951.

Banks, Robert. "Fifty Years of Theology in Australia, 1915–1965: Part One" *Colloquium* 9, no. 1 (1976) 36–42.

———, ed. *Reconciliation and Hope: New Testament Essays on Atonement and Eschatology Presented to L. L. Morris on His 60th Birthday.* Exeter, UK: Paternoster, 1974.

Barclay, Oliver R. *Evangelicalism in Britain 1935–1995: A Personal Sketch.* Leicester, UK: Inter-Varsity, 1997.

———. *Whatever Happened to the Jesus Lane Lot?* Leicester, UK: Inter-Varsity, 1977.

Barker, Frederic. "The Supposed Sacrament of Penance." In *A Course of Sermons on the Principal Errors of the Church of Rome; Preached in St. Andrew's Church, Liverpool by Ten Clergymen of the Church of England*. London: J. Hatchard & Son, 1838.

———. *On the Rise of the Errors of the Church of Rome. A Course of Sermons*. N.p., 1840.

Barnes, Ernest William. "The Future of the Evangelical Movement." In *Liberal Evangelicalism: An Interpretation by Members of the Church of England*, edited by T. Guy Rogers, 287–304. London: Hodder and Stoughton, 1923.

———. *Should Such a Faith Offend?* London: Hodder and Stoughton, 1928.

Barzun, Jacques. *From Dawn to Decadence: 500 Years of Western Cultural Life, 1500 to the Present*. New York: Harper Collins, 2000.

———. *Marx, Darwin, Wagner: Critique of a Heritage*. 2nd ed. Garden City, NY: Doubleday, 1958.

Bates, James Drane. "Email to Marcia Cameron." In *Phenomenal Sydney: Anglicans in a Time of Change, 1945–2013*, by Marcia M. Cameron, 268–72. Eugene, OR: Wipf & Stock, 2016.

Bebbington, David. *The Dominance of Evangelicalism: The Age of Spurgeon and Moody*. Leicester, UK: Inter-Varsity, 2005.

———. *Evangelicalism in Modern Britain: A History from the 1730s to the 1980s*. Grand Rapids: Baker, 1992.

———. *Holiness in Nineteenth Century*. Carlisle, UK: Paternoster, 2000.

———. *Patterns in History: A Christian Perspective on Historical Thought. With a New Preface and Afterword*. Grand Rapids: Baker Book House, 1990.

———. Review of *Four Views on the Spectrum of Evangelicalism*, by Kevin T. Bauder et. al. *Evangelical Studies Bulletin* 83 (2012) 1–6.

Bendall, Sarah, et al. *A History of Emmanuel College, Cambridge*. Woodbridge, UK: Boydell, 1999.

Bernard, John Henry. *A Critical and Exegetical Commentary on the Gospel According to St. John*. 2 vols. Edited by A. H. McNeile. Edinburgh: T & T Clark, 1928.

———, ed. *The Works of Bishop Butler: A New Edition with an Introduction and Notes by J. H. Bernard*. London: Macmillan, 1900.

Besant, Sir Walter. *All Sorts and Conditions of Men: An Impossible Story*. New ed. London: Chatto & Windus, 1884.

Bickersteth, Edward Henry. *Yesterday, To-day and Forever: A Poem, in Twelve Books*. 10th ed. London: Rivingtons, 1874.

Bicknell, E. J. *A Theological Introduction to the Thirty-nine Articles of the Church of England*. 2nd ed. London: Longmans, Green, 1925.

Binns, Leonard E. *The Evangelical Movement in the English Church*. London: Methuen, 1928.

Birks, Thomas Rawson. *The Difficulties of Belief: In Connexion with the Creation, Fall, Redemption and Judgment*. London: Macmillan, 1876.

———. "Introduction." In *A View of the Evidences of Christianity: In Three Parts*, by William Paley, 3–30. London: Religious Tract Society, 1859.

———. *Modern Utilitarianism; Or, the Systems of Paley, Bentham, and Mill Examined and Compared*. London: Macmillan, 1874.

———. *Supernatural Revelation, or First Principles of Moral Theology*. London: Macmillan, 1879.

Blanch, Allan M. *From Strength to Strength: A Life of Marcus Loane.* North Melbourne, Australia: Australian Scholarly, 2015.
Boardman, W. E. *The Higher Christian Life.* Boston: Henry Hoyt, 1859.
Boase, George Clement, "Jeune, Francis." In *DNB* 29:372-73.
Bolt, Peter G. *William Cowper (1778-1858): The Indispensable Parson: The Life and Influence of Australia's First Parish Clergyman.* Camperdown, Australia: Bolt, 2009.
Bolt, Peter G., and Mark D. Thompson, eds. *Donald Robinson: Selected Works.* 3 vols. Camperdown, Australia: Australian Church Record, 2008.
Boultbee, T. P. *The Alleged Moral Difficulties of the Old Testament. A Lecture delivered in connection with the Christian Evidence Society.* London: Hodder & Stoughton, 1872.
———. *A Commentary on the Thirty-Nine Articles: Forming an Introduction to the Theology of the Church of England.* 7th ed. London: Longmans, Green, 1884.
———. *An Introduction to the Theology of the Church of England in an Exposition of the Thirty-nine Articles.* London: Longmans, Green, 1871.
Boyce, F. B. *Fourscore Years and Seven: Memoirs of Archdeacon Boyce, for Over Sixty Years a Clergyman of the Church of England in New South Wales.* Sydney, Australia: Angus and Robertson, 1934.
Braga, Stuart. *A Century of Preaching Christ: Katoomba Christian Convention 1903-2003.* Sydney, Australia: Katoomba Christian Convention, 2003.
Bratt, J. D. "Kuyper, Abraham." In *BDE* 351-54.
Brett, G. S. "Green, Thomas Hill." In *Encyclopaedia of Religion and Ethics,* edited by James Hastings, 6:435-40. Edinburgh: T & T Clark, 1913.
Briggs, Charles A. *The Bible, the Church and the Reason: The Three Great Fountains of Divine Authority.* Edinburgh: T & T Clark, 1892.
Brine, T. "Foreword." In *The One Hundred Texts of the Society for Irish Church Missions,* v-ix. London: The Society for Irish Church Missions, 1939.
Brock, M. G., and M. C. Curthoys, eds. *Nineteenth-Century Oxford, Part 2.* The History of the University of Oxford 7. Oxford: Clarendon, 2000.
Bromiley, G. W. "Appendix I. '1900-1950.'" In *A History of the Evangelical Party in the Church of England,* 252-69. New ed. London: Church Book Room, 1951.
Brook, R. "The Bible." In *Foundations: A Statement of Christian Belief in Terms of Modern Thought,* 25-71. London: Macmillan, 1912.
Brooke, Christopher N. L. *A History of the University of Cambridge: Volume IV: 1870-1900.* Cambridge: Cambridge University Press, 1993.
Brown, Callum G. *The Death of Christian Britain: Understanding Secularisation, 1800-2000.* London: Routledge, 2009.
Brown, Colin. *From the Ancient World to the Age of Enlightenment.* Christianity and Western Thought: A History of Philosophers, Ideas and Movements 1. Leicester, UK: Apollos, 1990.
———. *Miracles and the Critical Mind.* Grand Rapids: Eerdmans, 1984.
———. *Philosophy and the Christian Faith.* London: Tyndale, 1968. Reprint, Downers Grove, IL: Inter-Varsity, n.d.
Browne, Edward Harold. *Exposition of the Thirty-nine Articles: Historical and Doctrinal.* 14th ed. London: Longmans, Green, 1894.
Bull, George. *Harmonia Apostolica.* London, 1670.
Bullock, F. W. B. *The History of Ridley Hall, Cambridge. Vol. 1, To the End of A.D. 1907.* Cambridge: Cambridge University Press, 1941.

———. *A History of Training for the Ministry of the Church of England and Wales from 1800 to 1874*. St Leonards-on-Sea, UK: Budd and Gillatt, 1955.

Burkitt, F. C. "The Eschatological Idea in the Gospel." In *Essays on Some Biblical Questions of the Day by Members of the University of Cambridge*, edited by Henry Barclay Swete, 183–214. London: Macmillan, 1909.

———. *The Gospel History and Its Transmission*. Edinburgh: T & T Clark, 1906.

Burroughs, E. A., "Evangelicalism and Personality." In *Liberal Evangelicalism: An Interpretation by Members of the Church of England*, edited by T. Guy Rogers, 51–100. London: Hodder and Stoughton, 1923.

Bury, J. B. *An Inaugural Lecture, Delivered in the Divinity School, Cambridge, on January 26, 1903*. Cambridge: Cambridge University Press, 1903.

Butler, Joseph. *Analogy of Religion, Natural and Revealed, to the Constitution and Nature*. London: Knapton, 1736.

Cable, K. J. "Barry, Alfred (1826–1910)." In *ADB* 3:105–7.

———. "The First and Second Book of Chronicles." In *The Heretics Club 1916–2006*, edited by William W. Emilsen and Geoffrey R. Treloar, 1–28. Sydney, Australia: Origen, 2009.

———. "Hammond, Thomas Chatterton (1877–1961)." In *ADB* 14:367–68.

———. "King, Robert Lethbridge (1823–1897)." In *ADB* 5:30–31.

———. "The Memorialists." *The Anglican Historical Society, Diocese of Sydney, Journal* 58, no. 2 (2013) 10–24.

———. "Smith, William Saumarez (1836–1909)." In *ADB* 11:675–77.

Caithness, James F. "Prefatory Note." *The Church of Christ. Minutes of Discussion at a Meeting Held at Caxton Hall, Westminster, on Monday, October 9th, 1922. Affirmative: Mr. Peter J. Hand. Negative: Rev. Thomas C. Hammond*, 3–4. 3rd ed. London: Chas. J. Thynne and Jarvis, 1922.

Calverly, E. L. "Momerie, A. W." In *DNB* 3:183. Supplement January 1901–December 1911.

Calvin, John. *Commentary on the Book of Psalms*. Vol. 2. Translated and edited by James Anderson. Grand Rapids: Eerdmans, 1949.

———. *Institutes of the Christian Religion*. Edited by John T. McNeill; translated and indexed by Ford Lewis Battles, in collaboration with the editor and a committee of advisers. London: SCM, 1960.

Cameron, Marcia Helen. "Aspects of Anglican Theological Education in Australia: 1900–1940, With Particular Reference to Four Colleges." PhD diss., Macquarie University, 1999.

———. "Moore College Under Nathaniel Jones 1897–1911." In *The "Furtherance of Religious Beliefs": Essays on the History of Theological Education in Australia*, edited by G. R. Treloar. A special combined edition of *Lucas: An Evangelical History Review* 19/20 (1995–1996) 96–123. Sydney, Australia: Centre for the Study of Australian Christianity, 1997.

———. *Phenomenal Sydney: Anglicans in a Time of Change, 1945–2013*. Eugene, OR: Wipf & Stock, 2016.

Cameron, Nigel M. de S. *Biblical Higher Criticism and the Defense of Infallibilism in Nineteenth Century Britain*. Lewiston, NY: Edwin Mellen, 1987.

Campbell, Constantine R. *Paul and Union with Christ: An Exegetical and Theological Study*. Grand Rapids: Zondervan, 2012.

Campbell, R. J. *The New Theology*. London: Chapman and Hall, 1907.

Carlyle, Edward Irving. "Momerie, Alfred Williams." In *DNB*. Second Supplement, vol. 3, 183.
Carnley, Peter Frederick, "T. C. Hammond and the Theological Roots of Sydney Arianism." *St Mark's Review* 198 (2005) 5–11.
———. *Reflections in Glass: Trends and Tensions in the Contemporary Anglican Church.* Pymble, Australia: HarperCollins, 2004.
Carter, Charles Sydney, and G. E. Alison, eds. *The Protestant Dictionary: Containing Articles on the History, Doctrines, and Practices of the Christian Church.* New ed. London: Harrison Trust, 1933.
Chadwick, Owen. *The Secularization of the European Mind in the Nineteenth Century.* Cambridge: Cambridge University Press, 1975.
———. *The Victorian Church, Part II: 1860–1901*. Ecclesiastical History of England 7. London: Adam and Charles Black, 1970.
Chapman, Allan. *Stargazers: Copernicus, Galileo, and the Telescope and the Church: The Astronomical Renaissance 1500–1700.* Oxford: Lion, 2014.
Chase, Frederick Henry. "The Gospels, in the Light of Historical Criticism." In *Essays on Some Theological Questions of the Day,* edited by Henry Barclay Swete, 371–419. London: Macmillan, 1905.
Chawner, William. *Prove All Things.* Cambridge, UK: Privately printed, 1909.
Cheetham, Henry. *The One Hundred Texts of the Irish Church Missions, Briefly Expanded.* 2nd ed. London: Bemrose and Sons, 1887.
Christensen, Torben. *The Divine Order: A Study in F. D. Maurice's Theology.* Leiden: Brill, 1973.
The Church of Christ. Minutes of Discussion at a Meeting Held at Caxton Hall, Westminster, on Monday, October 9th, 1922. Affirmative: Mr. Peter J. Hand. Negative: Rev. Thomas C. Hammond. London: Chas. J. Thynne and Jarvis, 1922.
The Churchman: A Monthly Magazine Conducted by Clergymen and Laymen of the Church of England. London: Elliot Stock, 1879–1976. (Quarterly from 1977 with title: *Churchman*. London: Church Society, 1977–.)
Church of England. *The Book of Common Prayer and Administration of the Sacraments, and other Rites and Ceremonies of the Church According to the Use of the Church of England . . . and the Form and Manner of Making, Ordaining, and Consecrating of Bishops, Priests, and Deacons.* Oxford: Oxford University Press, 1902.
Clark, Andrew. "Ince, William." In *DNB*. Second Supplement, vol. 2, 337–38.
Clark, Kitson. *Churchmen and the Condition of England 1832–1885: A Study in the Development of Social Ideas and Practice from the Old Regime to the Modern State.* London: Methuen, 1973.
Clarke, William Newton. *An Outline of Christian Theology.* Edinburgh: T & T Clark, 1902.
———. *The Use of the Scriptures in Theology.* Edinburgh: T & T Clark, 1905.
Claydon, E. H. B. Letters August 25 and September 12, 1913. In David J. Davies, Papers. MitchLib, MLL MSS 3179, Box 1.
Clouser, Roy A. *The Myth of Religious Neutrality: An Essay on the Hidden Role of Religious Belief in Theories.* Notre Dame: University of Notre Dame Press, 1991.
Coad, F. Roy. *A History of the Brethren Movement.* Exeter, UK: Paternoster, 1968.
Cole, Keith. "Aickin, George Ellis." In *ADEB* 2.
———. *A History of the Church Missionary Society of Australia.* Sydney, Australia: Church Missionary Historical Publications, 1971.

———. *History of the Diocese of Bendigo 1902-1976: An Anglican Diocese in Rural Victoria*. Bendigo, Australia: Keith Cole, 1991.

———. "Langley, John Douse." In *ADEB* 215-16.

Colenso, John William. *The Pentateuch and Book of Joshua Critically Examined*. London: Longman, Roberts and Green, 1862.

Comment and Criticism: A Cambridge Quarterly Paper for the Discussion of Current Religious and Theological Questions. Formerly *The New Commentator*. New York: Longmans, Green, 1913-1915.

Contentio Veritatis: Essays in Constructive Theology, by Six Oxford Tutors. London: John Murray, 1902.

"The Convention." *St. Paul's Gazette*. 10, no. 12 (1922) 4. (St Paul's Church of England, Chatswood, Australia.)

Conybeare, W. J. and J. S. Howson, *The Life and Epistles of St Paul*. New ed. New York: Longmans, Green, 1892.

Cooper, Robert Jermyn. *A Brief Defence of the Bible Against the Attacks of Rationalistic Infidelity: An Inquiry in Reference to Certain "Rationalist" Opinions, Especially Those Contained in the Volume "Essays and Reviews."* London: Rivingtons, 1861.

Cowper, William Macquarie. *The Episcopate of the Right Reverend Frederic Barker, D.D.: A Memoir*. London: n.p., 1888.

Cranmer, Thomas. "An Homily of the Salvation of Mankind By Only Christ our Saviour from Sin and Death Everlasting." In *The Two Books of Homilies, Appointed to be Read in Churches*, edited by John Griffiths, 24-35. Oxford: The University Press, 1859.

———. "An Homily of the Salvation of Mankind by only Christ our Saviour from Sin and Death Everlasting." In *The English Reformers*, 262-71. Library of Christian Classics 26, edited by T. H. L. Parker. London: SCM, 1966.

———. "An Homily or Sermon of Good Works Annexed unto Faith." In *The Two Books of Homilies, Appointed to be Read in Churches*, edited by John Griffiths, 48-65. Oxford: The University Press, 1859.

———. "An Homily or Sermon of Good Works Annexed unto Faith." In *The English Reformers*, 283-86. Library of Christian Classics 26, edited by T. H. L. Parker. London: SCM, 1966.

Crawford, R. M. "Wood, George Arnold." In *ADB* 12:556-58.

Crockford's Clerical Directory. London: Church House, 1891.

Cunningham, Audrey. *William Cunningham: Teacher and Priest. With a Preface by F. R. Salter*. London: SPCK, 1950.

Cunningham, William. "The Christian Standpoint." In *Essays on Some Theological Questions of the Day*, edited by Henry Barclay Swete, 1-53. London: Macmillan, 1905.

———. *Socialism and Christianity*. London: SPCK, 1910.

Curtis, W. A. "Infallibility of Holy Scripture." In *Encyclopaedia of Religion and Ethics*, edited by James Hastings, 7:261-63. Edinburgh: T & T Clark, 1913.

Dale, R. W. *The Atonement*. London: Hodder and Stoughton, 1875.

Daniel, Evan. *The Prayer-book: Its History, Language and Contents*. London: Wells Gardner, Darton, 1887.

D'Arcy, Charles F. "Christian Liberty." In *Anglican Essays: A Collective Review of the Principles and Special Opportunities of the Anglican Communion as Catholic and*

Reformed, edited by The Archbishop of Armagh et. al., 1–41. London: Macmillan, 1923.

———. *Christianity and the Supernatural*. 2nd ed. London: Longmans, Green, 1909.

———. *Idealism and Theology: A Study of Presuppositions*. The Anglican Church Handbooks, edited by W. H. Griffith Thomas. London: Hodder and Stoughton, 1899.

Darwin, Charles Robert. *The Descent of Man, and Selection in Relation to Sex*. 2 vols. London: John Murray, 1871.

———. *On the Origin of Species by Means of Natural Selection, or the Preservation of Favoured Races in the Struggle for Life*. London: John Murray, 1859.

Davidson, Randall T., director of compilation. "Report of the Committee appointed . . . to consider . . . the Critical Study of Scripture." In *The Five Lambeth Conferences*. London: Society for the Propagation of the Gospel, 1920.

Davies, David J. Answer to Question 9. In "Candidates for Ordination," Diocese of Ely. Photocopy of the form supplied by the Keeper of Diocesan Records, Department of Manuscripts, Cambridge University Library.

———. "Bishop Barnes. Personal Memories and Impressions." *Sydney Morning Herald*, Letters to Editor, February 13, 1926, 9.

———. "The Certainty of Christ." In David J. Davies, Papers, 1902–1935. MitchLib. MLL MSS 3179, Box 1.

———. *The Church and the Plain Man*. Sydney, Australia: Angus and Robertson, 1919.

———. "Communion Addresses." In David J. Davies, Papers. SMAMoore, Box 2.5.

———. "Discussion." *TSLR* 9 (1922) 23–26.

———. "The English Church in the Eighteenth Century." *ACQR* 3, no. 3 (1913) 217–33.

———. "From 1841 to 1845: 'The Catastrophe'." In *Church Chronicle*, August 1932. Reprinted in *From Oxford to the Bush: Essays on Catholic Anglicanism in Australia*, edited by John A. Moses, 41–47. Adelaide: SPCK Australia, 1997.

———. "Gains and Losses from the Great Reformation." In David J. Davies, Papers. SMAMoore, Box 2.2.

———. "Good Friday Meditation." In David J. Davies, Papers. SMAMoore, Box 2.1.

———. *Gunther Memorial Lecture. Sunday March 19, 1933*. Sydney, Australia: Robert Dey, 1933.

———. "The Interpretation of Scripture." In David J. Davies, Papers, 1902–1935. MitchLib. MLL MSS 3179, Box 1.

———. "The Interpretation of the V.S.L." *TSLR* 14 (1927) 31–42.

———. *The Labour Problem in Australia*. Melbourne, Australia: Diocesan Book Society for the Social Questions Committee of the Diocese of Melbourne, 1918.

———. "The Literary History of the V.S.L." *TSLR* 3 (1916) 5–21.

———. "Memoranda, Disputation of Brethren, May 21/14." In David J. Davies, Papers. MitchLib, MLL MSS 3179, Box 1.

———. "Modern Scholastics." In David J. Davies, Papers. SMAMoore, Box 2.3.

———. "Moore College Notes." *SDM* 4, no. 7 (1913) 21.

———. "The Need of India." In David J. Davies, Papers. SMAMoore, Box 2.1.

———. "A Notable Quatercentenary." In David J. Davies, Papers. SMAMoore, Box 2.2.

———. "Our Late Archbishop." With photograph titled "'The Brothers'—Conference of Evangelical Clergy at St. Aidan's College, Birkenhead, 15th, 16th, 17th July, 1909." Annotated by David J. Davies. *SDM* 24, no. 3 (1933) 8–10.

———. Papers, 1902–1935. MitchLib, MLL MSS 3179. Microform copy in Donald Robinson Library, Moore Theological College.
———. *The Pastoral Ideal and the Personal Touch: A Sermon.* Sydney: W. A. Pepperday, 1915.
———. "Preachers for the Month." *SDM* 3, nos. 2, 3, and 10 (1912) 3.
———. "Religious Thought in the Sixteenth Century," (1933). In David J. Davies, Papers. SMAMoore, Box 2.2. The same is found titled "Martin Luther's Contribution to the Religious Thought of the Sixteenth Century," in "Minute Book of The Heretics Club," vol. 2, April 24, 1933. USydArch.
———. Review of *The Doctrine of the Atonement*, by J. K. Mozley. *SDM* 7, no. 7 (1916) 14–15.
———. Review of *The English Church and the Reformation*, by C. Sydney Carter. *SDM* 4, no. 9 (1913) 24–26.
———. Review of *Liberal Evangelicalism: An Interpretation by Members of the Church of England*, edited by T. G. Rogers. *SDM* 14, no. 12 (1923) 14–16.
———. Review of *Primitive Christian Eschatology* by E. C. Dewick. *ACQR* 2, no. 4 (1912) 372–76.
———. Review of *Religion and the Rise of Capitalism: A Historical Study*, by R. H. Tawney. *SDM* 17, no. 7 (1926) 12–14.
———. Review of *The Tutorial Prayer Book for the Teacher and the Student, and the General Reader*, edited by Charles Neil and M. Willoughy. *SDM* 4, no. 5 (1913) 27–28.
———. *Roman Catholic Claims Tested by Scripture and History.* Sydney, Australia: n.p., n.d.
———. "The Social Problem Committee." *SDM* 4, no. 8 (1913) 7–9.
———. "The Social Question." *SDM* 3, no. 11 (1911) 21–22.
———. *Socialism and Society. A Paper Read Before the Sydney Junior Clerical Society at Christ Church S. Laurence.* April 21, 1913. Sydney, Australia: D. S. Ford, 1913.
———. "Socialism and Society." *ACQR* 3, no. 4 (1913) 304–21.
———. "Some Historical Aspects of Puritanism." 1. *ACQR* 2, no. 3 (1912) 241–58; 2. *ACQR* 2, no. 4 (1912) 324–36.
———. "Some Points Concerning the Oxford Movement." Heretics Club Paper, 1932. In David J. Davies Papers. SMAMoore, Box 2.2.
———. "Studies in Isaiah." In David J. Davies Papers. SMAMoore Box 2.5.
———. "Studies in Romans." In David J. Davies Papers. SMAMoore, Box 2.4.
———. "The Thirty-nine Articles" (1933). In David J. Davies Papers. SMAMoore, Box 2.2.
———. *The Wages System, or, Working for a Boss.* Melbourne, Australia: Social Questions Committee of the Diocese of Melbourne, 1922.
Dempster, J. A. H. "Miller, Hugh, 1802–1856." In *DSCHT* 564.
Denney, James. *The Atonement and the Modern Mind.* London: Hodder and Stoughton, 1903.
———. *The Church and the Kingdom.* London: Hodder and Stoughton, 1910.
———. *The Death of Christ: Its Place and Interpretation in the New Testament.* London: Hodder and Stoughton, 1902.
———. *The Death of Christ.* Edited by R. V. G. Tasker. London: Tyndale, 1951.
———. *Paul's Epistle to the Romans.* Expositor's Greek Testament 2. London: Hodder and Stoughton, 1900.

———. *Studies in Theology. Lectures Delivered in Chicago Theological Seminary.* 6th ed. London: Hodder and Stoughton, 1899.

Dewick, E. C. *Primitive Christian Eschatology.* Hulsean Prize Essay 1908. Cambridge: Cambridge University Press, 1912.

Dibelius, Martin. *A Fresh Approach to the New Testament and Early Christian Literature.* London: Ivor Nicholson and Watson, 1936.

———. *Gospel Criticism and Christology: A Series of Lectures Delivered at King's College in October 1934.* London: Ivor Nicholson and Watson, 1935.

Dickey, Brian. "Jones, Nathaniel." In *ADEB* 191–92.

Digges La Touche, E. *Christian Certitude: Its Intellectual Base.* London: James Clarke, 1910.

———. *Is Christianity Scientific?* Australian Church Manuals. Sydney, Australia: Angus and Robertson, 1913.

———. *The Need for an Evangelical Revival.* Papers for Evangelical Churchmen, No. 1. Sydney, Australia: Angus and Robertson, 1914.

———. *The Person of Christ in Modern Thought.* London: James Clarke, 1912.

———. *The Philosophy of Faith: Five Lectures.* London: Church Bookroom, 1922.

Dillman, August. *Handbuch der Alttestamentliche Theologie.* Leipzig: Hirzel, 1895.

Dimock, Nathaniel. *Confession and Absolution in the Church of England: A Letter to His Grace the Lord Archbishop of Canterbury Containing Some Observations of the "Freedom of Confession" by The Rev. Canon Carter.* London: Hardwicke, 1877.

———. *Light from History on Christian Ritual, Published under the direction of the Council of the National Protestant Church Union.* London: Charles Murray, 1900.

———. *On Eucharistic Worship in the English Church*, by an English Presbyter. London: Haughton, 1876.

———. *Some Notes on the Conference Held at Fulham Palace in October 1900, on the Doctrine of the Holy Communion and its Expression in Ritual.* London: Elliot Stock, 1901.

———. *Vox Liturgiae Anglicanae.* London: Elliot Stock, 1897.

Dods, Marcus. *The Bible: Its Origin and Nature.* Edinburgh: T & T Clark, 1905.

Dougan, Alan. *A Backward Glance at the Angus Affair.* Sydney, Australia: Wentworth, 1971.

Dowland, David A. *Nineteenth-Century Anglican Theological Training: The Redbrick Challenge.* Oxford: Clarendon, 1997.

Dowling, D. J. "Guinness, Henry Grattan." In *BDE* 272–74.

Downer, Arthur Cleveland. *A Century of Evangelical Religion at Oxford.* London: Church Book Room, n.d.

Driver, S. R. *Introduction to the Literature of the Old Testament.* Edinburgh: T & T Clark, 1898.

Drury, T. W. *How We Got Our Prayer Book.* London: Nisbet, 1901.

———. *Principles of the Book of Common Prayer.* London: Longmans, 1909.

———. *Two Studies in the Book of Common Prayer.* London: Nisbet, 1901.

Duffield, G. F. "Barnes, Ernest William." In *NIDCC* 106.

Dunning, Mrs. A. K. *Hampered: A Tale of American Family Life.* London: Religious Tract Society, 1884.

Dunstan, Alan, and John S. Peart-Binns. *Cornish Bishop.* London: Epworth, 1977.

Eddington, Arthur Stanley. *The Nature of the Physical World.* The Gifford Lectures, 1927. New York: Macmillan, 1928.

Edersheim, Alfred. *The Life and Times of Jesus the Messiah*. London: Longmans, Green, 1883.
Editor. "Church Book Room Notes." *Churchman* 35, no. 4 (1921) 221.
Edwards, Benjamin. *WASPS, Tykes and Ecumaniacs: Aspects of Australian Sectarianism 1945-1981*. Brunswick East, Australia: Acorn, 2008.
Edwards, David L. with John Stott. *Essentials: A Liberal-Evangelical Dialogue*. London: Hodder and Stoughton, 1988.
Edwards, Trevor. "Developments in the Evangelical Anglican Doctrine of the Church in the Diocese of Sydney, 1935-1985: With Special Reference to the Writing and Teaching of T. C. Hammond, D. W. B. Robinson and D. B. Knox." MTh diss., University of Sydney 1996.
Elliott-Binns, L. E. *The Development of English Theology in the Later Nineteenth Century*. London: Longmans, Green, 1952.
———. *English Thought 1860-1900: The Theological Aspect*. London: Longmans, Green, 1956.
———. *Religion in the Victorian Era*. London: Lutterworth, 1936.
Ellis-Jones, Ian. "The Relevance of Dr Samuel Angus for the Christian Church in Australia in the Twenty-first Century." http://www.sydneyunitarianchurch.org/RelevanceAngus_StACol.pdf
Emilsen, William W. "The Heretics: An Anecdotal Odyssey." In *The Heretics Club 1916-2006: Ninetieth Anniversary Papers*, edited by William Emilsen and Geoffrey R. Treloar, 73-79. Sydney, Australia: Origen, 2009.
Emilsen, William W., and Geoffrey R. Treloar, eds. *The Heretics Club 1916-2006: Ninetieth Anniversary Papers*. Sydney, Australia: Origen, 2009.
Essays and Reviews. London: John W. Parker, 1860.
Examination Statutes for the Degrees of B.A., B.Mus. B.C.L. and B.M. Oxford: Clarendon, 1885.
Farrar, Frederic W. *Darkness and Dawn: Or Scenes From the Days of Nero*. London: Longmans and Green, 1897.
———. *The Early Days of Christianity*. London: Cassell, 1884.
———. *The History of Interpretation: Eight Lectures Preached before the University of Oxford in the Year MDCCCLXXXV*. London: Macmillan, 1886.
Fausset, A. R., "Church." In *ECEBC* 130-31.
———. "Creation." In *ECEBC* 141-44.
———. "Dispensations." In *ECEBC* 173-74.
———. "Noah." In *ECEBC* 514-17.
———. "Thousand Years." In *ECEBC* 685-86.
Fausset, A. R., et al. *The Second Advent: Will It Be Before the Millenium?* New York: James Pott, 1887.
Feuerbach, Ludwig. *The Essence of Christianity*. Translated by Marion Evans. London: John Chapman, 1854.
Finney, Colin. *Paradise Revealed: Natural History in Nineteenth Century Australia*. Melbourne, Australia: Museum of Victoria, 1993.
Fishe, Henry. *Questions and Answers on the One Hundred Texts Taught in the Mission Schools for the Society of the Irish Church Missions, with Notes and Comments*. 2nd ed. London: Offices of the Irish Church Missions, 1901.
Fiske, Shanyn. *Heretical Hellenism: Women Writers, Ancient Greece, and the Victorian Popular Imagination*. Athens, OH: Ohio University Press, 2008.

Fletcher, Brian H. *The Place of Anglicanism in Australia: Church, Society and Nation.* Mulgrave, Australia: Broughton, 2008.

Flew, Antony, ed. *A Dictionary of Philosophy.* 2nd ed. New York: St Martin's, 1984.

Frame, Tom. *Anglicans in Australia: Evolution in the Antipodes.* Sydney, Australia: University of New South Wales Press, 2009.

———. *A House Divided: A Quest for Unity Within Anglicanism.* Brunswick East, Australia: Acorn, 2010.

Fraser, Alexander Campbell. *Philosophy of Theism. Being the Gifford Lectures Delivered Before the University of Edinburgh in 1894-95, 1895-96.* Edinburgh: W. Blackwood and Sons 1895.

French, Richard Valpy, ed. *Lex Mosaica: Or the Law of Moses and the Higher Criticism.* London: Eyre & Spottiswoode, 1894.

Frere, Walter Howard. *The English Church in the Reigns of Elizabeth and James I (1558-1625).* London: Macmillan, 1904.

———. *A New History of the Book of Common Prayer . . . on the Basis of the Former Work by Francis Procter, MA.* London: Macmillan, 1901.

Garnsey, Arthur. *How the Gospels Grew: Three Lectures Delivered in the Chapter House, St. Andrew's Cathedral, Sydney.* Sydney, Australia: n.p., 1935.

———. *A Plea for Liberty: Being a Memorial Sent to the Archbishop of Sydney by a Group of his Clergy, and Documents Relevant Thereto.* Sydney, Australia: n.p., 1938.

Garnsey, David. *Arthur Garnsey: A Man for Truth and Freedom.* Sydney, Australia: Kingsdale, 1985.

Geehan, E. R., ed. *Jerusalem and Athens: Critical Discussions on the Theology and Apologetics of Cornelius Van Til.* Nutley, NJ: Presbyterian and Reformed, 1971.

Gerber, Gordon B. *Memoirs of Rev. Gordon B. Gerber.* Unpublished excerpts kindly supplied by Philip Gerber.

George, Timothy. *Theology of the Reformers.* Leicester, UK: Apollos, 1988.

Gibbons, James Cardinal. *The Faith of Our Fathers: Being a Plain Exposition and Vindication of the Church Founded by Our Lord Jesus Christ.* 93rd rev. ed. Baltimore: John Murphy, 1917.

Gibson, Edgar C. S. *The Thirty-nine Articles of the Church of England: Explained with an Introduction.* 3rd ed. London: Methuen, 1902.

Girdlestone, R. B. et al. *English Church Teaching on Faith, Life and Order.* 3rd ed. London: Charles Murray, 1899.

Godfrey, W. Robert. "Biblical Authority in the Sixteenth and Seventeenth Centuries: A Question of Transition." In *Scripture and Truth*, edited by D. A. Carson and John D. Woodbridge, 225-43. Leicester, England: Inter-Varsity,1983.

Goe, F. F. "President's Address to Synod." *The Victorian Churchman*, September 28, 1894, 507-09.

———. "President's Annual Address to Church of England Assembly." *The Argus*, September 28, 1897, 6.

Goldman, Lawrence. *Dons and Workers: Oxford and Adult Education Since 1850.* Oxford: Clarendon, 1995.

Goode, William. *Divine Rule of Faith and Practice*, 2nd ed. London: John Henry Jackson, 1853.

———. *The Doctrine of the Church of England as to the Effects of Baptism in the case of Infants.* London: n.p., 1849.

———. *The Nature of Christ's Presence in the Eucharist: Or, The True Doctrine of the Real Presence Vindicated in Opposition to the Fictitious Real Presence Asserted by Archdeacon Denison, Mr. (late Archdeacon) Wilberforce, and Dr. Pusey: With Full Proof of the Character of the Attempt Made by Those Authors to Represent their Doctrine as that of the Church of England and her Divines*. London: T. Hatchard, 1856.

———. *A Vindication of the Doctrine of the Church of England on the Validity of the Orders of the Scotch and Foreign Non-Episcopal Churches*. London: Thomas Hatchard, 1852.

Goodhew, D. J. "Johnson, Douglas." In *BDE* 333–34.

Gore, Charles. "The Holy Spirit and Inspiration." In *Lux Mundi*, edited by Charles Gore, 315–62. London: John Murray, 1890.

———, ed. *Lux Mundi: A Series of Studies in the Religion of the Incarnation*. 10th ed. London: John Murray, 1890.

———. *The Ministry of the Christian Church*. London: Longmans, 1893.

———. "Preface to the Tenth Edition." In *Lux Mundi*, edited by Charles Gore, vii–xl. London: John Murray, 1890.

———. *St. Paul's Epistle to the Romans: A Practical Exposition*. 2 vols. London: John Murray, 1900.

Grave, S. A. *A History of Philosophy in Australia*. St Lucia, Australia: University of Queensland Press, 1984.

Green, John Richard. *A Short History of the English People*. London: John Murray, 1874.

Green, Thomas Hill. "Essay on Christian Dogma." In *Miscellanies and a Memoir. The Works of Thomas Hill Green 3*, edited by R. L. Nettleship, 161–85. 3rd ed. London: Longmans, Green, 1891.

———. *Prolegomena to Ethics*, edited by A. C. Bradley. 4th ed. Oxford: Clarendon, 1899.

Green, William Henry. *The Higher Criticism of the Pentateuch*. New York: Charles Scribner's Sons, 1896.

Grensted, L. W., ed. *The Atonement in History and Life: A Volume of Essays*. London: SPCK, 1929.

———. *Short History of the Doctrine of the Atonement*. London: Manchester University Press, 1920.

Gribben, Crawford, and Timothy C. F. Stunt, eds. *Prisoners of Hope? Aspects of Evangelical Millennialism in Britain and Ireland, 1800–1880*. Carlisle, UK: Paternoster, 2004.

Griffin, Edward H. "Personality the Supreme Category of Philosophy." *Presbyterian and Reformed Review* 13, no. 52 (1902) 505–23.

Griffiths, John, ed. *The Two Books of Homilies Appointed to be Read in Churches*. Oxford: The University Press, 1859.

Guinness, Mr. and Mrs. H. Grattan. *The Divine Programme of World's History*. London: Hodder and Stoughton, 1888.

Günther, W. J. "Presidential Address." In *Proceedings of the Third Session of the Tenth Synod of the Diocese of Sydney, New South Wales, September 25–30th, 1897*, 31–32. Sydney, Australia: Joseph Cook, 1897.

Gwatkin, Henry Melvill. *The Eye for Spiritual Things*. Edinburgh: T & T Clark, 1906.

———. *The Knowledge of God and Its Historical Development*. Gifford Lectures 1906. 2 vols. Edinburgh: T & T Clark, 1906.

Haeckel, Ernst. *The Riddle of the Universe at the Close of the Nineteenth Century.* Translated by J. McCabe. New York: Harper and Brothers, 1900.

Hague, Dyson. "Justification." In *Evangelicalism. By Members of the Fellowship of Evangelical Churchmen*, edited by J. Russell Howden, 79–106. London: Chas. J. Thynne and Jarvis, 1925.

Hammond, T. C. *Abolishing God: A Reply to Professor Anderson of Sydney University.* Melbourne, Australia: S. John Bacon, 1943.

———. "Addenda." In *The Church of Christ. Minutes of Discussion at a Meeting Held at Caxton Hall, Westminster, on Monday, October 9th, 1922. Affirmative: Mr. Peter J. Hand. Negative: Rev. Thomas C. Hammond*, edited by Peter J. Hand, 45–50. London: Chas. J. Thynne and Jarvis, 1922.

———. *Age-Long Questions: An Examination of Some of the Problems of Religion, with Special Reference to Butler's Analogy of Religion.* London: Marshall, Morgan and Scott, 1942.

———. *Authority in the Church: Being an Examination into the Position and Jurisdiction of Bishops in the Anglican Communion.* London: Church Book Room, 1921.

———. "Authority in Religion." *ICQ* 9, no. 36 (1916) 287–99.

———. "Authority in Religion II. The Place of Dogma." *ICQ* 10, no. 37 (1917) 25–39.

———. "Barthianism and Natural Theology." *Societas* (1945) 5–11.

———. *Bible Truths and Modern Fancies.* Melbourne, Australia: S. John Bacon, 1942.

———. "Butler's Analogy, 1736–1936." *EQ* 8, no. 4 (1936) 337–55.

———. *Can We Advance and Still Believe the Bible? Being a Verbatim Report of an Address Delivered at a Youth Rally in Collins Street Baptist Church, Melbourne, 19th September, 1942.* Melbourne, Australia: S. John Bacon, 1942.

———. *The Case for Protestantism: Being a Selection of Broadcast Addresses Delivered over Station 2CH, Sydney, New South Wales.* Greenacre, Australia: Gowans and Sons, 1960.

———. *Christian Science: Its Merits and Defects. A Lecture Delivered in the City of Dublin YMCA.* Dublin: Irish Union of Young Men's Christian Associations, 1907.

———. *Comments on the Discussion at Caxton Hall, Westminster, held October 9th, 1922: Hand v. Hammond.* London: Chas. J. Thynne and Jarvis, 1922.

———. *Concerning Penal Laws.* Dublin: Church of Ireland, 1930.

———. "Consciousness and the Sub-conscious." In *The Person of Christ in Modern Thought*, by Everard Digges La Touche, 403–15. London: Hodder and Stoughton, 1912.

———. "Conversations, Malines." In *PD* 148–50.

———. "Cranmer on the Lord's Supper." In T. C. Hammond, Papers. SMAMoore, Box 5.11.

———. *The Cross on the Communion Table.* Belfast: Irish Church Union, 1917.

———. *Does the Doctrine of Transubstantiation Involve a Material Change?* London: Church Book Room, 1928.

———. *Doubts of the Sons: Being an Examination of the Much Advertised Book, "Faith of our Fathers," by Cardinal Gibbons.* Dublin: Connellan Mission, n.d.

———. "Emancipation, Catholic." In *PD* 211–18.

———. "The Evangelical Revival and the Oxford Movement." *The Churchman* 47, no. 2 (1933) 1–12.

———. *Fading Light: The Tragedy of Spiritual Decline in Germany.* London: Marshall, Morgan and Scott, 1942.

———. "The Fascination of the Church of Rome: A Reply." *ICQ* 8, no. 9 (1915) 60–69.

———. "The Fiat of Authority." In *Evangelicalism*, edited by J. Russell Howden, 156–206. Republished as *Inspiration and Authority: The Character of Inspiration and the Problems of Authority*. Inter-Varsity Papers 3. London: Inter-Varsity, n.d.

———. "Five Addresses." In *The Katoomba Convention Book, 1937: Containing Contributions from the Most Rev. H. W. K. Mowll et al.*, 1–57. Glebe, Australia: Australasian Medical, 1937.

———. "Foreword." In *Inspiration and Authority: The Character of Inspiration and the Problems of Authority*, iii–iv. London: Inter-Varsity, n.d.

———. *How the Roman Church Treats the Bible*. Dublin: Church of Ireland, 1921.

———. "Immanence and Transcendence." *ICQ* 4, no. 15 (1911) 198–215.

———. In *Understanding Be Men: A Handbook on Christian Doctrine for Non-Theological Students*. London: Inter-Varsity, 1936.

———. In *Understanding Be Men: A Handbook on Christian Doctrine for Non-Theological Students*. 2nd ed. London: Inter-Varsity, 1936.

———. In *Understanding Be Men: A Handbook on Christian Doctrine for Non-Theological Students*. 4th ed. London: Inter-Varsity, 1951.

———. In *Understanding Be Men: A Handbook on Christian Doctrine for Non-Theological Students*. 5th ed. London: Inter-Varsity, 1954.

———. *Inspiration and Authority: The Character of Inspiration and the Problems of Authority*. London: Inter-Varsity, n.d.

———. "Irish Church." In *PD* 342–43.

———. *Light and Life*. Melbourne, Australia: S. John Bacon, 1943.

———. "Maynooth, the College of St Patrick." In *PD* 412–14.

———. *Memories Crowd Upon Me*. London: n.p., 1949.

———. "Moral Theology." In *PD* 440–42.

———. *The New Creation*. London: Marshall, Morgan and Scott, 1953.

———. *"The New Theology": An Examination and Criticism*. A lecture delivered in the City of Dublin Y.M.C.A., February, 1907. Dublin: Irish Union of Young Men's Christian Associations, 1907.

———. *The One Hundred Texts of the Society for Irish Church Missions*, edited by T. Brine. London: Society for Irish Church Missions, 1939.

———. *Perfect Freedom: An Introduction to Christian Ethics*. London: Inter-Varsity, 1938.

———. *Pivot Points in Revelation: Being a Series of Five Discourses Delivered at the Inter-Varsity Christian Fellowship Conference, Healesville, Vic*. 2nd ed. Sydney, Australia: Inter-Varsity Christian Fellowship of Australia, 1940.

———. "Post-Reformation Theology in the Church of Ireland." In *The Church of Ireland AD 432–1932: Report of the Church of Ireland Conference Held in Dublin, 11th–14th October, 1932, to Which Is Appended an Account of the Commemoration by the Church of Ireland of the 1500th Anniversary of the Landing of St Patrick in Ireland*, edited by W. Bell and N. C. Emerson, 97–105. Dublin: Church of Ireland, 1933.

———. "Preface." In *The Case for Protestantism: Being a Selection of Broadcast Addresses Delivered over Station 2CH, Sydney, New South Wales*. Greenacre, Australia: Gowans and Sons, 1960.

———. "Purgatory." In *PD* 557–58.

---. *Reasoning Faith: An Introduction to Christian Apologetics*. London: Inter-Varsity, 1943.

---. *Reformation and Modern Ideals*. Dublin: Connellan Mission, 1927.

---. "Rev. T. C. Hammond's Address." In *The Church of Christ. Minutes of Discussion at a Meeting Held at Caxton Hall, Westminster, on Monday, October 9th, 1922. Affirmative: Mr. Peter J. Hand. Negative: Rev. Thomas C. Hammond*, 18–28. London: Chas. J. Thynne and Jarvis, 1922.

---. "Rev. T. C. Hammond's Reply." In *The Church of Christ. Minutes of Discussion at a Meeting Held at Caxton Hall, Westminster, on Monday, October 9th, 1922. Affirmative: Mr. Peter J. Hand. Negative: Rev. Thomas C. Hammond*, 33–39. London: Chas. J. Thynne and Jarvis, 1922.

---. "The Schoolmen of the Later Middle Ages." In *The Evangelical Doctrine of Holy Communion*, edited by A. J. Macdonald, 118–48. Cambridge: W. Heffer & Sons, 1930.

---. "The Significance of the Death of Christ." In *From the Manger to the Throne: Outstanding Events in the Life of Our Lord*, edited by F. Donald Coggan, 39–49. London: Inter-Varsity, 1936.

---. *So Great Salvation*. Melbourne, Australia: S. John Bacon, 1943.

---. *The Thirty-nine Articles: A Safeguard Against Romanism*. London: Church Book Room, 1931.

---. "Unam Sanctam." In *PD* 719-23.

---. *The Way of Holiness*. Melbourne, Australia: S. John Bacon, 1952.

Hand, Peter J. "Addenda." In *The Church of Christ. Minutes of Discussion at a Meeting Held at Caxton Hall, Westminster, on Monday, October 9th, 1922. Affirmative: Mr. Peter J. Hand. Negative: Rev. Thomas C. Hammond*, 41–44. London: Chas. J. Thynne and Jarvis 1922.

---. "Mr. Hand's Address." In *The Church of Christ. Minutes of Discussion at a Meeting Held at Caxton Hall, Westminster, on Monday, October 9th, 1922. Affirmative: Mr. Peter J. Hand. Negative: Rev. Thomas C. Hammond*, 7–17. London: Chas. J. Thynne and Jarvis 1922.

---. "Mr. Hand's Reply." In *The Church of Christ. Minutes of Discussion at a Meeting Held at Caxton Hall, Westminster, on Monday, October 9th, 1922. Affirmative: Mr. Peter J. Hand. Negative: Rev. Thomas C. Hammond*, 29–32, 37–39. London: Chas. J. Thynne and Jarvis 1922.

Hardwick, C. H. *A History of the Articles of Religion: To Which is Added a Series of Documents, from A.D. 1536 to A.D. 1615; Together with Illustrations from Contemporary Sources*. London: John Deighton, 1851.

Harman, Allan. *Isaiah: A Covenant to Be Kept for the Sake of the Church*. Fearn, UK: Christian Focus, 2005.

Harnack, Adolf von. *History of Dogma*. Vol. 1. Translated by Neil Buchanan from the third German edition. London: Williams & Norgate, 1894.

Harris, Brian. "Beyond Bebbington: The Quest for an Evangelical Identity in a Post-Modern Era." *Churchman* 122, no. 3 (2008) 201–19.

Haslam, William. *From Death into Life: Or Twenty Years of My Ministry*. London: Marshall and Scott, 1880.

Headlam, A. C. "The New Theology." *Church Quarterly Review* 59, no. 128 (1907) 79–109.

Henslow, George. "Present-day Rationalism with an Examination of Darwinism." In *Christian Apologetics. A Series of Addresses Delivered before the Christian Association of University College, London*, edited by W. W. Seton, 1-24. London: John Murray, 1903.

Hervey, Lord Arthur. "Introduction." In *Lex Mosaica: Or the Law of Moses and the Higher Criticism*, edited by Richard Valpy French, xxiii-xxxvi. London: Eyre & Spottiswoode, 1894.

Heurtley, Charles A. *Justification: Eight Sermons Preached before the University of Oxford in the Year 1845*. Oxford: John Henry Parker, 1846.

Hewitt, Gordon. In *Tropical Africa, the Middle East, at Home*. The Problem of Success: A History of the Church Missionary Society 1910-1942 2. London: SCM, 1971.

Hilliard, David. "Dioceses, Tribes and Factions: Unity and Disunity in Australian Anglicanism." In *Agendas of Australian Anglicans: Essays in Honour of Bruce Kaye*, edited by Tom Frame and Geoffrey Treloar, 65-81. Adelaide, Australia: ATF, 2006.

Hinchcliff, Peter. "Religious Issues, 1870-1914." In *Nineteenth-Century Oxford, Part 2*. The History of the University of Oxford 7, edited by M. G. Brock and M. C. Curthoys, 97-112. Oxford: Clarendon, 2000.

Hodge, Charles. *Systematic Theology*. 3 vols. London: Thomas Nelson, 1875.

Hoffecker, W. Andrew, ed. *Understanding the Flow of Western Thought: Revolutions in Worldview*. Phillipsburg, NJ: Presbyterian and Reformed, 2009.

Holbach, Paul Henri Thiry. *The System of Nature, or, The Laws of the Moral and Physical World*. Translator unknown. 4 vols. London: G. Kearsley, 1796-1797.

Holland, Henry Scott. *The Ground of Our Appeal*. Oxford: Christian Social Union, 1890.

"An Homily Concerning the Coming Down of the Holy Ghost and the Manifold Gifts of the Same." In *The Two Books of Homilies Appointed to Be Read in Churches*, edited by John Griffiths, 453-69. Oxford: Oxford University Press, 1859.

Hooker, Richard. *Of the Laws of Ecclesiastical Polity, Eight Books*. Book 6. In *The Works of the Learned and Judicious Divine, Mr. Richard Hooker: With an Account of His Life and Death by Isaac Walton*. Oxford: Clarendon, 1865.

Hort, Fenton John Anthony. *The Christian Ecclesia*. London: Macmillan, 1897.

———. "Coleridge." In *Cambridge Essays, Contributed by Members of the University, 1856*, 292-351. London: John W. Parker, 1856.

Houghton, Walter E. *The Victorian Frame of Mind, 1830-1870*. New Haven, CT: Yale University Press, 1957.

Howard, R. T. "The Work of Christ." In *Liberal Evangelicalism: An Interpretation by Members of the Church of England*, edited by T. Guy Rogers, 121-46. London: Hodder and Stoughton, 1923.

Howden, J. Russell, ed. *Evangelicalism. By Members of the Fellowship of Evangelical Churchmen*. London: Chas. J. Thynne and Jarvis, 1925.

Howe, H. G. J. "The Plans of the G.A.O.T.U. and their Approaching Consummation." *TSLR* 9 (1922) 9-28.

———. *The Dawning of That Day*. 4th ed. Revised and enlarged. Sydney, Australia: H. G. J. Howe, 1922-1928.

———. *The Dawning of That Day*. 5th ed. London: Pickering and Inglis, 1930.

Hume, J. S. *A Treatise of Human Nature: Being an Attempt to Introduce the Experimental Method of Reasoning into Moral Subjects*. Edited by L. A. Selby-Bigge. Reprint, Oxford: Clarendon, 1888.

Hunkin, J. W. *The Gospel for Tomorrow*. Harmondsworth, UK: Penguin, 1941.

———. "The Kingdom of God." In *Liberal Evangelicalism: An Interpretation by Members of the Church of England*, edited by T. Guy Rogers, 174–98. London: Hodder and Stoughton, 1923.

Hutton, William Holden. *The English Church From the Accession of Charles I to the Death of Anne*. London: Macmillan, 1903.

Huxley, Thomas Henry. *Science and Christian Tradition*. London: Macmillan, 1894.

Illingworth, J. R. *Personality, Human and Divine*. London: Macmillan, 1894.

———. *The Problem of Pain: Its Bearing on Faith in God*. In *Lux Mundi: A Series of Studies in the Religion of the Incarnation*, edited by Charles Gore, 10th ed., 113–26. London: John Murray, 1890.

Ince, William. *The Scriptural and Anglican View of the Function of the Christian Ministry. A Sermon*. Oxford: Parker, 1895.

Inge, W. R. "The Person of Christ." In *Contentio Veritatis: Essays in Constructive Theology, by Six Oxford Tutors*, 59–104. London: John Murray, 1894.

———. "The Sacraments." In *Contentio Veritatis: Essays in Constructive Theology*, 270–311. London: John Murray, 1902.

James, William. *The Principles of Psychology*. London: Macmillan, 1890.

———. *The Varieties of Religious Experience: A Study in Human Nature*. Gifford Lectures 1901–1902. London: Longmans, Green, 1902.

Jay, Elisabeth. *Faith and Doubt in Victorian Britain*. London: Macmillan Education, 1986.

Jensen, Peter J. "Good News about Preaching." *Southern Cross: The News Magazine for Sydney Anglicans* 23, no. 1 (2017) 24– 25.

Jeune, Francis. "The Primary Charge." In *Primary Charge and Sermons*, 1–77. New ed. London: Church of England Book Society, 1885.

Johnson, Douglas. Letters to Warren Nelson, February 19, 1987, and October 12, 1988. Copy supplied by Warren Nelson.

Johnson, Stuart Buchanan. "The Shaping of Colonial Liberalism: John Fairfax and the Sydney Morning Herald, 1841–1877." PhD diss., University of New South Wales, 2006.

Johnstone, S. M. *The Book of St Andrew's Cathedral Sydney*. Sydney, Australia: Edgar Bragg and Sons, 1937.

Jones, Nathaniel. "Australian College of Theology." In Nathaniel Jones, Papers, 1886–1911. SMAMoore, Box 1, Bundle h.

———. *Arise; Shine: An Epiphany Study for the New Year*. Sydney, Australia: Madgwick, n.d.

———. "Address to Protestant Church of England Union Annual Re-union." *Australian Churchman*, November 8, 1902, 4–5.

———. *The Church's Commission*. Sydney, Australia: "Australian Churchman" Office, n.d.

———. "Consecration of Bishop of Bendigo." *The Victorian Churchman*, February 8, 1907, 46–48.

———. "Devotional Value of the Prayer Book." In *Official Report of the Church Congress: Held at Hobart on January 23rd, 24th, 25th, and 26th, 1894*, 153–55. Hobart, Tasmania: Diocesan Book Depot, 1894.

———. "Diaries." In Nathaniel Jones, Papers, 1886–1911. SMAMoore, Box 1. ("Diary for 1887," "Diary for 1888–1890," "Diary for the Year of Grace 1893," "Diary and Convention Notes 1907.")

---. "Fulfilment of Promise." *The Victorian Churchman*, July 5, 1895, 162–63.
---. *God's Way of Justification, as Set Forth in the Epistle to the Romans. An Outline of the Argument of Chs.1 to 5:11*. Sydney, Australia: "Australian Churchman" Office, n.d.
---. *A Handful of Corn Upon the Top of the Mountains: Bible Readings and Addresses.* Sydney, Australia: W. M. Madgwick and Sons, 1905.
---. *"He Is Ever the Same": An Exposition of the Twenty Third Psalm*. Sydney, Australia: "A. C. World" Office, n.d.
---. "The Ideal Life and How to Live It." *The Victorian Churchman*, August 11, 1899, 287–88.
---. *Jesus Only: A Message for the Unsettled*. Sydney, Australia: "Australian Churchman" Office, 1902.
---. *The Manifestation of God to Those Who Keep His Word. An Address Given at the Petersham Conference on Tuesday Evening, August 4th, 1903*. N.p., n.d.
---. *The New Cart*. Sydney, Australia: "Australian Churchman" Office, n.d.
---. "Notes for Speech at 1909 Sydney Diocese Election Synod." In Nathaniel Jones, Papers, 1886–1911. SMAMoore, Box 1, file 041/8.
---. "The Old Yoke and the New." *The Victorian Churchman*, June 6, 1890, 188.
---. *Our Daily Sacrifice*. Melbourne, Australia: H. Rayward, 1900.
---. *Our Priestly Privileges: A Sermon Preached at the Anniversary of the Protestant Church of England Union, in St. Barnabas' Church, Sydney, May 27th, 1902. A Study of Hebrews xiii. 9–16*. Sydney, Australia: "Australian Churchman" Office, 1902.
---. Oxford Student Notebook. In Nathaniel Jones, Papers, 1886–1911. SMAMoore, Box 1.
---. *Partners with the Holy Ghost. Address Delivered by The Rev. Canon Jones, M.A. at the Annual Meeting of the New South Wales Gleaners' Union, November 1, 1904*. Sydney, Australia: W. M. Madgwick and Sons, 1904.
---. "Practical Religion." *The Victorian Churchman*, February 12, 1892, 42.
---. *Resurrection Life: A Prayer Book Study for Easter Tide*. Introductory Note by W. H. Griffith Thomas. London: Elliot Stock, 1909.
---. "Sermon on John 1:42, at Moore College Reunion of Students." *Australian Churchman*, December 9, 1905, 6.
---. *The Teaching of the Articles: A Plain Exposition of the Doctrines of the Articles of the Church of England, with Their Scripture Proofs*. Sydney, Australia: W. M. Madgwick and Sons, 1904. Reprint, Sydney, Australia: Church Missionary Society Book Room, 1944.
---. *"Touch Me Not." An Examination of a Popular Theory of the Sacraments. A Sermon Preached in Moore College Chapel*. Sydney, Australia: "Australian Churchman" Office, n.d.
---. "The Value of the Prayer Book as a Manual of Doctrine." *The Victorian Churchman*, May 7, 1897, 78–79.
Jowett, Benjamin. *The Epistles of St Paul to the Thessalonians, Galatians, Romans. With Critical Notes and Dissertations*. 2 vols. London: John Murray, 1855.
---. "The Interpretation of Scripture." In *Essays and Reviews*, 330–433. London: John W. Parker, 1860.
Judd, Stephen. "Defenders of Their Faith: Power and Party in the Anglican Diocese of Sydney 1909–1938." PhD diss., University of Sydney, 1984.
---. "Talbot, Albert Edward." In *ADEB* 363.

Judd, Stephen, and Kenneth Cable. *Sydney Anglicans: A History of the Diocese*. Sydney, Australia: Anglican Information Office, 1987.

Julian, John, ed. *A Dictionary of Hymnology Setting Forth the Origin and History of Christian Hymns of all Ages and Nations*. London: John Murray, 1915.

Kant, Immanuel. *Kant's Kritik of Judgment*. Translated with introduction and notes by J. H. Bernard. London: Macmillan, 1892.

———. *Kant's Critique of Practical Reason and other Works on the Theory of Ethics*. Translated by Thomas Kingsmill Abbott. 5th ed., revised. London: Longmans, Green, 1898.

———. *Kant's Introduction to Logic, and his Essay on the Mistaken Subtilty of the Four Figures... With a Few Notes by Coleridge*. Translated by Thomas Kingsmill Abbott. London: Longmans, Green, 1885.

———. *Religion within the Boundary of Pure Reason*. Translated by J. W. Semple. Edinburgh: T. & T. Clark, 1838.

Kaye, Bruce, ed. *Anglicanism in Australia: A History*. Carlton South, Australia: Melbourne University Press, 2002.

———. *A Church Without Walls: Being Anglican in Australia*. North Blackburn, Australia: Dove, 1995.

Keble, John. "National Apostasy." In *Sermons Academical and Occasional*, 129–48. Oxford: John Henry Parker, 1847.

Kelvin, Lord William Thomson. "Remarks." In *Christian Apologetics*, edited by W. W. Seton, xi, 24–26. London: John Murray, 1903.

Kennedy, John. *A Popular Handbook of Christian Evidences*. London: Sunday School Union, 1880.

Kidner, Derek. *Psalms 1–72: Introduction and Commentary*. Leicester, UK: Inter-Varsity, 1973.

King-Hall, Admiral Sir George Fowler, KCB, CVO. "Diaries". http://sites.google.com/site/kinghallconnections/6900-g-cincaustralia.

Kirk, Kenneth. "The Atonement." In *Essays Catholic and Critical by Members of the Anglican Communion*, edited by Edward Gordon Selwyn, 3rd ed., 247–78. London: Society for Promoting Christian Knowledge, 1929.

Klapwijk, Jacob. "John Calvin." In *Bringing Into Captivity Every Thought: Capita Selecta in the History of Christian Evaluations of Non-Christian Philosophy*, edited by Jacob Klapwijk et al., 123–42. Lanham, MD: University Press of America, 1991.

Knox, D. Broughton. *Selected Works*. Vol. 1, *The Doctrine of God*, edited by Tony Payne. Kingsford, Australia: Matthias Media, 2000.

———. *Selected Works*. Vol. 2, *Church and Ministry*, edited by Kirsten Birkett. Kingsford, Australia: Matthias Media, 2003.

———. *Thirty-Nine Articles: The Historic Basis of Anglican Faith*. Rev. ed. Sydney, Australia: Anglican Information Office, 1976. Reprinted in Knox, D. Broughton. *Selected Works*. Vol. 2, *Church and Ministry*, edited by Kirsten Birkett. Kingsford, Australia: Matthias Media, 2003. 107–98.

Knox, Edmund Arbuthnott. "Foreword." In *Does the Doctrine of Transubstantiation Involve a Material Change?*, by T. C. Hammond, 2–4. London: The Church Book Room, 1928.

———. *On What Authority? A Review of the Foundations of Christian Faith*. London: Longmans, Green, 1922.

———. *Reminiscences of an Octogenarian, 1847–1934*. London: Hutchinson, 1934.

Knudsen, Robert D. "Progressive and Regressive Tendencies in Christian Apologetics." In *Jerusalem and Athens: Critical Discussions on the Theology and Apologetics of Cornelius Van Til*, edited by E. R. Geehan, 275-98. Nutley, NJ: Presbyterian and Reformed, 1971.

Kuhn, T. S. *The Structure of Scientific Revolutions*. 2nd ed. Chicago: University of Chicago Press, 1970.

Kuyper, Abraham. *Encyclopedia of Sacred Theology: Its Principles. With an Introduction by Professor B. B. Warfield*. London: Hodder and Stoughton, 1899. Reprinted as *Principles of Sacred Theology*. Grand Rapids: Baker Book House, 1980.

———. *The Work of the Holy Spirit*. New York: Funk and Wagnalls, 1900.

La Touche, E. Digges. See Digges La Touche, E.

Lake, Meredith. *Proclaiming Jesus Christ as Lord: A History of the Sydney University Evangelical Union*. Sydney, Australia: The EU Graduates Fund, 2005.

Langford, Thomas A. *In Search of Foundations: English Theology 1900-1920*. Nashville: Abingdon, 1969.

Larsen, David L. *The Creative Company: A Christian Reader's Guide to Great Literature and Its Themes*. Grand Rapids: Kregel, 1999.

———. *Crisis of Doubt: Honest Faith in Nineteenth-Century England*. Oxford: Oxford University Press, 2006.

Lawton, William James. "Australian Anglican Theology." In *Anglicanism in Australia: A History*, edited by Bruce Norman Kaye, 177-199. Carlton South, Australia: Melbourne University Press, 2002.

———. "'The Better Time to Be: The Kingdom of God and Social Reform; Anglicanism and the Diocese of Sydney 1885-1914." PhD diss., University of New South Wales, 1985.

———. *The Better Time to Be: Utopian Attitudes to Society Among Sydney Anglicans 1885 to 1914*. Kensington, Australia: New South Wales University Press, 1990.

———. "Nathaniel Jones: Preacher of Righteousness." In *God Who is Rich in Mercy: Essays Presented to Dr. D. B. Knox*, edited by Peter T. O'Brien and David G. Peterson, 361-75. Homebush West, Australia: Lancer, ANZEA, 1986.

Lessing, Gotthold Ephraim. "Bibliolatry." In *Cambridge Free Thoughts and Letters on Bibliolatry, Translated from the German of G. E. Lessing, by H. H. Bernard*, edited by Isaac Bernard, xxxix-xl. London: Trübner, 1862.

Lewis, C. S. *Mere Christianity*. London: Collins Fontana, 1952.

Lias, J. J. "The Witness of the Historical Books to the Accuracy of the Pentateuch." *The Record*, March 1899, 284.

Liddon, H. P. *Some Elements of Religion*. London: Rivingtons, 1872.

Linder, Robert D. "'Honest Jim' McGowen (1855-1922) as a Christian in Politics." *Lucas* 15 (1993) 44-59.

———. "McGowen, James Sinclair Taylor." In *ADEB* 233.

Lints, Richard. "The Age of Intellectual Iconoclasm: The Nineteenth Century Revolt Against Theism." In *Revolutions in Worldview: Understanding the Flow of Western Thought*, edited by Andrew Hoffecker, 281-317. Phillipsburg, NJ: Presbyterian and Reformed, 2007.

"List of Suggested Books." In *The Australian College of Theology Manual for the Year 1913*, 42. Sydney, Australia: Australian College of Theology, 1913.

Litton, Edward Arthur. *The Church of Christ in Its Idea, Attributes and Ministry: With a Particular Reference to the Controversy on the Subject Between Romanists and*

Protestants. London: Longman, Brown, Green, and Longmans, 1851. Reprinted with an introduction by F. J. Chavasse. London: James Nisbet, 1898.

———. *Gospel Not a Ceremonial Law. A Sermon Preached Before the University of Oxford, at St Mary's, on Monday, January 30th, 1854.* Oxford: W. Graham, 1854.

———. *A Guide to the Study of Holy Scripture*. London: Seeley, Jackson, and Halliday, 1871.

———. *Introduction to Dogmatic Theology on the Basis of the XXXIX Articles of the Church of England*. 2nd ed. London: Elliott Stock, 1902.

———. "Notes, Appendix and Preface." In William Paley, *A View of the Evidences of Christianity: In Three Parts*. London: Christian Evidence Committee of the Society for Promoting Christian Knowledge, 1872.

———. *A Sermon on John iii.5 . . . in reference to the recent legislative decision in the case of Gorham v. Bishop of Exeter*. London: Hatchard, 1850.

Loane, Marcus L. *Archbishop Mowll: The Biography of Howard West Kilvinton Mowll, Archbishop of Sydney and Primate of Australia*. London: Hodder and Stoughton, 1960.

———. *A Centenary History of Moore Theological College*. Sydney, Australia: Angus and Robertson, 1955.

———. *Makers of Our Heritage: A Study of Four Evangelical Leaders*. London: Hodder and Stoughton, 1967.

———. *Mark These Men: A Brief Account of Some Evangelical Clergy in the Diocese of Sydney Who Were Associated with Archbishop Mowll*. Canberra: Acorn, 1985.

———. Review of *The Better Time to Be: Utopian Attitudes to Society Among Sydney Anglicans, 1885–1914* by W. J. Lawton. *Lucas* 11 (1991) 41–42.

Lucretius Carus, T. *De Rerum Natura, V.* Edited by J. D. Duff. Cambridge: Cambridge University Press, 1953.

Luther, Martin. *First Principles of the Reformation, or, The Ninety-five Theses and the Three Primary Works of Luther Translated into English: Edited with Theological and Historical Introductions by Henry Wace and C. A. Buchheim*. London: John Murray, 1883.

———. *Luther's Primary Works: Together with his Shorter and Longer Catechisms: Translated into English, Edited with Theological and Historical Essays by Henry Wace and C. A. Buchheim*. London: Hodder and Stoughton, 1896.

Lyttleton, Arthur. "The Atonement." In *Lux Mundi. A Series of Studies in the Religion of the Incarnation*, edited by Charles Gore. 10th ed., 275–312. London: John Murray, 1890.

Machen, J. Gresham. *Christianity and Liberalism*. New York: Macmillan, 1923. Reprint, Grand Rapids: Eerdmans, 1956.

———. *The Virgin Birth of Christ*. New York: Harper, 1930.

Maclear, G. F. *An Introduction to the Thirty-nine Articles*. London: Macmillan, 1896.

Macquarrie, John. "Anglo-American Philosophies of Spirit: J. Ward, et al." In *Twentieth-Century Religious Thought*, 63–68. London: SCM, 1988.

———. "The Ethical Approach to Theism: W. R. Sorley, et al." In *Twentieth-Century Religious Thought*, 68–71. London: SCM, 1988.

Macran, F. W. *English Apologetic Theology*. Donellan Lectures 1903–1904. London: Hodder and Stoughton, 1905.

Magee, William. *Discourses and Dissertations on the Scriptural Doctrines of Atonement and Sacrifice*. Edinburgh: A & C Black, 1843.

Mahaffy, J. P. and J. H. Bernard. *Kant's Critical Philosophy for English Readers.* New and completed ed. London: Macmillan, 1889.

Malthus, Thomas. *Essay on the Principle of Population, as it Affects the Future Improvement of Society.* London: Printed for J. Johnson, in St. Paul's Church-Yard, 1798.

Manley, G. T. "The Inspiration and Authority of the Bible." In *Evangelicalism*, edited by J. Russell Howden, 121–55. London: Chas. J. Thynne and Jarvis, 1925.

———. "Materialism or Christianity." In *Christian Apologetics*, edited by W. W. Seton, 101–13: London: John Murray, 1903.

———. *The Gospel in the Psalms: Being a Study of the Commission to Evangelize the World as Foreshadowed in the Psalms.* London: Church Missionary Society, 1908.

———, ed. *The New Bible Handbook.* London: Inter-Varsity, 1950.

———. *The Return of Jesus Christ.* London: Inter-Varsity, 1960.

———. Review of *Reasoning Faith*, by T. C. Hammond. *Churchman* 59, no. 4 (1945) 186.

———, ed. *Search the Scriptures: The I.V.F. Bible Study Course.* London: Inter-Varsity, 1949.

Manual of the Australian College of Theology. Sydney, Australia: W. A. Pepperday, 1899–1900.

Manual for the Year: Australian College of Theology. Sydney, Australia: W. A. Pepperday, 1913.

Maple, G. S. "Barker, Frederic." In *ADEB* 21–26.

———. "Barker, Frederic." In *BDE* 30–32.

"Marriages." *The Argus.* Melbourne, February 15, 1888, 1. National Library of Australia digitized newspapers www.trove.nla.gov.au/newspaper/the Argus/articles/

Maurice, F. D. *The Doctrine of Sacrifice: Deduced from the Scriptures.* Cambridge: Macmillan, 1854. Reprint, London: Macmillan, 1893.

———. "On Justification by Faith." In *Theological Essays*, 189–213. 3rd ed. London: Macmillan, 1871.

McDowell, R. B. and D. A. Webb. *Trinity College Dublin, 1592–1952: An Academic History.* Cambridge: Cambridge University Press, 1982.

McGillion, Chris. *The Chosen Ones: The Politics of Salvation in the Anglican Church.* Crows Nest, Australia: Allen and Unwin, 2005.

McIntosh, John. "'External Prop' or 'Divine Fiat': D. J. Davies and T. C. Hammond on the Authority of Scripture." *Lucas* 2, no. 2 (2010) 67–91.

———. "How T. C. Hammond Defended the Faith—A Useful History." *Lucas* 2, no. 10 (2017) 81–100.

McNeile, A. H. "The Religious Situation in Cambridge." *The New Commentator: A Quarterly Cambridge Paper for the Discussion of Current Religious and Theological Questions* 1 (1913) 11–12.

Mede, Joseph. *A Translation of Mede's Clavis Apocalyptica*, by R. B. Cooper. London: Rivingtons, 1833.

Mildmay Conference. *"Our God Shall Come": Addresses on the Second Coming of the Lord. By the Reverend Prebendary Auriol et al. Mildmay Park, February 26th, 27th and 28th, 1878.* London: John F. Shaw, 1878.

Mill, J. S. *The Utility of Religion.* In *Three Essays on Religion*, 69–122. 2nd ed. London: Longmans, Green, Reader and Dyer, 1874.

"Minute Book of The Heretics Club," vol. 1, 1916–1927, vol. 2. 1928–1936. Box 1 Heretics Club, S117, USydArch.

Moberly, R. C. *Atonement and Personality.* London: John Murray, 1901.

Moberly, W. H. "The Atonement." In *Foundations: A Statement of Christian Belief in Terms of Modern Thought: By Seven Oxford Men*, 265–335. London: Macmillan, 1912.

Monier-Williams, Monier. *The Bible and the Sacred Books of the East: Four Addresses.* London: Religious Tract Society, 1887.

Moody, D. L. *Bible Characters.* London: Morgan and Scott, 1885.

Moorhouse, J. *Church Work, Its Means and Methods.* London: Macmillan, 1894.

Morris, Leon. *The Apostolic Preaching of the Cross.* 3rd rev. ed. London: Tyndale, 1965.

———. "Foreword." In *T. C. Hammond: Irish Christian: His Life and Legacy in Ireland and Australia*, by Warren Nelson, xiii–xiv. Edinburgh: Banner of Truth, 1994.

———. "Preface to the First Edition." In *The Apostolic Preaching of the Cross*, by Leon Morris, 7–8. 3rd rev. ed. London: Tyndale, 1965.

Motyer, Alec. *Isaiah: An Introduction and Commentary.* Tyndale Old Testament Commentaries 20. Leicester, UK: Inter-Varsity, 1999.

———. *The Prophecy of Isaiah: An Introduction and Commentary.* Leicester, UK: Inter-Varsity, 1993.

Moule, Handley C. G. "The Christian's Relationship to the World." *The Victorian Churchman*, March 14, 1890, 71.

———. *The Epistle of Paul the Apostle to the Romans.* Cambridge Bible for Schools and Colleges. Cambridge: Cambridge University Press, 1879.

———. *The Epistle of St Paul to the Romans.* The Expositor's Bible. 6th ed. London: Hodder and Stoughton, 1902.

———. *The Evangelical School in the Church of England: Its Men and its Work in the Nineteenth Century.* London: James Nisbet, 1901.

———. "Introduction: Some Recollections." In Alexander Smellie, *Evan Henry Hopkins: A Memoir, with an Introductory Chapter by the Late H. C. G. Moule*, 9–15. London: Marshall Brothers, 1920.

———. *Outlines of Christian Doctrine.* 4th ed. rev. London: Hodder and Stoughton, 1894.

Moyal, Ann. *A Bright and Savage Land: Scientists in Colonial Australia.* Sydney, Australia: Collins, 1986.

Mozley, Ann. "Clarke, William Branwhite (1798–1878)." In *ADB* 3:420–22.

Mozley, J. B. *Eight Lectures on Miracles, Preached before the University of Oxford in the Year MDCCCLXV*, 6th ed. London: Rivingtons, 1883.

Mozley, J. K. *The Doctrine of the Atonement.* London: Duckworth, 1915.

———. "Religious Life and Thought at Cambridge." *ACQR* 1, no. 1 (1910) 25–32.

———. *Some Tendencies in British Theology: From the publication of* Lux Mundi *to the Present Day.* London: SPCK, 1952.

Munden, A. F. "Birks, Thomas Rawson." In *BDE* 54–55.

Murray, John. Review of *So Great Salvation: The History and Message of the Keswick Convention*, by Steven Barabas. In *Studies in Theology*, Collected Writings of John Murray 4, 281–86. Edinburgh: Banner of Truth Trust, 1992.

Murray, Robert H. *Archbishop Bernard: Professor, Prelate and Provost.* London: SPCK, 1931.

Nairn, Bede. "McGowen, James Sinclair." In *ADB* 10:273–74.

Neatby, William Blair. *A History of the Plymouth Brethren*. 2nd ed. London: Hodder and Stoughton, 1901.
Neil, Charles, and M. Willoughby, eds. *The Tutorial Prayer Book for the Teacher, the Student, and the General Reader*. London: Harrison Trust, 1913.
Neill, Stephen. *A History of Christian Missions*. 2nd ed. Harmondsworth, UK: Penguin, 1984.
Nelson, Warren. *T. C. Hammond: His Life and Legacy in Ireland and Australia*. Edinburgh: Banner of Truth, 1994.
Newman, John Henry. *Lectures on Justification*. London: Rivingtons, 1838.
———.*Tract XC. On certain passages in the XXXIX Articles*. London: John Henry and James Parker, 1875.
Niebuhr, Reinhold. *An Interpretation of Christian Ethics*. London: SCM, 1936.
Noll, Mark A. *The Rise of Evangelicalism: The Age of Edwards, Whitefield and the Wesleys*. A History of Evangelicalism. Leicester, UK: Apollos, 2004.
O'Brien, James Thomas. *An Attempt to Explain and Establish the Doctrine of Justification by Faith Only: In Ten Sermons on the Nature and Effects of Faith, Preached in the Chapel of Trinity College, Dublin*. London: Macmillan, 1863.
O'Brien, Peter T., and David G. Peterson, eds. *God Who Is Rich in Mercy: Essays Presented to Dr. D. B. Knox*. Homebush West, Australia: Lancer, 1986.
O'Connor, J. J., and E. F. Robertson. "Arthur Stanley Eddington." http://www-history.mcs.st-and.ac.uk/Bibliographies/Eddington.html.
O'Neill, Onora. "Vindicating Reason." In *The Cambridge Companion to Kant*, edited by Paul Guyer, 280–308. Cambridge: Cambridge University Press, 1992.
O'Neill, W. M. "Muscio, Bernard." In *ADB* 10:650–51.
Ogden, C. K., and I. A. Richards, *The Meaning of Meaning: A Study of the Influence of Language upon Thought and of the Science of Symbolism*. London: Kegan Paul, Trench, Trubner, 1923.
Oman, J. W. *The War and its Issues*. Cambridge: Cambridge University Press, 1915.
Orr, James. *The Bible Under Trial: Apologetic Papers in View of Present-day Assaults on Holy Scripture*. London: Marshall Brothers, 1907.
———. *The Christian View of God and the World: As Centring in the Incarnation*. The Kerr Lectures 1890–91. Edinburgh: Andrew Elliott, 1893. Reprint, Grand Rapids: Eerdmans, 1948.
———. *The Problem of the Old Testament: Considered with Reference to Recent Criticism*. London: James Nisbet, 1907.
———. *The Ritschlian Theology*. London: Hodder and Stoughton, 1897.
———. *Sin as a Problem Today*. London: Hodder and Stoughton, 1910.
Orr, J. Edwin. *The Light of the Nations: Progress and Achievement in the Nineteenth Century*. Paternoster Church History 8. Exeter: Paternoster, 1965.
Ovey, Michael. "Is Christ's Incarnation the Culmination of the Cosmic Process?" In *"The Word became Flesh": Evangelicals and the Incarnation. Papers from the Sixth Oak Hill College Annual School of Theology*, edited by David W. Peterson, 1–49. Carlisle, UK: Paternoster, 2003.
Oxford University Calendar. Oxford: Clarendon, 1883 and 1887.
Oxford University Examination Papers. Second Public Examination. Honour School of Theology. Oxford: Clarendon, 1886.
Oxford University Gazette, 13 (1882–1883).
Packer, J. I. *Evangelism and the Sovereignty of God*. Chicago: Inter-Varsity, 1961.

———. "*Fundamentalism*" *and the Word of God: Some Evangelical Principles*. Leicester, UK: Inter-Varsity, 1958.

———. *Keep in Step with the Spirit*. Leicester, UK: Inter-Varsity, 1984.

———. "The Oxford Evangelicals in Theology." In *The Evangelicals at Oxford 1735–1871: A Record of an Unchronicled Movement with the Record Extended to 1905 and an Essay on Oxford Evangelical Theology by the Revd. Dr. J. I. Packer*, by J. S. Reynolds, 82–94. Oxford: Marcham Manor, 1975.

———. "Preface." In *Holiness: Its Nature, Hindrances, Difficulties and Roots*, by J. C. Ryle, vii–xii. Welwyn, UK: Evangelical, 1979.

———. Review of *The New Creation* by T. C. Hammond. *The Church Gazette*, January-February 1955, 22–23.

Paget, Stephen. *Henry Scott Holland: Memoirs and Letters*. London: John Murray, 1921.

Paley, William. *A View of the Evidences of Christianity: In Three Parts*. New ed., with Introduction, Notes, and Supplement by T. R. Birks. London: Religious Tract Society, 1859.

———. *A View of the Evidences of Christianity: In Three Parts*. New ed., with Notes, Appendix, and Preface by the Reverend E. A. Litton. London: Christian Evidence Committee of the Society for Promoting Christian Knowledge, 1872.

Pansy [Isabella Macdonald Alden]. *The King's Daughter*. Edinburgh: J. Gemmell, 1883.

Paproth, Darrell. "The Deeper Life Movement in Victoria 1880–1914." *Our Yesterdays: Journal of the Victorian Baptist Historical Society* (2002) 53–77.

———. "Hussey Burgh Macartney Jr.: Mission Enthusiast." Conference paper, at ANZ Missionaries at Home and Abroad, First Biennial Trans-Tasman Conference. Australian National University, December 2004.

Parker, T. H. L., ed. *English Reformers*. Library of Christian Classics 26. London: SCM, 1966.

Parer, Michael S. *Australia's Last Heresy Hunt: The Angus Case*. Sydney, Australia: Wentworth, 1971.

Passmore, John. *A Hundred Years of Philosophy*. 2nd ed. Harmondsworth, UK: Penguin, 1984.

———. "John Anderson and Twentieth-century Philosophy." In John Anderson, *Studies in Empirical Philosophy*, ix–xxiv. Sydney, Australia: Angus and Robertson, 1962.

———. "Philosophy." In *The Pattern of Australian Culture*, edited by A. L. McLeod, 131–69. Ithaca, NY: Cornell University Press, 1963.

Pettet, David B. *Samuel Marsden: Preacher, Pastor, Magistrate and Missionary*. Camperdown, Australia: Bolt, 2016.

Piggin, Stuart. *Firestorm of the Lord: The History and Prospects for Revival in the Church and the World*. Carlisle, UK: Paternoster, 2000.

———. "A History of Theological Education in Australia." In *The Furtherance of Religious Beliefs: Essays on the History of Theological Education in Australia*, edited by G. R. Treloar. A special combined edition of *Lucas* 19/20 (1995–1996) 24–43.

———. *Spirit of a Nation: The Story of Australia's Christian Heritage*. Sydney, Australia: Strand, 2004.

———. "Towards the Renewal of the Anglican Church of Australia: An Historical and Sociological Evaluation of Bruce Kaye's Strategies." Paper presented at the Australian Anglican History Seminar, Sydney, September 27–28, 1997.

Pollock, J. C. *A Cambridge Movement*. London: John Murray, 1953.

Porter, Muriel. *The New Puritans: The Rise of Fundamentalism in the Anglican Church.* Melbourne, Australia: Melbourne University Press, 2006.
Powell, Baden. "On the Study of the Evidences of Christianity." In *Essays and Reviews,* 94–144. London: John W. Parker, 1860.
Price, C. P. "The Fascination of the Church of Rome." *ICQ* 7, no. 28 (1914) 316–26.
Proctor, F. B. *Classified Gems of Thought from the Great Writers and Preachers of All Ages: A Dictionary of Ready Reference on Religious Subjects. With a Preface by Henry Wace.* London: Hodder and Stoughton, 1886.
Pusey, E. B. *An Historical Enquiry into the Probable Causes of the Rationalist Character Lately Predominant in the Theology of Germany.* London: Rivingtons, 1828.
———. "Preface." In *Daniel the Prophet: Nine Lectures, Delivered in the Divinity School of the University of Oxford,* iii–xxi. 2nd ed. Oxford: James Parker, 1867. Reprint, New York: Funk & Wagnalls, 1885.
Pym, David. *The Religious Thought of Samuel Taylor Coleridge.* New York: Barnes and Noble, 1978.
Quinton, Anthony. "Russell, Bertrand Arthur William." In *The Fontana Biographical Companion to Modern Thought,* edited by Alan Bullock and R. B. Woodings, 661–62. London: Collins, 1983.
Ramsey, Arthur Michael. *F. D. Maurice and the Conflicts of Modern Theology.* Cambridge: Cambridge University Press, 1951.
———. *From Gore to Temple: The Development of Anglican Theology between* Lux Mundi *and the Second World War, 1889–1939.* London: Longmans, Green, 1960.
Randall, Ian M. *Spirituality and Social Change: The Contribution of F. B. Meyer (1847–1929).* Carlisle, UK: Paternoster, 2003.
Rashdall, Hastings. *The Idea of Atonement in Christian Theology.* Bampton Lectures 1915. London: Macmillan, 1919.
Rawlinson, A. E. J. "The Principle of Authority." In *Foundations: A Statement of Christian Belief in Terms of Modern Thought: By Seven Oxford Men,* 361–407. London: Macmillan, 1912.
Rawlinson, George. *The Alleged Historical Difficulties of the Old and New Testaments, and the Light Thrown on Them by Modern Discoveries.* London: n.p., 1871.
———. *The Antiquity of Man Historically Considered.* London: Religious Tract Society, 1883.
———. "Moses: The Author of the Levitical Code of Laws." In *Lex Mosaica: Or the Law of Moses and the Higher Criticism,* edited by Richard Valpy French, 19–52. London: Eyre and Spottiswoode, 1894.
Reardon, Bernard M. G. *Religious Thought in the Victorian Age: A Survey from Coleridge to Gore.* 2nd ed. London: Longman, 1995.
The Record. London: A. Mackintosh, 1828–1948.
Reid, J. R. *Marcus L. Loane: A Biography.* Brunswick East, Australia: Acorn, 2004.
Reimarus, Hermann Samuel. *Fragments from Reimarus: Consisting of Brief Critical Remarks on the Objects of Jesus and his Disciples as seen in the New Testament.* Translated from the German of G. E. Lessing. Edited by Charles Voysey. London and Edinburgh: Williams and Norgate, 1879.
Report of the Royal Commission on Ecclesiastical Discipline. London: His Majesty's Stationery Office, 1906.
Reventlow, Henning Graf. *The Authority of the Bible and the Rise of the Modern World.* Philadelphia: Fortress, 1985.

Reynolds, J. S. *Evangelicals at Oxford: 1735-1871: A Record of an Unchronicled Movement with the Record Extended to 1905. With an Essay on Oxford Evangelical Theology by the Revd. Dr. J. I. Packer*. Appleford, UK: Marcham Manor, 1975.

Ricardo, David. *On the Principles of Political Economy and Taxation*. London: John Murray, 1821.

Riesen, R. A. "Smith, George Adam." In *DSCHT* 780-81.

Ritschl, Albrecht. *The Christian Doctrine of Justification and Reconciliation*. Edinburgh: T & T Clark, 1900.

Robert, Dana L. "Premillennialism." In *Evangelical Dictionary of World Mission*, edited by Scott Moreau, 783-84. Carlisle, UK: Paternoster, 2000.

Robertson, James. *The Early Religion of Israel as Set Forth by Biblical Writers and by Modern Critical Historians*. The Baird Lecture for 1889. Edinburgh: William Blackwood, 1892.

Robin, A. de Q. *Charles Perry, Bishop of Melbourne: The Challenges of a Colonial Episcopate, 1947-1876*. Nedlands, Australia: University of Western Australia Press, 1967.

Robinson, D. W. B. "Church." In *NBD* 228-31. Reprinted in *Donald Robinson: Selected Works*, vol. 1, *Assembling God's People*, edited by P. G. Bolt and M. D. Thompson, 222-29. Camperdown, Australia: Australian Church Record, 2008.

———. "'The Church' Revisited: An Autobiographical Fragment." *The Reformed Theological Review* 48 (1989) 4-14. Reprinted in *Donald Robinson: Selected Works*, vol. 1, *Assembling God's People*, edited by P. G. Bolt and M. D. Thompson, 259-71. Camperdown, Australia: Australian Church Record, 2008.

———. *The Meaning of Baptism*. Beecroft, Australia: Evangelical Tracts and Publication, 1958. Reprinted in *Donald Robinson: Selected Works*, vol. 2, *Preaching God's Word*, edited by P. G. Bolt and M. D. Thompson, 227-51. Camperdown, Australia: Australian Church Record, 2008.

———. "The Origins of the Anglican Church League." *Lucas* 21 and 22 (1996), 137-65.

Robinson, Thomas. *The Christian System: Unfolded in a Course of Practical Essays on the Principal Doctrines and Duties of Christianity*. 3 vols. London: Printed for the author, 1805.

Rogers, T. Guy. "Introduction." In *The Inner Life: Essays in Liberal Evangelicalism*, 2nd series, vii-xiv. London: Hodder and Stoughton, 1925.

———, ed. *Liberal Evangelicalism: An Interpretation by Members of the Church of England*. 2nd series. London: Hodder and Stoughton, 1923.

———. "Religious Authority." In *Liberal Evangelicalism: An Interpretation by Members of the Church of England*, 28-50. London: Hodder and Stoughton, 1923.

Rogers, Thomas. *The English Creede, Consenting with the True Aunciency Catholique, and Apostolique Church in all Points, and Articles of Religion which euery Christian is to Knowe and Beleeue that Would Be Saued*. London: John Windet, for Andrew Maunsel, 1585.

Ross, K. R. "Denney, James." In *DSCHT* 239-40.

Row, C. A. *Christian Evidences Viewed in Relation to Modern Thought*. Bampton Lectures for 1877. 5th ed. London: Norgate, 1888.

———. *A Manual of Christian Evidences*. Theological Educator Series, edited by W. Robertson Nicoll. London: Hodder and Stoughton, 1886.

Rupke, Nicolaas A. "Christianity and the Sciences." In *World Christianities c.1815–c.1914*, 164–80. Cambridge History of Christianity 8, edited by Sheridan Gilley and Brian Stanley. Cambridge: Cambridge University Press, 2006.

Russell, Bertrand. "A Free Man's Worship." In *Independent Review* 1, no. 3 (1903). Reprinted in *Mysticism and Logic, and Other Essays*, 46–57. London: George Allen and Unwin, 1917.

———. "On Induction." In *The Problems of Philosophy*, 93–108. London: Oxford University Press, 1912.

———. *The Principles of Mathematics*. Cambridge: Cambridge University Press, 1903.

Ryle, Herbert Edward. *The Canon of the Old Testament: An Essay on the Gradual Growth and Formation of the Hebrew Canon of Scripture*. London: Macmillan, 1892.

Ryle, John Charles. *Coming Events and Present Duties: Being Miscellaneous Sermons on Prophetical Subjects. Arranged, Revised, and Corrected by the Rev. J. C. Ryle*. 2nd ed. London: Hunt, 1879.

———. *Expository Thoughts on the Gospels for Family and Private Use*. London: Chas. J. Thynne and Jarvis, 1856.

———. *Expository Thoughts on the Gospel of St Matthew, with Text Complete and Explanatory Notes*. Popular ed. London: Hodder and Stoughton, 1890.

———. *Holiness: Its Nature, Hindrances, Difficulties and Roots*. Welwyn, UK: Evangelical, 1979.

———. *Knots Untied: Being Plain Statements on Disputed Points in Religion from the Standpoint of an Evangelical Churchman*. Edited and introduced by G. E. Duffield. London: James Clarke, 1964.

———. *Light from Old Times: Or, Protestant Facts and Men. With an Introduction for Our Own Days*. 4th ed. London: Chas. J. Thynne and Jarvis, 1903.

Salmon, George. *Evolution, and Other Papers*. London: Christian Knowledge Society, 1906.

———. *An Historical Introduction to the Books of the New Testament*. 7th ed. London: John Murray, 1894.

———. *The Human Element in the Gospels: A Commentary on the Synoptic Narrative*. London: John Murray, 1907.

———. *The Infallibility of the Church: A Course of Lectures Delivered in the Divinity School of the University of Dublin*. 3rd ed. London: John Murray, 1899.

———. *On the Properties of Surfaces of the Second Degree Which Correspond to the Theorems of Pascal and Brianchon on Conic Sections*. London: Taylor and Francis, 1844.

Salmond, S. D. F. *The Christian Doctrine of Immortality*. Edinburgh: T & T Clark, 1903.

Salter, F. R. "Preface." In *William Cunningham—Teacher and Priest*, by Audrey Cunningham, vii–xv. London: SPCK, 1950.

Sanday, William, and Arthur C. Headlam. *A Critical and Exegetical Commentary on the Epistle to the Romans*. 5th ed. The International Critical Commentary. Edinburgh: T & T Clark, 1902.

Sayce, A. H. *Early History of the Hebrews*. London: Rivingtons, 1897.

———. *Fresh Light from the Ancient Monuments: A Sketch of the Most Striking Confirmation of the Bible, from Recent Discoveries in Egypt, Palestine, Assyria, Babylonia, Asia Minor*. London: Religious Tract Society, 1883.

Scales, D. A. "Illustrations of Compromise in Church History." *Churchman* 102, no. 3 (1988) 228–33.

Schaff, Philip, ed. *The Greek and Latin Creeds, with Translations.* 6th ed. The Creeds of Christendom: With a History and Critical Notes 2. New York: Harper and Brothers, 1931.

Schleicher, B. A. "The Results of Recent Criticism on the Old Testament." In *The Official Report of the Church Congress: Held at Hobart on January 23rd, 24th, 25th, and 26th, 1894,* 18–19. Tasmania: Diocesan Book Depot, 1894.

"Schleicher, John Theophilus." In *Crockford's Clerical Directory.* London: John Hall, 1885. Also in *The Sydney Diocesan Directory for the Year of Our Lord 1886.* Sydney, Australia: The Diocese of Sydney, 1886.

Schleiermacher, Friedrich. *The Christian Faith. English Translation of the Second German Edition* [of *Der Christliche Glaube*]. Edited by H. R. Mackintosh and J. S. Stewart. Edinburgh: T & T Clark, 1928.

Schniewind, J. B. "Autonomy, Obligation, and Virtue: An Overview of Kant's Moral Philosophy." In *The Cambridge Companion to Kant,* edited by Paul Guyer, 309–41. Cambridge: Cambridge University Press, 1992.

Schweitzer, Albert. *The Quest for the Historical Jesus: A Critical Study of its Progress from Reimarus to Wrede; With a Preface by F. C. Burkitt.* London: A. and C. Black, 1910.

Scofield, C. I., ed. *The Holy Bible, Containing the Old and New Testaments: Authorized Version, with a New System of Connected Topical References to All the Greater Themes of Scripture, with Annotations, Revised Marginal Renderings, Summaries, Definitions, and Index: to Which Are Added Helps at Hard Places, Explanations of Seeming Discrepancies, and a New System of Paragraphs.* New York: Oxford University Press, 1909.

Seeberg, Reinhold. *Text-Book of the History of Doctrines.* 2 vols. Translated by Charles E. Hay. Grand Rapids: Baker, 1966.

Sellers, Ian. "Rashdall, Hastings." In *NIDCC* 825–26.

Selwyn, E. G. "The Historic Christ." *Comment and Criticism* 2, no. 2 (1914) 62–69.

Service Register, Holy Trinity Church, Cambridge (June 18, 1905 to August 24, 1911). Record of David J. Davies's Bible studies, provided to the author by the Reverend Noel Pollard, Archivist at Holy Trinity Church, Cambridge on April 13, 1996.

Seton, W. W., ed. *Christian Apologetics: A Series of Addresses Delivered Before the Christian Association of University College London, by George Henslow, Henry Wace, D. S. Margoliouth, R. E. Welsh, George T. Manley, Cecil Wilson. With an Introduction by G. W. Maclaren.* London: John Murray, 1903.

Shiner, Rory. "An Appreciation of D. W. B. Robinson's New Testament Theology." In *Appreciation, Donald Robinson: Selected Works* 3, edited by Peter G. Bolt and Mark D. Thompson, 9–62. Camperdown, Australia: Australian Church Record, 2008.

Sibtain, Nancy de S. P., with Winifred M. Chambers. *Dare to Look Up: A Memoir of George Alexander Chambers.* Sydney, Australia: Angus and Robertson, 1968.

Sidgwick, Henry. *Lectures on the Ethics of T. H. Green, Mr. Herbert Spencer, and J. Martineau.* London: Macmillan, 1902.

Simeon, Charles. *Horae Homileticae, or, Discourses (in the Form of Skeletons) upon the Whole Scriptures.* London: Printed by Richard Watts, 1819.

Simpson, Patrick Carnegie. *The Fact of Christ: A Series of Lectures.* London: Hodder and Stoughton, 1901.

Sinclair, William. "St. Augustine of Hippo." *Churchman* 13 (1899) 374–87.

Sinker, Robert. *Daniel and the Minor Prophets.* London: Dent, 1902.

———. *Essays and Studies*. London: George Bell and Sons, 1900.
———. *"Higher Criticism": What Is It, and Where Does It Lead Us?* London: James Nisbet, 1899.
———. *Saul and the Hebrew Monarchy*. London: Dent, 1903.
———. "The Seventh Century." In *Lex Mosaica: Or the Law of Moses and the Higher Criticism*, edited by Richard Valpy French, 449–90. London: Eyre and Spottiswoode, 1894.
Smeal, Jane, and Helen G. Thompson. *Life and Letters of Silvanus Phillips Thompson*. London: T. Fisher Unwin, 1920.
Smellie, Alexander. *Evan H. Hopkins: A Memoir. With an Introductory Chapter by H. C. G. Moule*. London: Marshall Brothers, 1920.
Smith, George Adam. *The Book of Isaiah*. 2 vols. The Expositor's Bible. London: Hodder and Stoughton, 1888.
———. *Modern Criticism and the Preaching of the Old Testament*. London: Hodder and Stoughton, 1901.
Smith, Jonathan (of the Wren Library, Trinity College, Cambridge). Letter to the author, April 9, 2005.
Smith, S. E. Langford. Letter to Davies, May 18, 1914. In David J. Davies, Papers, 1902–1935. MitchLib. MLL MSS 3179, Box 1, large bundle. (Microform copy available in Moore Theological College Library.)
Smith, M. "Pennefather, William (1816–1873)." In *BDE* 514–16.
Smith, William Saumarez. *The Blood of the New Covenant: A Theological Essay*. Cambridge: Macmillan and Bower, 1889.
Sorley, W. R. *The Ethics of Naturalism*. 2nd ed. Edinburgh: Blackwood, 1904.
———. *A History of British Philosophy to 1900*. Cambridge: Cambridge University Press, 1965.
Spinoza, Benedict de. "The Ethics." In *De Intellectus Emendatione-Ethica*, The Chief Works of Benedict de Spinoza, Translated from the Latin, With an Introduction 2, translated by R. H. M. Elwes. 2nd ed. London: George Bell and Sons, 1887.
Stanton, Henry Vincent. *The Gospels as Historical Documents*. Cambridge: Cambridge University Press, 1903.
St. Clair, June, and Terry St. Clair. "V. Wor. Bro. Ven. Archdeacon David John Davies MA, BD 1879–1935." *Masonic Historical Society of New South Wales Bulletin* 38 (1997) 7–11.
Stirling, James Hutchison. *The Secret of Hegel: Being the Hegelian System in Origin, Form and Matter*. London: Longman, Green, Longman, Roberts and Green, 1865.
Stonehouse, N. B. "Martin Dibelius and the Relation of History and Faith." *WTJ* 2 (1940) 105–39. Reprinted in *Paul Before the Areopagus and Other New Testament Studies*, by N. B. Stonehouse, 151–85. Grand Rapids: Eerdmans, 1957.
Storr, Vernon F. "The Bible and its Value." In *Liberal Evangelicalism: An Interpretation by Members of the Church of England*, edited by T. Guy Rogers, 80–100. London: Hodder and Stoughton, 1923.
———. *The Development of English Theology in the Nineteenth Century 1800–1860*. London: Longmans, Green, 1913.
———. *Freedom and Tradition: A Study of Liberal Evangelicalism*. London: Nisbet, 1940.
Stott, John R., and David L. Edwards. *Essentials: A Liberal-Evangelical Dialogue*. London: Hodder and Stoughton, 1988.

Strauss, David Friedrich. *The Life of Jesus, Critically Examined*. Translated by Marian Evans. London: Chapman, 1846.

Streeter, Burnett Hillman, ed. *Foundations: A Statement of Christian Belief in Terms of Modern Thought. By Seven Oxford Men*. London: Macmillan, 1912.

———. "The Historic Christ." In *Foundations: A Statement of Christian Belief in Terms of Modern Thought. By Seven Oxford Men*, 73–145. London: Macmillan, 1912.

Strong, Thomas Banks. "Heurtley, Charles Abel." In *DNB*. Supplement, vol. 2 (1901), 416–17.

Swete, Henry Barclay, ed. *Essays on Some Theological Questions of the Day by Members of the University of Cambridge*. London: Macmillan, 1905.

———, ed. *Essays on Some Biblical Questions of the Day by Members of the University of Cambridge*. London: Macmillan, 1909.

Swifte, Yasmine Gai. "Charles Dickens and the Role of Legal Institutions in Social and Moral Reform: Oliver Twist, Bleak House, and Our Mutual Friend." MA diss., University of Sydney, 1999. http://hdl.handle.net/2123/409.

The Sydney Diocesan Directory for the Year of Our Lord 1886. Sydney, Australia: John Sands, 1886.

The Sydney Diocesan Directory for the Year of Our Lord 1920. Sydney, Australia: John Sands, 1920.

The Sydney Diocesan Directory for the Year of Our Lord 1934. Sydney, Australia: John Sands, 1934.

Sydney Diocesan Magazine: The Official Organ of the Lord Archbishop Month by Month. Sydney, Australia: Church of England, 1910–1958.

Taylor, Jeremy. *The Real Presence and Spiritual of Christ in the Blessed Sacrament proved against the Doctrine of Transubstantiation: A Dissuasive from Popery, and Five Letters to Persons Changed or Tempted to a Change in Their Religion*. Revised and corrected by Charles Page Eden. London: Longman, Brown, Green, and Longmans, 1849.

———. *XXV Sermons Preached at Golden-Grove Being for the Winter Half-year, Beginning on Advent-Sunday, Untill Whit-Sunday*. London: Printed by E. Cotes, for Richard Royston, 1653.

Tennant, Frederick Robert. "The Being of God, in the light of Physical Science." In *Essays on Some Theological Questions of the Day*, edited by Henry Barclay Swete, 55–146. Cambridge: Cambridge University Press, 1905.

———. *The Origin and Propagation of Sin*. Cambridge: Cambridge University Press, 1902.

———. *Philosophical Theology*. Vol. 2, *The World, the Soul and God*. Cambridge: Cambridge University Press, 1930.

———. *The Sources of the Doctrine of the Fall and of Original Sin*. Cambridge: Cambridge University Press, 1903.

Thomas, M. Guthrie Clark. *William Henry Griffith Thomas 1861–1924*. London: Church Book Room, 1949.

———. *The Catholic Faith: A Manual of Instruction for Members of the Church of England*. London: Hodder and Stoughton, 1904. Rev. ed. London: Church Book Room, 1952.

———. *The Holy Spirit of God*. London: Longmans, Green, 1913.

———. *The Principles of Theology: An Introduction to the Thirty-nine Articles*. London: Longmans, Green, 1930.

———. "*A Sacrament of Our Redemption*": *An Enquiry into the Meaning of the Lord's Supper in the New Testament and the Church of England*. London: Bemrose and Sons, 1905. 2nd ed. London: Church Book Room, 1920.

Thompson, Mark D. *A Sure Ground on Which to Stand: The Role of Authority and Interpretive Method in Luther's Approach to Scripture*. Carlisle, UK: Paternoster, 2004.

Thompson, Silvanus P. "Resurrection." In *A Not Impossible Religion*, 43–61. 2nd ed. New York: John Lane, 1918.

Toon, Peter. *Evangelical Theology 1833–1856: A Response to Tractarianism*. London: Marshall, Morgan and Scott, 1979.

Toulouse, M. G. "Evangelical Liberalism." In *Dictionary of Christianity in America*, edited by Daniel G. Reid et al., 411. Downers Grove: Inter-Varsity, 1990.

Treloar, Geoffrey R., ed. *The Furtherance of Religious Beliefs: Essays on the History of Theological Education in Australia*. A special combined edition of *Lucas: An Evangelical History Review* 19/20, 1995–1996.

———. "Hammond, Thomas Chatterton." In *BDE* 586–87.

———. *Lightfoot the Historian: The Nature and Role of History in the Life and Thought of J. B. Lightfoot (1828–1889) as Churchman and Scholar*. Tübingen: Mohr Siebeck, 1998.

———. "Smith, William Saumarez." In *ADEB* 345–47.

———. "T. C. Hammond the Controversialist." *Sydney Anglican Historical Society Journal* 51, (2006) 20–35.

Trench, R. C. *Notes on the Miracles of Our Lord*. 11th ed. London: Macmillan, 1878.

Trevelyan, G. M. Note to Davies on Completion of Part 1 of the Tripos. In David J. Davies, Papers, 1902–1935. SMAMoore, Box 2.

Trinity College Dublin: A College Miscellany. 6 vols. Dublin: TCD, 1895–1979.

Troeltsch, Ernst. "Historical and Dogmatic Method in Theology." 1898. In *Religion in History*, translated by James Luther Adams and Walter F. Bense, 11–32. Minneapolis: Fortress, 1991.

Turton, W. H. *The Truth of Christianity*. 6th ed. London: Wells, Gardner, Darton, 1907.

Tyrrell, George. *Christianity at the Cross-roads*. London: Longmans, Green, 1909.

University of Oxford, *The Examination Statutes: For the Degrees of B.A., B.Mus., B.C.L., and B.M. Together with the Decrees of Convocation and Regulations of the Boards of Studies and Boards of Faculties, at Present in Force Relating Thereto. Revised to the End of Trinity Term*. Oxford: Clarendon, 1885.

Upton, W. Prescott. *The Churchman's History of the Oxford Movement*. London: Church Book Room, 1933.

Ussher, James. *Answer to a Jesuit*. Cambridge, UK: Pitt Press, 1835.

Van Til, Cornelius. *A Christian Theory of Knowledge*. Philadelphia: Presbyterian and Reformed, 1969.

———. *Christian Apologetics*. 2nd ed. Edited by William Esgar. Phillipsburg, NJ: Presbyterian and Reformed, 2003.

———. *The Defense of the Faith*. 4th ed. Edited by K. Scott Oliphant Phillipsburg, NJ: Presbyterian and Reformed, 2008.

———. *An Introduction to Systematic Theology: Prolegomena and the Doctrines of Revelation, Scripture, and God*. 2nd ed. Edited by William Edgar Phillipsburg, NJ: Presbyterian and Reformed, 2007.

The Victorian Churchman: A Church of England Newspaper. Melbourne, Australia: Mason, Firth & McCutcheon, 1890–1919.

Vidler, Alec R. *F. D. Maurice and Company: Nineteenth Century Studies.* London: SCM, 1966.

———. *A Variety of Catholic Modernists.* Cambridge: Cambridge University Press, 1970.

Vos, Geerhardus. "Christian Faith and the Truthfulness of Bible History." *PTR* 4 (1906) 289–305. Reprinted in *Redemptive History and Biblical Interpretation: The Shorter Writings of Geerhardus Vos,* edited by Richard B. Gaffin Jr., 458–71. Phillipsburg, NJ: Presbyterian and Reformed, 1980.

———. "The Scriptural Doctrine of the Love of God." *Presbyterian and Reformed Review* 13 (1902) 1–37. Reprinted in *Redemptive History and Biblical Interpretation: The Shorter Writings of Geerhardus Vos,* edited by Richard B. Gaffin Jr., 425–57. Phillipsburg, NJ: Presbyterian and Reformed, 1980.

Wace, Henry. "The Gospel and the Political World." *Some Questions of the Day: Biblical, National, and Ecclesiastical,* 88–97. London: James Nisbet, 1912.

———. "Introductory Remarks on the Study of Dogmatic Theology." In *Introduction to Dogmatic Theology on the Basis of the XXXIX Articles of the Church of England, Second Edition; with an Introduction by Henry Wace,* by E. A. Litton, v–xv. London: Elliott Stock, 1902.

———. "On the Primary Principles of Luther's Life and Teaching." In *First Principles of the Reformation: Or, the Ninety-five Theses and the Three Primary Works of Luther. Translated into English. Edited with Theological and Historical Introductions by Henry Wace and C. A. Buchheim,* ix–xxxvi. London: J. Murray, 1883.

———. "On the Primary Principles of Luther's Life and Teaching." In *Luther's Primary Works: Together with his Shorter and Larger Catechisms. Translated into English,* edited by Henry Wace and C. A. Buchheim, 425–48. London: Hodder and Stoughton, 1896.

———. *Prophecy Jewish and Christian: Considered in a Series of Warburton Lectures at Lincoln's Inn.* London: John Murray, 1911.

———. "Summary." In *Lex Mosaica: Or The Law of Moses and the Higher Criticism. With an Introduction by the Late Right Reverend Lord Arthur Hervey, D.D. Bishop of Bath and Wells,* edited by Richard Valpy French, 609–14. London: Eyre and Spottiswood, 1894.

Wace, Henry, and C. A. Buchheim, eds. *First Principles of the Reformation: Or the Ninety-five Theses and the Three Primary Works of Dr Martin Luther. Translated into English. Edited with Theological and Historical Introductions by Henry Wace and C. A. Buchheim.* London: John Murray, 1883.

———. *Luther's Primary Works: Together with his Shorter and Larger Catechisms. Translated into English. Edited with Theological and Historical Essays by Henry Wace and C. A. Buchheim.* London: Hodder and Stoughton, 1896.

Wace, Henry, ed. *Criticism Criticised.* London: The Bible League, 1902.

Ward, James. *Naturalism and Agnosticism.* 2 vols. Gifford Lectures 1896–1898. London: Black, 1899.

———. *The Realm of Ends, or Pluralism and Theism.* Gifford Lectures 1907–1910. Cambridge: Cambridge University Press, 1911.

Ward, Mrs. Humphry. *Robert Elsmere.* London: Macmillan, 1888.

Warfield, B. B. "Atonement." In *The New Schaff-Herzog Encyclopedia of Religious Knowledge* 6:349-56. New York: Funk and Wagnalls, 1908-1912. Reprinted in *Studies in Theology*, 261-79. The Works of Benjamin Breckenridge Warfield 10. New York: Oxford University Press, 1932. Republished as "The Chief Theories of the Atonement." In *The Person and Work of Christ*, by B. B. Warfield, edited by Samuel G. Craig, 351-69. Philadelphia: Presbyterian and Reformed, 1950.

———. "The Biblical Idea of Revelation." In *The Inspiration and Authority of the Bible*, by B. B. Warfield, 71-102. Philadelphia: Presbyterian and Reformed, 1950.

———. "Calvin's Doctrine of the Knowledge of God." *PTR* 7 (1909) 219-325. Reprinted in *Calvin's Doctrine of the Knowledge of God*, edited by Samuel G. Craig, 29-130. Philadelphia: Presbyterian and Reformed, 1956.

———. "The Chief Theories of the Atonement." In *The New Schaff-Herzog Encyclopedia of Religious Knowledge* 5:349-66. New York: Funk and Wagnalls, 1908-1912. Reprinted in *The Person and Work of Christ*, by B. B. Warfield, edited by Samuel G. Craig, 351-69. Philadelphia: Presbyterian and Reformed, 1950.

———. "The 'Higher Life' Movement." *PTR* 16 (1918) 572-622, and *PTR* 17 (1919) 37-86. Reprinted in *Perfectionism*, by B. B. Warfield, edited by Samuel G. Craig, 216-311. Philadelphia: Presbyterian and Reformed, 1958.

———. "Inspiration." In *ISBE* 3:1473-83. London: Henry Camp, 1915. Republished as "The Biblical Idea of Inspiration." In *The Inspiration and Authority of the Bible*, by B. B. Warfield, edited by Samuel G. Craig, 131-66. Philadelphia: Presbyterian and Reformed, 1950.

———. "Modern Theories of the Atonement." *PTR* 1 (1903) 81-92. Reprinted in *Studies in Theology*, by B. B. Warfield, 283-297. New York: Oxford University Press, 1932. Reprinted in *The Person and Work of Christ*, by B. B. Warfield, edited by Samuel G. Craig, 373-87. Philadelphia: Presbyterian and Reformed, 1950.

———. *Perfectionism*. Edited by Samuel G. Craig. Philadelphia: Presbyterian and Reformed, 1958.

———. "Revelation." In *ISBE* 4:2573-82. London: Henry Camp, 1915. Republished as "The Biblical Idea of Revelation." In *The Inspiration and Authority of the Bible*, by B. B. Warfield, edited by Samuel G. Craig, 71-102. Philadelphia: Presbyterian and Reformed, 1950.

———. Review of *The Bible: Its Origin and Nature* by Marcus Dods. *PTR* 4 (1906) 109-15. Reprinted in *Critical Reviews*, 118-27. The Works of Benjamin Warfield 10. New York: Oxford University Press, 1932. Reprint, Grand Rapids: Baker, 1991.

———. Review of *The Doctrine of the Atonement* by J. K. Mozley. *PTR* 15 (1917) 467-76. Reprinted in *Critical Reviews*, 464-75. The Works of Benjamin Warfield 10. New York: Oxford University Press, 1932. Reprint, Grand Rapids: Baker, 1991.

———. Review of *Foundations. A Statement of Christian Belief in Terms of Modern Thought: By Seven Oxford Men*. *PTR* 11 (1913) 526-38. Reprinted in *Critical Reviews*, 320-34. The Works of Benjamin Warfield 10. New York: Oxford University Press, 1932. Reprint, Grand Rapids: Baker, 1991.

———. "The Victorious Life." *PTR* 16 (1918) 321-73. Reprinted in *Perfectionism*, by B. B. Warfield, edited by Samuel G. Craig, 349-99. Philadelphia: Presbyterian and Reformed, 1958.

Warre-Cornish, F. *A History of the English Church in the Nineteenth Century*, Parts 1 and 2. London: Macmillan, 1910.

Warschauer, Joseph. *Problems of Immanence: Social Studies Critical and Constructive*. London: J. Clarke, 1909.
Waterland, Daniel. *A Review of the Doctrine of the Eucharist*. Oxford: Clarendon, 1853.
Webb, C. C. J. *A Study of Religious Thought in England from 1850*. Oxford: Clarendon, 1933.
Welch, Claude. *Protestant Thought in the Nineteenth Century*. Vol. 1, *1799-1890*. New Haven: Yale University Press, 1972.
Wellings, Martin. *Evangelicals Embattled: Responses of Evangelicals in the Church of England to Ritualism, Darwinism and Theological Liberalism, 1890-1930*. Carlisle, UK: Paternoster, 2003.
West, Janet. *Innings of Grace: A Life of Bishop Hilliard*. Sydney, Australia: Trinity Grammar School, 1997.
———. "A Principal Embattled." Moore College Library Lecture, 1988. In David J. Davies, Papers. SMAMoore, Box 1.12.
Westcott, Brooke Foss. *The Epistle to the Hebrews. The Greek Text with Notes and Essays*. 2nd ed. London: Macmillan, 1892.
———. *The Historic Faith: Short Lectures on the Apostles' Creed*. 4th ed. London: Macmillan, 1890.
———. *The Victory of the Cross: Sermons Preached during Holy Week, 1888, in Hereford Cathedral*. New York: Macmillan, 1888.
Westcott, Brooke Foss, and Fenton John Anthony Hort, eds. *The New Testament in the Original Greek*. Cambridge: Macmillan, 1881.
Wilcock, Michael. *The Message of the Psalms 1-72: Songs for the People of God*. Leicester, UK: Inter-Varsity, 2001.
Williams, R. R. "Editorial." In *The Liberal Evangelical: Being the Bulletin of the Anglican Evangelical Group Movement* 6, no. 1 (1950) 349-50.
Wordsworth, Christopher. *Miscellanies Literary and Religious: In Three Volumes*. London: Rivingtons, 1879.
Wright, Charles H. H., ed. *Archbishop Cranmer on the True and Catholic Doctrine and Use of the Sacrament of the Lord's Supper, with a preface by the Very Rev. Henry Wace*. London: Chas. J. Thynne and Jarvis, 1907.
———. *Daniel and his Prophecies*. London: Williams and Norgate, 1906.
———. *The Intermediate State and Prayers for the Dead*. London: J. Nisbet, 1900.
———. *An Introduction to the Old Testament*. 5th ed. London: Hodder and Stoughton, 1900.
Wright, Charles H. H., and Charles Neil, eds. *The Protestant Dictionary: Containing Articles on the History, Doctrines, and Practices of the Christian Church*. London: Harrison Trust, 1904.
Wright, E. Blackwood. "Rites and Ceremonies." In *PD* 608-10.
Wright, John Charles. "President's Address." In "Proceedings of the First Session of the Fifteenth Synod of the Diocese of Sydney, NSW, Dec. 6th-Dec. 10th, 1909." *Sydney Synod Reports*, 28-40. Sydney, Australia: William Andrews, 1910.
Yates, Nigel. *Anglican Ritualism in Victorian Britain, 1830-1910*. Oxford: Clarendon, 1999.
Young, E. J. *Studies in Isaiah*. London: Tyndale, 1955.

Index

A

Abbott, Thomas Kingsmill, 190, 192, 194
Abelard, Peter, 36
ACL—Anglican Church League, 263
ACR. See Australian Church Record
Acton, John Emerich Edward, Lord, 130, 190, 210
Advent Testimony and Preparation Movement, 46
agnosticism, 14, 29, 38–39, 125, 142–43, 164–65, 196, 233, 250–51
Aickin, George Ellis, 142
Alcock, John, 76
Alford, Henry, 97, 129
Allenby, Edmund Henry Hynman, 46, 167
amillennialism, 44, 47, 49
Anderson, Francis, 4, 142, 182, 197
Anderson, John, 182, 197, 253–54
anglican, 54, 68, 71, 74, 76, 84, 88
Anglican Church Handbooks, 29, 108, 141, 152
Anglican Church League, 138, 145, 152, 179, 184
Anglican Church/Anglicans
    Anglican communion, 44, 203, 206, 213, 268
    church members, 50, 223, 240
    clergy, 36, 44, 142, 241, 259, 262
    Evangelicals, 1, 40, 44, 48, 205, 238, 258, 268
    history, 3, 4, 265
    liturgy, 223, 256
    Sydney Anglicans, 1, 49, 205, 268
    theology, 3, 41, 189, 193, 199–200, 202, 223, 238, 265, 267
Anglican Church/Anglicans. *See also* Anglo-Catholicism, Church of England, Diocese of Sydney, English Reformation, Evangelicalism, General Synod, High Church, Lambeth Conference, Liberal Evangelicalism, Moore College, Ridley College, Synod-Sydney Anglican, Tractarianism
Anglican Evangelical Group Movement, 33, 36, 138–39, 183, 184, 217, 218
Anglican Fellowship, Sydney, 5, 184
Anglo-Catholicism
    doctrinal position, 22
    growth of, 12, 15, 69, 82, 87, 93, 152, 187, 215, 267
    opposition to, 2, 42, 62, 65, 77, 87, 174, 267
    presence in Sydney, 93, 152, 185
    ritualism, 42, 77, 96, 152, 202–3, 265
    Romanising influence, 83, 86, 180, 197, 212, 214
    sacramentalism, 42, 98, 99
    students at Moore College, 262, 268
    T.C. Hammond's relations with, 192, 205–6, 226, 228, 255, 258, 266
    theology, 22, 24, 40, 70, 83, 88–89, 92–93, 95, 97, 109, 119, 129, 134–35, 145, 157, 159, 213

Anglo-Catholics
    Bicknell, E.J., 266
    Frere, W.H., 152, 213
    Froude, R.H., 217
    Gibson, E.C.S., 83
    Gladstone, W.E., 217
    Gore, C., 84, 134–36, 164, 217, 222
    Keble, J., 145, 179, 215–17
    Maclear, G.F., 83, 129
    Newman, J.H., 22–23, 41, 180–81
    Pugin, A.W.N., 23
    Pusey, E.B., 16–17, 217
    Rawlinson, A.E.J., 198, 218
    Strong, P.N.W., 40
    Wordsworth, J., 18
    Yonge, C.M., 40
Angus, Samuel, 143, 165, 175, 181, 183, 185, 240–42
Anselm, 35, 36, 177
Anti-Ritualist Society, 203
anti-Roman Catholic feeling, 42, 55, 57, 181, 209
Aquinas, Thomas, 208, 210, 215, 233, 251
Archdall, Mervyn, 34, 42–43, 61–62, 86, 94, 119, 143, 148–49, 151, 161–62
Arianism, 131
Arise, Shine, 112, 118
Aristotle, 245
Arminianism, 13, 27, 57, 91, 181, 216
Arnold, Matthew, 13, 16
Articles of Religion. *See* Thirty-nine Articles
Ascension of Christ, 86, 138
Askwith, Edward Harrison, 128, 129
Atonement, doctrine of
    broadening of position of some Evangelicals, 34, 51
    central to the Christian faith, 34–36, 51, 134, 169, 171, 173, 191, 194, 223–27, 234, 235–36, 239
    conservative response to liberals, 27, 35, 51
    D.J. Davies's position, 62, 128, 134–37, 139, 169, 171–73, 179, 185, 235, 264
    liberal essay in *Lux Mundi*, 18
    liberal position, 85, 128, 135, 137, 169, 224, 235
    objections to Evangelical position, 35–36
    rejection of traditional position, 12, 18, 70, 223, 224
    substitutionary doctrine, 19, 34–36, 134, 136, 191, 194, 223, 227, 259
    T.C. Hammond's position, 35, 171, 191, 223–25, 227, 234–36, 239, 259
Auberlen, Karl August, 94
Augsburg Confession, 175
Augustine of Hippo, 44, 83, 88, 110, 177, 226–27, 233, 256
Australasian Church Quarterly Review, 142, 152
Australian Church Record, 144, 152, 230, 263
Australian College of Theology, 61, 145, 258
authority in religion, 197–99
authority in the Church, 213–14, 228
authority, external, 13, 132, 138, 153, 175, 198, 201, 221, 232, 266
autonomy. *See also* neutrality (religious)
autonomy, human intellectual and/or moral, 13, 16–18, 33, 127

B

Babbage, Stuart Barton, 64
Bain, Alexander, 250, 252
Baker, Harold Napier, 142, 145
Balfour, Arthur James, 12, 46, 196
Balleine, George Reginald, 44, 48, 152
Balliol College, Oxford, 15, 18
Bampton Lectures, 41, 70–71, 76, 219
Bancroft, Richard, 97
baptism, 91, 97, 203, 256
baptismal regeneration, 58, 98
Bardsley, Cyril Charles Bowman, 217
Barker, Frederic
    appointment as Bishop of Sydney, 13, 54
    death, 56
    early ministry, 23, 54–55, 57

INDEX

Evangelical convictions, 21, 55, 59, 63, 262
Evangelical influence in Sydney, 5, 22, 53, 60, 64, 200, 263
foundation of Moore College, 2, 5, 53, 55, 261
opposition to Roman Catholicism, 54
recruitment of clergy, 34, 42, 54–55
selection of principals of Moore College, 5, 55, 59, 63, 100, 261
Barnes, Ernest William, 128, 133, 138, 185
Barry, Alfred, 34, 56, 58–59, 61, 73, 261
Barth, Karl, 254
Bathurst, diocese of, 2, 56, 58, 267
Baur, Ferdinand Christian, 16
Bearham, George, 179
Bebbington quadrilateral of priorities, 9
Bebbington, David William, 28, 44
Begbie, Herbert Smirnoff, 60, 106, 151, 237, 239
Bellarmine, Robert, 207, 208
Bellerby, Alfred, 133
Bengel, Albrecht, 44
Berkeley, George, 195
Bernard, John Henry, 190–92, 203, 213–214
Besant, Walter, 75
Bible. *See* Scripture
Bible Churchmen's Missionary Society, 138, 218
Bible League, Oxford, 31
Bickersteth, Edward Henry, 45–46
Bicknell, Edward John, 266
Bingham, Geoffrey Cyril, 7
Binns, Leonard Elliott
  later known as Elliott-Binns, 138
Birks, Thomas Rawson, 14, 27–28, 33–35, 46, 50, 126
Boardman, William Edwin, 48
Boultbee, Thomas Pownall, 28, 30, 41, 83, 129, 189
Bourne, Francis Adolphus, 207
Boyce, Francis Bertie, 60, 141, 154
British and Foreign Bible Society, 143, 157
British Weekly, The—'Advanced Liberal' newspaper, 46

Broad Church, 27, 56, 59, 61, 76, 93, 127, 261
Broughton, William Grant, 21, 54
Brown, David, 46
Browne, Edward Harold, 37, 55, 83
Bull, George, 22, 134
Burkitt, Francis Crawford, 129, 146
Bury, John Bagnell, 130–31, 165, 190
Bush Church Aid Society, 264
Bushnell, Horace, 35
Butler, Joseph, 13, 27, 32, 39, 150, 190–91, 195–196, 233, 242, 244, 251

C

Cable, Kenneth John, 4, 8
Calvin, John, 89–90, 92, 111, 244–45, 256–57
Calvinism, 13, 53, 57, 117, 216, 233, 245, 260
Cambridge and District Clergy Union, 137
Cambridge Apostles, 132
Cambridge Inter-Collegiate Christian Union, 7, 31–32, 64, 125, 133–34, 250, 266
Cambridge Society of Heretics, 138, 143, 163
Cambridge Triumvirate, 32
Cambridge University Adam Smith Club, 137
Camden Society, Cambridge, 23
Cameron, Marcia, 6
Campbell, Reginald John, 194
Candole, Henry Lawe Corry Vully de, 33, 133, 139, 142
Carey, Harvey McKay, 251
Carnley, Peter Frederick, 3
Carter, Charles Sydney, 152
Cashel, Frederick, 68
Catholic, The—monthly magazine of the Irish Church Missions, 206
Caxton Hall discussion, 209
Chadwick, Owen, 19
challenges to Christian faith, 11–14, 16, 18–21, 25–26
Chambers, George Alexander, 4, 90, 126, 161

Charles I, King, 44
Chase, Frederic Henry, 129
Chavasse, Francis James, 141
Chawner, William, 138
Christ Church St Laurence, Sydney, 24, 93
Christian Association of University Colleges, 39
Christian Brethren. *See* Plymouth Brethren
Christian Observer—Evangelical newspaper, 41
Christian Social Union, Cambridge, 131
christology, 84, 99, 104, 150–51, 157, 159, 195, 204, 218, 234, 256
Christopher, Alfred Millard William, 73, 77
Church and the Plain Man, The, 144, 146, 155, 159, 161, 264. *See also* Moorhouse Lectures
Church Association, Cambridge, 42
Church Congress, 1894, Hobart, 81, 108
Church Missionary Association, NSW, 50, 119
Church Missionary Society, 1–2, 12, 138, 162, 188, 191, 217, 259, 264
Church of England
    Church of England in Australia, 43, 54, 57, 144, 152, 205, 214, 263, 267
    differing traditions within, 58, 97, 207, 261–62
    doctrine, 82, 87, 95
    Evangelical party, 44, 139
    growth of liberalism, 1, 11, 139–40, 250
    growth of ritualism, 11, 24, 42
    liturgy, 42, 61, 72, 109, 144
    moral earnestness, 47
    Protestant and Reformed character, 87, 121, 174, 193, 199, 203, 214
    Thirty-nine Articles, 42, 47, 86–87, 180, 181
    threat of erastianism, 21
    Tractarianism, effect of, 12, 217
Church of England Men's Society of New South Wales, 145

Church of Ireland, 12, 21, 30, 44, 49, 76, 187–88, 190, 192–93, 201–6, 212–14, 226–27
Church of Ireland Gazette, 209
Church of Scotland, 95
Church Standard—Anglo-Catholic church newspaper, 152
Churchman, The—Evangelical journal, 41, 92, 124, 214
CICCU. *See* Cambridge Inter-Collegiate Christian Union
Clarke, William Branwhite, 21, 37
Clarke, William Newton, 36, 145, 159–60, 173
Claydon, Ernest Henry Beales, 150
CMS—Church Missionary Society, 133, 218, 258
CMS College, Islington, 133
Cole, Edmund Keith, 258
Colenso, John William, 14, 16, 29
Coleridge, Samuel Taylor, 14, 16, 18, 30, 168, 173
Congregational Church, Pitt Street, Sydney, 172
Conybeare, William John, 129
Council of Trent, 24, 41, 89, 96, 180, 199, 215–16, 228, 266
Cowper, William, 22, 53
Cowper, William Macquarie, 54–55, 59, 64, 81
Cranmer, Thomas, 24, 90, 193, 230, 259, 267
creeds, 86, 111, 166, 198, 200, 210, 216, 232, 235, 251
Crosslinks. *See* Bible Churchmen's Missionary Society
Crozier, John Baptist, 213
Cunningham, William, 15, 127, 131–32, 137, 139, 155

D

d'Arcy, Charles Frederick, 29, 190, 195, 218
Dale, Robert William, 35, 171
Daniel, Book of, 32, 37, 75, 78, 168, 193
Darby, John Nelson, 44, 75

INDEX

Darwin, Charles, 19–21, 37–39, 165, 191, 251
Darwin, Erasmus, 19
Darwinism, 12–14, 51
Davies, David—father of D.J. Davies, 123
Davies, David John
- 'The Heretics', 174, 176–79, 183
- appointment as principal, Moore College, 123, 126, 139, 141–42, 196, 261, 264
- Archbishop Wright—relations with, 136, 154, 196, 261, 264
- associates of Davies, 40, 48, 64, 125, 128, 132–33, 142–43, 147–48, 150, 161–62, 180, 185, 265
- atonement, doctrine of, 35, 134–37, 139, 169, 171–72, 179, 185, 235
- background and early years, 15, 123, 124
- Bible–his view of the Bible, 14, 30, 127, 129–30, 137, 146, 148–52, 157–62, 164, 166–68, 175, 178–80, 183, 185, 219, 220, 264
- constitution of the Church of England in Australia, 144, 152, 180, 263
- critics of, 149–51, 157, 159, 161–62, 165, 176
- death, 64, 133, 184, 262, 266
- disappointment at election of Archbishop Mowll, 179, 265
- doctrinal position, 35, 43, 51, 149–50, 160, 165, 173, 179–82, 203, 216, 247
- doctrinal position—sacraments, 145, 178
- freemason, 139, 144, 153, 161–62, 167–69, 172
- Group Brotherhood, 33, 35–36, 62, 64, 123, 125, 128, 139–41, 169, 264
- Gunther Memorial Lecture, 181–83
- Heretics Club, 163–64, 166
- impact on his students, 184, 265
- influence at Moore College, 27, 151, 162, 174, 265, 268
- influence in the Diocese of Sydney, 6, 36, 62, 142, 144, 152, 154, 157, 163, 183–85, 265
- junior cleric and Cambridge don, 133–38
- liberal position, 4–5, 29, 62, 64, 127, 131, 133–36, 138–39, 145–51, 153, 156–61, 163, 165–66, 170–79, 181, 183, 185, 198, 201, 210, 227, 236–37, 248, 262, 264–65
- marriage, 141
- Moorhouse Lectures, 144, 155–61
- preaching, 85, 133, 136, 142, 145, 167, 169–72
- principal of Moore College, 1, 62–63, 133, 143, 145, 147, 162, 183–85, 218, 263
- published work, 146, 181–83
- student years, 15, 18, 20, 35, 42, 63, 123–33, 136, 146, 159, 190, 266
- theology, 89, 126–31, 135–36, 138, 148–49, 152, 155, 160–61, 165–67, 169, 171–72, 174, 177, 179–80, 182–83, 216, 221–22, 231–32, 235, 262

Davies, Grace Augusta—wife of D.J. Davies, 63, 141, 184
Davies, Sarah—mother of D.J. Davies, 123
Deaconess House, 2, 265
deism, 16, 19
Denman, Stephen Henry, 60
Denney, James, 35, 84, 132, 134, 169, 191, 195, 223
Descent of Man, 20, 38
Deuteronomy, 31
Dewick, Edward Chisholm, 146, 147
Dibelius, Martin, 253
Dickey, Brian Kenneth, 8
Digges La Touche, Everard
- death, 152
- doctrinal position, 62, 166
- Donnellan Lecturer, 147, 195
- Evangelical position, 39, 143, 148–51, 162
- impact on Moore College students, 147–48, 159
- lecturer, Moore College, 40, 142, 145–48

Digges La Touche, Everard (*continued*)
    opposition to D.J. Davies, 145, 147–48, 152, 157, 161, 218
    scholarship, 147, 158, 253
    theology, 40, 150, 253
Dillman, Christian Friedrich August, 32
Dimock, Nathaniel, 42, 216
Diocese of Sydney, 1, 3–4, 32, 40, 50, 56, 63, 65, 144, 187, 217, 228, 261, 265, 268
Dispensationalism, 44, 50, 158, 242
doctrine of God, 27–28, 191
Dods, Marcus, 158–61
Donatist Dispute, 211
Donnellan Lectures, 143, 147, 190–191, 195
Driver, Samuel Rolles, 17, 20, 69, 193
Drury, Thomas Wortley, 42, 146
Dutch Reformed Church, 40, 76

E

Ecclesiological Society, 23
Eddington, Arthur Stanley, 126, 132, 179
Edersheim, Alfred, 70
Edwards, Benjamin, 7
Einstein, Albert, 243
Elland Society, 124, 141
Elliott, Edward Bishop, 45
Elliott-Binns, Leonard Elliott, 11, 138
Emmanuel College, Cambridge, 11, 133, 137–39, 180
English Church Union, 24, 42
Epicurus, 19
Erastianism, 21, 24, 174
eschatology, 46, 50, 101, 108, 129, 146–47
Essays and Reviews, 13, 16, 19, 28–29, 45, 60, 69–70, 72
ethics, 125, 243–46
Eusebius of Caesarea, 204
evangelical
    Evangelical party, 67, 134
    influence at Moore College, 1–2, 4, 27, 53–54, 58–59, 261, 268
    influence in the Diocese of Sydney, 1–3, 49, 54, 61, 63–64, 67, 200, 265–66, 268
    response to liberalism, 32, 181
    school of thought, 61, 175, 228, 262
Evangelical Churchman's Association, Melbourne, 108
Evangelical Revival, 160, 191, 216, 217
Evangelical spectrum
    broadening, 9, 26–27, 32, 34, 59, 61, 64, 138–40, 144, 162, 178, 181, 262, 264, 268
    conservative, 50, 57, 73, 82, 101, 119–20, 166, 227, 229, 260, 262, 266
    liberal, 50, 62, 123, 133
    premillennial thinking, 49, 59, 80, 85, 100
Evangelicalism *See also* Liberal Evangelicalism
    challenges faced by, 20, 27–43, 61, 70, 144, 148, 150, 181, 216, 234, 241
    characteristics, 43, 50, 61, 65, 67, 73, 80, 85, 99, 101, 115, 120–21, 155, 160, 188, 205, 229, 231, 262, 264
    conservative, 1, 63–64, 82, 119, 144, 150, 152, 158, 161, 166, 173, 183–85, 187, 193, 198, 258
    history of, 44, 48
    opposition to Anglo-Catholicism, 2, 41, 62, 205
Evangelicalism—publication by the Fellowship of Evangelical Churchmen, 218
Evangelicals
    Archdall, M., 34, 42, 43, 61–62, 86, 94, 119, 143, 148–49, 151, 161–62
    Begbie, H.S., 60, 106, 151, 237, 239
    Birks, T.R., 27–28, 33–35, 46, 50, 126
    Boultbee, T.P., 28, 30, 41, 83, 129, 189
    Chambers, G.A., 4, 90, 126, 161
    Chavasse, F.J., 141
    Christopher, A.M.W., 73, 77
    Cowper, W., 53
    Cowper, W.M., 54–55, 59, 64, 81
    Digges La Touche, E., 39–40, 62, 142, 145, 147–52, 157–59, 161–62, 166, 195, 218
    Dimock, N., 1
    Drury, T.W., 42
    Goodhew, R.H., 259

INDEX

Grubb, G.C., 49–50, 60, 67, 77, 120
Hervey, A.C., 31
Heurtley, C.A., 37, 41, 71, 83
Hilliard, W.G., 144, 267
Hodge, C., 29, 36, 171
Hodgson, W., 55, 58, 60
Howe, H.G.J., 106, 144, 161, 167–68
Johnson, D., 230
Johnstone, S.M., 143–44, 148–49, 151, 161
King, R.L., 55, 58, 61
Kirkby, S J., 60, 64, 145, 149, 266
Knox, D.B., 2–4, 97, 179, 259
Knox, D.J., 98, 259
Knox, E.A., 14, 25, 34, 43, 133, 215, 218–19
Langford Smith, S.E., 60, 151, 161
Litton, E.A., 28–30, 35–38, 41–42, 47, 50, 135, 139, 169, 192, 203, 213
Macartney, H.B., 49
Manley, G.T., 39, 191, 223
Moule, H.C.G., 22
Robinson, D.W.B., 216, 259
Robinson, R.B., 60, 106, 162, 237, 259
Robinson, Thomas, 68, 91
Ryle, J.C., 32, 41, 45, 49, 57, 59, 73, 76, 78, 141
Salmon, G., 39, 123, 129, 190, 192, 227, 253
Short, K.H., 258–59
Simeon, C., 37, 53–54, 57, 216
Thomas, W.H. Griffith, 29, 31, 39–40, 42, 61, 68, 73, 90, 108, 116, 118, 141, 193, 258, 266
Tress, H.L., 64, 161–62, 167, 266
Wace, H., 31–32, 47, 73, 113, 139, 176–79, 187, 191–93, 218
Williams, A.L., 56, 58, 60
Evans, Daniel, 76
evolution, 39, 182
external authority, 132, 138, 153, 175, 198, 201–221, 232, 266

F

Fall of Man, 237, 245

Farrar, Frederic William, 70, 76, 219
Fausset, Andrew Robert, 37, 45–46, 95
Fellowship of Evangelical Churchmen, 218
Fletcher, Brian Hinton, 5
Frame, Thomas Robert, 3
Fraser, Alexander Campbell, 195
Free Church of Scotland, 37
free will, 13
freemasonry, 139, 144, 153, 157, 162, 168–69, 172, 179
Fremantle, William Henry, 45
Frere, Walter Howard, 152, 213
Froude, Richard Hurrell, 217

G

Garnsey, Arthur Henry, 7, 142, 184, 241, 249–50
Garnsey, David Arthur, 7
General Synod, Church of England in Australia, 144
General Synod, Church of Ireland, 204, 213
Genesis, Book of, 20, 38, 51, 157, 240, 252
Gibbon, Edward, 210
Gibbons, James, 208–9
Gibson, Edgar Charles Sumner, 83
Gifford Lectures, 126, 131–32, 165
Girdlestone, Robert Baker, 32, 71
Gladstone, William Ewart, 217
Glanville, George Corrie, 144, 162
Gleaners' Union, 119
God, immanence of, 14, 29, 194–96, 233
God, sovereignty of, 13
God, transcendence of, 14, 29, 51, 196–97, 233, 252
Goe, Field Flowers, 60, 74, 81
Goode, William, 41, 95, 216
Goodhew, Richard Henry 'Harry', 259
Gore, Charles, 15, 84, 134–36, 164, 217, 222
Goulburn, diocese of, 2, 56, 58, 142
Graf-Kuenen-Wellhausen hypothesis, 30
Green, John Richard, 75
Green, Thomas Hill, 15, 29, 69, 72, 125, 127, 135, 149, 155, 190, 195, 245–47, 251

Green, William Henry, 31
Grensted, Laurence William, 224
Griffin, Edward H., 195
Griffith Thomas, W.H. *See* Thomas, W.H. Griffith
Grindal, Edmund, 213
Group Brotherhood, 33, 35–36, 47, 61–62, 64, 123, 125, 133, 138–39, 141–42, 169, 217–18, 264
Grubb, George Carleton, 49–50, 60, 67, 77, 120
Guinness, Fanny Emma, 46
Guinness, Henry Grattan, 46
Gunther Memorial Lectures, 181, 242, 249
Günther, William James, 34
Gwatkin, Henry Melvill, 64, 129, 131, 135, 138, 165, 211

H

Haeckel, Ernst Heinrich Philipp August, 14, 20, 36, 250
Hammond, Colman, father of T.C. Hammond, 188
Hammond, Elizabeth, mother of T.C. Hammond, 188
Hammond, James Henry, brother of T.C. Hammond, 188
Hammond, Margaret, wife of T.C. Hammond, 193
Hammond, Robert Brodribb Stewart, 50
Hammond, Thomas Chatterton
  apologetics, 249, 253, 267
  appointment as principal, Moore College, 5, 27, 64–65, 162, 184, 229–30, 262–63, 266
  Archbishop Mowll—relations with, 43, 249–50, 265, 267–68
  associates of Hammond, 29, 39–40, 43, 65, 143, 179, 195, 215, 225, 230, 239, 259, 266–67
  atonement, doctrine of, 191, 194, 223–25, 227, 234–36, 239, 259
  background and early years, 7, 188–89
  Bible—his view of, 5, 159, 197, 199, 203, 219–22, 227, 232, 236, 238, 240, 252, 256, 258
  Church of Ireland, 13, 25, 193–94, 203–4, 210, 212–14, 226
  conservative position, 250, 262
  constitution of the Church of England in Australia, 5, 205, 214, 267
  controversialist, 7, 196, 205, 207–8, 210, 212, 214, 216–17, 238, 249, 253–54, 257, 267
  counters sinless perfectionism, 7
  doctrinal position, 3, 7, 28, 43, 65, 191, 205, 208, 223–25, 229–30, 236, 262
  doctrinal position—sacraments, 203, 257, 267
  ethics, 28, 243–46, 249–50, 260, 267
  Gunther Memorial Lectures, 242, 249
  impact on his students, 65, 258–59, 267
  influence at Moore College, 6, 193, 240, 259, 262, 268
  influence in the Diocese of Sydney, 200, 205, 240, 242, 250, 260, 268
  Inter-Varsity Fellowship, 200, 228, 240, 249, 267
  Irish Church Missions, 189, 206, 208, 217, 230, 250
  Katoomba Christian Convention, 50, 106, 237–38
  marriage, 193, 205
  Memorialists, 5, 7–8, 250, 265, 267
  negative view of, 5
  philosophical outlook, 14
  premillennialism—views on, 27, 47, 49
  principal of Moore College, 1, 3, 32, 55, 95, 197, 217, 220, 225, 249
  published work, 8, 189, 196, 208, 215, 217–19, 227, 229–47, 249, 253–57, 266
  Red Book Case, 7–8, 205, 214, 267
  retirement, 65, 229
  Roman Catholic Church, 202, 206, 208–9, 211–12, 215
  sermons, 243, 259

INDEX

student years, 18, 20, 32–33, 35, 42, 189–93, 204, 246, 266
theology, 29–30, 73, 89, 96, 131, 171, 181, 187–88, 194–201, 215–16, 218, 223, 226–27, 229–48, 250–57, 260, 266
visit to Australia in 1926, 65, 174, 176, 197, 217, 241, 263, 265
Hammond, Thomas Chatterton. *See also* titles of his major books—*In Understanding Be Men, New Creation, One Hundred Texts, Perfect Freedom, Reasoning Faith, So Great Salvation*
Handful of Corn Upon the Top of the Mountains, 101
Hardwick, Charles, 83
Harford-Battersby, Thomas Dundas, 48
Harnack, Carl Gustav Adolph von, 32
Harris, Brian, 9
Haslam, William, 73, 76–77
Head, Frederick Waldgrave, 137
Headlam, Arthur Cayley, 70, 135, 194
Heber, Reginald, 54
Hegel, Georg Wilhelm Friedrich, 15, 17–18, 28, 30, 150, 190, 197, 220, 240–41
Hegelian idealism, 30, 197, 220, 240–41
Henderson, Grace, 74
Henslow, George, 20
Henson, Herbert Hensley, 199
Heretics—The Heretics Society (Cambridge), 138, 143, 163
Heretics, The (Sydney), 8, 138, 143, 146, 163–65, 173–74, 176, 179, 241
Hervey, Arthur Charles, 31
Heurtley, Charles Abel, 37, 41, 71, 83
High Church
 appeal of Tractarianism, 22
 episcopal authority, 95, 97
 presence in Sydney, 9, 54, 57–59, 70, 152, 261
 sacramentalism, 97–98, 256
 students at Moore College, 59, 261–62, 268
 T.C. Hammond's relations with, 187, 192, 201, 226–28, 238, 260
High Churchmen

Bancroft, R., 97
Bernard, J.H., 190–92, 203, 213–14
Bull, G., 22, 134
Evans, D., 76
Hutton, W.H., 152
Ince, W., 71, 97
Laud, W., 44, 256
Schleicher, B.A., 57–59, 70, 261
Wordsworth, C., 214
Wordsworth, J., 71
higher Christian life, 103
higher criticism, 31, 33–34, 57, 71, 86, 136, 148, 150, 153, 241
Hill, Thomas Ernest, 56
Hilliard, David, 2
Hilliard, William George, 144, 267
Hodge, Charles, 29, 36, 171
Hodgson, William, 55, 58, 61
Holbach, Paul-Henri Thiry d', Baron, 19
holiness
 H.C.G. Moule—teaching on holiness, 59, 102, 106, 121, 257, 266
 holiness of God, 21, 90–91, 103, 109
 Keswick view of holiness, 1, 48–49, 59, 63, 76, 82, 101, 106, 121, 124, 262, 267–68
 Nathaniel Jones—teaching on holiness, 63, 68, 76–77, 80, 87–90, 102–3, 106–9, 112, 114, 119–21, 237, 262–63, 266
 personal holiness, 48, 50, 103, 106–7, 112, 120–21, 263, 268
 premillenarianism—connection with holiness, 26, 43, 50, 81, 106, 262
 search for holiness, 26, 40, 47–49, 59, 88–89, 120, 257
 T.C. Hammond—teaching on holiness, 237, 255, 257, 262, 268
Holland, Henry Scott, 15
Holy Communion, 42, 109, 171, 238
Holy Spirit
 D.J. Davies—teaching on the Holy Spirit, 151–52, 160, 179
 doctrine of the Holy Spirit, 86, 110–11, 232, 235–36, 239, 245, 248, 256
 inspiration of the Scriptures, 30, 151–52, 199, 221, 232

Holy Spirit (*continued*)
  Nathaniel Jones—teaching on the Holy Spirit, 78, 83, 86, 88–89, 91, 102, 109–110, 112, 117, 119, 248
  Roman Catholic doctrine of the Holy Spirit, 207
  T.C. Hammond—teaching on the Holy Spirit, 199, 232, 235–36, 239, 248, 256–57
  work of the Holy Spirit in the Christian believer, 7, 48, 78, 88, 91, 102, 109, 112, 117, 120, 135, 160, 221, 236, 248, 256–57
  work of the Holy Spirit in the church, 236
Holy Trinity Church, Cambridge, 27, 33–34, 53, 130, 133–34, 136–71
Holy Trinity Church, Dublin, 68
Hooker, Richard, 86, 94, 96, 110, 129, 207, 212
Hopkins, Evan Henry, 48–49, 76, 79, 102, 121
Hort, Fenton John Anthony, 16–17, 71
House of Commons, UK Parliament, 173, 214–15
House of Lords, UK Parliament, 24
Howard, Richard Thomas, 169–70, 224
Howe, Harry George James, 106, 144, 161, 167–68
Howson, John Saul, 129
Hume, David, 28, 251
Hunkin, Joseph Wellington, 47, 133, 138, 183–84
Hutchison, Wilfred, 249
Hutton, William Holden, 152
Huxley, Thomas Henry, 13, 20, 27, 39, 88, 91, 164–65, 196, 251–52

I

ICM—Irish Church Missions, 187–189, 206, 208, 217, 230
idealism
  challenge to the concept of God, 84, 191, 194
  Coleridge, S.T, 14
  dominance of, 15, 51, 190, 195, 241
  Hegelian idealism, 197, 241
  influence on D.J. Davies, 29, 126, 142, 169, 179, 182
  Kantian idealism, 14, 17, 94, 132, 175, 182, 254
  opposition to theism, 17, 29
Illingworth, John Richardson, 126, 129, 149
immanence of God, 29, 194–96, 233
immanentism, 15, 196, 198, 228
In Understanding Be Men, 228–30, 266–67
Incarnation, 109, 166, 195, 235, 244
Ince, William, 71, 97
infallibility of the Bible, 159, 164, 175, 198, 218
Inge, William Ralph, 127, 146, 172
inspiration of the Bible, 30–32, 35, 40, 64, 118, 147, 158, 160, 162, 164, 171, 175, 218–23, 232, 266
Inter-Varsity Fellowship of Evangelical Unions, 39, 197, 200, 217, 223, 228–30, 232, 238, 240, 243, 249, 268
Irish Book of Common Prayer, 25
Irish Church Missions, 187, 189, 205–6, 212, 250
Irish Church Quarterly, 202
Irish Church Union, 204
Isaiah, Book of, 133, 136, 153
IVF *See* Inter-Varsity Fellowship of Evangelical Unions

J

James, William, 195
Jetson Exhibition, 124
Jeune, Francis, 28
Johnson, Douglas, 230
Johnson, Richard, 21, 53
Johnstone, Samuel Martin, 143–44, 148–49, 151, 161
Joint Board of Theological Studies, 143
Jones, Grace, wife of Nathaniel, 34, 75, 78, 80
Jones, John, father of Nathaniel Jones, 68

INDEX

Jones, Nathaniel. *See also* titles of his main work—*A Handful of Corn Upon the Top of the Mountains, Arise, Shine, Our Daily Sacrifice, Teaching of the Thirty-nine Articles, Resurrection Life*; See also Prayer Book *and* Thirty-nine Articles
  associates of Jones, 42, 61–62, 68, 73, 75, 86, 94, 108, 118, 143–45, 200, 258, 264
  Bible—his view of the Bible, 84–85, 87–89, 92–93, 96, 99, 101–2, 107, 110–11, 118, 120, 232, 263
  critics of, 4, 113
  death, 141, 264
  Dickens—interest in, 75
  doctrinal position, 4, 27–28, 34, 39, 43, 59–60, 67, 70, 82, 84–100, 120, 132, 156, 158, 181, 216, 237, 242, 248, 257, 262–63, 264
  doctrinal position—sacraments, 97–99, 105
  early ministry, 74–76, 80–81, 108
  early years, 68
  Evangelical convictions, 27
  health problems, 74, 78, 116
  holiness—his view of, 27, 88, 107, 266
  impact on his students, 4, 47, 82, 104, 106, 145, 161–62, 167, 176, 237, 239, 263–66
  influence at Moore College, 1, 4, 59–60, 73, 82, 90, 108, 261, 268
  influence in the Diocese of Sydney, 5, 34, 60–61, 263, 265
  Katoomba Christian Convention, 101–5
  lasting influence, 2, 50, 62–65, 98, 100, 179, 184–85, 203, 217, 227, 259, 263–65
  marriage, 74
  nominates Griffith Thomas as archbishop, 61
  piety, 75–76, 78–79, 105, 109–112, 121, 263, 268
  premilleniallist views, 4, 27, 44–45, 48, 63, 67–68, 81, 85, 104, 106, 120, 158, 262–63
  principal of Moore College, 1, 22, 43, 67, 74, 81–82, 93, 106, 261
  published work, 82–83, 86, 109, 111–19, 160
  sermons, 67, 75–78, 107–9, 119–20
  student years, 14, 17, 22, 29–30, 35, 41–42, 44, 60, 68–73, 92, 125–26, 131
Jowett, Benjamin, 18, 28, 69–70
Judd, Stephen, 4, 8
Junior Clerical Society of Sydney, 154
jus liturgicum, 43
justification by faith, 64, 70, 89
justification by faith, doctrine of
  evangelical position, 41, 102, 105–6, 119–20, 134, 216, 227, 236–37
  Reformation doctrine, 47, 98, 112, 115, 176–77, 180, 256, 266
  T.C. Hammond's position, 215, 225–227, 236, 255
justification, doctrine of
  Anglo-Catholic doctrine, 22
  D.J. Davies's position, 134–36, 139, 179, 236, 264–65
  liberal position, 257
  rejection of Evangelical position, 134
  Roman Catholic doctrine, 41, 90, 181, 215, 237, 256

K

Kant, Immanuel, 4, 14, 17, 28, 94, 127, 132, 134, 173, 175, 190, 194, 196, 198, 221, 246, 253–54
Katoomba Christian Convention, 50, 101, 106, 229, 237–38, 263–64, 268
Kaye, Bruce Norman, 4, 5
Keble, John, 21–22, 93, 145, 179, 215–17
Kelvin, William Thomson, Lord, 39, 191
Keswick, 1, 6, 12, 26–27, 48–50, 59, 61, 63, 67, 73, 76–77, 80, 82, 101–3, 106, 112, 114, 118, 121, 124, 184–85, 216, 237, 257, 262, 267–68
Keswick Convention, 48–49, 79, 103, 133
Keynes, John Maynard, 132
King, Robert Lethbridge, 55, 58, 61
King's College, London, 73

King-Hall, George Fowler, 147
Kingsley, Charles, 75
Kirk, Kenneth Escott, 224
Kirkby, Sydney James, 60, 64, 145, 149, 266
Knox, David Broughton, 2–4, 97, 179, 259
Knox, David James, 60, 64, 98, 161, 259
Knox, Edmund Arbuthnott, 14, 25, 34, 43, 61, 63, 133, 215, 218–19
Kuyper, Abraham, 33, 40, 136, 245, 257

L

La Touche, Digges. *See* Digges La Touche, which is the correct name
Lady of England, a, 75
Lambeth Conference, 1897, 34, 43, 59, 81
Langford Smith, Sydney Edgar, 60, 151, 161
Langley, Henry Archdall, 81
Langley, John Douse, 81, 107
Langshaw, Reginald Norman, 185
Last Things, 147, 238
Lateran Council, 211, 215
Latimer, Hugh, 129
Laud, William, 44, 256
Lawe, Grace Augusta, 141
Lawton, William John, 4, 6
Lees, Harrington Clare, 138
Lessing, Gotthold Ephraim, 199
Lias, John James, 32
Liberal Evangelicalism
 impact on Diocese of Sydney, 1, 123, 133, 141
 impact on Moore College, 1, 162
 opposition to ritualism, 51, 262
 theological outlook, 36, 92, 125, 128, 131, 133, 135, 138, 141, 183, 237, 262, 264
 view of Scripture, 127, 129, 131, 133, 163, 236
Liberal Evangelicalism—publication by Group Brotherhood, 47, 128, 133, 169, 218, 224
Liberal Evangelicals. *See also*—Wright, J.C.

Davies, D.J., 1, 27, 29–30, 33, 35–36, 40, 42–43, 48, 51, 62–64, 85, 89, 123–85, 190, 196, 198, 201, 203, 210, 216, 218–22, 227, 231–32, 235–36, 238, 247–48, 261–66, 268
Glanville, G. C., 144, 162
Grensted, L.W., 224
Gwatkin, H.M., 129, 131, 135, 138, 211
Hunkin, J.W., 133
Talbot, A.E., 62, 123, 129, 132–33, 140, 142, 145, 147, 184, 247
Liddon, Henry Parry, 37, 92
Lightfoot, Joseph Barber, 17, 34, 56, 57, 71, 164
Little Flock theory, 4, 67, 81, 263
Litton, Edward Arthur, 13, 28, 30, 35–38, 41–42, 47, 50, 135, 139, 169, 192, 203, 213
Loane, Marcus Lawrence
 associates, 64, 82
 biographer of Archbishop Mowll, 7
 historian of Moore College, 4–5
 Katoomba Christian Convention, 106
 principal of Moore College, 40, 255, 258–59
 staff member of Moore College, 6, 64, 185, 266
 view of Archbishop Mowll, 7
 view of D.J. Davies, 124, 145, 179, 181, 183, 185
 view of Nathaniel Jones, 4, 101, 121
 view of T.C. Hammond, 6, 255, 260
 writings, 6
Loane, Patricia, 65
London University, 230
London University College Christian Association, 191
Lord's Supper, 35, 42, 97–98, 105, 112, 114, 173, 178, 193, 215, 223, 230, 259, 267
Lucretius, 19
Luther, Martin, 89–90, 110, 115, 136, 174–79
Lux Mundi, 15, 18, 40, 60, 69, 93, 126, 135, 164
Lyell, Charles, 19

INDEX

M

Macartney, Hussey Burgh, 49, 50
Machen, John Gresham, 129, 173
Maclear, George Frederick, 83, 129
Macran, Frederick Walter, 18, 191
Macran, Henry Stewart, 190
Magee, William, 227
Mahaffy, John Pentland, 190
Major, Henry Dewsbury Alves, 134
Malthus, Thomas, 19
Manley, George Thomas, 39, 191, 223
Mann, William John George., 162
Mansel, Henry Longueville, 28
Margoliouth, David Samuel, 32, 191
Marsden, Samuel, 21, 53
Marshall, Walter, 7
Martineau, Harriet, 125
Mason, Arthur James, 129
materialism, 14, 39, 252
Maurice, Frederick Denison, 15–16, 18, 35, 70, 127, 131, 135, 171, 173
McGillion, Chris, 3
McGowen, James Sinclair Taylor, 154
McNay, John, 188, 193
McNeile, Alan Hugh, 192
McTaggart, John McTaggart Ellis, 125
Mede, Joseph, 44
Melbourne, diocese of, 2, 38, 49–50, 56, 58, 60, 74, 81, 107–8, 110, 137–38, 145, 179–80
Memorial—protest to Archbishop Mowll, 249–50, 265
Memorialists, 7–8, 267
Mildmay Conference, 45, 48, 68, 124
Mill, John Stuart, 14, 27–28, 69, 72, 91
millennialism, 10
Miller, Hugh, 37
Mitchell, Joseph, 74
Moberly, Robert Campbell, 18, 223
Modern Churchmen's Union, Cambridge, 128, 133, 138, 183
Modern Utilitarianism (book by T.R. Birks), 27
modernism, 47, 63, 91, 127–29, 134, 143, 147, 169, 172, 181, 183, 185, 221, 241, 257

Momerie, Alfred Williams, 73
Monier-Williams, Monier, 70
Moody, Dwight Lyman, 48, 68–69, 71, 76, 78–79, 123
Moore College
  appointment of D.J. Davies as principal, 126, 139–40, 196
  appointment of Nathaniel Jones as principal, 51, 67, 74, 78, 81, 108, 261
  appointment of T.C. Hammond as principal, 187, 197, 228–30, 263
  Davies's liberal influence, 50, 62, 123, 133, 143, 148, 150–51, 160, 173, 220, 241
  Digges La Touche's impact on, 40, 143, 148
  Evangelical character of, 1–3, 9, 26, 55, 59–60, 63, 65, 79–81, 100, 106–7, 261–262, 264, 268
  foundation and early years, 2, 53, 55–58, 60
  long-lasting influence of Nathaniel Jones, 4, 34, 41, 43, 47, 73–74, 82, 95, 98, 100, 104, 108, 119, 121, 161, 167, 179, 189, 265
  T.C. Hammond's conservative Evangelical influence, 32, 193, 195, 197, 217, 225, 229, 240, 242, 249, 255, 266–68
  teaching at Moore College, 27, 29, 51, 58, 63, 152–53, 174, 216, 238, 249, 255
Moore College Committee, 62–63, 161–62, 165, 167, 183–84, 263
Moore College staff members
  Chambers, G.A., 4, 90, 126, 161
  Cole, E.K., 258
  Digges La Touche, E., 142, 145, 147
  Glanville, G.C., 144, 162
  Kirkby, S.J., 145
  Knox, D.B., 259
  Morton, A.W., 258
  Patton, J.V., 145
  Robinson, D.W.B., 216
  Smith, B.L., 259
  Talbot, A.E., 145, 147

Moore College staff members. *See also* Loane, Marcus Lawrence
Moore Theological College. *See* Moore College
Moore, George Edward, 125, 132
Moore, Thomas, 55
Moorhouse Lectures, 144, 155, 161
Moorhouse, James, 110
Morling, George Henry, 7
Morris, Leon Lamb, 225, 259
Morton, Archibald Wentworth, 258
Moule, Handley Carr Glyn
  Bishop of Durham, 125
  doctrinal position, 13, 29, 38, 67, 73, 79, 83, 92, 94, 97–98, 102, 106, 108, 111, 129, 134–35, 189, 192, 195
  Evangelical position, 49, 91, 102, 114, 121, 139, 169, 266
  exegesis, 102, 257
  opposition to Anglo-Catholicism, 22, 41, 42
  premillennial views, 47, 59, 67, 263
  Professor of Divinity, 31
  theologian, 31, 35, 41, 49, 158, 263
Mowll, Howard West Kilvinton
  associates, 161, 187, 249–50, 265–68
  Bishop of West China, 161
  close association with Bishop E. A. Knox, 43, 63
  conservative Evangelical position, 5, 7, 43, 63–64, 184, 261, 265–66, 268
  early ministry, 43
  elected archbishop, 60, 63, 161, 163, 176, 179, 183–184, 261–262, 265
  Katoomba Christian Convention, 237
  Memorialists, 5, 249–50, 265–67
  opposition to ritualism, 43
  Red Book Case, 267
  role in diocese, 4, 64, 106, 184–85, 187
  selection of principals of Moore College, 27, 64, 258, 262
  student years, 31, 63, 133, 250, 266
Mozley, John Kenneth, 36, 75, 84, 127, 146, 169, 171
Murray, Andrew, 76
Muscio, Bernard, 126

N

Nash, Clifford Harris, 7
national apostasy
  Keble's Assize sermon in 1833, 93, 179, 215
National Assembly of the Church of England, 25
naturalism, 34, 38, 126
Neale, John Mason, 23
Neil, Charles, 193, 267
Nelson, Warren, 8, 214
neutrality (religious), 28, 50, 158, 197, 253
New Creation, The, 229, 236, 255, 257, 267
New Education Fellowship, 254
New South Wales Council of Churches, 144
New Testament
  canon of the New Testament, 129, 151, 168, 199, 222, 232, 252
  commentary on, 18, 44, 96–97, 129, 223–24, 226–27
  critical study of, 31–34, 128, 192, 209, 224, 241, 250, 253, 256
  defense of, 18, 87
  Mowll's statement of support, 64
  negative criticism of, 16
  reading of the New Testament, 109, 111
  reliability of the New Testament, 17
  teaching of the New Testament, 94, 109, 143
  text of, 22, 24, 71, 94, 149–50, 167, 189, 225, 244
  theology of the New Testament, 35, 87–88, 94–95, 120, 135, 169–70, 172, 183, 222, 224, 231, 257
Newman, John Henry, 22–23, 41, 83, 180–81, 208–209, 217

O

O'Brien, James Thomas, 227
Ogden, Charles Kay, 138
Old Testament

canon of the Old Testament, 31–32,
  84, 86, 150–51, 168, 222, 252
critical study of, 30, 33, 58, 60,
  128–29, 136, 164, 193, 220, 224,
  231, 241–42
historicity of, 17, 32
progressive revelation, 31, 34, 131,
  136, 148, 153, 158, 170, 183, 220
responses to criticism, 30–33, 69–70,
  136, 150–51, 222
teaching of the Old Testament, 31,
  84, 109, 111, 147, 258
theology of the Old Testament, 17,
  111, 120, 170, 183, 219
Olevianus, 257
Oman, John Wood, 199
One Hundred Texts, 189, 229
Origin of Species, 13, 19–20, 37, 60, 251
original sin, 18, 88, 194
Orr, James, 29, 32–35, 136, 195, 219,
  233, 251
Our Daily Sacrifice, 109, 112, 118
Oxford Assize sermon, 21–22, 145, 179,
  215–16
Oxford Movement, 12, 23, 216

P

Packer, James Innell, 29, 49, 255
Paget, Francis, 69
Paine, Thomas, 19
Paley, William, 13, 20, 27–28
Papal Infallibility, 175, 207–8
Parker Society, 41
Parker, Matthew, 213
Parry, Reginald St John, 124
Patton, James Valentine, 144–45
Paul IV, Pope, 212
Pelagianism, 27, 88, 92, 236
Pennefather, William, 45, 48, 68
Pentateuch, 14, 16–17, 29, 31
Perfect Freedom, 229, 243, 250, 255
Perry Divinity Hall, Bendigo, 74, 76, 108
Perry, Charles, 38, 56, 74
Piggin, Stuart, 3, 6
Pivot Points, 229, 240, 242–43
Plato, 15, 190, 245

Plymouth Brethren, 50, 81–82, 93–95,
  97, 200
Porter, Muriel, 3
postmillennialism, 26, 45–46
Powell, Baden, 28
Prayer Book
  Anglo-Catholic attempts at revision,
    25
  Cranmer's role in, 24
  devotional value of, 48, 101, 108–9,
    112, 114, 118
  expression of Reformation doctrine,
    25, 42, 95, 150, 171, 173, 187,
    228, 263, 265
  High Church changes in 1661, 22
  liturgical chaos of ritual innovation,
    25
  Nathaniel Jones and, 73, 76, 78,
    81, 88, 95, 99, 101, 107–9, 112,
    114–18, 121, 263
  revision of, 144, 173, 176, 214, 265
  services, 23, 35, 72, 107–8, 115–18,
    121, 171, 223
  T.C. Hammond and, 189, 194, 258,
    267
  teaching of, 76, 88, 118, 152, 258, 267
  theology of, 42, 44, 67, 108–9, 114,
    136, 170, 173, 213, 260, 263, 267
predestination, 87, 91–92, 181
premillennialism, 1, 26, 37, 43–50, 59,
  61, 63, 67–68, 73, 80–82, 85, 100,
  106, 118, 120–21, 124, 147, 158,
  161, 167–68, 184–85, 216, 238,
  262–63, 266, 268
Presbyterian, 76, 82–85
Presbyterian Church of New South
  Wales, 183
Privy Council, 25, 204
Procter, Francis—Prayer Book historian,
  213
Proctor, Francis Bartlett—author,
  Classified Gems of Thought, 76
progressive revelation. *See* Revelation,
  progressive
Protestant Church of England Union,
  42, 119
Protestant Dictionary, The, 193, 227

protestantism, 3, 119, 127, 173, 181, 202, 205, 207, 230, 267
Psalms, 30, 110
Pugin, Augustus Welby Northmore, 23
puritans, 44, 255
Pusey, Edward Bouverie, 16–17, 58, 69–70, 75, 217

R

Radford, Lewis Bostock, 142, 146
Ramsey, Arthur Michael, 224
Rashdall, Hastings, 224
rationalism, 2, 11–12, 24, 39, 42, 55, 72, 245, 261–62
Rawlinson, Alfred Edward John, 198, 218
Rawlinson, George, 31, 70
Real Presence
    Anglo-Catholic doctrine of, 22, 24
Reasoning Faith, 229, 249–50, 252, 255
Record, The—Evangelical Church of England newspaper, 41, 49, 57, 113, 124, 128
Red Book Case, 7–8, 205, 214, 267
Reformation
    Anglo-Catholic view of, 22
    Church of Ireland, 194, 212, 226, 266
    Counter Reformation, 208, 212
    D.J. Davies's 'Heretics' papers, 174–79
    D.J. Davies's view of, 136, 174
    English Reformation, 99, 121, 187–88, 200, 203–4, 211, 213–14, 265
    justification by faith—doctrine of, 47, 180, 236–37, 256, 266
    legacy of, 35, 42, 57, 59, 65, 87, 93, 101, 115, 118–19, 152, 160, 173–75, 185, 200, 227, 265
    Prayer Book, 98–99, 108
    principles of, 24, 73, 86–87, 89, 101, 118, 163, 175, 180, 185, 199
    Reformation Evangelicalism, 25, 76, 80, 95, 109, 197, 206, 229–40, 255, 262
    T.C. Hammond—Reformation Evangelical, 5, 193, 198, 202, 204–5, 208–9, 211, 216–17, 229, 257, 260, 262, 266
    theology, 41–42, 67, 72, 82, 120, 176, 192, 200, 204–5, 213, 216, 223, 226, 228, 232, 235, 238, 240, 247, 260
    Thirty-nine Articles, 83, 87, 215, 265
Religious Discussion Society, Emmanuel College, 138
Renan, Ernest, 14
Resurrection, 40, 44, 85, 104, 114–16, 118, 138–39, 150–51, 165–66, 224, 234, 239, 245, 253, 255, 257
Resurrection Life, 112, 114, 116–18
revelation
    broadening of Evangelical position, 218
    D.J. Davies's position, 148–49, 167, 170, 197, 220–21
    God's revelation of himself, 44, 151, 172, 229, 231, 240–41, 244, 247
    in creation, 27, 37, 151, 182, 236
    in Scripture, 27, 30–32, 157, 159, 178, 200–201, 219, 231, 242, 244–45, 252, 257
    personality of Christ, 149, 151
    progressive, 34, 136, 148, 153, 158, 170, 183, 220
    rejection of Evangelical position, 252–53
    T.C. Hammond's position, 158, 198, 201, 231, 235, 242–45, 250
Revelation, Book of, 167–68, 240
Reynolds, John Stewart, 71
Ridley College, Melbourne, 142, 179, 259
Ridley Hall, Cambridge, 1, 11, 31, 33, 42, 55, 64, 125, 133, 138, 146, 159, 266
Ritschl, Albrecht, 35, 169, 173, 181
ritualism
    archbishops of Sydney intolerance of, 43, 57, 62, 264, 266, 268
    associated with Oxford Movement, 12, 22–23, 77, 96
    challenge to Evangelicals, 11, 24, 26, 42–43, 45, 55, 71, 261, 263, 265

Moore College principals opposed to,
2, 7, 51, 65, 96, 152, 162, 202–3,
262–63, 266
Prayer Book restrictions on, 23, 228,
265
ritualism in Sydney, 24, 119, 261, 265
sacramentalism, associated with,
23–24, 77
spread of, 23, 25, 40, 45
Robertson, James, 31
Robinson, Donald William Bradley, 216,
256, 259
Robinson, Richard Bradley, 60, 106, 162,
237, 259
Robinson, Thomas, 68, 91
Rogers, Thomas, 97
Roman Catholic Church, 54
Roman Catholicism
and the Reformation, 177–78, 204,
207, 211
D.J. Davies's critique of, 177–78, 181,
209, 266
doctrine, 89, 159, 173, 177, 181, 189,
206, 209, 215, 223, 230, 232, 234,
237–38, 256, 260, 266
growing influence in England, 42,
87, 206
Hammond's opposition to, 188–89,
193, 197, 202, 204, 206, 208–212,
215, 225, 250
Nathaniel Jones's critique of, 83–84,
86, 88, 91, 96, 119, 181
presence in Sydney, 82
Roman Catholic Church in Ireland,
187–88, 202, 206, 208, 210–11
Roman Catholic Relief Act 1778, 211
Roman Catholic Relief Act 1829,
209, 211
Roman Catholic theologians, 35, 41,
147, 233
Romanising influences in the Church
of England, 24, 42, 45, 180, 204
theological disputation, 181, 209, 211,
215, 217, 225, 230–31, 250, 255
Roman Catholics
Bellarmine, R., 207
Gibbons, J., 208
McGillion, C., 3, 209

Newman, J.H., 41, 181, 208–9, 217
Romans, Letter to the, 49, 70, 102, 115,
134–36, 171, 233, 257
Romanticism, 47
Row, Charles Adolphus, 76
Royal Commission on Ecclesiastical
Discipline, 25, 43
Rupke, Nicolaas Adrianus, 36
Ruskin, John, 70
Russell, Bertrand Arthur William, 125–
26, 132, 150, 251
Ryle, Herbert Edward, 32–33, 128
Ryle, John Charles, 13, 32, 41, 45, 49, 57,
59, 73, 76, 78, 141

S

Sabellianism, 86
sacraments, 41–42, 96–97, 119, 177, 214,
226, 238, 257, 263
Salmon, George, 18, 39, 123, 129, 190,
192, 227, 253
salvation, 83, 87, 89, 93, 102, 180, 240
sanctification, doctrine of, 44, 73, 89,
102, 105–6, 114, 181, 216, 236–
37, 255, 257
Sanday, William, 18, 70, 135
Sankey, Ira David, 48
Sayce, Archibald Henry, 31, 70, 129
Schleicher, Bernard Alexander, 57–59,
70, 261
Schleicher, John Theophilus, 58
Schleiermacher, Friedrich Daniel Ernst,
35
Schweitzer, Albert, 17, 33, 147
Scripture
authority of, 7, 16, 25, 31, 33, 35, 51,
64, 73, 79, 82, 84, 86, 93, 96, 99,
101–2, 107, 120, 151, 162–63,
174, 177–78, 189, 197, 199, 221,
228, 232, 235, 238, 266
canon of Scripture, 32, 86, 150, 175,
222–32
clarity (perspicuity) of Scripture, 232
critical study of, 34, 36–37, 178, 239,
255

Scripture (*continued*)
  D.J. Davies's position, 14, 62, 64, 127, 146, 148, 151–53, 157–61, 164, 167–68, 173, 235
  Evangelical defense of, 37–38, 51, 87, 96, 99, 120, 150–51, 175, 179–80, 226–27, 234, 236
  God revealed in, 27, 30–31, 88, 105, 148–50, 159, 218–19, 222, 231, 239, 245
  hard literalism, 159
  human element in Scripture, 158–59
  in relation to Church Tradition, 41, 98, 177, 180, 222, 232
  inspiration of, 31, 34, 36, 40, 162, 171, 223, 232, 266
  liberal view of, 16, 26, 33, 146, 148, 150, 159, 169, 185, 198
  moral character of, 36, 120, 160, 169
  Nathaniel Jones' position, 73, 79, 82, 84, 87–89, 93
  negative criticism of, 12, 14, 16–17, 29, 32, 45, 50, 70, 86, 131, 157–58, 184, 199, 243, 250, 253
  reliability of, 139, 150–51
  study of, 72
  sufficiency of, 30, 61, 86, 101, 107, 109, 151, 159, 180, 220, 222, 232, 238, 257
  T.C. Hammond's position, 189, 207, 222, 227, 229, 233, 235–36, 239, 245, 247, 258, 260, 265
Scripture Union, 264
Second Coming of Christ, 40, 45, 68, 103–4, 106
Sedgwick, Adam, 37
Shaftesbury, Anthony Ashley Cooper, 7th Earl of Shaftesbury, 45, 59, 68, 75, 85
Shedd, William Greenough Thayer, 171
Short, Kenneth Herbert, 258–59
Sidgwick, Henry, 125
Simeon, Charles, 37, 53–54, 57, 216
Simpson, Patrick Carnegie, 224
Sinker, Robert, 30–31, 33, 128, 139
sinless perfectionism, 49, 60, 88, 90, 237, 268
Smith, Bruce Leslie, 259

Smith, George Adam, 136
Smith, Robert Pearsall, 48
Smith, William Saumarez
  criticism of Scripture, 34
  death, 60–61
  early ministry, 58
  Evangelical sympathies, 60
  granted title of Archbishop of Sydney, 81, 261
  Lambeth Conference, 1897, 34, 81
  liberal tendency, 57
  opposition to ritualism, 57
  role in diocese, 57–59
  selection of principals of Moore College, 57, 59–60, 67, 81, 261
So Great Salvation, 237, 255
Social Problem Committee of the Diocese of Sydney, 144, 154, 157, 264
Society of Junior Historians, Cambridge, 137
sola fide, 89, 176
sola gratia, 89, 176
sola scriptura, 86–89, 176
solus Christus, 87, 93, 176
Sorley, William Ritchie, 126
sovereignty of God, 92, 233–34, 243, 244, 246
Sozomen, 204
Speier, Diet of, 174
Spencer, Herbert, 20, 38–39, 125–126, 196, 251
Spinoza, Benedict de, 29, 194
Spurgeon, Charles Haddon, 36
St Aidan's College, Birkenhead, 55, 57, 60, 142
St Aldate's Church, Oxford, 73, 77
St Andrew's Cathedral, Sydney, 23, 55, 62, 64, 123, 140, 142, 154, 181, 184, 241–42, 258
St Andrew's Church, Summer Hill, Sydney, 148, 152
St Andrew's College, University of Sydney, 83, 143
St James' Church, King Street, Sydney, 24, 93
St James' College, Sydney, 54
St Kevin's Church, Dublin, 193, 202–3
St Paul's Cathedral, Melbourne, 107, 179

St Paul's Church, Chatswood, 161, 167
St Paul's College, University of Sydney, 7, 57, 142–43, 241, 249
St Philip's Church, York Street, Sydney, 54, 81, 107, 249, 259
Standing Committee of Sydney Synod, 62, 161–62
Stanton, Vincent Henry, 18, 33, 129
Storr, Vernon Faithfull, 11, 183
Strauss, David Friedrich, 14, 16, 241
Streeter, Burnett Hillman, 148
Strong, Augustus Hopkins, 171
Strong, Charles, 240, 242
Strong, Philip Nigel Warrington, 40
Student Christian Movement, 64, 125, 133–34, 145, 238, 250, 268
Student Theological Society, Trinity College, Dublin, 191
Swete, Henry Barclay, 63
Sydney Diocesan Magazine, 144, 146, 169, 173
Sydney Doctrine Commission, 3
Sydney University Evangelical Union, 237, 240, 268
Sydney University Extension Board, 142, 146
Sydney, diocese of. *See* Diocese of Sydney Synod, Sydney Anglican, 2, 34, 57, 59, 61–62, 64, 141, 154–55, 161, 163, 165, 173, 176, 183

T

Tait, Arthur James, 33, 64, 138, 142
Talbot, Albert Edward, 7, 62, 123, 129, 132–33, 140, 142, 145, 147, 184, 247
Tawney, Richard Henry, 173
Taylor, James Hudson, 45
Taylor, Jeremy, 129, 227
TCD. *See* Trinity College, Dublin
Teaching of the Thirty-nine Articles, 90–100
Temple, William, 149
Tennant, Frederick Robert, 127
Thirty-nine Articles
 criticism of, 28
 D.J. Davies's position, 145, 151, 163, 175, 179–81, 216
 Evangelical defense of, 26, 73, 82, 93, 96–97, 99, 135, 163
 expression of Reformation doctrine, 35, 83, 90–91, 96, 99–100, 112, 267
 Nathaniel Jones's position, 60, 67, 73, 82, 84–100, 112, 117, 263, 265
 T.C. Hammond's position, 189, 194, 215, 258, 260
 teaching of, 82, 91, 98, 258, 266
 theology of, 25, 28, 41, 44, 47, 72, 82–99, 101, 129, 215–16, 232, 260
 Tractarian interpretation of, 41, 214–15
Thomas Moore Estate, 55, 59, 64, 81
Thomas, William Henry Griffith, 29, 31, 39–40, 42, 61, 68, 73, 90, 108, 116, 118, 141, 193, 258, 267
Thompson, Silvanus Phillips, 166
Toon, Peter, 36
Tract XC, 41, 83, 180–81
Tractarianism, 12, 15–16, 21–23, 37, 40–42, 48, 54, 59, 61, 69, 72, 76, 92, 95, 180–81, 217, 260, 266
transcendence of God, 29, 51, 194, 196–97, 233, 252
transubstantiation, 214
Treloar, Geoffrey R., 8
Trench, Richard Chenevix, 75
Tress, Herbert Langley, 64, 161–62, 167, 266
Trevelyan, George Macaulay, 131
Trinity College, Cambridge, 15, 18, 31, 69, 124–28, 131–32, 266
Trinity College, Dublin, 13, 20, 39, 48, 68, 123, 143, 189–92, 195, 203–4, 213, 239, 246, 266
Trinity, doctrine of, 13, 40, 85–86, 127, 232, 235, 244
Troeltsch, Ernst, 32, 165
Tübingen School, 16, 18, 192
Tucker, Charlotte Maria
 alias, a Lady of England, q.v., 75
Tyrrell, George, 147

U

Universities Preliminary Theological Examination, 74, 82
University of Sydney, 4, 7, 37, 54, 57, 126, 197, 251
Upwey Convention, 230
Ussher, James, 97, 199, 226–27, 256
utilitarianism, 27, 69

V

Victorian Churchman, The, 60, 76–77, 106
virgin birth, 138–39, 150, 165
Vos, Geerhardus Johannes, 33

W

Wace, Henry, 31–32, 47, 73, 113, 139, 176–79, 187, 191–93, 218
Wade, Arthur Leslie, 60
Waldegrave, Samuel, 24, 42
Walsh, Charles Richard, 162
Ward, James, 126
Warfield, Benjamin Breckinridge, 35, 48, 159, 193, 198, 219, 223, 237
Warman, Frederic Sumpter Guy, 152
Warre-Cornish, Francis Warre, 23
Waterland, Daniel Cosgrove, 97
Wellhausen, Julius, 30, 129, 220
Wesley, Charles, 44, 91, 152
Wesley, John, 44, 91, 152
Westcott, Brooke Foss, 16–17, 34, 56–57, 70–71, 74, 86, 101, 104, 107, 115, 117
Westminster Confession of Faith, 175, 199
Whitehead, Alfred North, 126, 132
Whitgift, John, 210
Wilberforce, William, 53
Williams, Arthur Lukyn, 56, 58, 60
Willoughby, James Mason, 267
Wilson, Daniel, 54
Wood, George Arnold, 142
Wordsworth, Christopher, 214
Wordsworth, John, 18, 71
World Missionary Conference, 137
Wright, Charles Henry Hamilton, 30, 32, 193, 227
Wright, John Charles
  death, 63, 163, 181, 261
  early ministry, 43, 61, 133
  election as archbishop, 61, 141
  Evangelical origins, 124
  liberal tendency, 33, 61–62, 64, 136, 140–41, 162, 263
  opposition to ritualism, 43, 62, 264, 266, 268
  role in diocese, 5, 123, 136, 142, 144, 152, 154, 249, 263, 264
  selection of Davies as principal of Moore College, 62, 123, 141, 196, 261, 264
  student years, 14, 61, 63
Wycliffe Hall, Oxford, 1, 11, 31, 42, 55, 61, 71, 118, 133, 138, 141

Y

YMCA. *See* Young Men's Christian Association
Yonge, Charlotte Mary, 40
Young Earth Creationism, 51
Young Men's Christian Association, 188–89, 195
Young, Joseph, 151

Z

Zwingli, Huldrych, 238